He 162

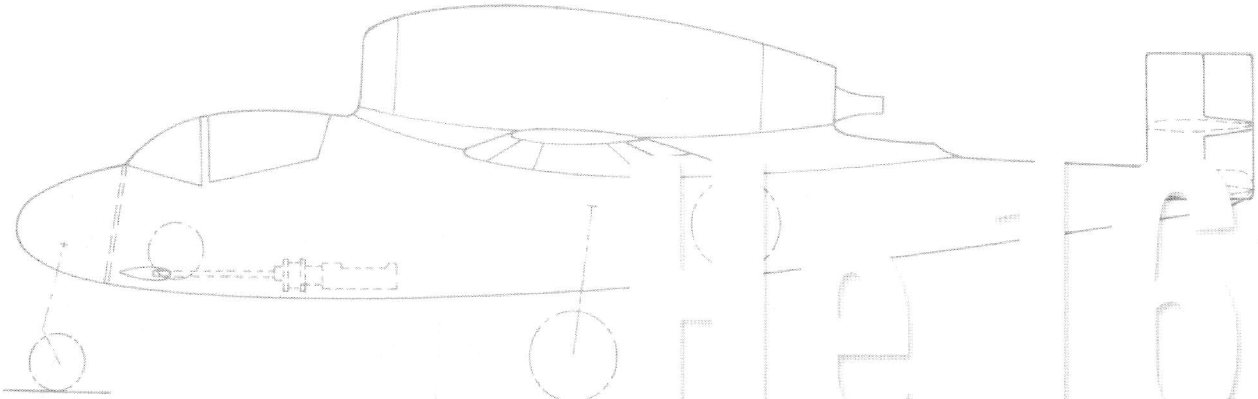

CLASSIC

An Imprint of
Crécy Publishing

Heinkel He 162

From Drawing Board to Destruction: The *Volksjäger*

ROBERT FORSYTH AND EDDIE J. CREEK

The Authors

Robert Forsyth is an author, editor and publisher, specialising in military aviation and military history. After working in the shipping industry, he co-founded a publishing and book production business in 1995 specialising in reference books on military aviation, armoured warfare, vintage motor sport, history, biography and wildlife.

He is the author of thirty books on the aircraft, units and operations of the Luftwaffe, an interest he has held since boyhood, and he has been consulted for television on the same subject. He has written articles for *The Aviation Historian, Aerojournal, Aeroplane Monthly, Aviation News, Combat Aircraft,* and *FlyPast*, has appeared on various podcasts and on-line TV, and is a member of the Editorial Board of *The Aviation Historian*.

Aside from his aviation interests, as a fan of British blues, he is also author of *Climax Blues Band – An Illustrated History*.

Eddie J. Creek, a former architect, was one of the founding members of *Gruppe 66*, the first independent and international Luftwaffe research group in 1966. Throughout the 1970s and 1980s he travelled to Germany extensively to interview veterans and meet other researchers. He is co-author of a number of landmark books on Luftwaffe aircraft including the Putnam volume, *German Aircraft of the Second World War* (1972), *Jet Planes of the Third Reich* (1982) and *Arado Ar 234* (1992) as well as Me 262 (1997-2000 - four volumes), *On Special Missions – The Luftwaffe's Research and Experimental Squadrons 1923-1945* (2003) all with J. Richard Smith and, with Robert Forsyth, *Me 264 Amerika Bomber – The Luftwaffe's Lost Transatlantic Bomber* (2006) and *Blitz Bombers – Kampfgeschwader 76* and the *Arado Ar 234: Luftwaffe Jet Bombers on the Western Front 1944-1945* (2020). He has contributed to more books than he cares to remember.

Heinkel He 162

First published 2009

ISBN 978-1-80035-299-5

Produced by Chevron Publishing Limited
Project Editor: Robert Forsyth and Edwin R. Oliver
Book design: Mark Nelson

Published by Crécy Publishing Ltd.
An imprint of Crécy Publishing Ltd.
1a Ringway Trading Estate,
Shadowmoss Road, Manchester, M22 5LH

Visit the Crécy Publishing website at:
www.crecy.co.uk

Printed in Malta by Melita

CLASSIC
An Imprint of
Crécy Publishing

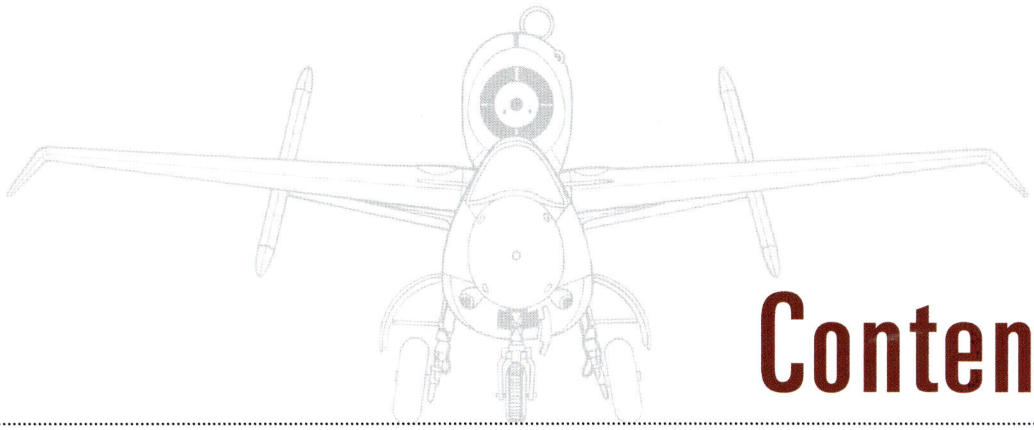

Contents

Introduction and Acknowledgements

IN his biography of Marshal of the Royal Air Force, Sir Arthur 'Bomber' Harris[1], the Chief of RAF Bomber Command, historian Henry Probert refers to the observations of Professor Richard Overy on the impact of the Allied strategic bomber offensive upon Nazi Germany's ability to wage war; Probert states:

> '*Overy places its effects in three categories, first of all those that were intended... The system of distributing weapons was seriously affected, as were research and technological innovation; the supply of oil and chemicals was particularly heavily hit. Added to these were the effects of area bombing in disrupting essential services, causing massive diversions of resources to damage repair, and forcing dispersal of different elements of the production processes, with consequent far-reaching implications for transportation. Then there was the workforce, whose productivity was hard to sustain and even harder to increase in the face of air raid alarms and absenteeism. Management too, constantly being enjoined to raise production, had somehow to cope with the endless disruption being caused by bombing. To add to the toll there were the social effects, not least those occasioned by the official and unofficial evacuation of civilians from larger towns and cities – nine million of them by January 1945...*'

At a macro level this is, undoubtedly, an accurate assessment of the problems facing the Germans by January 1945 and yet, despite such awesome difficulties, at a micro level there are a number of astonishing cases of how the German war machine and its production infrastructure kept going. One such example was to be found in the commissioning, development and manufacture of the Heinkel He 162 jet fighter, the so-called '*Volksjäger*' – 'People's Fighter' – an aircraft which had been produced in record time – a little more than three months from drawing board to the flight of the first prototype – and which combined the very latest engine technology with the crudest 'emergency' construction at very reasonable cost in both fiscal terms and in terms of man-hours. By January 1945 it was undergoing various modifications and refinements.

Was the He 162 beautiful or was it an ugly duckling? Aesthetically and aerodynamically, it was certainly a contradiction: built of wood, often in caves using the most primitive means with glue that would not hold its wings to its fuselage, and often using slave labour, it featured BMW's most state-of-the-art power plant. A leading British test pilot would opine that it had the makings of being a 'phenomenal machine'.

Was it a justified project, or was it – as Professor Willy Messerschmitt maintained – 'only a hope'? One Allied technical intelligence assessment team sent to Germany at the end of the war rated the He 162 as an 'outstanding achievement from whatever aspect it may be considered.'

Therein lies the root cause of the fascination which surrounds it. Therein lies the reason why the authors have undertaken this study.

We have been fortunate enough to have been able to draw upon many hundreds of pages of Heinkel, Reich Air Ministry and *Luftwaffe* documents, correspondence, signals, and technical drawings, most of which – fortunately – survived to fall into British custody in the immediate aftermath of the war. We have also had the great benefit of a multitude of personal papers and a substantial collection of fascinating photographs with which to piece together the elements of desperation, commitment, accomplishment, failure, triumph and tragedy which form the story of the *Volksjäger*.

Lack of publishing 'space' has precluded us from using, to even greater detail, the thousands of pages of captured Ernst Heinkel Aktiengesellschaft (EHAG) works teleprint signals, cables and letters issued between January and May 1945. These were microfilmed by the American Historical Association (AHA) for the Study of War Documents in Alexandria, Virginia in the immediate post-war period and portray in minute detail the day-to-day management by EHAG of the building of the He 162 – everything, for example, from essential construction issues (though we have used a great deal of these) to how many bottles of cognac were stored in the corporate drinks cabinet on the day that senior ministerial officials and officers came to watch the (fateful) flight of the He 162 V1 on 10 December 1944; from crucial supplies issues (which are included in this book) to the cost and feasibility of travel from Schwechat to Rostock for a single company employee in April 1945. That opportunity awaits the next researcher who may have more 'space' in future. However, it is our hope that, if nothing else, we have been able to present the reader with a most comprehensive account possible of the He 162's relatively brief, but dramatic, existence from the perspectives of its gestation, its development, its limited operational deployment and the plans for its enhancement, to its handling and assessment by the Allies right up to the early 1950s.

In the compilation of the material for this book, the authors wish to place on record their gratitude to the following researchers and historians for their kind assistance: firstly to Eric Mombeek for allowing us to quote from his own research into the operations of JG 1 in 1944-45; to Philippe Couderchon for his permission to use information and photographs collected during his research into French testing of the He 162 in the immediate post-war years; to Simon Schatz for the benefit of his advice on various aspects of the He 162 and for his superb colour renditions; to J Richard Smith for making available an unpublished draft on the history of the *Volksjäger*; to Ted Oliver for kindly reading through the first draft manuscript and for his kind comments and advice, especially in the areas of projects and pulsejets; to Nick Beale, Rick Chapman, Steve Coates, Manfred Griehl, Mike Norton, Lorenz Rasset (†), Arno Rose, and Werner Stocker for their help with information, documents and translation assistance, and to the Archive of Modern Conflict (AMC), Captain Eric Brown, CBE, DSC, AFC, RN, Hans-Hermann Cammann, Jim Crow, Martin Handig, Volker Koos, *Dipl.-Ing.* Karl Kössler, *Österreichische Flugzeug Historiker* (Austrian Aircraft Historians), Gordon Permann, Peter Petrick, *Dr.* Jochen Prien, Stephen Ransom, Günter Sengfelder, Marton Szigeti, Chris Thomas, David Wadman and David Williams for kindly allowing us to publish photographs.

Robert Forsyth
Eddie J. Creek
January 2009

1. Henry Probert *Bomber Harris: His Life and Times*, Greenhill Books, London, 2006.

'A Shot in the Dark'

Volksjäger – The People's Fighter

IF it can be said that adversity generates creativity, then the story of the development of the Heinkel He 162 jet fighter is testimony to such a precept. From the summer of 1944, the adversity facing the political and military leadership of the Third Reich was formidable. Ironically however, facing such adversity prompted many inventive proposals for national defence, practical and impractical, on a determined and even manic scale.

By early July 1944, the Allied armies were consolidating their bridgehead in Normandy and their air forces seemed dominant to the point of impunity. With the key city of Caen under threat from the British, on 8 July the German *Führer*, Adolf Hitler, told his commanders that 'Every square kilometre must be defended tenaciously'. But this was just one day after RAF bombers had dropped 2,500 tons of bombs on Caen, reducing it to rubble. One German unit which had fought to hold the city tenaciously for 33 days was the 12. SS Panzer Division '*Hitler-Jugend*' ['Hitler Youth']. Made up largely of young soldiers drawn straight from the ranks of the Hitler Youth, the Division suffered a 60 per cent casualty rate during the battle for Caen and its strength in tanks and armoured vehicles was reduced by half. The battle-hardened commander of the *Hitler Jugend*, SS-*Standartenführer* Kurt Meyer, was forced to concede: 'Officers and men know that the struggle is hopeless.'[1]

To a great extent, Hitler attributed much of the blame for his armies' predicament in France on a lack of vigor displayed by the *Luftwaffe* over the battlefront – and, for that matter, in the skies over Germany's cities which were suffering regular day and night bombardment from Allied heavy bombers. On 20 June, following a conversation with *Generalleutnant* Adolf Galland, the *General der Jagdflieger*, *Oberst* Ulrich Diesing, the *Chef der TLR* (Chief of the Air Equipment and Armaments Department), had addressed the *Jägerstab* (Fighter Staff), a committee comprised of industrialists and representatives of the *Reichsluftfahrtministerium* (RLM) which had been set up in February and tasked with regenerating Germany's flagging and bomb-stricken fighter production industry. Diesing endeavoured to put forward the *Luftwaffe's* point of view: 'Yesterday I spoke with General Galland who has come back from the front. General Galland stated quite clearly that as far as performance goes, our fighters are adequate and indeed, in most cases superior at the altitudes at which the invasion fighting is taking place... But that unfortunately they were by no means sufficient in numbers. The morale of our fighter pilots, however, is high as in the days of our great offensives on the Western and Eastern Fronts... The problem now is to provide the necessary numbers...'[2]

Hitler, however, believed that it was not solely a question of aircraft production: he had read the conference transcripts of the *Jägerstab*, and its accomplishments had been impressive.

Hauptdienstleiter Dipl.-Ing. Karl-Otto Saur was the tireless and bluntly spoken head of the *Jägerstab*, a man *Generalleutnant* Karl Koller, head of the *Luftwaffe* Operations Staff, considered to be a '...thoroughly self-opinionated and conceited individual, reserved and deceitful in his relations with the *Luftwaffe*.' An engineer and a dedicated member of the Nazi Party, Saur had, in fact, worked in a relatively minor position for

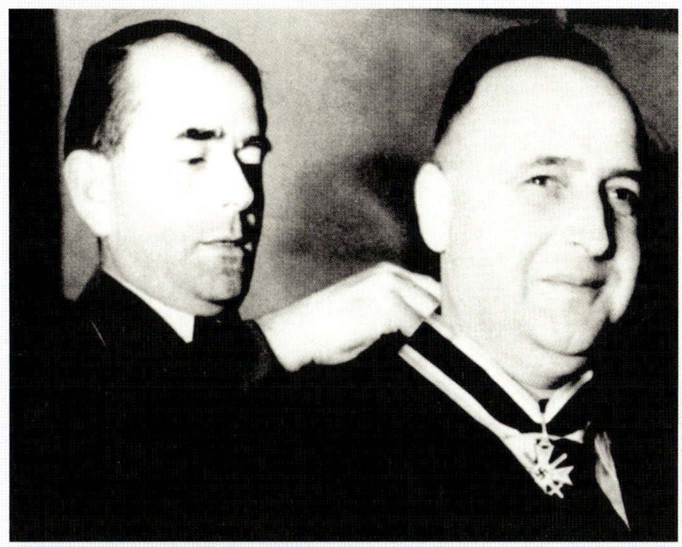

The Minister for Armaments and War Production, Albert Speer, fastens the Ritterkreuz des Kriegsverdienstkreuzes mit Schwertern (Knight's Cross of the War Service Cross with Swords) around the neck of a smiling Hauptdienstleiter Dipl.-Ing. Karl-Otto Saur. Saur, a driving force behind the initial development of the He 162, was described by Hitler as the 'genius in our armaments industry.'

the *Organisation Todt* civil and military engineering group and then for the German Armaments Minister, Albert Speer, as director of his Technical Department – effectively in charge of armaments production. In late 1944, Hitler would describe Saur as the 'genius in our armaments industry.'[3]

On 1 August 1944, Saur addressed his team proclaiming: 'For a whole week we have been making the greatest efforts with regard to aircraft sponsored by the *Jägerstab* and this applies in particular to those of us who have worked at this task unremittingly and with fanatical devotion... Yesterday our final output reached 3,145 aircraft sponsored by the *Jägerstab*, a total of 3,678 operational aircraft and a total of 4,675 military aircraft of all types. This enormous increase is 500 aircraft above output in June and 600 above that for May. Thus production has increased by 100 aircraft in two months; fighter production alone has increased from 2,300 to 3,100, that is by 800 aircraft in two months.'[4]

Thus, by August, Hitler reasoned that with the *Jägerstab* performing such production miracles, the failure of the *Luftwaffe* to stem the tide of the Allied air and land offensives was down to incompetence and lack of fibre within its own organisation. Even the bomber crews were beginning to level criticism at their compatriots in the fighter arm. Koller, standing in for the Commander-in-Chief of the *Luftwaffe*, *Reichsmarschall* Hermann Göring, who had been ominously absent from Hitler's headquarters for some time with an apparent abscess to the throat, took the full blast of Hitler's wrath. He wrote despairingly: 'At every conference the *Führer* rants on for hours about the *Luftwaffe*...

The so-called 'Father of Heroes': Generaloberst Alfred Keller, a recipient of the Pour le Mérite for his service as an air commander during the First World War, had voiced his opinions on an evident 'lack of guts' among the German Jagdflieger. He led the civilian, but Nazi Party-controlled, flying training and sports association, the Nationalsozialistisches Fliegerkorps (NSFK), and became enthused by the concept of the Volksjäger, remaining committed to it until the end of the war.

He levels the meanest accusations about our meagre aircraft figures, our technical blunders, our non-completion of the replenishment of units in the Reich...'

In France, Hitler was trying to push the invaders back to the sea. He had to prevent them from consolidating their hold in Normandy, but time was running out. The *Wehrmacht* had failed in its critical drive on Mortain and Avranches and the Allies were blasting shattered German divisions to pieces with their fighter-bombers. Agitated by the very adverse military situation now developing, Hitler had little patience left with the *Luftwaffe*. Unable to contain his anger any further at its perceived abject failure as a fighting force and its evident inability to effectively defend the Western Front and homeland against the Allied air forces, Adolf Hitler summoned Göring. For the *Reichsmarschall*, it was a humiliating experience. In the presence of Army Generals Jodl and Guderian, Hitler chided: 'The *Luftwaffe's* doing nothing! It's no longer worthy to be an independent service – and that's your fault!'

As the two *Wehrmacht* generals diplomatically left the room, tears trickled down the *Reichsmarschall's* cheeks.

Behind the scenes, Saur had produced a document which had emanated from the representative of an aircraft factory in Paris who had apparently conferred with a disillusioned *Luftwaffe* fighter commander serving in France. According to Galland: 'The outcome was a "Factual Report by an Unprejudiced Outsider on the Real Conditions of Aerial Warfare on the Invasion Front." This report reached the higher officials much quicker than usual and, of all people, came into the hands of Saur, who believed he could now prove that the fatal paralysis of the *Luftwaffe* could not be blamed on his section of the war industry. The letter strengthened the thesis that the *Jagdwaffe* had become a bottomless barrel into which gigantic production figures were poured in vain. Hitler in his turn drew the most amazing conclusions from it…'[5]

That Hitler was basing his military judgements on the recommendations of a man who '…took pains to eliminate all competition from other people for the *Führer's* favour and to get himself into a powerful position of his own' is perhaps indicative of where he was beginning to channel his trust.

The ever-industrious Saur searched for an alternative to depending on the *Luftwaffe* for fighter operations and it was not long before he conjured up an idea which saw the rapid deployment of a small, cheap, high-performance jet fighter which could be mass-produced in what he somewhat omniously referred to as a 'forced action'.

Furthermore, despite what may have been his vindictive machinations against the Military, Saur was not alone in his views. Even within certain quarters of the senior command of the *Luftwaffe* there was a sense that all was not well. *Generaloberst* Alfred Keller, the erstwhile commander of *Luftflotte* 1 and a recipient of the *Pour le Mérite* from his time as commander of *Bombengeschwaders* 1 *der OHL* in 1917, had voiced his opinions on an evident 'lack of guts' among the German *Jagdflieger*.[6] In late June 1943, Keller had relinquished command of *Luftlotte* 1 and was placed on the *Führer-Reserve* at the OKL in order to assume command of the civilian, but Nazi Party-controlled, flying training and sports association, the *Nationalsozialistisches Fliegerkorps* (NSFK). The NSFK had been formed in April 1937 under the leadership of *Generalleutnant* Friedrich Christiansen, another highly decorated officer and holder of the *Pour le Mérite* whom the Nazis felt would help to attract older pilots to joining a Party organisation. An auxiliary branch of the NSFK was the *Flieger Hitler-Jugend* (Flying Hitler Youth) which offered aircraft model-building courses and glider flying to boys of school age.[7]

Such was Keller's faith in the zeal and dedication to duty of his *Flieger Hitler-Jugend* that he believed that given the right aircraft, boys as young as 15 to 17 years of age could be quickly trained to fly in combat following a limited period of glider tuition and be capable of shooting down an enemy aircraft on every mission they flew. If the simple but reliable piece of design that was the new *Volkswagen* could be driven by virtually anyone with the minimum of instruction, then why not the same for an aircraft?[8]

As Adolf Galland related sardonically to a USAAF Intelligence officer in late May 1945: 'A few weeks after the 162 programme had spontaneously sprung into being, another equally spontaneous idea was conceived in the brains of a few amateurs in influential places; they thought that youthful glider pilots, having finished their glider training and a short re-training period in He 162s, could be sent

Above: Known originally as the KdF Wagen, ('Kraft durch Freude' – Strength through Joy), the iconic small, air-cooled Volkswagen was developed in wartime Germany as a vehicle for the people, although, in reality, it was used exclusively by the Military. The Volkswagen was intended as a cheap-to-build, shining symbol for the working classes in protest against the identification of the motor car with 'bourgeois' society. With the Volksjäger, it was hoped to embrace the same cheap-to-build principles for a fighter aircraft.

To fly the Volksjäger, the NSFK intended to call upon groups of eager and politically ardent teenage boys and youth in the Hitler-Jugend (Hitler Youth). Within the Third Reich, aviation had long been seen as glamourous and heroic, and the German leadership had little doubt in the notion of hurriedly training Hitler Youth to fly a simple aircraft in combat, using spirit and fanaticism to win the day over technology and enemy air superiority. Here a group of Hitler Youth are seen earlier in the war during a visit to inspect installations on the Baltic coast.

Generalleutnant Adolf Galland, the General der Jagdflieger, was extremely sceptical about the prospect of a Volksjäger from every viewpoint – the technical, the tactical and the ability of industry to cope. He apparently attempted to dissuade Generaloberst Keller from embarking on what he viewed as a nonsensical and wasteful NSFK-promoted scheme. He described the He 162 programme to Allied officers in 1945 as '... another spontaneous idea conceived in the brains of amateurs.' Galland is seen here in the company of NSFK officers no doubt 'towing the Party line.'

into the air. The Hitler Youth would change the situation in the air and show the German Air Force what it was all about. Saur gave Göring the idea which he jumped at immediately – as he did to all proposals which were out of the ordinary and sufficiently crazy. Good old *Generaloberst* Keller, whom we called the 'Father of Heroes' and who was in command of the NSFK, was won over for this. One day he came to see me in order to discuss the preparations. He intended tackling the problem without any technical knowledge, merely aided by his NSFK '*Standartenführer*' and '*Gruppenführer*'. The position of the NSFK was very doubtful as there was a serious quarrel between them and the Hitler Youth and the General in command of air-training. These three powerful authorities couldn't be combined and tried to eliminate each other all the time. Keller, as leader of the NSFK, thought he had found a new way of justifying the existence of his *Korps*. However, I dissuaded him after a few days.'[9]

However, relayed to an increasingly desperate Göring, the idea was seized upon. The *Reichsmarschall* fantasised about squadrons of fanatical, NSFK-trained *Hitler-Jugend* taking to the skies to wreak carnage and revenge on the Allied air forces. By drawing on such a vast, untapped well of manpower, the rate of supply of pilots would be equal to the number of aircraft which Saur projected enthusiastically would roll off the assembly lines in underground and strategicially distant factories using round-the-clock production.[10]

Eventually, the idea filtered through to *Oberst* Siegfried Knemeyer, the TLR *Flieger-Entwicklungs-Chef*. Prior to the war, Knemeyer had worked on the development of instrument flying and had qualified as an engineer. A skilled pilot and with a considerable knowledge of electronics, he later served with the *Aufklärungsgruppe Ob.d.L.*, flying test flights and operational missions in many different aircraft over Europe and North Africa. In April 1943, he was appointed Technical Officer to the *Angriffsführer England*, the command responsible for bombing raids against the British Isles and was then assigned to Göring's personal staff where he applied pressure to encourage development of the Me 262 jet fighter.

However, while Knemeyer recognised that in the Me 262 Germany possessed the technology it needed to respond effectively to the ever-growing threat of Allied heavy bombers and their escort fighters operating from altitude against strategic homeland targets, by the summer of 1944, there was also a pressing need for the *Luftwaffe* to combat the increasing numbers of *low-level* attacks mounted by Allied fighters against its airfields. This was, indeed, becoming a deadly problem: as one former *Staffelkapitän* from JG 3 remarked to a fellow captured airman after he was shot down in his Bf 109 over Normandy in July 1944, 'Allied numerical superiority is quite colossal... You could say that their superiority in numbers is in the ratio of twenty to one, and then their materiel is better, and also their personnel. All our pilots are inexperienced, while theirs are all fairly experienced. Better aircraft too – but there's nothing we can do about that. We had to stand on our airfield looking up at the sky, watching them fly over. We had six aircraft on the ground ready for operations and they used to circle about up there with between 80 and 100 aircraft. To take off is suicidal.'[11]

Below left: Reichsmarschall Hermann Göring, Commander-in-Chief of the Luftwaffe, siezed upon the concept of the Volksjäger, viewing it as a means of expedience with which to reinstate his force's rapidly diminishing favour with Hitler, the German High Command and the people. According to Adolf Galland, at the thought of the He 162, Göring proclaimed: 'Hundreds! Thousands! Umpteen thousands! Until the enemy has been chased back beyond the borders of Germany.'

Typical of the scenario facing the Luftwaffe were the all too familiar events surrounding the death on 3 September 1944 of *Hptm.* Emil 'Bully' Lang, *Gruppenkommandeur* of II./JG 26 who was credited with 173 victories of which 144 were over the Eastern Front and 29 in the West (including nine Spitfires, nine P-51s, six P-47s and

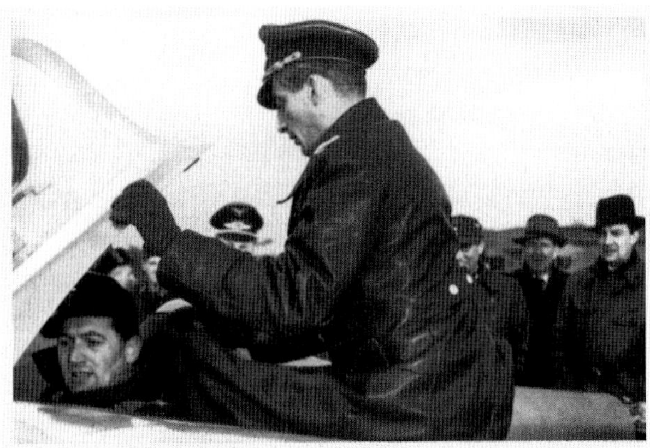

Oberst Siegfried Knemeyer was a skilled pilot with a considerable knowledge of electronics, who was in charge of aeronautical and technical development within the RLM. In the summer of 1944, Knemeyer proposed that a high-speed fighter be developed which could take off when enemy aircraft had been sighted, operate from short runways and be produced '...on such a scale as would enable the enemy to be engaged anywhere and during the whole of their flight.' He too would become a keen proponent of the Volksjäger concept. Knemeyer is seen here sitting on the edge of the Horten H IIIe tailless glider at Oranienburg in 1944 with Hptm. Theodor Rosarius, commander of the 2./Versuchsverband Ob.d.L, in the cockpit.

four P-38s), 28 of which were claimed over the Invasion Front, the highest number of Allied fighters lodged by a German pilot. He was a recipient of the *Eichenlaube* to the *Ritterkreuz*. Lang was caught by a USAAF P-47 as he endeavoured to get his malfunctioning Fw 190 A-8 airborne from Brussels-Melsbroek airfield, struggling in a steep climb with his gear down. The pilot of the P-47 recalled: 'I was closing very rapidly and the 190 was still in a vertical turn. I throttled back to pick up my lead but was still going too fast, so I could only get to about an 80 percent lead. I fired a short burst from this position from 200 yards. The range was very close and I could distinctly see the crosses on his wings and the egg blue finish on the aircraft. I fired until I was afraid I'd collide with him, so I eased off. As I pulled up for another pass, I saw him upside down. Then he hit and skidded along the ground and burst into flames.'

It was against such a grim background that Knemeyer supported the idea of a cheap, mass-produced aircraft; as he wrote in July 1945: 'In the summer of 1944, the Me 109 and Fw 190 were no longer able successfully to combat the increasing low-flying attacks over Western Germany. This was due to the fact that the superiority in speed of the German aircraft was inadequate on account of the proximity of the enemy air bases, and thus it was practically impossible to vector the German aircraft to a successful interception.

'Shortage of equipment precluded the combatting of enemy low-level attacks by a system of standing patrols, thus it became absolutely essential to develop a high-speed single-seater fighter which had a sufficiently good performance which would enable it to take off when the enemy aircraft were actually sighted. In addition, due to the bombing of the large airfields with long runways, these new fighters had to be able to take off in a very short distance and thus enable small landing grounds to be used. The mass production of such an aircraft had to be on such a scale as would enable the enemy to be engaged anywhere and during the whole of their flight.

'By limiting the endurance and the armament requirement for this new aircraft, the existing jet fighter [the Me 262], would have fulfilled the requirements. However, this aircraft had to be ruled out since it was not possible to produce the numbers which would have been required for combatting these low-flying attacks and, in particular, because the provision of two power units per airframe was quite beyond the capacity of industry.'

Indeed, by the summer of 1944, skilled labour for aircraft and aero-engine manufacture was becoming an increasingly scarce commodity in wartime Germany, as more and more workers were conscripted for military service and supply shortages began to bite. It thus became inevitable that more reliance was placed on semi-skilled and unskilled labour, a large proportion of which were forced or slave workers. If Saur's, Keller's and Knemeyer's collective vision was to be realised, the methods of construction would need to be kept as simple as possible. In considering the prevailing tactical situation, Knemeyer viewed the following items as being key requirements for any such aircraft:

- High speed at low and medium altitudes (with a minimum speed of 750 km/h at sea level)
- Capable of unassisted take-off in less than 600 metres
- Minimum production build-up to obtain the necessary large-scale production
- The extensive employment of wood in construction
  Under no circumstances was there to be any interruption to the Me 262 and Ar 234 jet aircraft manufacturing programmes, both in stages of relative infancy
  Rather, the exploitation of dormant production capacity was envisaged, through the cancellation of the Ta 154/254 and Ju 252 programmes. The assigned component manufacturers had previously been engaged in the manufacture of furniture, but had transferred to the aircraft industry and been engaged in the production of all-wood aircraft
- The use of only one jet engine. Since production of the Jumo 004 turbine was already at maximum output, it was planned to adopt the BMW 003.

Furthermore, according to Knemeyer, because of restrictions imposed by the neccesity of an envisaged early start in large-scale production, there was to be an avoidance of '...any constructional, aerodynamic, or mechanical risk.' The jet engine was to be mounted '... above the wing despite the loss of logitudinal stability, but a corresponding decrease in the risk of fire' and there was to be a '... preclusion of any possibilty of increasing speed through the use of higher powered jet units.' Knemeyer stated, 'Such power units were meant to be used [only] for increasing the load without loss of speed.'[12]

The concept of mounting a jet engine above the wing was not entirely new: in February 1943, in response to a specifiation for a high-speed, piston-engined, anti-shipping aircraft intended for deployment against the anticipated Allied invasion of Europe, the Henschel Flugzeugwerke at Berlin-Schönefeld offered a design known as the Hs 132 centred around a small, mid-wing monoplane with twin end-plate fins and rudders and a single turbojet mounted above the fuselage. The fuselage was to be of metal construction, while the wings were to made of wood with a plywood skin. The most radical feature was the cockpit, in which the pilot was to lie prone behind a glazed nose so as to be able to withstand forces of up to 10 g. This way, the Hs 132 would attack ships in a shallow dive, reaching speeds of up to 910 km/h and dropping its 500 kg or 1,000 kg bombs at the target with the aid of a primitive computer. Three subtypes were planned, powered by either BMW 003 E-2, Junkers Jumo 004 B or Heinkel-Hirth HeS 011 engines, with an armament of two 20 mm MG 151/20 cannon – with an option for two MK 103s, if ordnance was reduced.

The finished design bore a striking resemblance to the aircraft that would eventually emerge as the Heinkel He 162, but Henschel only progressed as far as developing a wind tunnel model and producing the fuselage and wings of the first prototype.[13]

A wind tunnel model of the Henschel Hs 132 built by the Aerodynamische Versuchsanstalt at Göttingen with a BMW or Heinkel-Hirth jet engine mounted above the fuselage in a dimensionally identical way to what would become the Heinkel He 162. The pilot was to lie prone behind a glazed nose so as to be able to withstand forces of up to 10 g and attack ship targets in a shallow dive, reaching speeds of up to 910 km/h.

Much – if not all – of Knemeyer's requirements was encapsulated into an RLM specification of early July 1944 for a fast jet aircraft under the designation '1 TL – *Jäger*' which was to be completed in the almost unfeasibly short period of eight weeks. Furthermore, a mock-up was to be ready by 1 October, and a first prototype ready to fly by 1 December, with series production commencing from 1 January 1945.[14]

Under somewhat co-incidental circumstances, on 12 July 1944, Knemeyer is believed to have expressed his approval for a project being developed

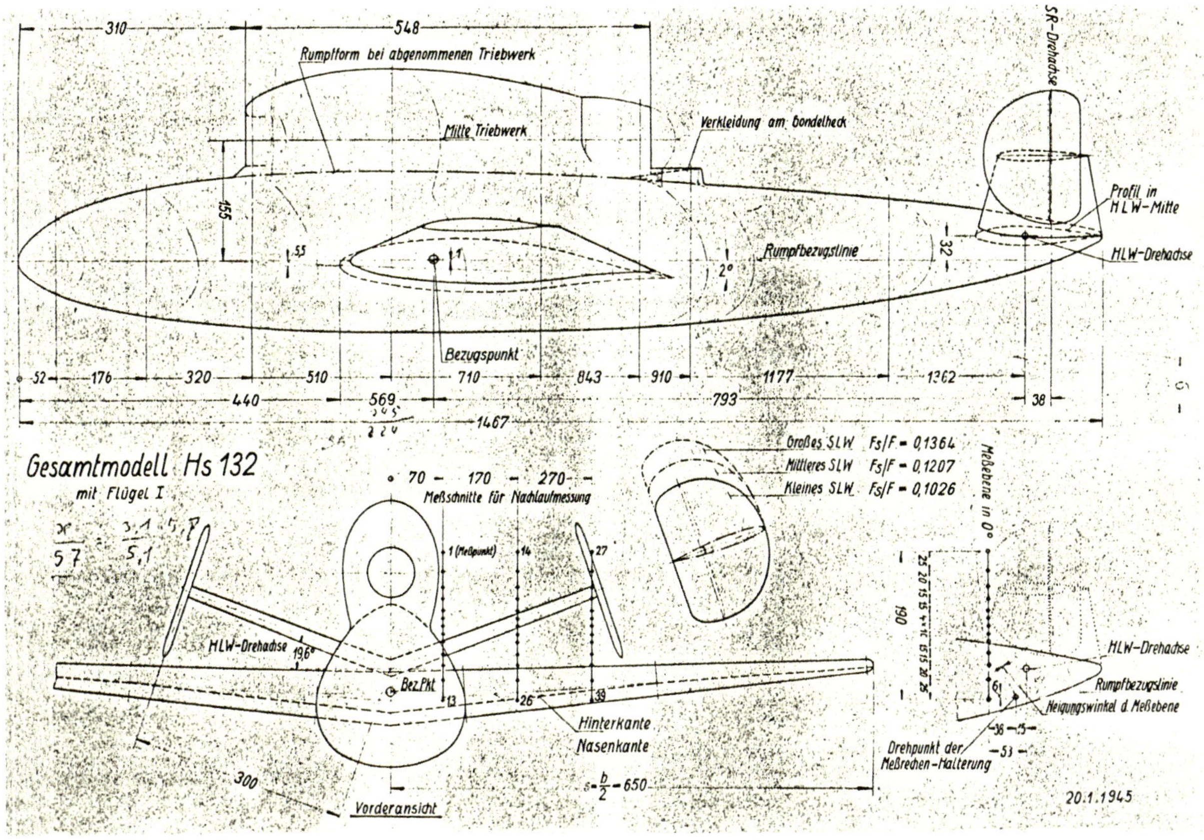

A drawing of the Hs 132, dated 20 January 1945, taken from a document prepared by the Aerodynamische Versuchsanstalt at Göttingen.

Below: The HeS 011 jet engine suffered a protracted development due to its complex diagonal flow compressor. The model seen here, the V4, suffered from so many problems that it had to be redesigned.

by the leading aircraft firm, Ernst Heinkel AG (EHAG) in Vienna, for a high-performance jet fighter, powered by two HeS 011 or Jumo 004 C turbojets and known as the P.1073. It appears that the origins of this project lay partly in a request by the RLM of 15 February 1944 for design studies to be made for a single-seat interceptor to be powered by the envisaged Heinkel-Hirth He 109-011 engine and partly in the fact that *Professor* Ernst Heinkel had been frustrated by two significant events.[15] The first of these was that despite his He 280 jet fighter being the first such aircraft in the world to have flown under turbojet power on 30 March 1941, the project had been abandoned in March 1943 by the RLM because of ongoing problems with engine design and delivery delays and the subsequent development of jet engine technology was taken up by his rival, Messerschmitt. Secondly, he had been irked by his unexpected financial position, which had been compromised by the relegation and very recent cancellation by Albert Speer of the He 177/He 277 bomber programme in July 1944 in order for national aircraft production to concentrate on fighters.[16] Heinkel was thus determined to secure a major fighter contract and his energies became channelled in that direction – but as he recounted in his memoirs, it was the ensuing adversities facing production of the Me 262, as outlined by Knemeyer, that essentially spawned work on what would become known as the '*Volksjäger*': 'The recognition of this fact encouraged Saur and his circle in July 1944 to develop a so-called "rush-job", a simple, single-engined jet which required little material to build. Saur's unrealistic notion that this plane should be a "people's fighter", in which Hitler Youth, after a short training, could fly for the defence of Germany, displayed the unbalanced fanaticism of those days. But the basic idea of simplification could have solved the problem of many German bottlenecks, had it been used at the right time. The Soviets gave proof of this.

'But when I, too, received orders at Vienna to build a light jet fighter of this type, I knew quite well that this was only a last vain resistance to an inevitable fate. Nevertheless, my having been shut out of the revolutionary development of jet aircraft, in spite of having been the first to take it up, had left such a mark in me that I was eager to prove my supremacy in the field once more.'[17]

At the Heinkel *Entwurfbüro* (Project Office) in the Vienna district of Schwechat, *Dipl.-Ing.* Siegfried Günther, the company's Senior Design Engineer, and according to one former Heinkel worker '... reputed to be one of the inventive brains of the Heinkel concern',[18] had completed work on his plans for the P.1073 by early July.

Siegfried Günter, and his identical twin, Walter, was born on 8 December 1899. During the First World War, the Günther twins joined the same artillery regiment in 1917 and subsequently were captured by the British on the same day! Both spent time in England as PoWs. Following the Great War, they both enrolled in at the Technical University in Hannover to study aircraft design. Siegfried was the mathematician of the pair, while Walter was more artistic with a true flare for design. In their spare time, the twins built gliders, and one of their efforts, built with their friends Walter Mertens and Werner Meyer-Cassel, caught the attention of businessman Paul Bäumer, who witnessed the craft flying over the famous Wasserkuppe plateau in the Rhön Mountains where so much advancement in German sailpane development took place during the inter-war years. Bäumer immediately offered the twins jobs with his Bäumer Aero company in

The Junkers Jumo 004 B jet engine which powered Me 262 and Ar 234 jet fighters and bombers in numbers from the autumn of 1944 onwards. This example is believed to be the first examined by the British at the Royal Aircraft Establishment in Farnborough in 1945 having been removed from an Ar 234 of 9./KG 76 which was forced down over the Western Front by USAAF fighters in February of that year.

Left: The He 280 jet fighter provided Ernst Heinkel with a source of both accomplishment and frustration. The aircraft had been the first such aircraft to take to the skies in March 1941, but development was eventually abandoned in March 1943 because of ongoing problems with engine design and delays, and subsequent jet engine technology was taken up by Heinkel's rival, Messerschmitt. Here, the He 280 V3 taxies in following a flight by Fritz Schäfer from EHAG's Rostock plant in the summer of 1942. Standing on the port wing is Heinkel test pilot, Flugbaumeister Gotthold Peter, who would be killed in 1944 flying the He 162.

Berlin. There they began designing motor gliders and, increasingly, fast sports machines, including one in which Bäumer was killed in a crash in 1928.

In 1931, the twins applied for positions with the then Ernst Heinkel Flugzeugwerke at Warnemünde. The eye of Ernst Heinkel too had been caught by one of the twins' designs and Heinkel later recorded his first impressions of Siegfried Günther: 'A thirty-year-old man stood in my office. He was extraordinarily solemn and in suitably old-fashioned clothes. He wore a stiff collar and a dickey. His jacket was carefully buttoned, his cuffs protruded well out of the sleeves and on his nose was perched a pair of rimless glasses. The young man looked sober, not to say shy. One could easily have imagined him to be a parson or school-teacher, but under no circimstances an aeroplane designer and one who had succumbed to the intoxication of speed into the bargain.'

A little later, after Heinkel had met Walter, he recorded: 'They were both bachelors, took rooms with a widow and hardly ever went out in society. If they had a passion, it was for good food and fast cars. With their small, pretty little Fiat, they drove at speed which in their case was as incongruous as seeing a country parson in a racing car... This very strange pair represented what unconsciously I had been seeking. The brothers could complete and co-ordinate what I saw roughly in my mind. They combined technical efficiency with a feeling for artistic beauty. They could design the aerodynamic shape I was looking for.'[19]

Indeed, the Günther twins went on to design some of the most important and famous aircraft associated with Heinkel, including the He 51, He 70, He 111 and He 177.

In the summer of 1944, Ernst Heinkel Aktiengesellschaft was in an ideal position to take on the production of a new aircraft type since the company's manufacturing capacity had been freed up following the cancellation of the He 177 four-engine strategic bomber. The He 162 thus became an extremely attractive proposition to Ernst Heinkel whose financial position had felt the impact of the He 177 cancellation. Here a number of license-built He 177s are seen under construction at the Flugzeugwerke Eger factory at Cheb in the Czechoslovakia.

Dr Ernest Heinkel (right) sketches in a pencil adjustment to a plan of a He 111 on the drawing board in July 1941. With him is Siegfried Günter who would go on to become EHAG's Senior Design Engineer, and according to one former Heinkel worker '... reputed to be one of the inventive brains of the Heinkel concern'. Günter was involved with the designs of the He 51, He 70, He 177 and, in late 1944, the He 162 Volksjäger.

With mud still on their boots from having watched the test flight of the He 280 V1, Ernst Heinkel and Ernst Udet pose alongside company engineers and test pilots at the following champagne reception. At far right is Siegfried Günter, while fifth from right (in Luftwaffe uniform) is test pilot, Paul Bader, and left of Bader is Karl Bütter. Günter can be viewed as the design 'brains' behind the He 162 project which took place four years after this photograph was taken, while Bader would test-fly the aircraft and designer Butter, would be heavily involved in the plans for the aircraft. Udet committed suicide in November 1941.

The P.1073, as originally conceived in Heinkel's proposal of 10 July 1944, was described as a '*Schneller Strahljäger*' ('High Speed Jet Fighter') and was foreseen as a possible replacement for the Me 262, but possessing a much higher critical Mach number in the order of 0.94 and an increase in speed of at least 70 km/h. Most of the initial studies featured a 35 degree swept-back wing and a V-type tailplane, with two staggered He S 11 engines mounted dorsally and ventrally on the fuselage, but later plans included single-engined proposals. The HeS 011 engine would provide a maximum speed of 1010 km/h at 6000 m. However, due to the non-availability of the He S 11, for the immediate future at least, it was proposed to use Jumo 004 C engines, which would offer a maximum speed of 940 km/h at 6000 m. Flight endurance at full power was one hour at 11000 m, while climbing time to the same height was ten minutes, with a range of 1000 km.

In order to accommodate the nose wheel, the ventrally-mounted engine would be offset to the right, and for the same reason, the proposed MK 103 cannon was to be fitted asymmetrically with two MG 151 cannon installed on each side of the fuselage.[20]

It seems interest in the concept of a cheap, mass-produced, high-speed jet fighter tailed off at this point – albeit temporarily – although quiet, determined work to promote the idea continued within the RLM until, in the evening of 7 September 1944, a top priority teleprint message arrived at the EHAG *Entwurfbüro* in Schwechat from the Heinkel works at Oranienburg addressed to *Professor* Heinkel, Siegfried Günther and *Ing.* Heinz Meschkat.[21] Perhaps with some degree of subversion, the message had probably originated with *Dipl.-Ing.* Karl Frydag, Heinkel's RLM-assigned *Generaldirektor* (General Manager). Frydag, was a man of considerable capacity for work, for simultaneous

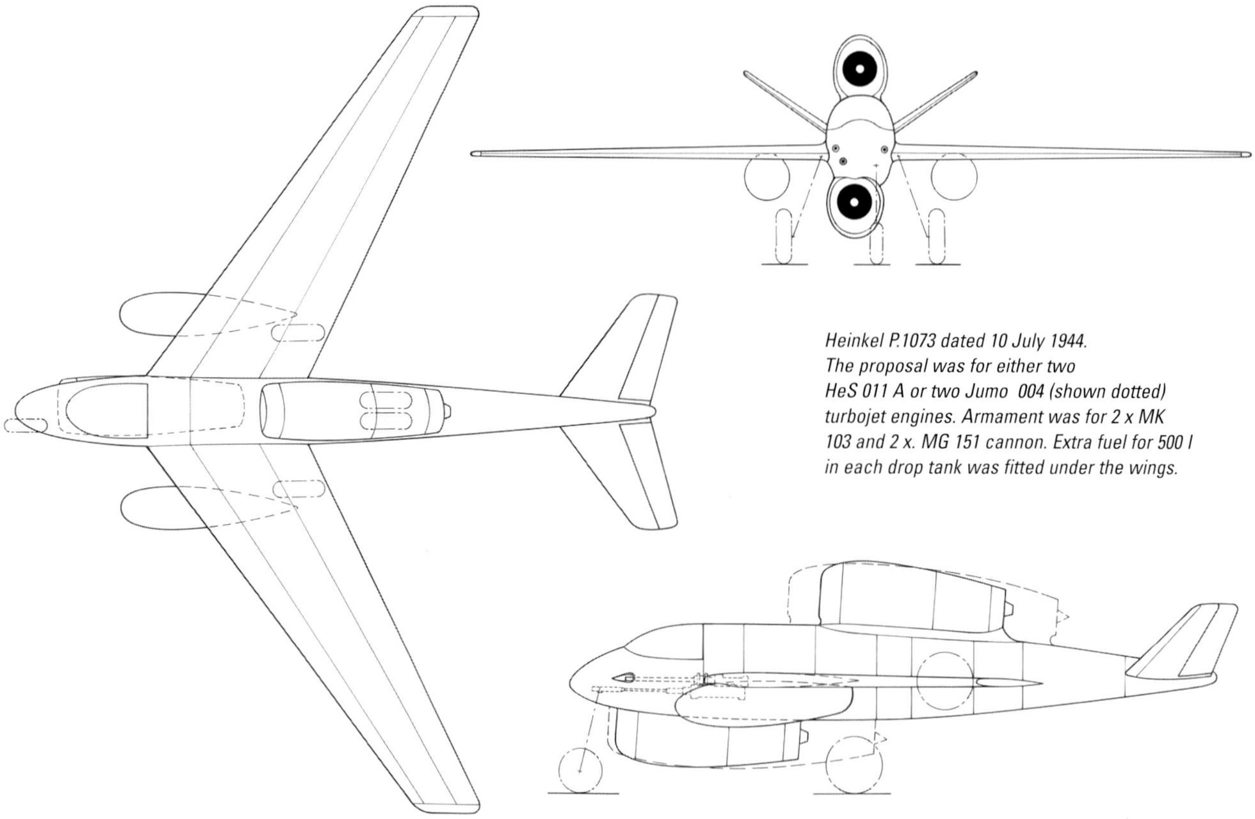

Heinkel P.1073 dated 10 July 1944. The proposal was for either two HeS 011 A or two Jumo 004 (shown dotted) turbojet engines. Armament was for 2 x MK 103 and 2 x. MG 151 cannon. Extra fuel for 500 l in each drop tank was fitted under the wings.

As leader of the Main Committee for Aircraft Construction, Dipl.-Ing. Karl Frydag, also Generaldirektor of EHAG, ensured that the company had as much notice as possible of the Volksjäger tender. He played a forceful role maintaining the momentum of the He 162 production programme in 1945 and at the end of the war offered a robust reposte to Willy Messerschmitt's suggestions that the He 162 was a wasteful and needless commodity.

to his function at Heinkel, he acted as Technical Director of the Henschel Flugzeugwerke at Berlin-Schönefeld.[22] Somewhat conveniently – and more importantly – he was also leader of the influential *Hauptausschuss Flugzeugbau* (Main Committee for Aircraft Construction) in the Armaments Ministry, and thus a close associate of Karl-Otto Saur with whom he had regular discussions on aircraft production.[23] The message from Oranienburg contained still unreleased detailed specifications from the RLM for a 'Tl-*Jäger*' which was due to be tendered shortly to Heinkel (officially), Arado, Blohm und Voss, Fieseler, Focke-Wulf, Messerschmitt, Junkers and Siebel and which called for a fighter to be built from existing components and powered by a BMW 003 engine. That specification was eventually released the next day by *Oberst* Ulrich Diesing, the *Chef TLR* (Head of Air Technical Equipment) at the RLM under the designation '*Volksjäger*' – 'People's Fighter'.[24]

The BMW 003 was the engine that German aircraft manufacturers were waiting for, but its development had been dogged by endless problems associated with turbine failures. The engine had first been developed in 1939 by BMW at Spandau as the P.3302 and first ran in August of the following year, though early testing proved disappointing with only 150 kp thrust given at 8000 rpm on the test bed. BMW experienced trouble with breaking components and poor combustion efficiency, but by the summer of 1941, the P.3302 had been improved sufficiently to generate some 450 kp of thrust on the test bed. Two engines were then mated with the Me 262V1 at Messerschmitt's plant in Augsburg, but again, there were troubles with the turbines, mainly due to fatigue in welded joints and heat-induced brittleness in the turbine blades.

Although still underpowered at a new rating of 550 kp of thrust, another pair of engines was fitted to the Me 262V1 in early 1942, and on 23 March the aircraft took off with Messerschmitt test pilot, Fritz Wendel, at the controls using the underwing turbojets and a nose-mounted Jumo 210G piston engine. Wendel recorded that on reaching an altitude of 1,000 m, he levelled off, and at a speed of 400-450 km/h, despite continually throttling back, could not bring the engines below 7,000 rpm, as a result of which, their thrust was still more than 200 kg each. When the fuel guage indicated 100 litres, Wendel noticed a large variation in fuel injection on the left turbojet which simultaneously began to run rough. He then moved the left throttle lever to the 'stop' position and in so doing, inadvertently throttled the right engine so far back that it too cut out, falling from 7,000 rpm to below 2,000 rpm idling speed. During his landing approach at an IAS of 240 km/h, the wing nose flaps were extended fully, the aircraft made a normal landing, and stopped after a run of two-thirds of the airfield length, when both steering mechanisms of the sprung undercarriage snapped off at their welding points for unknown reasons. The incident quashed any chance of BMW providing jet engines for the Me 262.

Despite this, BMW persevered throughout 1942, but could not overcome difficulties with vibration fractures in the rotor blades of the

The BMW 003 engine suffered a problematic gestation between 1942 and 1944 and its manufacture was subject to delays. This new example was found at Leck by Allied troops and was probably for use as a spare. The aircraft in the background is a Focke-Wulf Fw 190 D-9, W. Nr. 210249 and carries a chevron and vertical bar before and aft of the fuselage cross.

compressor, problems with the baffle plate combustion chamber, turbine blade failures and overheating as a result of insufficient oil feed during starting or acceleration. By the end of the year however, it seemed most of these difficulties had been ironed out by introducing a new seven-stage compressor, improved cooling and a new method of blade fixing. A new engine, the BMW 109-003, was placed under test at Spandau under the supervision of chief designer, Hans Roßkopf. Modifications were introduced to solve the compressor blade problems and in October 1943, the engine underwent flight tests when it was fitted to a Ju 88 as a test bed. Things went well enough for BMW to want try out their engine as the sole powerplant on an aircraft, but further manufacturing delays served to hamper this desire and by July 1944, work on a first batch of 100 BMW 003s at a dedicated company flight-test centre at Oranienburg was still ongoing.[25]

In September 1944, plans were drawn up for the mass production of the BMW 003 to commence in November 1944 at an initial rate of 75 engines per month, which would rapidly rise to 2,365 per month by June 1945, and reach a peak of 6,000 monthly by January 1946. The very protracted development of this engine was nearing completion when the RLM ordered that the BMW 003 would have to be adapted to operate on J2 (a combination of diesel fuel and kerosene) instead of B4 (87 octane aviation fuel), due to serious shortages of the latter. Throughout the BMW 003 test programme only B4 fuel had been used, but when conversion to J2 was attempted it proved virtually impossible, in the event of a flame-out, to relight the engine in flight. This requirement delayed the start of production considerably as development of a new fuel system was found necessary, and the problem was eventually overcome by adopting a system similar to that fitted to the rival Jumo 004 B.[26]

Meanwhile at Schwechat, the Heinkel team quickly went into action, fully intending to exploit the 'insider information' they now held in what was an unfair advantage over their competitors. The day after receiving the Oranienburg signal – 8 September – the P.1073 project file was pulled out of the drawer at the *Entwurfbüro* and adapted by scaling-down the basic P.1073 layout to a size corresponding to the smaller, and less powerful, BMW turbojet, combined with an unswept wing and twin fins and rudders. In August, Heinkel was advised by the RLM that a single-engined configuration was essential on account of the saving in production effort and a probable shortage of powerplants. As the entire Jumo 004 production output was reserved for the Me 262 and Ar 234 B, the only other turbojet readily available for installation in any new fighter was the BMW 003. The resulting – and interim – P.1073-15 was deliberately designed to meet the RLM specification.

Thus, Heinkel had enjoyed a two-day head start by the time a teleprinter message marked 'Very Urgent' and 'Strictly Confidential' clattered into the offices of Blohm und Voss in Hamburg from the RLM in Berlin shortly before midday on Sunday, 10 September, addressed to the company's designer, *Dr.-Ing.* Richard Vogt. The message laid out an RLM requirement for a cheap-to-build jet fighter. The same message was also sent to Arado, Fieseler, Focke-Wulf, Messerschmitt, Junkers and Siebel. The requirement called for a maximum speed of 750 km/h at sea level, a take-off distance of not more than 500 m, the ability to operate from poor airfields, and an endurance of at least 30 minutes at sea level at 100 per cent thrust. The proposed fighter was to incorporate an armament of two 30 mm MK 108 cannon with 80-100 rpg, or alternatively two 20 mm MG 151/20 cannon with 200-250 rpg, and be equipped with instrumentation and basic FuG 15 or FuG 16 VHF radio transceiver equipment for fair weather operations only. As far as practical, wood and steel were to be employed in the fighter's construction, though armour plating was to be incorporated to allow adequate defence for the pilot and the aircraft's 30 mm ammunition against attack from the front using 13 mm ammunition. The fuel tanks were also to be armour-plated, but the manufacturers were asked to investigate whether the take-off run could be reduced if the ammunition load and weight of armour plating were reduced. Perhaps the most demanding stipulation however, was that the competing proposals should be ready for examination by TLR/Fl-E2/III (Fighter Aircraft Development Group) within three to five days![27] However on the 12th, OKL confirmed by telegram that this deadline was extended to the 14th.[28]

According to *Generalleutnant* Adolf Galland, who, as *General der Jagdflieger*, claimed to have been excluded from the matters until the late summer of 1944, utmost secrecy surrounded the whole tender process – something which is difficult to conceive given the number of ministry officials and company employees that would have been involved in the process.[29]

Dutifully – and despite the extremely short time frame set by the RLM, all but three of the contenders went to work. It seems that Fieseler and Siebel were unable to comply with the specification, while Messerschmitt declined to tender for reasons which its chairman made abundantly clear and which will be explained later in this chapter. This left Arado, Blohm und Voss, Focke-Wulf, Heinkel and Junkers in the running. Each company submitted at least one design, but Focke-Wulf actually submitted two.

Continued on page 19

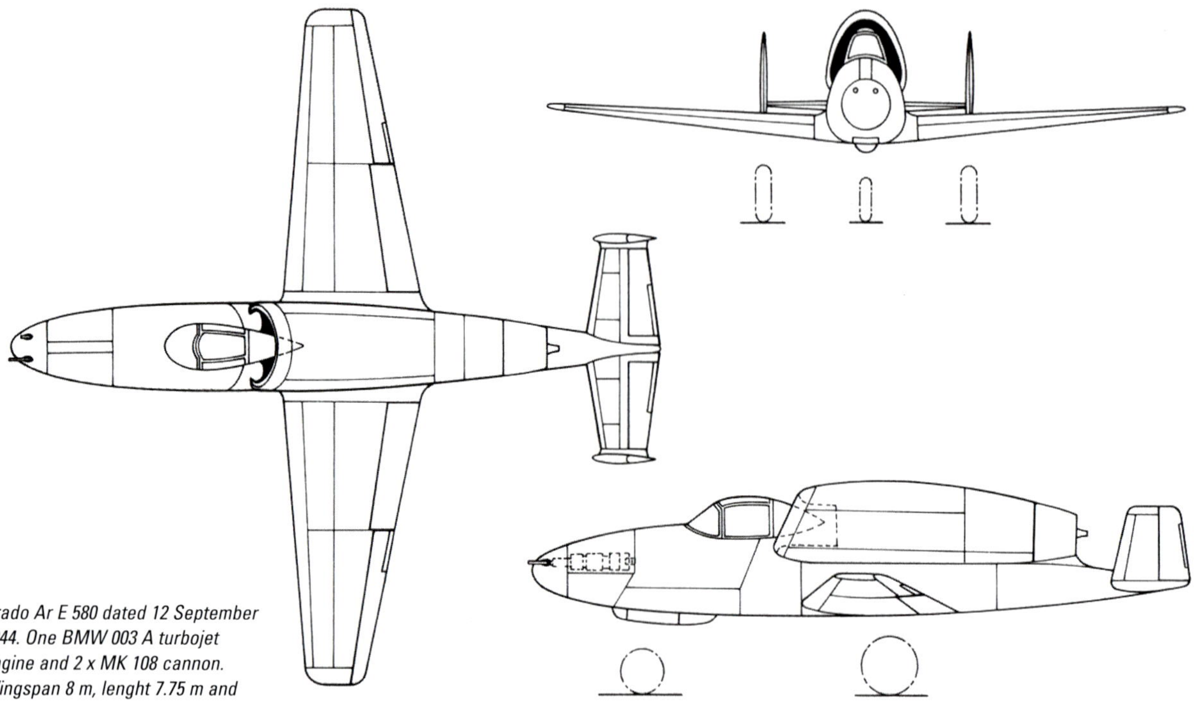

Arado Ar E 580 dated 12 September 1944. One BMW 003 A turbojet engine and 2 x MK 108 cannon. Wingspan 8 m, lenght 7.75 m and total height with wheels down 2.5 m.

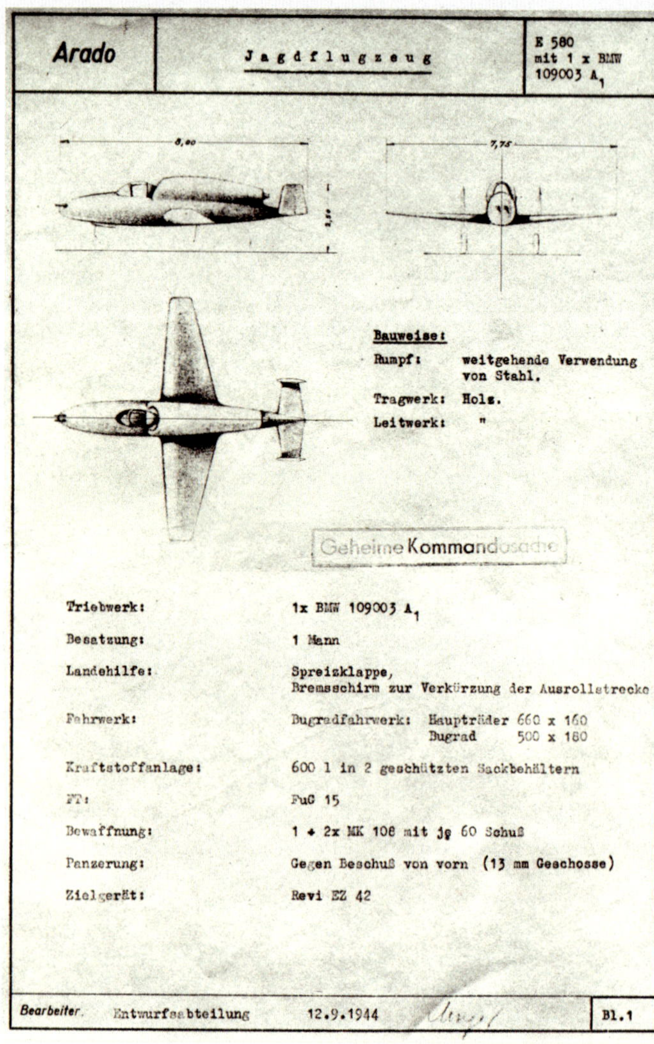

Arado | Jagdflugzeug | E 580 mit 1 x BMW 109003 A_1

Bauweise:
Rumpf: weitgehende Verwendung von Stahl.
Tragwerk: Holz.
Leitwerk: "

Geheime Kommandosache

Triebwerk: 1x BMW 109003 A_1
Besatzung: 1 Mann
Landehilfe: Spreizklappe, Bremsschirm zur Verkürzung der Ausrollstrecke
Fahrwerk: Bugradfahrwerk: Haupträder 660 x 160, Bugrad 500 x 180
Kraftstoffanlage: 600 l in 2 geschützten Sackbehältern
FT: FuG 15
Bewaffnung: 1 + 2x MK 108 mit je 60 Schuß
Panzerung: Gegen Beschuß von vorn (13 mm Geschosse)
Zielgerät: Revi EZ 42

Bearbeiter. Entwurfsabteilung 12.9.1944 Bl.1

Right: The first page of the Arado Volksjäger.project E 580 as submitted to the RLM.

Arado E 580

This was a design based on an Arado project from 1943, for a large aircraft with slightly swept-back wings, twin tail fins and powered by an unspecified turbojet mounted above the fuselage, providing 1,500 kg thrust.

Arado used this earlier design as a basis for a smaller, unswept, low-wing derivative with which to meet the RLM specification of 10 September 1944. Designated E 580 (the 'E' standing for '*Entwurf*'), the design had a wingspan of 7.75 m, a length of 8 m, and a wing surface of 10 sq. m. It was noteworthy for the unusual feature of the intake of the BMW 003 being partially obscured by the roof of the cockpit canopy.

The E 580 was to feature a tricycle undercarriage with wide-track main wheels and was to carry two 30 mm MK 108 cannon, but it did not appear to include two 20 mm MG 151/20 cannon as per the RLM request. In this configuration, the aircraft would weigh 2635 kg and possess a top speed of 750 km/h, with a rate of climb of 17 m/s at ground level and 4 m/s at 9800 m. The E 580 would be able to take off within 570 m and held a range of 610 km with an endurance of 22 minutes.

Dipl.-Ing. Rüdiger Kosin head of Arado's design office recalled that a representative of the RLM *Technisches Amt* arrived without warning at the company's premises in Landeshut, Silesia in mid-September 1944 in order to supervise the design of the project. Kosin recalled that, 'He seemed to know exactly what the final design should look like. He didn't budge from the department for two whole days and tried throughout that time to steer the project in the direction he wanted it to go.'

This may perhaps explain the E 580's striking similarity to the eventual Heinkel design. The Arado design was ready for submission on 12 September 1944.

Blohm und Voss P 211

Designed by *Dr.-Ing.* Richard Vogt, the P 211 *'Einstrahltriebkleinstjäger'* ('single jet-propelled mini-fighter') was based on an earlier Blohm und Voss design known as the P 211.01 comprising swept-back wings fitted to a tubular steel spar from which a BMW 003 engine would be suspended.

When Vogt and the Blohm und Voss design team assessed the 10 September RLM tender with its stringent deadline, they decided to simplify the P 211.01. The resulting P 211.02 was to be constructed in an eight-stage assembly

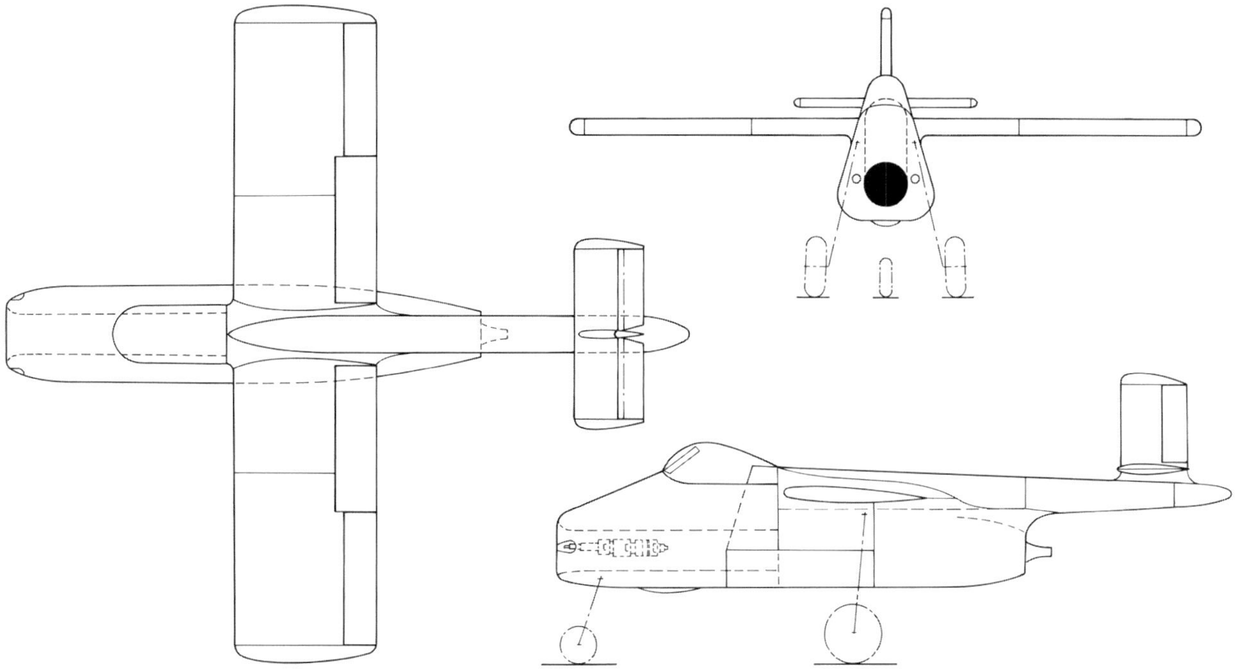

Blohm & Voss P 211 dated 29 September 1944. One BMW 003 A turbojet engine and 2 x MK 108 cannon. Wing span 7.6 m, Length 78.06 m and total height with wheels down 3.3 m.

Two views of the induction pipe on which it was proposed that the pilot of the BV 211 would sit. This was connected to a long boom which also served as a fuel tank and tail. Note also the fairing and connection points for the wing join to which the metal wing centre section would be fitted.

sequence from a mix of 50 per cent steel, 23 per cent wood, only 13 per cent Duralumin (which was in short supply to Germany by mid-1944) and 6 per cent miscellaneous materials. The 8.08 m long, 7.6 m span, high-wing P.211 featured a pod and boom fuselage in which the pilot was housed above the turbojet intake duct that gave stability to the nose section and from which extended a retractable tricycle undercarriage. The BMW 003 exhausted below the boom – which also served as a fuel tank – and tail.

Weighing 3100 kg, the P 211's maximum speed was forecast at 767 km/h with a rate of climb of 14.05 m/s at ground level and 2.46 m/s at 9000 m and a range of 720 km. The aircraft would be able to take off in 650 m if on a concrete runway and in 800 m if on grass and would be armed with two 30 mm MK 108 cannon.

Professor Ernst Heinkel and his *Generaldirektor*, *Dipl.-Ing.* Karl Frydag, opined to Allied interrogators in July 1945 that they believed the Blohm und Voss project was '... very promising, but would have taken some time in terms of experimental and development work.'

Focke-Wulf *Volksflitzer* and *Volksflugzeug* (or *Volksjäger*)

Focke-Wulf's design office at Bad Eilsen approached the 10 September RLM tender by scaling down the design of the company's April 1943 project known as the Fw 226 *Flitzer* ('Streaker'). Having proven success in its Fw 189 design, Focke-Wulf copied that aircraft's twin-boom layout for the *Flitzer* but incorporated both a jet engine – originally the HeS 011 – as well as an option for rocket power. By July 1944 therefore, three options existed: as a jet fighter with rocket power boost for quick, high-altitude interception work; a jet fighter with additional rocket boost for climb to medium altitudes; or a jet-powered fighter only, without rocket assistance but with two hours flying time at 10000 m.

The aircraft would carry either two 30 mm MK 108 cannon in the forward fuselage beneath the cockpit or two 30 mm MK 108 cannon in the fuselage and two 20 mm MG 151 cannon in the wings with provision for a ZFR telescopic gunsight. In the former configuration, the loaded weight of the *Flitzer* with 830 kg of fuel would be 3660 kg, while in the latter configuration, it would be 4350 kg with 1250 kg of fuel.

By simply substituting the HeS 011 for a BMW 003 and removing the rocket power, Focke-Wulf created, somewhat half-heartedly, the mid-wing '*Volksflitzer*'. Armament was to consist of two MK 108s and all-up flight weight would have been 3000 kg, while endurance would have been approximately 50 minutes at 10000 m.

A more serious proposal was the Focke-Wulf '*Volksflugzeug*' which featured a long intake duct for a BMW 003 with either a high swept or unswept wing with a span of 7.5 m and a distinctive swept back tailplane mounted on top of the tail fin. Measuring 8.80 m in length, and weighing 3050 kg, the *Volksflugzeug* would have needed a 1000 m take-off run and would have climbed at 14.5 m/s reaching a maximum speed of 820 km/h with some 45-50 minutes endurance at 10000 m.

In reality, the *Volksflitzer* would have demonstrated significantly lower performance characteristics than the *Volksflugzeug*, but Focke-Wulf apparently gave little priority to either design, treating them as little more than 'flights of fantasy' while working on more sophisticated designs such as the the planned Ta 183.

Junkers – possibly EF 123 or EF 124

Designed by *Professor* Heinrich Hertel, Junkers' Head of Aircraft Development, the Junkers proposal is believed to have centred around a ventrally-fitted BMW 003, with high, unswept wings and a single tail fin. The project progressed to model stage and is thought to have been assigned the design number EF 123 or EF 124, as Junkers used 'E' for '*Entwicklungflugzeug*' ('Developmental Aircraft') rather that 'P' – Project numbers.

Of the Junkers proposal to install a powerplant underneath the fuselage in order to attain a smaller surface of resistance, *Professor* Ernst Heinkel and his *Generaldirektor*, *Dipl.-Ing.* Karl Frydag, commented to Allied interrogators in July 1945: 'In our opinion this installation is dangerous in cases of forced landing and tends to catch fire. Besides, the powerplant beneath the fuselage would be destroyed in most cases of forced-landing, whereas the powerplant over the fuselage (in the case of the He 162), as experience has shown, never led to accidents in forced-landings.'

No armament information or technical specifications are known.

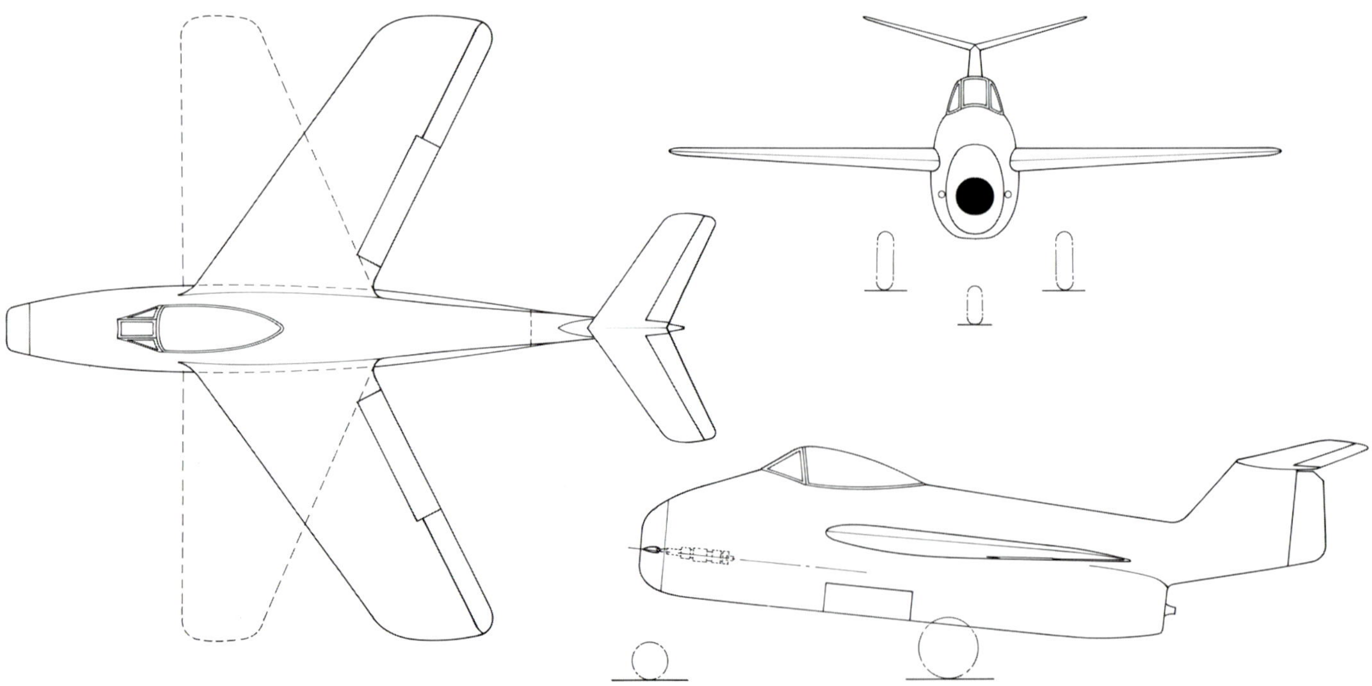

Focke-Wulf 'Volksflugzeug' dated 20 September 1944. One BMW 003 A turbojet engine and 2 x MK 108 cannon.

However, over the next three days, as the respective contenders deliberated and scoffed over their drawing boards, Heinkel and Günter reworked their P.1073-15 design and, with modifications that would appear were largely the work of the company's Rostock-Marienehe personnel, issued a new design for a '*Kleinstjäger*' ('Midget Fighter'), the P.1073-18, dated 11 September. The design retained a high unswept wing and twin fins and rudders, with a BMW 003 mounted in a dorsal location on the fuselage. Firepower was to comprise two 20 mm MG 151/20 cannon carrying 150 rpg installed symmetrically in the foreward fuselage, either side of the cockpit and below the pilot. The tricycle undercarriage was also retained, with the nosewheel retracting forward into the tip of the nose and ahead of the pilot. Together with 50 kg of armour plate, equipment (145 kg), and pilot (90 kg), the 'military weight' totalled 500 kg. With an airframe weight of 725 kg, the BMW 003 weight of 725 kg, fuel and tank combined weighing 550 kg, the overall weight of the aircraft was foreseen at 2500 kg. From the plans, it was foreseen that the aircraft would also be able to carry one SC 250 bomb as an offensive load, and figures were also submitted for an armament configuration of two MK 108s as an alternative to the MG 151 arrangement.

Speed was calculated at 810 km/h at ground level, 860 km/h at 6000 m and 800 km/h at 11000 m. Endurance was projected at 20 minutes at ground level and 33 minutes at 6000 m, while range would be 270 km at ground level and 440 km at 6000 m. Climbing speed was calculated at 22 m/s at ground level, 13.5 m/s at 6000 m and 4.5 m/s at 11000 m, which was shown to be a considerable improvement over a Bf 109 G with a DB 605 A engine under operational conditions. The P.1073-18 would be able to take off on a 650 m runway.[30]

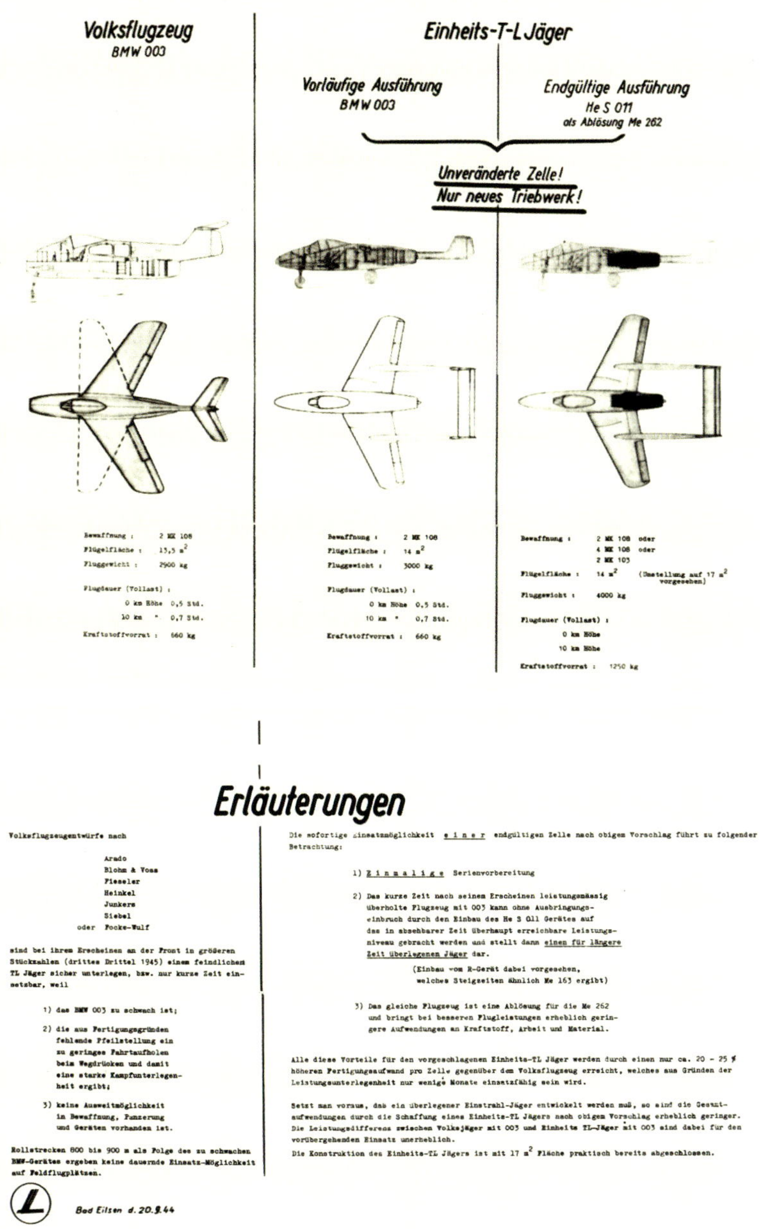

Volksflugzeug
BMW 003

Einheits-T-L Jäger

Vorläufige Ausführung
BMW 003

Endgültige Ausführung
He S 011
als Ablösung Me 262

Unveränderte Zelle!
Nur neues Triebwerk!

Bewaffnung : 2 MK 108
Flügelfläche : 13,5 m^2
Fluggewicht : 2900 kg
Flugdauer (Vollast) :
0 km Höhe 0,5 Std.
10 km " 0,7 Std.
Kraftstoffvorrat : 660 kg

Bewaffnung : 2 MK 108
Flügelfläche : 14 m^2
Fluggewicht : 3000 kg
Flugdauer (Vollast) :
0 km Höhe 0,5 Std.
10 km " 0,7 Std.
Kraftstoffvorrat : 660 kg

Bewaffnung : 2 MK 108 oder
4 MK 108 oder
2 MK 103
Flügelfläche : 14 m^2 (Umstellung auf 17 m^2 vorgesehen)
Fluggewicht : 4000 kg
Flugdauer (Vollast) :
0 km Höhe
10 km Höhe
Kraftstoffvorrat : 1250 kg

Erläuterungen

Volksflugzeugentwürfe nach

Arado
Blohm & Voss
Fieseler
Heinkel
Junkers
Siebel
oder Focke-Wulf

sind bei ihrem Erscheinen an der Front in größeren Stückzahlen (drittes Drittel 1945) einem feindlichen TL Jäger sicher unterlegen, bzw. nur kurze Zeit einsetzbar, weil

1) das BMW 003 zu schwach ist;
2) die aus Fertigungsgründen fehlende Pfeilstellung ein zu geringes Fahrtaufholen beim Wegdrücken und damit eine starke Kampfunterlegenheit ergibt;
3) keine Ausweitmöglichkeit in Bewaffnung, Panzerung und Geräten vorhanden ist.

Rollstrecken 800 bis 900 m als Folge des zu schwachen BMW-Gerätes ergeben keine dauernde Einsatz-Möglichkeit auf Feldflugplätzen.

Die sofortige Einsatzmöglichkeit e i n e r endgültigen Zelle nach obigem Vorschlag führt zu folgender Betrachtung:

1) E i n m a l i g e Serienvorbereitung
2) Das kurze Zeit nach seinem Erscheinen leistungsmässig überholte Flugzeug mit 003 kann ohne Ausbringungseinbruch durch den Einbau des He S 011 Gerätes auf das in absehbarer Zeit überhaupt erreichbare Leistungsniveau gebracht werden und stellt dann einen für längere Zeit überlegenen Jäger dar.
(Einbau vom R-Gerät dabei vorgesehen, welches Steigzeiten ähnlich Me 163 ergibt)
3) Das gleiche Flugzeug ist eine Ablösung für die Me 262 und bringt bei besseren Flugleistungen erheblich geringere Aufwendungen an Kraftstoff, Arbeit und Material.

Alle diese Vorteile für den vorgeschlagenen Einheits-TL Jäger werden durch einen nur ca. 20 - 25 % höheren Fertigungsaufwand pro Zelle gegenüber dem Volksflugzeug erreicht, welches aus Gründen der Leistungsunterlegenheit nur wenige Monate einsatzfähig sein wird.

Setzt man voraus, daß ein überlegener Einstrahl-Jäger entwickelt werden muß, so sind die Gesamtaufwendungen durch die Schaffung eines Einheits-TL Jägers nach obigem Vorschlag erheblich geringer. Die Leistungsdifferenz zwischen Volksjäger mit 003 und Einheits TL-Jäger mit 003 sind dabei für den vorübergehenden Einsatz unerheblich.
Die Konstruktion des Einheits-TL Jägers ist mit 17 m^2 Fläche praktisch bereits abgeschlossen.

Bad Eilsen d. 20.9.44

Two pages from an 'Explanation' document issued by Focke-Wulf on 20 September 1944 showing the differences and changes in design to the company's three submissions for the Volksjäger project, including the accommodation for either a BMW 003 or HeS 011 engine in the Volksflitzer concept.

Taken from an undated Junkers document entitled simply 'Volksjäger Projekt', these three views, each bearing a Junkers photograph reference, show what is believed to be a model of either the EF 123 or EF 124.

As an alternative to the MG 151/20, Heinkel proposed to fit two Rheinmetall-Borsig belt-fed, electrically ignited 30 mm MK 108 cannon in the P.1073. Good for close-range fire, it was a powerful weapon, but its cheapness and ease of manufacture made it prone to jamming and other forms of malfunction. Nevertheless, the weapon achieved devastating results against Allied bomber formations when used to good effect by skilled pilots flying the Fw 190 and Me 262.

Heinkel planned to install a pair of 20 mm Mauser MG 151/20 cannon into the P.1073, and it eventually armed the He 162. Originally designed to fire a 15 mm projectile, the calibre was increased when it was found that a 15 mm shell did not carry a sufficient quantity of explosive. The gun was widely used, proved to have a high rate of fire and excellent ballistics. In its final form the weapon weighed 42.4 kg and had a muzzle velocity of 790 metres per second.

One-by-one, the submissions from all five companies were delivered to the RLM in time to conform to the required deadline, although Arado did make the note on its submission that, '*As a consequence of the limited time available (2 days) the project as submitted could only be generated in draft form*.'[31] But from one quarter there was bitter disdain; *Professor* Willy Messerschmitt gave vent to his feelings in a note prepared for Albert Speer and Ernst Heinkel in October: 'The Me 262 must form the backbone of the *Luftwaffe* air defence in the deciding battles of the spring of 1945. The Me 262 is a reality, the *Volksjäger* only a hope. I cannot understand the need to develop a further aircraft when we already possess a superior machine. For about a year the Me 262 has been developed and parts are still required. Workmanship is lacking which endangers the performance of the machine and yet while we are 'screaming' for materials and parts, someone wants to develop a new aircraft.'[32]

On 14 September representatives from the contending companies met at the RLM at the start of a two-day meeting to formally present their proposals in person to a panel of senior *Luftwaffe* technical officers and Ministry officials. Each representative was permitted five minutes to outline their respective project.[33] With stupendous irony, the man selected by the RLM to 'assess' all the proposals was none other than the Technical Director of EHAG at Wien-Schwechat, *Dipl.-Ing.* Carl Francke, who also happened to be representing Heinkel at the meeting!

After consideration, the proposals from Focke-Wulf were judged unrealistic, with a sense that the company was participating only for the

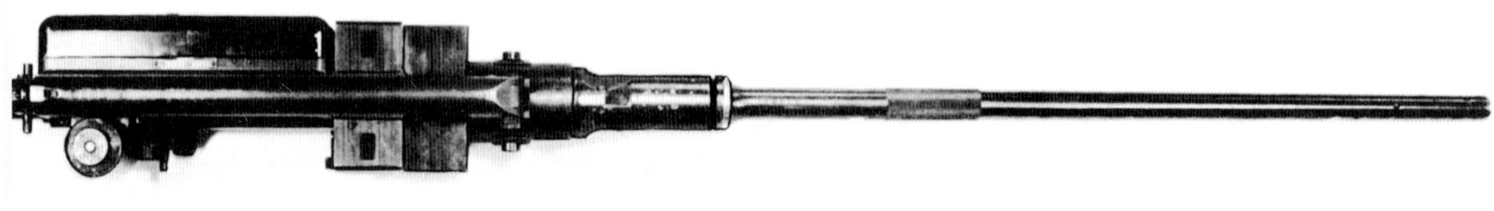

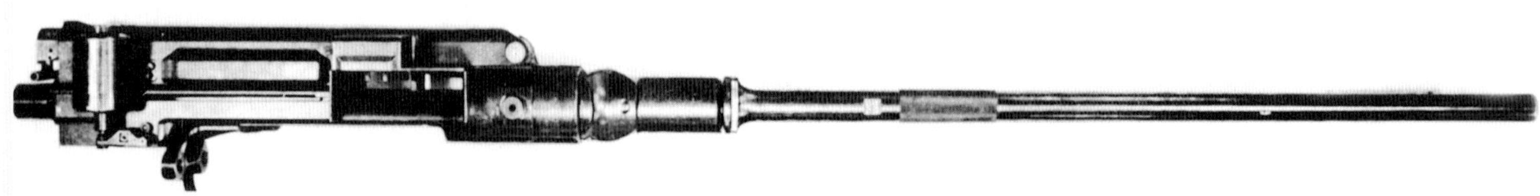

Me 262s of Erprobungskommando 262 at Lechfeld in the summer of 1944. The Erprobungskommando was the first test unit to be equipped with the new jet fighter which heralded a new dawn in air combat – and Willy Messerschmitt would attempt to guard, jealously and zealously, his position at the forefront of German technological advance. In October 1944, he wrote: 'The Me 262 must form the backbone of the Luftwaffe air defence in the deciding battles of the spring of 1945. The Me 262 is a reality, the Volksjäger only a hope.'

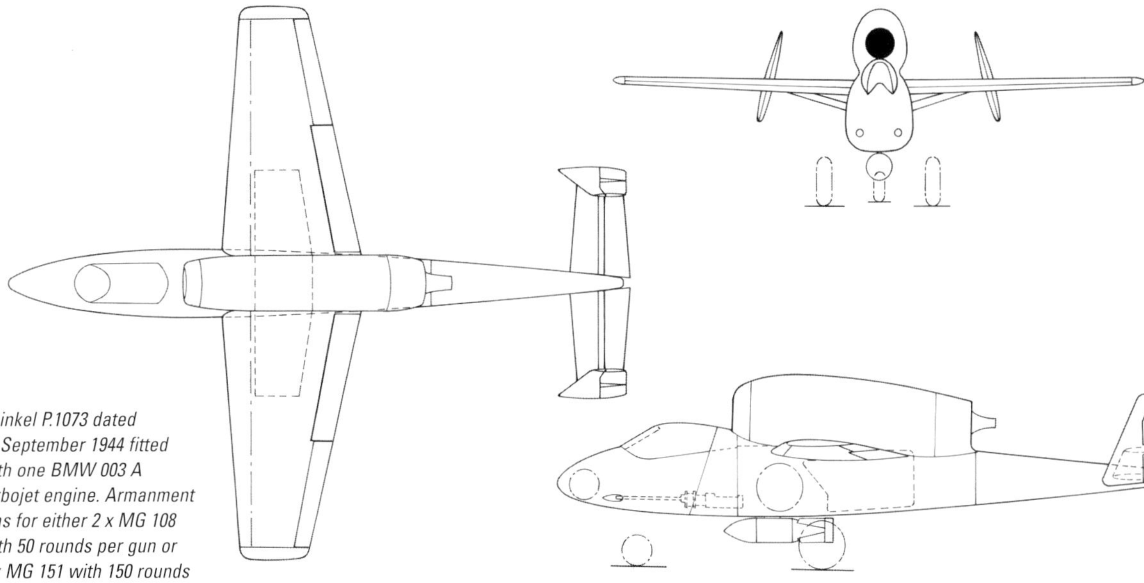

Heinkel P.1073 dated 11 September 1944 fitted with one BMW 003 A turbojet engine. Armanment was for either 2 x MG 108 with 50 rounds per gun or 2 x MG 151 with 150 rounds per gun plus a single SC 250 bomb under the fuselage.

purposes of gathering information. However, it is unlikely that this would have caused much upset to Focke-Wulf judging by the contents of a memo sent to the RLM by the company's design team in which they warned: 'By the time it reaches the front in any meaningful numbers (third quarter of 1945), any *Volksjäger*-type aircraft is certain to be inferior to enemy jet fighters and its operational life span would be brief because: the BMW 003 is too weak a powerplant; the lack of wing sweep, dictated on production grounds, will limit dive speed and impair combat performance; there is no design capacity for improvements in armament, armour or other equipment.'[34]

The Arado and Junkers proposals were completely rejected, and Heinkel's P.1073-18 was also regarded as unsuitable. It remained for the Blohm und Voss proposal, the P.211-01, to be viewed the best of those projects submitted, both from aerodynamic and engineering viewpoints. Francke, representing EHAG, protested that the other submissions had their weights and performances calculated by a different formula to that employed by his company, thus placing the Heinkel proposal in an unfavorable light.

Dr.-Ing. Richard Vogt, the Technical Director and Chief Designer at Blohm und Voss scornfully observed that despite knowing – purportedly – of the so-called '*Volksjäger*' requirement for 'one month' via *Dipl.-Ing.* Francke, Heinkel had still not adhered – or been able to adhere – closely to the RLM's specification requirements in terms of armament and endurance. Far from a 'simple-to-build' fighter, the P.1073 was actually very complex in its design which would result in the need for dedicated cranes to be available at all operational airfields in order to remove and

Professor Willy Messerschmitt, whose company had produced the Me 262 jet fighter, wrote a stinging critique of the Volksjäger project which, in particular, was directed at the efforts by Heinkel whose project he viewed as unnecessary and wasteful.

Dipl.-Ing. Carl Francke, the Technical Director of EHAG, seen here to the left sitting next to Ernst Heinkel, undertook the dual role of representing his firm's interest in the Volksjäger tendering process as well as assessing all competing entries. He would later demonstrate a tireless dedication to EHAG's efforts in the production of the He 162.

Dr.-Ing. Richard Vogt, the Technical Director and Chief Designer at Blohm und Voss, objected most strongly to what he felt were the unfair and prejudiced methods used in the Volksjäger tendering process: 'Francke gave only five minutes and sat timing it with his watch,' Vogt complained.

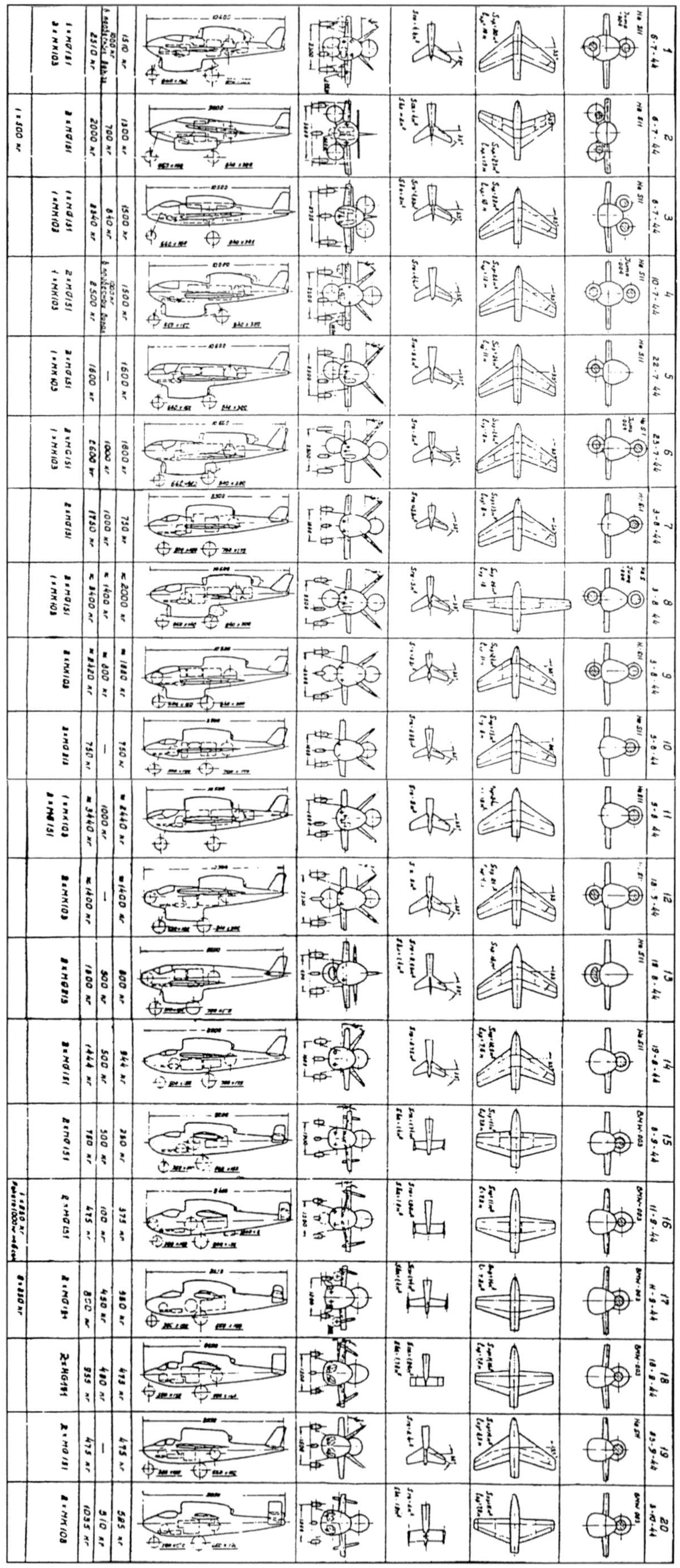

After the Russian occupation in 1945, remaining EHAG personnel drafted an overview of the He 162 design evolution from the beginnings in July 1944 up to early October 1944. The above chart shows 20 designs that lead to its inception and ultimately to the preliminary He 162 A-1.

lift away the dorsally-mounted engines. To remove the P.1073's wings required even more work: the removal of the engine, its casing and fuel pipes.[35]

Vogt also wrote after the meeting that '... Messerschmitt were not interested in the *Volksjäger* project because it offered no technical advance over the Me 262.'

'For the discussion relating to the Blohm und Voss project, Francke gave only five minutes and sat timing it with his watch in his hand. It was obvious that he was not the least bit interested in this proposal. This, despite *Oberstleutant* Knemeyer and the advisors, *Stabsing.* Malz and Schwarz, saying that the Blohm und Voss project had much to its credit even though the weight given in the specification was slightly higher. However this could have been solved through further discussion and further work.'

The following day, despite initial rejection, all the other participants began recalculating the weights and performance of their proposals on the same basis as that used by Heinkel. The revised specification from Blohm und Voss found favour with *Oberst* Diesing, the *Chef TLR*, principally because the positioning of the engine did not obstruct the pilot's view, the design used less Duralumin in its construction – a material in short supply – and it could be assembled reasonably quickly.

By contrast, the Heinkel design was found to be lacking, both in terms of range and endurance. Its armament was also considered insufficient and there were some concerns as to whether EHAG would be able to comply with the demands of production. The 'projected programme' was given as follows:

1 October 1944	– Mockup inspection
10 December 1944	– Ready for take-off (first aircraft)
January 1945	– Start of large quantity production
April 1945	– Production output of 1,000 aircraft
	– Increased production up to 2,000 per month.[36]

However, the EHAG representatives managed to allay any fears and assured the panel that the company would be able to meet the delivery date requirement and would need fewer man-hours of construction. Certainly, capacity would be available following the cancellation of the He 177 and the He 219 night fighter.[37] In addition the undercarriage legs from the Bf 109 would be used, saving the need for new forgings, tools and wheels.

At this point, despite the inherent advantages in its construction, concerns arose regarding the Blohm und Voss P 211: it was thought a power loss could result in its long 2.5 m intake duct. Furthermore, its shape could induce drag, and because the air intake was only just over a metre off the ground, the risk existed of dirt and foreign bodies being ingested resulting in engine damage – a very real danger if the aircraft was to operate from rough, forward airfields.[38]

So it was, that after lengthy deliberation, the Heinkel project won the day – but only the day.

Another meeting held on the 17th to chew the matter over, proved inconclusive.[39] The debate continued on 19 September when a further meeting was held under the chairmanship of *Generaling.* Roluf Lucht, the head of the *Entwicklungs Hauptkommission Flugzeuge* (Chief Development Commission for Aircraft) – a committee which had been formed only four days earlier on the orders of Speer – at which all the competing proposals were reviewed again, these including the existing Arado, Blohm und Voss and Heinkel projects, and, apparently, new submissions from Fieseler, Focke-Wulf, Junkers and Siebel. It was again agreed that the Blohm und Voss P.211-01 was superior in every respect to all other contenders, but the meeting ended in a heated argument between Karl Frydag, who disagreed with the decision, and *Stabsing.* Schwarz, the deputy leader of the Fighter Aircraft Development Group of TLR/Fl-E2, and, yet again, no final selection was made.[40]

According to one of the participants in this meeting, *Dr.-Ing.* Vogt of Blohm und Voss, the Siebel proposal was hardly considered and yet it was very evident that the Heinkel proposal had already been accepted beforehand without sufficient comparison with the Blohm und Voss

General Stabsing. Roluf Lucht, the head of the Entwicklungs Hauptkommission Flugzeuge, was an éminence grise who exerted considerable influence over the early stages of the Volksjäger programme and who favoured the Heinkel proposal.

proposal. Vogt commented: 'The manner in which these critical questions were dealt with during the committee meeting shook me to the core. It was impossible to speak of a review of the agenda topics, let alone a serious examination... Heinkel's *Generaldirektor* Frydag stated that the Blohm und Voss proposal contained a number of technical drawbacks, but no discussions regarding similar shortcomings to the Heinkel proposal were mentioned.'

Vogt concluded from this meeting that from the perspective view of Blohm und Voss, further work on the *Volksjäger* project was pointless.

Astonishingly, amidst all this deliberation, EHAG had quietly finished work on a small-scale mock-up of the projected *Volksjäger* and invited the RLM to inspect it at their convenience.

Then, on 21 September, a conference was held at OKL's forward headquarters at Rosengarten, near Rastenburg, in East Prussia, to finalise the selection of the new fighter. This conference was attended by *Reichsmarschall* Göring, *Generaloberst* Robert *Ritter* von Greim (commander of *Luftflotte 6*), *Generalmajor* Adolf Galland, *Generalleutnant* Karl Koller (the former Chief of the *Luftwaffe* Operations Staff), *Oberst* Ulrich Diesing *(Chef TLR)*, Karl Frydag, *Generalstabsing.* Lucht and Karl-Otto Saur. The Heinkel design was clearly favored by the Armaments Ministry faction under Saur, who, for political reasons, had already officially crowned the proposed aircraft the '*Volksjäger*' following Diesing's earlier specification to industry. Galland, who staunchly advocated the Me 262, recalled in his memoirs that: 'From the beginning I had strongly opposed the *Volksjäger* project. In contrast to the creators of this idea, my objections were based on factual reasons such as insufficient performance, range, armament, poor visibility, and dubious air worthiness. Furthermore, I was convinced that this aircraft could not be brought into worthwhile operation before the end of the war. The terrific expenditure of labour and material was bound to be at the expense of the Me 262. To my mind, all resources ought to be concentrated on this well-tested fighter in order to make the best of the possibilities remaining to us. If we scattered our strength once more in the last phase of the war, then all our efforts would be in vain.'[41]

In a report prepared by British Air Intelligence in late June 1945, there is the remarkable suggestion that some degree of 'sharp practice' may have been employed by those officers championing the cause of the *Volksjäger*; Group Captain S.D.Felkin, the well-known intelligence officer attached to the Air Ministry's A.D.I.(K) and a man greatly experienced in interrogating German aviation personaities of all ranks, recorded: 'A curious light is thrown on these events by a document which purports to record the interrogation of *Flugbaumeister* Malz of the single- and twin-engine fighter section of Fl.-E 2 of the RLM department dealing with the development of aircraft types. Malz is recorded as having made the astounding statement that when Lucht, Diesing and Knemeyer made their decisive report on the 162 to Göring, certain technical documents required to support their case were lacking and that, in consequence, Malz was ordered to have faked pictures of the 162 prepared by a cinema expert on such subjects. The faked pictures included views purporting to show the 162 above the clouds and executing a roll.'[42]

On 23 September, during discussions at his Rastenburg headquarters, Hitler accepted Saur's advice and ordered the rapid design and mass production, without testing, of the Heinkel proposal for the *Volksjäger* (actually described as the '*Einstrahltriebkleinstjäger*'), which was to be produced under the *Jägerstab's* Production Programme 226 at a provisional rate of 1,000 machines per month by April 1945.[43] Speer, also present at this meeting, noted that Hitler instructed the design to

Generalkommissar Phillipp Kessler would play a key role in co-ordinating the production of the He 162 in late 1944/early 1945. An engineer by training, he was awarded the Knight's Cross to the War Service Cross with Swords.

be carried forward with a 'vigorous drive' with the manufacturer, the industrial and governmental authorities and the military all working with appropriate co-ordination and co-operation.[44]

The same day, *Generalstabsing.* Lucht and representatives of the *Entwicklungs Hauptkommission Flugzeuge* inspected the small-scale mock-up of the Heinkel P.1073 at Wien-Heidfeld and were handed a ten-page report, with accompanying drawings, prepared that day in which the P.1073 was described as a '*Strahljäger*' – a jet fighter. Armament had settled on two MK 108s each carrying 50 rounds, while the aircraft had an overall weight of 2571 kg and a maximum speed of 840 km/h at 6000 m, with a corresponding range of 430 km and an endurance of 33 minutes.[45] At this point, the balance began to shift in Heinkel's favour.

Next day, 24 September, following a suggestion from Speer, Hitler nominated *Generalkommissar* Phillipp Kessler, Director General of the Bergmann Electricity Corporation and Chairman of the Armaments Advisory Board, as *Kommissar* of the '*Einstrahltriebkleinstjäger*' programme and of propulsion unit production. A former artilleryman and an engineer by training, Kessler had worked as Chief Engineer for Siemens-Schuckert prior to joining Bergmann in 1932. He had also served as Speer's *Kommissar* for ball-bearing production and in May 1944 had been awarded the *Ritterkreuz des Kriegsverdienstkreuzes mit Schwertern* (Knight's Cross to the War Merit Cross with Swords) for his vigorous role in sustaining ball-bearing production earlier on 22 May 1944.[46]

In a move redolent of the fanatic, yet wholly unrealistic mindset of the Nazi leadership at this time, on 26 September, Hitler issued a decree calling for the formation of the *Volkssturm*, a last-ditch people's militia for the defence of the German homeland. Inspired by the concept of the *Volkssturm*, Saur, with the aid of the *Reichsjugendführer* (Reich Youth Leader), *Reichsleiter* Artur Axmann, then proposed a scheme to provide the necessary pilots for the thousands of He 162 fighters which were expected to roll off the production lines in 1945. This was *Generaloberst* Keller's vision taking on a real dimension. According to Werner Baumbach, the acclaimed *Luftwaffe* bomber commander and *Ritterkreuzträger*, Keller authorised an entire year's intake of the Hitler Youth to begin immediate glider training with the NSFK, after a short period of which they were to transfer directly to the He 162, but without any intermediate powered flying experience. Gunnery training was to be provided on the ground.[47] These *Volksjäger* units were seen as the aerial counterpart of the *Volkssturm*.

On 24 October 1944, a meeting in Berlin, chaired by Lucht, discussed a variety of training aircraft including the Bü 181, Ar 96, Ar 396, the Skoda Kauba, Si 204, Bf 109, Fw 190 and Ta 152 as well as how best to train in preparation for the He 162. In the case of the *Volksjäger*, discussion centred around the training of boys to become pilots but somehow without the need for fuel. Therefore there was a requirement for a towable, high-performance glider which would be comparable to an actual He 162, but which would be sparing of precious fuel. According to Lucht, the meeting did not offer any immediate soloutions, but it was suggested that this matter should be looked into further. The construction of such a machine was envisaged to be handled jointly between EHAG (allowing six weeks) and the NSFK (allowing a further six weeks), under direction of the *Entwicklungs Hauptkommission Flugzeuge*.

The proposal was for a glider weighing between 400-500 kg, with a speed of 4 m per second. The craft was to replicate, as far as possible, the take-off and landing attributes of a He 162, using a 150 hp motorised winch which, with a 1000 m long cable, would release at 250 m, although if extended to 1500 m could release at 400 m, which was considered sufficient for the pilot to aquire a feel for flight without having to leave the vicinity of an airfield. However, it was proposed that this could be increased to a release height of 1000 m using a 700 hp winch with a tow cable of 2500 m.

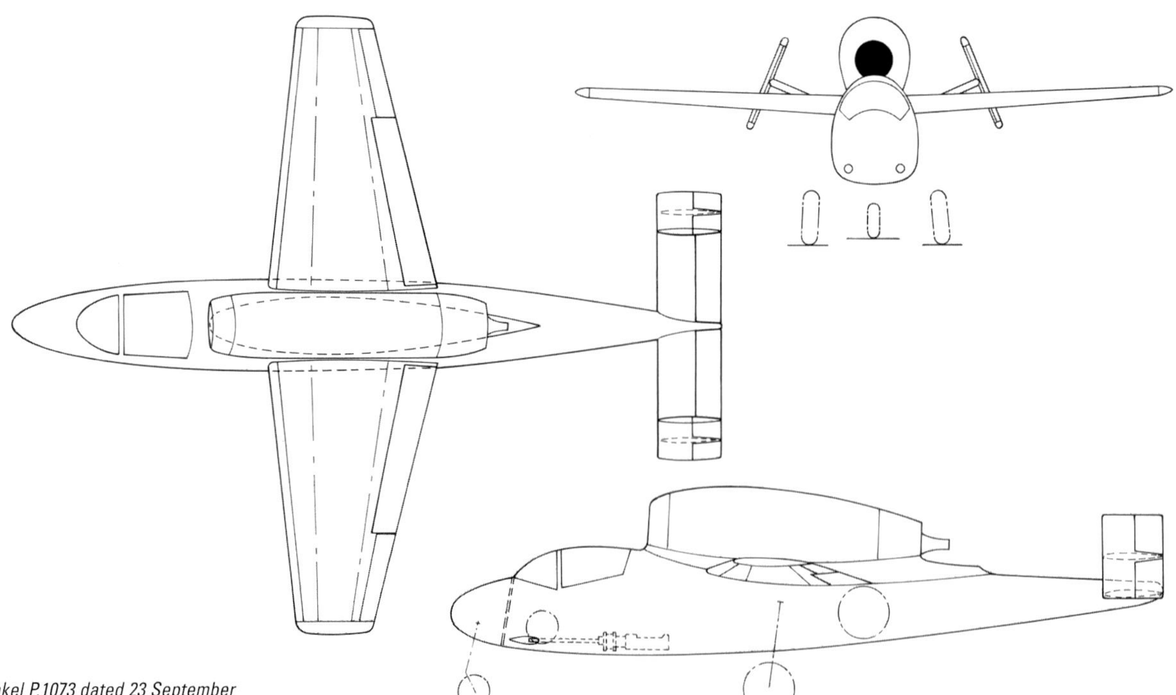

Heinkel P.1073 dated 23 September 1944 fitted with one BMW 003 A turbojet engine. Armanment was for 2 x MG 151 cannon.

It was the intention to build ten such glider trainers by 29 December 1944 under the direction of *Oberst* Schaede, including two to be fitted with Maybach Panzer Motoren. If these ten prototypes proved successful, then the plan was to construct a further 200 examples.[48]

News seems to have filtered through to Göring who was visiting Hitler at Rastenburg and as Adolf Galland recalled: 'Göring himself became a victim of the national frenzy with which the planning of the *Volksjäger* programme had infected almost everyone connected with air defence. "Hundreds! Thousands! Umpteen thousands!", exclaimed Göring, "Until the enemy has been chased back beyond the borders of Germany."'[49] However, in reality Göring had little influence in the matter since the decision to proceed with the *Volksjäger* had been taken by Hitler and Speer.

In his memoirs, Baumbach recorded: 'With the help of Artur Axmann, the sensible *Reichsjugendführer*, and his *Stabsführer*, Moeckel, who was killed in a motor accident shortly afterwards, I managed to convince nearly everyone of the absurdity of this idea. Even the He 162 called for thorough fighter training and could not "be flown by any Hitler Youth". But Saur continued to advocate his project with might and main, and no technical or other argument could convince him that the "*Volksjäger*" was no "people's fighter".'[50]

Yet even on 28 September, it seems there was still doubt about Heinkel, for the RLM requested that Blohm und Voss return for a meeting on 2 October to discuss their proposal. No one seems to have informed the Ministry of Armaments and War Production however, for the following day, Albert Speer issued a directive to the effect that production of the *Volksjäger* was to commence immediately without need for the outcome or consequence of trials. In any case, the provisional Heinkel mock-up had been cleared by TLR/Fl-E2 and *E-Stelle* Rechlin.[51]

At midday on 29 September 1944, amidst feelings of excitement, anticipation and, undoubtedly, some trepidation, Ernst Heinkel assembled his senior managers and engineers for a meeting at his villa in Wien to discuss plans for production of the *Volksjäger* – or as Heinkel saw it, for reasons of personal prestige, the 'He 500'. In attendance were Siegfried Günter, Karl Schwärzler (Chief Designer at Wien and Rostock), Otto Butter (the Deputy Chief Designer and known as the inventor of shot-riveting), Karl Hayn (EHAG Works Director), Ulrich Raue (Works Director, Schwechat) and Karl-Otto Burmeister (Senior Production Advisor). Carl Franke had returned from the meetings in Berlin and opened discussions with the announcement: 'We have the contract for the *Kleinstjäger*. Proviso: first flight on 1 December 1944; main series production, March 1945. We had not reckoned with such little time.'

Heinkel: 'We have to keep to the proposed schedule. All the people involved will still have duties to perform. I can get 150 construction workers from Messerschmitt.'

Günter: 'From tomorrow I can deliever the first project documents and the rest can follow latest within two weeks.'

Hayn: 'By the end of December 1944 I must have all the serious construction information. Then, by the end of January, I can deliver the necessary working proposals and by the end of February, I will need all the tools and machinery so that from March I can deliver the series production.'

Heinkel: 'Before that I want to know when the prototype and drawings will be ready as we have only nine weeks before the first flight.'

Schwärzler: 'We can finalise the schedule when we have the project drawings.'

Heinkel: 'Schwärzler, it's no good putting obstacles in the way; we have to move ahead as per schedule.'

Karl Schwärzler, EHAG's Chief Designer at the Wien and Rostock plants (photographed here after the war) completed detailed drawings of the He 162 in little over a month from being commissioned. It was an extraordinary accomplishment.

Schwärzler: 'The earliest I can comment on this is tomorrow.'

Francke: 'Butter, when can you produce a list of all the material needed for the prototype, including drawings and parts?'

Butter: 'We need five weeks for construction.'

Raue: 'If we need more than five weeks, can we run over? But as from tomorrow we'll need all the support we can get.'

Butter: 'The construction schedule can be maintained, dare I say, if the following can be put in place: the necessary number of co-workers; a division of labour; construction alterations; an understanding with department management over the need for overtime. I am concerned regarding the outsourced Messerschmitt workers. From my 450 men, I will search out the best 250 who will remain in the Fichtegasse office. All the others will be responsible for other work in the main office. As an incentive, we should get 10,000 cigarettes and 500 bottles of vermouth wine to distribute as a goodwill gesture.'

Raue: 'I'd like the same as well.'

Francke: 'I believe that Butter and Raue can maintain the deadline as long as *Dr.* Heinkel can agree.'

Heinkel: 'I agree totally.'[52]

On the last day of the month, *Oberstleutnant* Knemeyer formally announced the Heinkel project as the winner of the *Volksjäger* competition and this ended all further discussion on the merits of its selection, despite continued protests from *Dr.-Ing.* Vogt of Blohm und Voss, who was advised of the decision by teleprinter message and whose P.211 was still facing problems with design. According to Vogt, Lucht apologised personally for not being aware of the fact that discussions had taken place directly between Frydag and Saur behind his back and which had brought matters to a close. It appeared that Frydag's main grounds for objecting to the Blohm und Voss project was the positioning of its engine and its extended air intake which would have severe effects on the aircraft's performance.[53]

The placing of a development contract was, however, little more than a formality, for the detailed design of the Heinkel fighter had actually begun six days earlier, on 24 September. Despite Heinkel requesting the designation 'He 500', by 3 October the RLM had allocated the defunct type number '8-162' to the aircraft, in a misguided attempt to confuse Allied intelligence as to the aircraft's true identity.[54]

Heinkel got to work on the new He 162 without delay. On 1 October, preparations commenced for the start of series manufacture with prototype drawings being issued to the experimental workshops at Wien-Heidfeld on the 15th as well as commencement of jig and tool design.[55] But only four days after work started, the *Chef* TLR requested further changes in addition to those already requested involving the BMW engine installation, wing configuration and the installation of the undercarriage and fuel tank. These centred on a redesign of the planned canopy jettisoning system, the installation of RATO units and an enhanced oxygen system for high-altitude.[56]

On 4 October, EHAG issued a new '*Baubeschreibung*' (specification) covering the He 162 which included a BMW 003 A-1 engine, two 30 MK 108 cannon with 50 rpg and a speed of 780 km/h at 11 kilometres, with an endurance of 57 minutes and a range of 660 km.

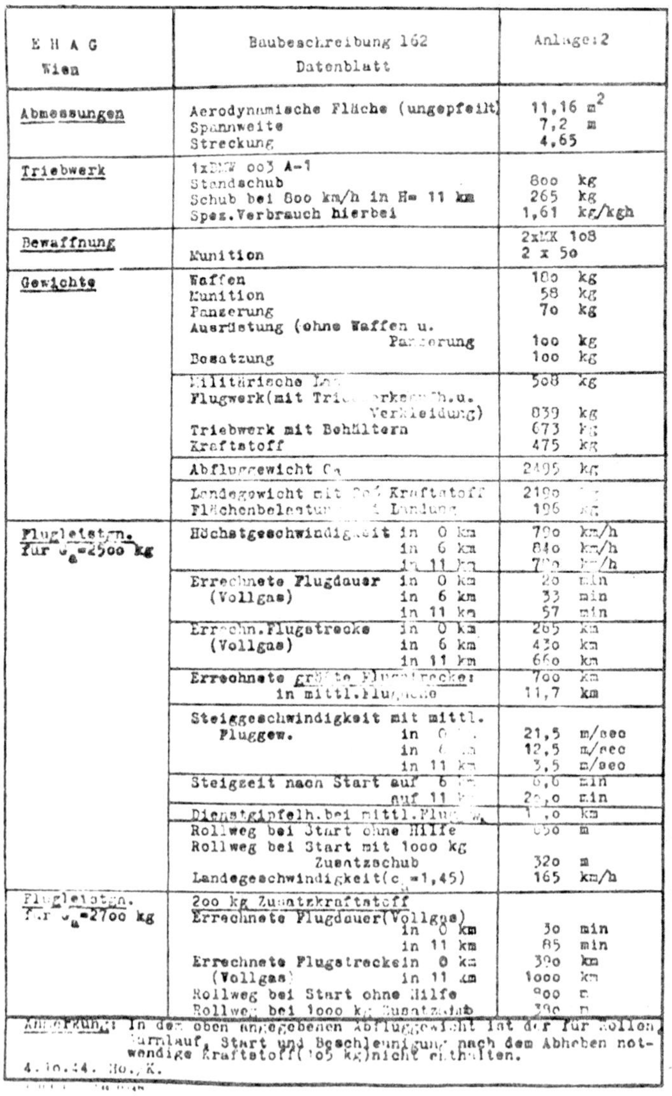

E H A G Wien	Baubeschreibung 162 Datenblatt	Anlage:2
Abmessungen	Aerodynamische Fläche (ungepfeilt)	11,16 m²
	Spannweite	7,2 m
	Streckung	4,65
Triebwerk	1xBMW 003 A-1	
	Standschub	800 kg
	Schub bei 800 km/h in H= 11 km	265 kg
	Spez.Verbrauch hierbei	1,61 kg/kgh
Bewaffnung		2xMK 108
	Munition	2 x 50
Gewichte	Waffen	180 kg
	Munition	58 kg
	Panzerung	70 kg
	Ausrüstung (ohne Waffen u. Panzerung	100 kg
	Besatzung	100 kg
	Militärische La[illegible]	508 kg
	Flugwerk(mit Tri[illegible]h.u. Verkleidung)	839 kg
	Triebwerk mit Behältern	673 kg
	Kraftstoff	475 kg
	Abfluggewicht Ga	2495 kg
	Landegewicht mit [illegible] Kraftstoff	2190 [illegible]
	Flächenbelastun[illegible] Landung	196 kg
Flugleistgn. für Ga=2500 kg	Höchstgeschwindigkeit in 0 km	790 km/h
	in 6 km	840 km/h
	in 11 km	7[illegible] km/h
	Errechnete Flugdauer (Vollgas) in 0 km	20 min
	in 6 km	33 min
	in 11 km	57 min
	Errechn.Flugstrecke (Vollgas) in 0 km	265 km
	in 6 km	430 km
	in 11 km	660 km
	Errechnete größte Flugstrecke: in mittl.Flughöhe	700 km 11,7 km
	Steiggeschwindigkeit mit mittl. Fluggew. in 0 km	21,5 m/sec
	in 6 km	12,5 m/sec
	in 11 km	3,5 m/sec
	Steigzeit nach Start auf 6 km	6,6 min
	auf 11 km	2[illegible],0 min
	Dienstgipfelh.bei mittl.Flugw.	[illegible],0 km
	Rollweg bei Start ohne Hilfe	[illegible]50 m
	Rollweg bei Start mit 1000 kg Zusatzschub	320 m
	Landegeschwindigkeit(ca =1,45)	165 km/h
Flugleistgn. für Ga=2700 kg	200 kg Zusatzkraftstoff	
	Errechnete Flugdauer(Vollgas) in 0 km	30 min
	in 11 km	85 min
	Errechnete Flugstrecke in 0 km	390 km
	(Vollgas) in 11 km	1000 km
	Rollweg bei Start ohne Hilfe	900 m
	Rollweg bei 1000 kg Zusatzschub	390 m

Anmerkung: In dem oben angegebenen Abfluggewicht ist der für Rollen, Warmlauf, Start und Beschleunigung nach dem Abheben notwendige Kraftstoff (105 kg) nicht enthalten.
4.10.44. Ho./K.

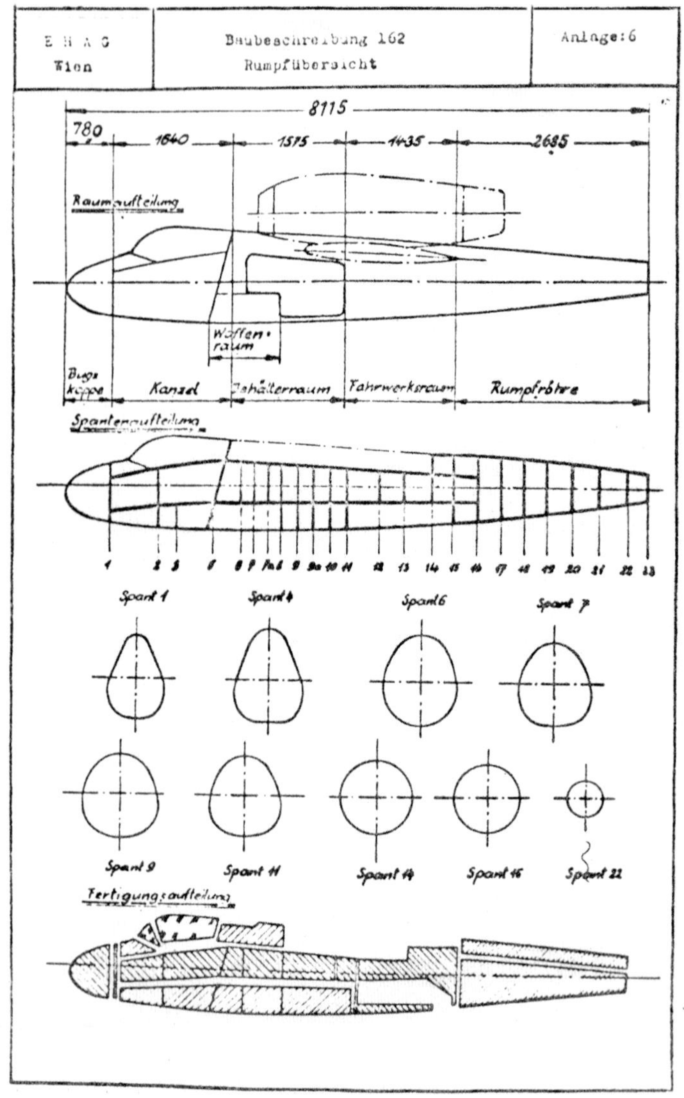

Above and opposite page: Three documents from the EHAG Baubeschreibung 162 dated 4 October 1944. A general data sheet (left); the design of the fuselage (centre) and the armament layout (right).

Three days later, a large conference was held at Heinkel's offices on the Fichtegasse in Wien, which, intriguingly included design, technical and engineering representatives from Messerschmitt, Junkers, Focke-Wulf and Dornier. The aim was to discuss the construction and general technical feasibility of the He 162 in order to see 'who' was able to do 'what' – presumably as a construction consortium. All aspects of the proposed aircraft were examined including fuselage, tail assembly and the connection of the tail assembly to fuselage, wing-fuselage connections, functioning of the undercarriage, nosewheel hydraulics and door, armour plating, seat position, cockpit canopy, wings, controls and steering.

The general conclusion was that more time might be needed to undertake detailed development of the various fixings and parts.[57]

By now, senior operational and tactical officers from the Staff of the *General der Jagdflieger* began to show interest in the new fighter concept. On 8 October, the Austrian *Ritterkreuzträger*, *Major* Hartmann Grasser, a former *Jagddivision* commander and *Kommandeur* of III./JG 1 and II./JG 110 with 103 victories to his credit, accompanied by *Flg.Stabs.Ing.* Rauchensteiner, visited Heinkel to inspect the mock-up produced by his fellow countrymen.

By the end of the month, the *Volksjäger* project was given the highest priority by the *Führer*. EHAG responded to this and in an unparallelled feat, the Heinkel design team under Günter and Schwärzler managed to complete the detailed drawings by 5 November. The production drawings, which amounted to approximately 1,000, were completed, and series production of He 162 components commenced. The total number of manhours expended in the design departments, including the preparation of production drawings, was of the order of 200,000 hours. This scale of effort was only achieved by Heinkel employing almost their entire design staff of 370 men on the He 162 comprising, and temporarily dropping all other work.

As indication of Heinkel's commitment to the project, the following staff were assigned to the preparation of the prototype and production drawings:

Division Leaders	-	12
Group Leaders	-	25
Senior Designers	-	20
Designers & Technicians	-	50
Draughtsmen	-	143
Stress men	-	50
Jig and Tool Draughtsmen	-	20
Standards and Tolerances	-	20
Checkers	-	30
		370

Under 'normal' circumstances, Heinkel would employ around 150 personnel on such a project.

This remarkable operation was accomplished as a result of many of the Heinkel design staff sleeping by their drawing boards during this period, and working a minimum of 72 hours per week, and a maximum

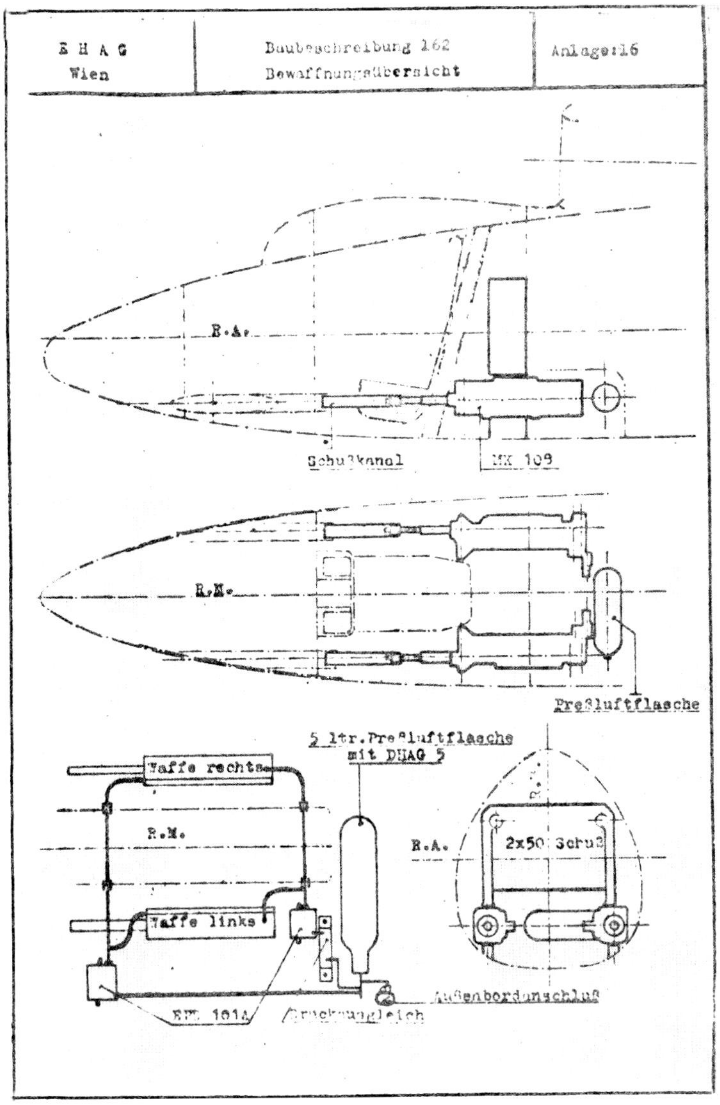

of about 90 hours, for some two to three months.[58] Even wind tunnel tests conducted at the AVA Göttingen were completed.[59]

But such accomplishments counted for little with Professor Willy Messerschmitt; on 23 October, from his company's offices housed in a former mountain infantry barracks at Oberammergau deep in southern Bavaria, Professor Willi Messerschmitt drafted a scornful and damning indictment of the *Volksjäger* programme, a copy of which was sent to Albert Speer and Ernst Heinkel among others[60]: 'I regard the project for producing a cheap fighter with a BMW 003A propulsion unit for operational use in large numbers in the spring of 1945 as having failed – at any rate in its present-day form.

'The technical requirements postulated are erroneous as the functions of the *Volksjäger* can be better carried out by already existing and proved aircraft. A development which does not conform in performance to existing technical possibilities is always behind the times… In my opinion there is not the slightest possibility that the *Volksjäger* programme can become sufficiently advanced by spring 1945 to warrant our counting on the aircraft becoming operational in large numbers. It is a delusion to think that the 162 can be developed and produced by "surplus manufacturing capacity" without disturbing production of current types, and in particular, of the Me 262. Me 262 production is not yet well established. Jigs, skilled labour and control personnel are still lacking… The Me 262 is a really superior weapon … whilst the 162 is only a hope… No effort would be too great to realise the most rapid development possible of an aircraft with a superior performance to the Me 262; we do not, however, need a machine with an inferior performance, which is what is contemplated in the case of the 162. This type should therefore be rejected.'

Whilst the superiority – in most respects – of the Me 262 cannot be questioned, ironically Messerschmitt's diatribe serves only to lend some credence to the *Volksjäger* concept. By highlighting the delays affecting production of the Me 262, Messerschmitt was actually demonstrating his own 'delusion' of fast and reliable Me 262 output.

Because the German aviation industry tended to use a large amount of general-purpose (rather than specialised) machinery, a high proportion of skilled labour was required for the workforce. According to the Aircraft Industry Report of the US Strategic Bombing Survey, German airframe plants employed about 450,000 persons in October 1944. About 23 per cent, or 103,500, were women. The total number of Germans employed, both men and women, was only 52 per cent of the entire workforce. The remaining 48 per cent, or 216,000, was composed of political prisoners, prisoners of war, Jews, and foreign nationals of both sexes. Of the total workforce, some 36 per cent, or 162,000, were foreigners, many of which were forced workers.[61]

Furthermore, the Me 262 had been designed and developed to the production standards of 1940-43, which aimed at a 'zero defects'-level of manufacturing quality, and this only added to the difficulties resulting from the shortage of skilled labour. Series manufacture of the Me 262 had begun in March 1944, but, owing to the fact that no other fighter type was taken out of production, to ensure that the necessary labour and materials were released, only 122 machines had been completed by 10 August of that year.

In view of the Allies air supremacy, the reduced training period for *Luftwaffe* fighter pilots, and the poor reliability of the turbojet engines then available, a long service life was not expected for jet aircraft. It was calculated that an Me 262 would be a total loss after 5 to 10 combat missions. In addition, the Me 262 required two turbojet engines, and correspondingly more fuel, the supply of which was growing extremely scarce due to Germany's rapidly deteriorating military position. Thus, the concept of a single-engined turbojet fighter of about half the size and weight of the Me 262, but with a similar performance, became increasingly attractive on account of the potential savings in materials and production time. Because of design and load limitations, such a fighter, with only one powerplant, would not stand any chance of success unless compromises were made in its armament, armour, flight duration and equipment.

The Me 262 had first taken to the air using pure jet power on 18 July 1942 – over two years earlier – when company test pilot, Fritz Wendel, made a trouble-free flight from Leipheim, following a delayed gestation, largely attributable to the setbacks and problems with engine development and supply from BMW and Junkers. From then on, until mid-1944, development on the Me 262 stuttered ahead using a series of prototypes to test all aspects of the aircraft. There were highs and lows however: *Dipl.-Ing.* Heinrich Beauvais, crashed the Me 262V3 in August 1942 after three abortive attempts to take off; on 18 April 1943, *Oberfeldwebel* Wilhelm Ostertag was killed when one of the Jumo 004 turbojets on the Me 262 V2 flamed out, throwing the aircraft into a steep dive from which it never recovered. Later, in May 1944, *Unteroffizier* Kurt Flachs was killed when the Me 262V7 crashed on its 31st flight. The first series production aircraft suffered problems from tyre bursts, electrical and mechanical problems and persisting engine flame-outs: in June 1944 alone, the S7 crashed on the 1st following an engine fire, the Me 262 S1 suffered a damaged starboard wing on the 11th, while the fuselage nose, wings and both engines of the S3 were damaged in a crash landing at Lechfeld on the 16th.

The first assessment of the aircraft under operational conditions had been undertaken by *Erprobungskommando* 262, commanded since August 1944 by *Hauptmann* Horst Geyer. This small test unit was based at at Lechfeld, Rechlin-Lärz and Erfurt-Bindersleben and comprised a number of pilots of varying experience drawn from numerous *Jagd-* and *Zerstörergeschwader*. In September, Adolf Galland assigned the staff echelon of the *Kommando* to form the nucleus of a new III. *Gruppe*, *Ergänzungsjagdgeschwader* 2 at Lechfeld intended to oversee all future jet fighter training, while the component *Einsatzkommandos* of E.Kdo 262 were moved north to the concrete runways at Hesepe and Achmer which provided a suitable environment from which to embark on regular missions in the defence of the Reich using the undoubted

An early model of the He 162 used for aerodynamic tests. Unfortunately, the scale is not known.

Right: Wind tunnel testing of the He 162 design began as early as October 1944 and by early 1945 had advanced on a significant scale at the AVA Göttingen, the LFA Braunschweig and the DVL at Berlin-Adlershof, the model seen here being tested at the latter site.

Ominous events overshadowed the early phases of the Me 262 development programme when, in mid-1944, a number of early series aircraft suffered mishaps. Here the Me 262 S7, W.Nr. 130 012, VI+AL, is seen having crash-landed at Lechfeld on 1 June following an engine fire. One of the Jumo 004 turbojet engines was ripped off as a result of the crash and the nose and wings were also damaged. Such events were 'overlooked' by Willy Messerschmitt.

Me 262 A-1s of Kommando Nowotny, the Luftwaffe's first truly operational jet fighter unit, with their distinctive tail markings, yellow fuselage bands and large tactical numerals on their noses, are prepared for a mission on the concrete perimeter track at Achmer in the autumn of 1944. Named after its Austrian commander, Major Walter Nowotny, the acclaimed Ritterkreuzträger, the unit's pilots struggled to master the speed and handling of the jet and many of its aircraft were damaged or destroyed in accidents or shot down in early combat operations.

techological superiority of the new Messerschmitt to intercept Allied heavy bombers and their piston engine escort fighters.

On paper, this appeared acceptable enough, but the reality was very different. Despite a strength of some 30 Me 262 A-1as, most of the *Kommandos'* pilots remained largely untrained on the jet fighter and their new bases lay directly in the approach paths of those USAAF bombers, and their escorts, which were beginning to appear in ever greater numbers in German airspace.

It was at this time that *Generalleutnant* Galland plucked the 255-victory fighter ace and holder of the *Ritterkreuz* with Diamonds – Germany's highest military award – Walter Nowotny, from languishing in a training command in France in order to lead the newly formed '*Kommando Nowotny*' which had been established from the Achmer and Hesepe units and which was to prove the jet fighter in combat. Problems pestered *Kommando Nowotny* from the start: despite a somewhat crude training programme, it was found that only 15 pilots – those possessing any experience at all on the Me 262 – were capable of flying the type. By late September however, the *Kommando* had some thirty Me 262s. The following month saw the first tentative operations, but in the first half of October, no fewer than ten jets were either destroyed or damaged due to take-off or landing accidents. Nowotny's pilots, most of them drawn from conventional single-engined fighter units, lacking sufficient training in instrument flying and with only two or three intended training flights, found the Me 262 with its effortless speed, short endurance and rapid descent, difficult to handle.

The *Kommando* attempted to fly its first operational sortie 'in force' on 7 October against one of the largest American daylight bombing raids so far mounted, aimed at oil refineries and storage tanks in central Germany. Taking off from Hesepe, *Lt.* Schall and *Feldwebel* Lennartz each managed to claim a B-24 shot down, thus bringing home the *Kommando's* first victories. However, it would be different for those aircraft operating from Achmer: three jets were shot down on take-off there.

Isolated victories against Mustangs in mid-October did little to counter the scything opinions of Fritz Wendel who visited *Kommando Nowotny* as part of a Messerschmittt technical field team: '*Kommando Nowotny* has been in action since 3 October 1944. Up until 24 October sorties had been flown on a total of three days. The Inspector of the Day Fighters, *Oberst* Trautloft, was at the base during the first days and had made great personal efforts to ensure the success of the first fighter sorties with the Me 262... He saw to it that several successful fighter pilots were taken from other units to form the core of this unit. The commander, *Major* Nowotny is a successful Eastern Front pilot but is unfamiliar with the present situation in the West and, at 23, is not the superior leader personality necessary to guarantee the success of this vital operation.'

Wendel went on to demolish the unit's operational and tactical methods and lack of coherent objective, pointing out contradictary opinions within its personnel and concluded by stating that: 'Instruction on the aircraft type is particularly bad with *Kommando Nowotny*. The importance given to the technical side may be illustrated by the fact that the *Gruppe* Technical Officer at Achmer is not a technician. The *Staffel* Technical Officer at Hesepe is also a complete layman who has himself recently destroyed two aircraft as a result of carelessness and inadequate training.'

Despite these inauspicious events, the very same month Messerschmitt penned his scathing prognosis on the prospects of the He 162 in which he argued: 'I remember how we struggled to improve the performance of the aircraft we have built to date and how the slightest inferiority in the performance of enemy aircraft has immediately become evident in aerial combat. Exactly the same struggle to increase the speed by a single kilometre per hour and to improve range, armour

Messerschmitt test pilot, Fritz Wendel, seen here left with Willy Messerschmitt, issued a stark warning about the quality of training and state of readiness of Kommando Nowotny in the autumn of 1944. He observed that less combat-experienced pilots found the prospect of learning to fly the Me 262 daunting.

and armament naturally now lies before us in the case of jet aircraft. In my opinion it is incomprehensibly short-sighted to begin this struggle by taking a retrograde step of our own volition at a moment when we have attained a measure of superiority.'

'The demand for the *Volksjäger* is founded on the assumption that as the enemy's superiority is based on numbers, we, in order to equalise that position, must take the field with a cheap, mass-produced article which is within our own productive capacity. It is true enough that we need very large numbers of fighters and for this reason I have maintained for years that our fighter production should be raised to the utmost with all our means, even at the cost of bomber production, and thus reach those figures which are actually producing today under the more difficult conditions of the sixth year of the war.

'It is, however, wrong to assume that we can achieve by the spring or summer of 1945 a greater number of aircraft with a newly-developed type than with already existing types...'

Messerschmitt was unable to accept that a '*Volksjäger*' could be produced satisfactorily within the constraints of time and labour: '... the *Volksjäger* will go through the initial stages leading up to full series production and this process will be hastened to the utmost and consequently uneconomical of man-hours. At present no definitive experience is available, and the series will therefore have to suffer from constant modifications. Our own experience has shown that during the initial stages of series production an expenditure of some seven times the normal number of working hours must be reckoned with at the beginning. In the cases of a forced devlopment, the initial stages are even more expensive.'[62]

However, Siegfried Knemeyer refuted such a view in his report to Allied interrogators of July 1945: 'At no time was the danger of a false step underestimated, and all concerned realised that they were dealing with a new, high-speed aircraft. On the contrary, it was abundantly clear that a major mistake must of neccesity lead to the cancellation of the new type. It was, however, hoped that the risk of development would be reduced to a minimum by the co-opting of all technicians and development personnel and by careful limitations in the apportionment of the work. Finally, in the autumn of 1944, we could afford to use the development and production capacity of the aircraft industry for a short time on a 'shot in the dark' project owing to the fact that production of bomber aircraft had been stopped.'[63]

As to the operational prospects of the He 162, Messerschmitt was equally dubious: 'The desire to throw very large numbers of the *Volksjäger*, which is still to be developed, into operations so early as the spring battles of 1945, with the hope that it will prove a decisive factor, appears to me to be a misleading conception. It is expected that within six months an aircraft can be designed, built, tested and manufactured in a large series which must embrace the results of testing and the elimination of defects! It is expected in addition that within this period of six months the whole necessary organisation within the German Air Force can be built up, including the training of air crews and ground staff, the setting up of pools for the front, repair factories, supply organisations etc.'

Yet the aircraft designer's choice of the word 'hope' to describe the *Volksjäger* was entirely apt – for that is just what the programme offered the leaders of the Third Reich, while production of the technically complex Me 262 presented formidable challenges – as even Messerschmitt himself admitted in his October paper, set against the shaky and less-than-impressive debut of *Kommando Nowotny*: 'The Me 262 has been in production for about a year and is still in serious difficulty. The desired output is not being attained, workmanship in the shops is bad and endangers both the performance and characteristics of the aircraft, and even, to some extent, its safety in flight. Even today, we still do not possess half the jigs neccesary for mass production. We have to beg and struggle to procure bottleneck components and even raw material quotas and it is in such a situation that it is proposed to develop and manufacture a completely new aircraft type, to utilise two large aircraft factories for the purpose, to develop and build jigs – even in duplicate – for this new type, whilst explaining to us that all this will be achieved by the use of production capacity which is not required by the Me 262! The 162 programme will not be excecuted with free surplus manufacturing capacity as it is stated, but will be built up with resources which even today are not available for the Me 262.'

As will be seen in the following chapter, Karl Frydag would subsequently offer a robust and reasoned rejection of many of Messerschmitt's allegations. However, the next six months would testify to whether Messerschmitt's biased predictions would be proved correct or whether the tenacious, creative and dedicated development team and workforce at Heinkel Rostock and Wien could deliver the 'undeliverable' and prove him wrong.

Blitz! Blitz!

From Drawing Board to Deployment

FROM the moment EHAG commenced work on what would become the Heinkel He 162, the company's management agreed that it would deploy maximum possible assets in terms of personnel, space and time toward the project. Indeed, Karl Schwärzler, the Chief Designer at Wien (Vienna) and Rostock, considered that in developing any new aircraft type, the correct policy was to employ the maximum effort towards it in order to bring ideas to fruition before they became obsolete.[1]

The modern entrance to EHAG's plant at Oranienburg. Although it is unlikely that Oranienburg actually manufactured the He 162, the plant did take in machines from the Rostock works that needed upgrading.

Heinkel ensured that the RLM would give it 'maximum freedom' and drop virtually all interference and control. By being prepared to accept risks, coupled with the rapidity with which the drawings were produced and by employing jig and tool draughtsmen alongside designers, it became practicable for Heinkel to start production manufacture four to six weeks *before* the flight of the first prototype. Furthermore, by establishing a '*Fertigungsberatung*' (Production Consultancy) of six men, forming a liaison between production and prototype design, it was possible to ensure that the prototype drawings were used extensively for series manufacture. This, again, facilitated the bringing of the aircraft into production quickly.

EHAG's plans were that production would be spread across its plants at Rostock-Marienehe, Oranienburg and Barth, although an output of 50 He 162s was planned by Wien-Schwechat with the sensible aim of avoiding a loss of contact between design and production. If necessary, EHAG was not afraid to switch almost its entire production capability at Schwechat over to the He 162. Schwechat had enjoyed a good reputation as a centre for production. Between 1942 and 1944, the plant had played an instrumental role in the construction of the He 219 night fighter. It was not until the first serious air raid in early 1944 that the factory was hindered in producing components to supply its own needs. Despite the Allied bombing raids of 1944, one former Heinkel employee was unable to recall any significant impact on production. Following the raid of 26 June 1944, for example, all four main *Hallen* – numbers 39, 40, 41 and 50 – remained largely intact, though some bomb damage was evident in 39 and 41.

EHAG also took over the facilities of nearby companies for its manufacturing efforts; for example the Schwechat Brewery close to the junction of the Schwadorf-Fischamend road, allowed its cellars to be used for pattern-making, mostly by political detainees formerly employed at the main plant. Two workshops, under the direction of Karl Hayn (EHAG Works Director), were established here and code-named '*Santa* I' and '*Santa* II'.[2] However, the total workforce at Schwechat had fallen from approximately 12,000 in January 1944 to some 8,000 in September. One rumour circulating amongst Schwechat workers said that cement intended for a large air raid shelter mined into the quarries north of the plant had been sidelined for use in *Professor* Heinkel's private shelter beneath his villa in Wien![3]

Another major initiative was the sharing of production with the Junkers firm, whose capacity at its plants was now largely freed up following the sharp decrease in its production of bombers. Junkers would therefore assume two-thirds of the production work for the He 162 at its plant at Bernburg, while decisions regarding tools and other preparatory measures would be a matter of collaboration between the two companies. With this in mind, EHAG took over a warehouse in Mariahilfer Strasse, Wien, where the designers from both Heinkel and Junkers conducted their preparatory work for series manufacture while, simultaneously, the drawings for the first full-scale models were being completed.

The Nazis never shied away from the grim issue of slave labour. To enhance production of the *Volksjäger*, some 8,000 forced labourers were eventually drafted into the He 162 programme at Rostock, accounting for 55 per cent of the EHAG workforce there, while at Oranienburg the percentage figure was even higher, with 5,900 workers

A view inside a timber component workshop at the Heinkel satellite production facility at Warnemünde on the Baltic coast to the north of Rostock. By early 1945, almost every Heinkel production centre was engaged to some degree in the He 162 programme.

representing 65 per cent of total labour. The Wien facilities would employ a further 2,000 forced workers, accounting for 33 per cent of the labour force. Forty-five per cent of the workforce at Heinkel's partner, Junkers, was made up of forced labour, equating to 22,500 workers. In addition, the infamous underground facility, the '*Mittelwerke*' at Nordhausen, would contribute to the production of the He 162 under the code name '*Schildkröte*' ('Tortoise').[4] The *Mittelwerke* comprised some 7,000 malnourished slave labourers working in airless, poorly lit, cramped, noisy and dirty conditions alongside about 1,000 Germans. The concentration camp at Ravensbrück would be a source of labour for the EHAG facility at Barth, while the Sachsenhausen and Mauthausen camps were able to supply Oranienburg and Schwechat/Heidfeld with additional 'workers'. At the *Mittelwerke* it was estimated that it would take 750 man-hours to build one He 162 while 300 man-hours to build a BMW 003 turbo engine.[5] Heinkel's deployment of forced labour was deliberate, calculated and unprecedented.[6]

Broadly, the plan, with a target of May 1945, was as follows[7]:

EHAG Nord Rostock-Marienehe - 1,000 aircraft per month
EHAG Süd Wien-Schwechat - 1,000 aircraft per month
EHAG Mitte Oranienburg - planned two-seat production only
Junkers (Bernburg) - 1,000 aircraft per month
Mittelwerke Nordhausen - 1,000 aircraft per month

It was projected that monthly BMW 003 engine output would reach 1,000 units by May 1945 and would remain at that level at least until April the following year, with aircraft production mirroring that figure (as above).[8]

It was planned that the issuing of orders to and co-ordination of the almost bewildering network of the much needed and appointed sub-contractors would be effected from Mariahilfer Strasse in Wien, also under the management of Karl Hayn. Liaison with the sub-contractors would be co-ordinated by fifty 'competent' employees from the design staff, who would monitor all sub-contracted items in order to ensure that subsequent assembly would proceed without delay.[9] That was the theory.

The task facing Hayn and his group was daunting: fuselages were to be made at the EHAG facilities at a *Waldwerk* (forest factory) at Barth and at an underground facility at Mödling in the Hinterbrühl, the site of a former chalk mine in Lower Austria, which was code-named '*Languste*' ('Lobster') and located some 20 kilometres south of Wien. Junkers would contribute from another underground facility – in this case, a salt mine – near Stassfurt.

Metal components would be sourced from Heinkel satellite facilities at Pütnitz (for Rostock) and Theresienfeld (for Wien), while Junkers would source from Aschersleben, Stassfurt, Halberstadt, Leopoldshall and Schönebeck. Engines would come from BMW at Spandau and Zühlsdorf, while armaments would be supplied by the Deutsche Waffen- und Munitionsfabrik at Posen on behalf of Rheinmetall-Borsig (for the MK 108) and Mauser at Oberndorf and Berlin (for the MG 151). Zeiss-Ikon would provide the Revi 16 gunsight from Berlin-Zehlendorf and Dresden, while Askania would supply the EZ 42 from Berlin-Friedenau.

Paint and lacquer would be sourced from both Austrian and German suppliers, while three main sub-contractors were selected for the manufacture of wooden components: the Hermann Wächter firm in Neustadt an der Orla, the Erfurt *Reparaturwerk* and the May firm in Stuttgart-Esslingen, all of whom had previously undertaken work on wooden airframes, such as the manufacture of wings for transport gliders and the Me 163 rocket-powered interceptor, as well as the all-wood Ta 154.

The following account will highlight the He 162 development and production process effected by the RLM and its departments and

A view of one of the main storage buildings in the extensive Heinkel works at Wien-Schwechat in Austria which played a key role in the production of the He 162 during late 1944/early 1945.

A contemporary postcard of a peaceful view of holidaymakers at the entrance to the underground lake grotto near Mödling in the Hinterbrühl, Austria during the late 1930s. This was one part of the expansive Hinterbrühl cave and mine area south of Wien, which, a few years later, would be given over to the production of the He 162 jet fighter.

Above: An entrance to the infamous underground Mittelwerke at Nordhausen in the Harz mountains. Heinkel could draw upon a force of 7,000 malnourished slave labourers working in airless, poorly lit, cramped, noisy and dirty conditions at Nordhausen to help build the He 162, with an estimated 300 man-hours needed to produce each machine.

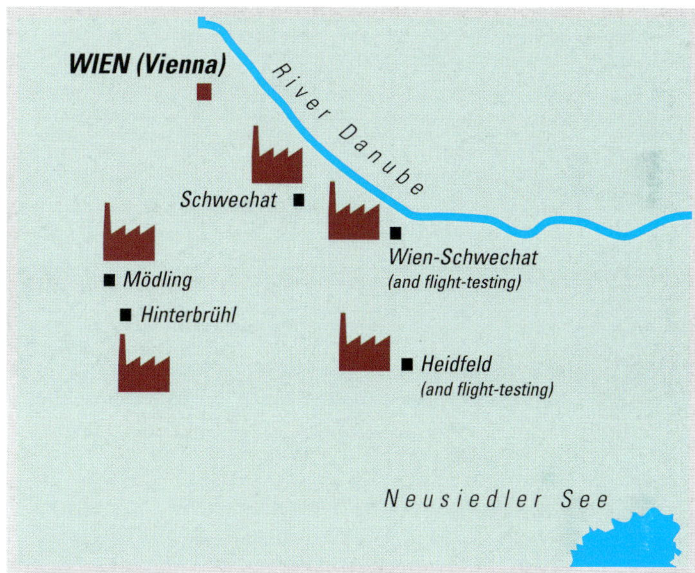

AUSTRIA

He 162 Production sites

GERMANY

He 162 Production sites

He 162 Airfields

outstations, and EHAG, its associates and sub-contractors in fortnightly periods from 23 October 1944 to April 1945; this way, the reader will hopefully gain an insight into the speedy pace of work adopted by all concerned, with the exception of one or two sub-contractors.

Also of note is the fact that many of the hundreds of teleprint messages, telegrams and memos sent out by EHAG, often from its design offices, under Karl Schwärzler, on Fichtegasse in central Wien, from December 1944 through to April 1945 are headed '*Blitz! Blitz!*' – literally 'Lightning!' but best translated as 'Top Urgent!' – another indication of the urgency and pressure under which Heinkel worked.

Monday, 23 October – Sunday, 5 November 1944

Construction work on the He 162 prototypes began on 25 October 1944 and, by 1 November, stability and functional experiments, the production of wind tunnel models as well as the preparation and evaluation of wind tunnel data and the writing of maintenance manuals for the He 162, were being carried out in Rostock.[10]

On 1 November the *Chef* TLR (E-2) issued a *Flugzeug Baureihen* (Aircraft Type Specification) for the '8-162', listing an aircraft equipped with a BMW 003 E-1 engine, armed with either two Rheinmetall-Borsig 30 mm MK 108 cannon each with 50 rpg – as the He 162 A-1 – or two Mauser 20 mm MG 151/20 cannon each with 120 rpg, as the He 162 A-2. The specification listed a 960-litre fuel tank and the design was to be equipped with FuG 24Z and FuG 25a IFF radio equipment.[11]

On 4 November, the *Erprobungsstelle* (*E-Stelle*) *der Luftwaffe* at Tarnewitz, the main weapons evaluation centre, confirmed that a 30 mm MK 108 cannon had been fitted successfully to the He 162 mock-up and had been test-fired without breakdown or jamming, although a belt feed had not been tested. Furthermore, the ballistics specialists at Tarnewitz stated that of the first ten prototype aircraft, eight would be fitted with MK 108s, while two – the V5 and V6 – would carry MG 151/20s.[12]

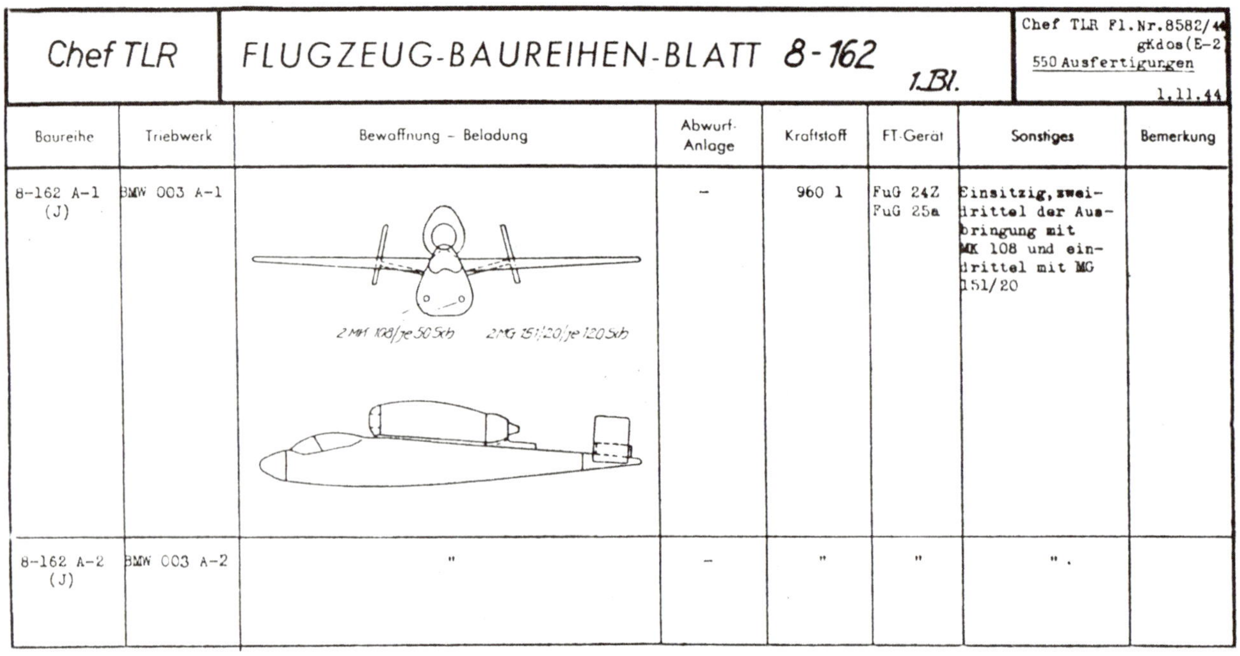

Chef TLR | FLUGZEUG-BAUREIHEN-BLATT 8-162 | 1.Bl. | Chef TLR Fl.Nr.8582/44 gKdos(E-2) 550 Ausfertigungen 1.11.44

Baureihe	Triebwerk	Bewaffnung – Beladung	Abwurf-Anlage	Kraftstoff	FT-Gerät	Sonstiges	Bemerkung
8-162 A-1 (J)	BMW 003 A-1	2 MK 108/je 50 Sch 2 MG 151/20/je 120 Sch	–	960 l	FuG 24Z FuG 25a	Einsitzig, zweidrittel der Ausbringung mit MK 108 und eindrittel mit MG 151/20	
8-162 A-2 (J)	BMW 003 A-2	"	–	"	"	" .	

Above: A facsimile of a document issued by the RLM, Chef TLR showing the official 8-number designation issued for the He 162 dated 1 November 1944.

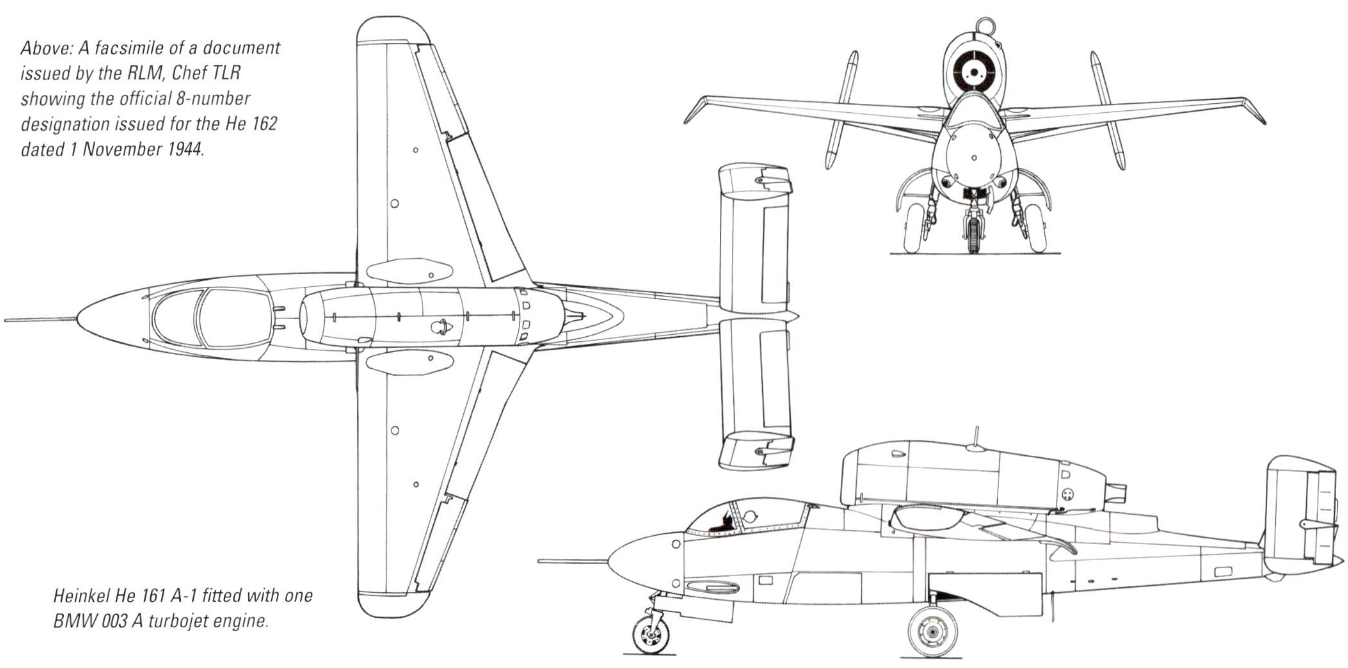

Heinkel He 161 A-1 fitted with one BMW 003 A turbojet engine.

Monday, 6 November – Sunday, 19 November 1944

Word of the He 162 had – not surprisingly – reached deep into the darker corridors of power. Under request, and having consulted with *Generalleutnant* Galland and *Professor* Willy Messerschmitt about the prevailing fighter situation, on 9 November SS-*Obergruppenführer und General der Waffen*-SS Gottlob Berger, the *Chef des* SS-*Reichssicherheitshauptamt*, wrote to *Reichsführer*-SS Heinrich Himmler detailing the construction of the He 162, assuring him that justification to build the aircraft lay in the fact that it would use less raw materials and half as much fuel consumption as the Me 262, therefore making the most of the limited resources available to the Third Reich. Berger advised Himmler that the plan was that one-third of *Volksjäger* production would be assigned to EHAG and the remaining two-thirds to Junkers, while the most promising engine belonged to BMW. Interestingly, according to Berger, the construction of the wings was to be the responsibility of a 'working co-operation' between the SS, the NSFK, appointed carpenters and industry, under the leadership of *Dr.* Kurt May of SS-*Führungshauptamt Amt* X.[13] It was envisaged that such co-operation would capitalise on an element of the joinery industry which was under-used – a rare thing in late-war Germany. The firms would be grouped into three '*Baukreise*' (construction groups). The plan was to build 1,000 machines per month by March, but there was even an investigation underway into producing 2,000 aircraft per month! In order to realise this ambition the redoubtable *Generalkommissar* Phillipp Kessler would be appointed to oversee the production programme. 'Of course at the moment there are still a few problems, especially in the area of transport and materials and the workforce...' Berger advised the *Reichsführer*. 'It is important that, right now, flying personnel need to be brought together and that such personnel should be released from disbanded bomber units, in particular pilots, and also from parachute units and elements of the infantry. Especially important is the military training of the NSFK and their conversion [on to the He 162].'

Berger further advised that main series production was to be commenced in the shortest period of time. 'Following the *Führer* Order of 12 October 1944, *Herr Generalkommissar* Kessler, the project leader, will forthwith be known under the name '*Gewaltaktion*' ('Forced Action'), while management of the timber industry sector is the responsibility of SS-*Hauptsturmführer Dr.* May and his staff...'

Berger received a somewhat indifferent reply on 25 November from SS-*Standartenführer Dr.* Rudolf Brandt of Himmler's personal staff, who advised that due to the more pressing matters in the *Reichsführer's* workload, Brandt had considered it best not to show him the letter, but from the information presented by Berger, the matter seemed well in hand.[14]

There was some debate at this time as to the type of gunsight to be fitted to the He 162; the *E-Stelle* Tarnewitz seems to have favoured the installation of the improved *Revi* 16 G reflector gunsight as opposed to the 16 B, whereas EHAG's Technical Director, *Dipl.-Ing.* Carl Francke, was interested in the new, larger EZ 42 gyroscopic sight under development by Askania at Berlin-Friedenau and Carl Zeiss at Jena.[15] On 16 November, Francke requested that a Heinkel weapons specialist be sent to Askania to find out more since, according to Francke, the EZ 42 had '...passed all tests and performed very well.'[16] This would turn out to be a somewhat over-optimistic view.

Already, there was a hive of activity around the He 162. On the 13th, *Obersturmführer* Fiedler and *Sturmführer* Rab of the NSFK arrived at Schwechat to oversee the construction of a glider-trainer version of the He 162[17] and to discuss a glider training programme, presumably with the intention of preparing potential Hitler Youth fliers for graduation on to the jet fighter. Francke instructed that *Oberstinq.* Zieglãnder was to supervise the preparation of the timber with the sub-contractors. On 17 November, Francke noted that in consultation with the *General der Fliegerausbildung* a powered trainer version of the He 162 was to be considered. Curiously it was agreed that the design should feature '... room for two men in the cockpit by lengthening the fuselage. Emergency exit for the second man will be through the cockpit floor. A major advantage is that flight characteristics will not change very much. Construction is being initiated.'

Both RLM and Heinkel officials were co-ordinating the preparation of the wooden components from various sub-contractors. Parts were already being delivered from these suppliers: the Heinkel *Wochenbericht* (Weekly Report) for 13-17 November states, with typical terseness, that on the 16th a nosewheel door, a gun-barrel shroud, a carrier for a 'container', plywood skinning and dural fuselage skinning had been '... delivered on time', while on the 17th a meeting about the nosewheel mechanism was interrupted by an air-raid alarm which lasted for two hours. Despite the threat of bombs, it was agreed that construction plans would be completed by the VDM company and delivered to the tool company on the 25th.[18] Elsewhere on the 17th, the Heinkel Technical Department was able to report that the first prototype of the He 162 – the He 162V1 – was due to roll out on time and that the wing section and engine for the aircraft were to be transported to Wien by road by Sunday, 19th. Furthermore, the '... Rest of the parts are all on hand. Could have been here a day or two earlier', although Francke did observe that there was not enough fuel for the full transportation of said parts. Furthermore, he recorded that '... There are 50 too few German skilled workers for the series construction in Wien. Requirement not yet critical and the company will try to recruit as necessary.'

It is relevant to note here that at the beginning of the following week, on 20 November, EHAG was having to exert pressure just to commandeer 10 railway wagons from the *Wehrinspektion Wien* (Defence Inspectorate Wien) and forty tyres from the local administrative authority, such was the shortage of transport supplies. 'Please inform us if anything goes wrong,' Francke asked his transport co-ordinator.[19]

Another large-scale wind tunnel model (1:1.5) had been completed and was at Braunschweig, although it was recognised that a planned tow-model intended for stability tests and the aircraft's clear-vision canopy would take longer to arrive due to problems with the sub-contractors.

To the north, in Rostock, on the 17th, *Generalkommissar* Kessler, running the '*Einstrahltriebkleinstjäger*' programme (see Chapter One), called together a 'major conference' at EHAG Rostock in order formally to authorise the commencement of series production of the He 162 there and to co-ordinate local production facilities and 'official authorities'.[21]

Meanwhile, technicians at *Abteilung* E3 of the *Chef* TLR, the department responsible for power units, worked to marry a BMW 003 engine to a He 162 cockpit using a test jig which incorporated a fuel tank and suspension springs in order to simulate the exact working viability of the combination in combat and to avoid independent

The EZ 42 gyroscopic gunsight, manufactured by Askania and Carl Zeiss, was intended to be widely fitted into the Luftwaffe's Me 262s in order to improve accuracy in deflection shooting – but pilots who flew machines so fitted found the equipment problematic. This did not prevent EHAG's Technical Director, Carl Francke, from favouring it for use wthin the He 162.

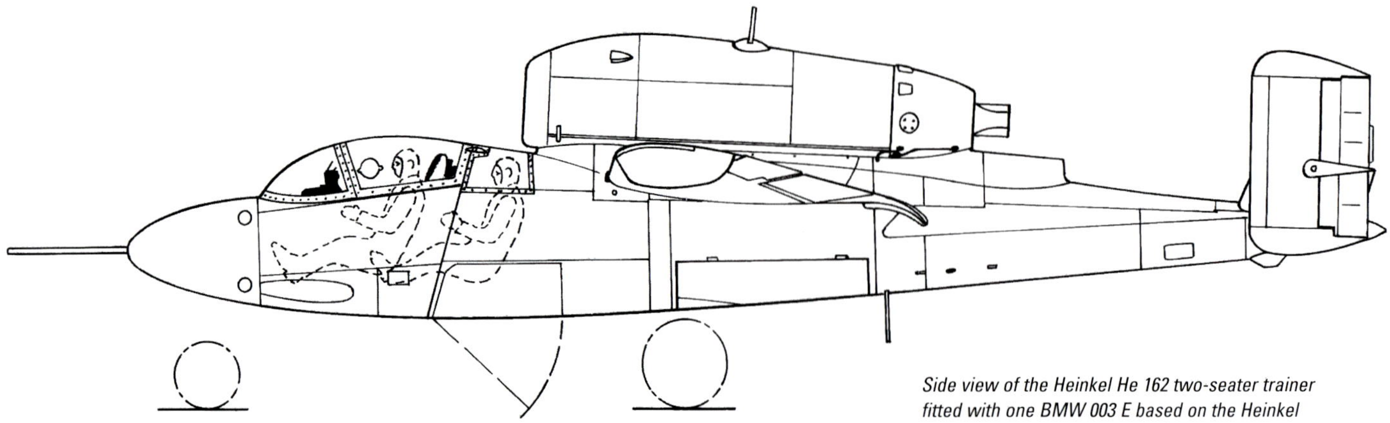

Side view of the Heinkel He 162 two-seater trainer fitted with one BMW 003 E based on the Heinkel drawing below. Note that the pilot in the second seat would be ejected downwards in an emergency.

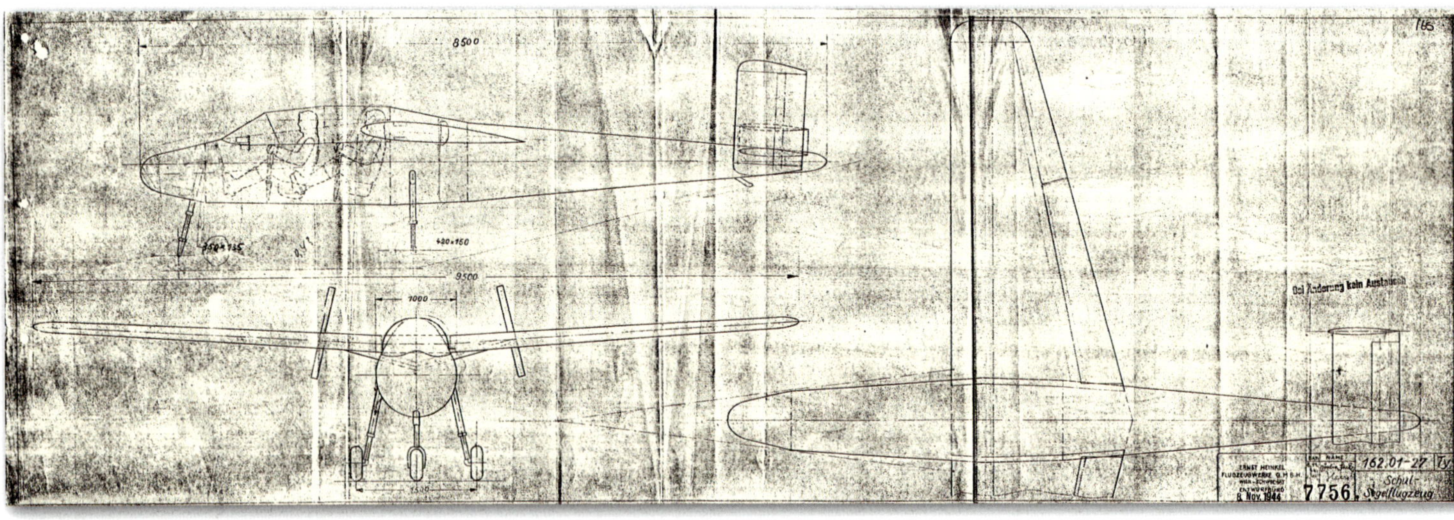

Heinkel drawing of the proposed glider trainer version of the He 162 as at 8 November 1944.

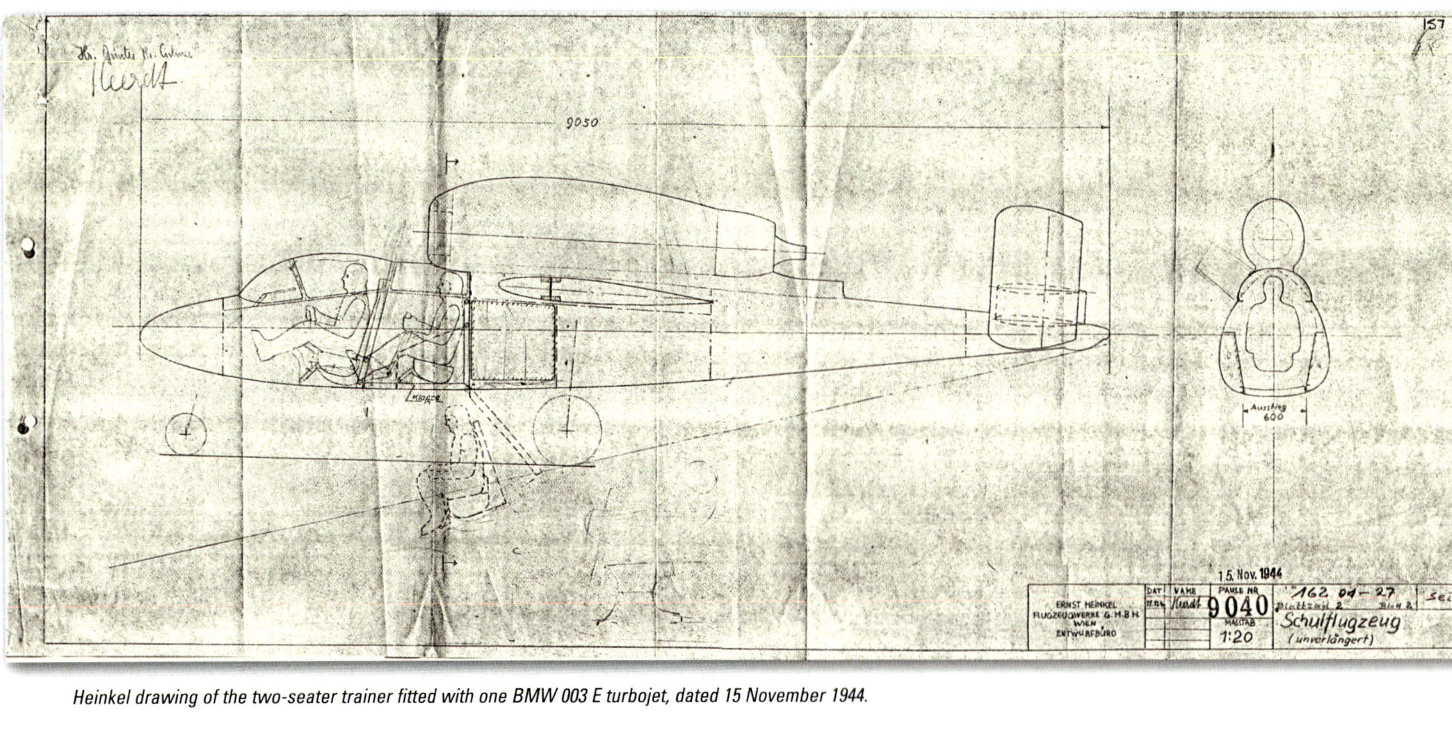

Heinkel drawing of the two-seater trainer fitted with one BMW 003 E turbojet, dated 15 November 1944.

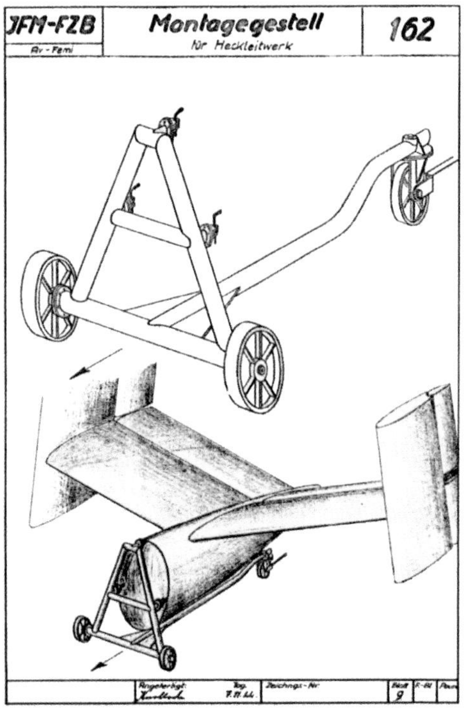

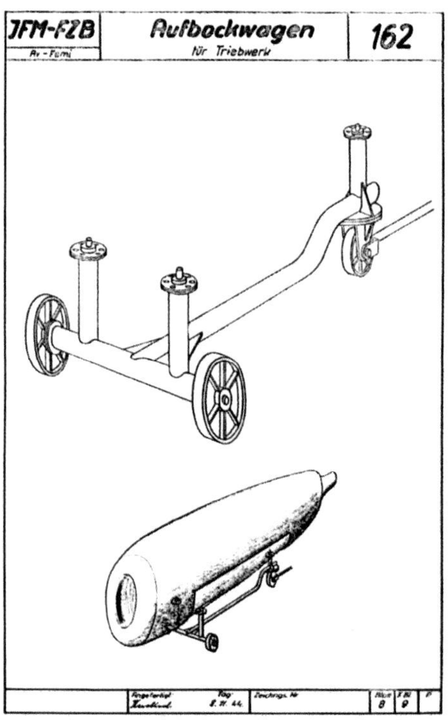

A set of five elementary sketches produced by Junkers in early November 1944 show the different types of transport trailers designed for moving partially assembled He 162s on the production line. In the drawings, top right, trailers are used to transport engines either singly or in convoy, while to top left, a different type of trailer is shown for the movement of tail sections. Note that the fitting of the the tail section and assembly of the final aircraft were to be performed on these trailers, representing a quick and simple mobile production method.

development of engine and cockpit. From this experiment, insight was gained into the optimum positioning of the engine for maximum performance as well as the performance characteristics of electrical systems, fuel feed and consumption.[22]

There is evidence of some simmering discontent within the departments at EHAG immediately following the completion of the first protoype. On the 18th Francke drafted a confidential memo to his core management team, including *Professor* Heinkel, on a matter that was clearly bothering him:

'With the conclusion of the construction of the 162, remarks are being made that the Technical Department has nothing to do and could do without some of its personnel. *Dr.* Heinkel and *Gen. Dir.* Frydag have expressed the opinion that the personnel of the Technical Department could be reduced because the work of control and development could be handled by between 300 and 400 workers and further developments other than the 162 would not be needed for this war.

'There is so much development work in Wien at this time that the personnel of the Technical Department are totally occupied, working a 72-hour week, plus overtime, (72-hour weeks are not the practice at Messerschmitt, Focke-Wulf or Junkers).'

Francke drew attention to the fact that, in terms of the He 162, the Heinkel Technical Department was overseeing general project management, the planned installation of the BMW 003 and HeS 011 engines, the possibility of downward-swept wings, the construction of both powered and glider trainer versions and the building of another rocket-powered, shoulder-mounted, straight wing fighter project, the P.1077, known as the *Julia* and in which the pilot lay prone with spartan instrumentation in the cockpit. In addition, work was being undertaken on a rebuild of the cockpit for the Hütter 211 prototype long-range reconnaissance and heavy night fighter commissioned by the RLM in late 1944 (whose design was greatly influenced by the He 219), plus general project management of the He 219 night fighter as well as the building of a new laminar wing for the Dornier Do 335 heavy fighter.

The downward hanging wing tips to which Francke referred in his memo were designed by *Dr.* Alexander Lippisch, the acclaimed aerodynamicist who had been consulted by EHAG to improve lateral stability on the He 162. It was convenient that Lippisch, who had played an instrumental role in the development of the Me 163 rocket-powered interceptor whilst working for Messerschmitt in 1943, was at this time resident in Wien as head of the *Institut für Flugzeuggestaltung der Luftfahrtforschung Wien* (IFLW) and therefore close at hand (although he still retained a consulting position for further development of the Me 163).[23]

Carl Francke

Carl Francke was an experienced aviator who had flown as a member of the German team competing in the Europa-Rundflug air race in 1934 under Theo Osterkamp. In the summer of 1937, while Head of Department E7 at the *Erprobungsstelle* Rechlin, he had also piloted the Bf 109 V8 and V13 in award-winning high-speed, and Climb and Dive flights at the 4th International Flying Meeting at Dubendorf in Switzerland. As a member of the *Luftwaffe* he had served as a test pilot at the *Erprobungsstelle* (*See*) at Travemünde, where he had made a name for himself by being heavily involved in testing seaplanes as well as new types of fighter designs and compiling the standard manual for flight-testing. Transferring to Rechlin, he flew the first prototype of the He 177 heavy bomber in November 1939, as well as more 'exotic' types such as the Focke-Wulf Fw 61 V2 autogyro and the Me 321, the world's largest glider. He joined EHAG in late 1943.[20]

Above: Carl Francke (centre in white overalls) following his victorious flight at the International Flying Meeting at Dubendorf in Switzerland in July 1937. With him are Robert Lusser (right), who was head of Heinkel's sports aircraft design at this time and who would later move to Willy Messerschmitt's BFW, and Hans Seidemann (in Luftwaffe uniform), another sporting pilot, who would later serve in the Luftwaffe as commander of *Fliegerkorps* Tunis in North Africa.

Below: Carl Francke seen to the left in Luftwaffe officer's cap and leather overcoat, with (right) looking in the opposite direction, Ernst Udet (to centre) together with other dignitaries who had come to witness the first test flight of the He 280 V1 in September 1940.

Carl Francke (standing on wing to left) leans over the canopy of the He 280 V2 as the *Generalluftzeugmeister*, Ernst Udet, assesses the cockpit following the aircraft's second flight by Paul Bader on 5 April 1941. Bader is seen crouching on the wing next to Francke. While Francke's personality would dominate Heinkel's production of the He 162 in late 1944/early 1945, Bader would act as 'Typenbegleiter' ('Project Leader' or 'Development Co-ordinator') for the type.

In late November 1944, engine technicians at the Erprobungsstelle Rechlin constructed a test rig intended to simulate the functioning of He 162 controls and the BMW 003 engine in combat and to avoid independent development of the engine and cockpit.

A view looking into a He 162 cockpit mock-up and simulator constructed by the Erprobungsstelle Rechlin. A number of in-flight instrument gauges, including the turn and bank indicator, airspeed indicator, rate-of-climb indicator, altimeter and compass, have had tape crosses applied to the glass to signify that they are not in a functional state, while the engine instrument gauges – temperature, fuel pressure, fuel level and rpm – appear to be connected, thus indicating that the simulator is for engine-testing.

Lippisch had proposed fitting small '*Ohren*' ('ears') to the wing tips of the He 162 and when incorporated into the design of the aircraft, this distinctive feature became known as the 'Lippisch ears'.

Francke also emphasised that only 69 men of the Technical Department had been assigned to the He 162 project, although he foresaw this number increasing with an intake of technicians from the *Mittelwerke* at Nordhausen. 'The number of staff of the Technical Department is laughably small in comparison to the staff of the other companies mentioned above,' Francke noted caustically. Furthermore: 'I am not of the opinion that the 162 is the last development of this war, even for Heinkel. If the enemy appears with jets next spring that are somewhat faster that the 162 or 262, then we shall have to develop an aircraft quickly that is similar to the 162 but with swept-back wings and a more powerful powerplant. It was only possible to achieve the on-schedule development of the 162 because of the unconditional procurement of personnel from various jurisdictions. It would be foolish to now drop such an effective tool. In conclusion, it should be stated that the constant removal of poor personnel is the order of the day, but that the transfer or surrender of good personnel is not only inadvisable, but also dangerous. This is especially the case in regards to future transfers and call-ups for military service.'[24]

Above: The downward-pointing 'Lippisch ear' of He 162 M23 (A-2) W.Nr. 220 006, VI+IP, as photographed following recovery by the Allies at München-Riem in the summer of 1945. The wing flap has been damaged by bomb debris.

Above: The acclaimed aerodynamicist, Dr. Alexander Lippisch, designed the small, distinctive 'ears' to the wing tips of the He 162 which became known as 'Lippisch ears' and which were intended to improve lateral stability. Lippisch is seen here in the uniform of the Deutscher Luftsport-Verband, with the insignia on his arm of the SA-Fliegersturm which was disbanded in 1933. This photograph is believed to have been taken in 1936.

Left: A BMW 003 engine wired up for testing on a stand. This view has been taken from the tail assembly looking along the partly completed fuselage.

Monday, 20 November – Sunday, 3 December 1944

On 21 November, Francke wrote to the senior management of EHAG advising that '… On 1.12.44 there is to be a big meeting at Rechlin. Our mock-up [of the He 162] is to be presented. The first mock-up of the 162 is looking good externally and by latest 25.11 is to start its journey to Rechlin (even by a railway freight wagon if nothing else is possible).' *Ing.* Meschkat was ordered to arrange the transport and to handle dismantling and re-assembly at Rechlin.[25]

The gun manufacturer, Rheinmetall-Borsig, whose 30 mm MK 108 was being built into a number of the He 162 prototypes, advised Heinkel that with such armament installed, the *Volksjäger* would need to launch attacks against formations of heavy bombers from a height of 1000-1500 m above and behind, then to dive below the formation and to pull up at an 80-degree angle, closing to between 600 to 800 m before opening fire. Fire was to cease when a 60-degree angle had been reached and the engagement broken off. 'We need to know the speed in such an attack,' Francke noted, 'and duration of effective firing times when attacking B-17s and B-29s. The calculation of these data is due on 25.11.1944.'[26]

Francke's reference to the American 'B-29' Superfortress is indicative of the belief by the Germans that the USAAF would soon be operating its formidable new heavy bomber types over Europe.

At midday on the 21st, Francke despatched a telling note via courier to *Generalstabs-Ingenieur Dipl.-Ing.* Roluf Lucht, a senior engineer with the RLM and, since September 1944, chairman of the Emergency Aircraft Commission: 'You intend to have a development meeting of the *Hauptkommission* on Friday of this week, which I am supposed to attend. Please inform my courier when and where this meeting is to take place so I can make the proper arrangements to attend. Because of the constant air raids on Wien, communication with the outside world is very limited. I need, at least, to be able to use the telephone, so that the He 162 deadlines are not jeopardized…'[27]

Equally frustrating for Francke was the news that one of EHAG's wing and tail section timber sub-contractors, the Nels company in Stuttgart, was requesting an extension to its delivery deadline. 'This is completely unacceptable,' Francke noted. 'I urge that the sub-contractors at Stuttgart-Esslingen make up the difference, if other sub-contractors do not deliver on time. The wings for the prototypes, and series aircraft, are to be delivered on time.'[28]

The next day, Francke advised *Prof.* Heinkel, *Dipl.-Ing.* Frydag and other members of the He 162 production team of his concerns about the capabilities of the timber firms appointed as sub-contracted suppliers. 'It cannot possibly be predicted today,' wrote Francke, 'if the wood construction firms that we have hired (under the leadership of *Dr.-Ing.* May) will be able to fulfil their contract in regards to wings, tail assemblies and flaps. However we have already observed how inflexible the firms that we have hired are in regards to development and prototype construction. Furthermore, they lack skilled workers. The delayed delivery of the wings and tail assemblies forces us to lose the reserves we had taken out of the prototype and are lost again for the V1 fuselage. I consider it necessary, therefore, to remove the *Languste* shop from the timber construction process of the prototype. This is especially necessary when we consider the '*Julia*' project and the different variants of the 162.'

Dr.-Ing. May, in charge of co-ordinating Heinkel's wood suppliers and sub-contractors from Berlin, again incurred Francke's wrath later the same day following receipt of a telegram regarding the Wächter company, a particular supplier: 'It seems there has been non-delivery of metal fittings and delay on the 162 wing,' Francke fumed in a note to *Prof.* Heinkel and Karl Frydag. 'The Kalkert concern also lacks the parts needed. *Dr.-Ing.* May is not screaming for the parts because he knows he can use the excuse of non-delivery to delay his own deadline. The distribution of completed sub-assemblies on our part is not working. I suggest that a man be found here in Wien who will be able to deal with the problem. We cannot afford to allow the timber workshops, whose deliveries are way off, to blame us for the delays.'[29]

Francke went on to propose some urgent and quite radical solutions including the taking over of two local timber firms in Wien and their transfer to the Heinkel underground '*Languste*' facility at Mödling in the Hinterbrühl. Alternatively, if that was not possible, the establishment of a new timber works run along the lines of a concentration camp with appropriate management personnel, being made available. Failing that, EHAG could take over the Gebhardt timber firm in Krems, some 80 km west of Wien on the Danube.[30] Early in December, the firms of Deutsche Edel-Möbel AG and Müller-Strobel in Buttschowitz near Brünn in Czechoslovakia, which had had some experience in the production of timber tail surfaces for the Bf 109, were recruited to manufacture 'wooden parts' for the He 162 programme. As Francke's secretary noted of the latter company: 'This manufacturing set-up should be fine and would be able to overcome the delays at *Dr.* May's concern. Only quality technical labour and no forced labour is being used. They have about 25,000 square metres of wood on hand. They promised to make up, with extra shift work, the total the *Dr.* May concern would have produced in a much shorter time period (30 wings in November, 27 in December). Drawings are on their way from Esslingen to Buttschowitz.'

Generalkommissar Kessler chaired another meeting about the He 162 on 23 November, this time at Junkers in Bernburg, with a view to finalising arrangements for Junkers' involvement in the production of the *Volksjäger.*[31] That day, Carl Francke also visited Berlin and used the opportunity to confront *Dr.* May on the issue of a 10-day delay in the delivery of He 162 wing sets and May's allegation that this was as a result of construction drawings arriving late from EHAG. 'I have checked out these assertions:' Francke responded angrily in a letter marked '*Blitz! Blitz! Blitz!*' immediately following the meeting. 'The plans were sent to you via courier. The last on 30.10. … Mistakes did not appear in the plans…'[32]

Next, Francke – evidently on the warpath – wrote to Frydag in another *Blitz! Blitz!* communication: 'I have confronted *Dr.* May in Berlin concerning the 10-day delay of the wings. *Dr.* May asserted that he had received plans too late, and that there were mistakes on them… These accusations are all unwarranted… After all that has happened, the fact remains that *Dr.* May is unable to provide wings on time. I think you should have the men from Nels report to you in Berlin to find out what is going on.'[33]

On the 24th, Francke noted that the He 162 V1 was 'nearing completion' and that its wing had been fitted, but that its engine had been found to be damaged in transit. BMW were arranging a representative to attend Schwechat to assist with installation. Much was relying on the engine producers: from May, it was projected that BMW would be producing 6,000 units per month, supplemented by a further 2,000 units per month from the *Mittelwerke.*[34]

Francke also noted: 'The wings for the V2 are being ferried from the Albrecht factory at Weidramsdorf on the morning of 28 November.'

But there were problems: 'The metal parts of the wings were not finished correctly by EHAG, but these will be delivered on 29 November. The wing construction sub-contractor in Stuttgart-Esslingen is not capable of sticking to the schedule. The delay of 10 days as advised by *Dr.* May will be made up by the other two contractors.'[35]

However, Francke was able to confirm that the He 162 mock-up was on its way to Rechlin and that an aerodynamic oscillation and vibration test model was on its way to the *Aerodynamische Versuchsanstalt* (AVA) at Göttingen.

That day, *Dipl.-Ing.* Karl Frydag, Heinkel's General Manager visited Wien from Berlin; according to Francke, he and his companion, Otto Lange '… were definitely impressed with the work accomplished.'

However at 2030 that evening, Francke's secretary was forced to telegram a colleague over what appeared to be utter confusion and a lamentable collapse in communication amongst EHAG personnel working on the He 162, regarding the acquisition of a consignment of key components. The telegram is most revealing:

'Insane events! Höpken just arrived by train without the parts! Menzer got involved and sent his man, *Herr* Friedrich, to Niebusch [a contractor]. Hence the parts were sent on his travel ticket. There was nothing Höpken could do. Friedrich ran into difficulties in Breslau, left the parts there and continued his journey without them!!!!!!!!!! Can you believe it?' (The ten exclamation marks are as per the original document.)

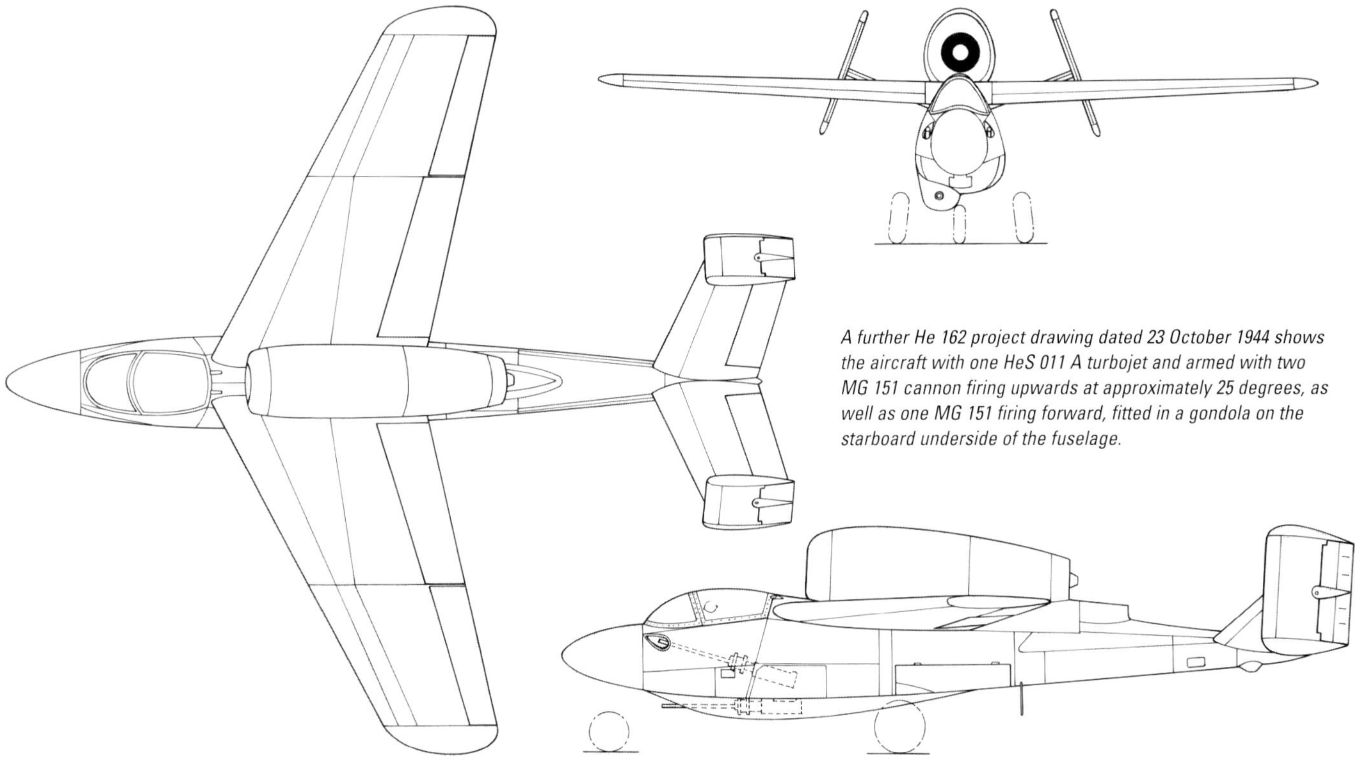

A further He 162 project drawing dated 23 October 1944 shows the aircraft with one HeS 011 A turbojet and armed with two MG 151 cannon firing upwards at approximately 25 degrees, as well as one MG 151 firing forward, fitted in a gondola on the starboard underside of the fuselage.

By 25 November, the *E-Stelle* Tarnewitz was still awaiting the appointment of a dedicated technician to oversee the installation of the Revi 16 B gunsight into the He 162.[36]

On the 26th, Francke was demanding to know of his senior colleagues within the Technical Department when the presumed and actual delivery dates were for metal fitting and internal wing parts as well as similar dates for both pattern and drill attachments/jigs and fully completed wings and tail assemblies.[37] On the 27th Francke lamented to Frydag: 'The first tail unit has arrived after a difficult journey and was attached, thank God! It has been installed into the V1, but it doesn't fit! A substitute is being arranged.'

'Originally, Niebusch was supposed to build the tail unit for the whole series. In the meantime, an organisation called Heinke has joined in, claiming that Niebusch is a part of the Heinke organisation. Similar developments are noticeable with other wood construction firms. That is why,' Francke warned, 'many organisations appear that take on work that demands a high degree of urgency, are then incapable of carrying out the work and pass it on to smaller sub-contractors (an easy way to make quick money). I do not consider these procedures favourably, since we have become inflexible due to all the changes we have to make. The quotas increase because of bottlenecks caused by these changes.'[38]

Francke fired off a *Blitz! Blitz!* communication to May in Berlin advising that there were to be '... a number of changes to be made to the 162 timber construction parts. They have to be incorporated as quickly as possible (wing fuel tanks).' Francke asked for a meeting by 2 December latest, either in Berlin or Wien, to discuss the matter further.[39]

During a conference with Hitler on the 28th, Albert Speer presented the *Führer* with drawings and technical data and advised him that the prototype He 162 would be ready to fly, on schedule, on 10 December.[40] Around this time, design proposals were first presented by Francke for a swept-back wing to be fitted to the HeS 011-engined variant of the He 162.[41] By 1 December matters had been put in place to include a FuG 24 radio transmitter and homing loop as standard; Francke sent a representative urgently to the firm of Reh & Co., the manufacturers of the FuG 24, at Cranzahl in the Erzgebirge, to collect one set. Francke informed *Herr* Reh that the Heinkel representative was '... obligated to bring the transmitter to Wien as soon as possible. We want to use it in the V1 in order to have ground-to-air communication on the first flight. We need to know what the test pilot is saying. I shall, as we have agreed, take responsibility that it will not get out that the transmitter is already in our hands. I hope to have the test aircraft flown before the official first flight date. Keep this strictly confidential.'[42]

The same day, in Wien, in a telling and somewhat prophetic note, again marked *Blitz! Blitz!*, the tireless Francke wrote to *Dr.* Gründer at Junkers in Dessau regarding the plans for building glider training variants: 'We have to construct the glider training aircraft out of timber, but they are not robust enough,' he warned. 'I have asked Lucht for 20 timber specialists to be sent by 31.12.44. If they do not arrive soon, then there won't be much point after that time.'[43]

There were also problems being encountered at Hinterbrühl with flaps manufactured by the Krems company; in a communication to *Prof.* Heinkel, and others, Francke complained '... Two weeks ago the flaps were delivered from Krems. One fitted, the other did not. Today, Krems still does not know about this. It is imperative in such cases that a well functioning communication channel from *Languste* is set up. For these purposes engineers from the Engineer Corps are to be employed with the *Stab* Kessler. The first liaison engineer in *Languste* steers any problems back through the communications channel to the original sub-contractor. Example: a tail unit has arrived and has this, or that, fault. A quick sketch needs to be made... With this sketch, the liaison engineer travels to all the sub-contractors involved in the tail unit construction or hands the sketch over to other liaison engineers. The liaison engineers are sent out with this information...'[44]

There was some good news when BMW advised that the 003 engine for the He 162 V2 was on its way to Berlin-Spandau by armoured train, with six more engine units due to arrive between 1 and 10 December.

Momentum was maintained when – in an event unparalleled in the history of aviation – the first prototype of the He 162, the V1 (later the M1), W.Nr. 200 001, was completed, fitted with 30 mm MK 108 cannon and ready for take-off at Heidfeld on 1 December – less than 70 days after the authorization of the *Volksjäger* programme,[45] although Karl Schwärzler, Heinkel's Chief Designer at Wien and Rostock, expressed concerns about the weakness of the undercarriage and as a result, only taxying trials were undertaken the next day.[46]

There were other pressures on Heinkel: the military desperately needed more manpower and requested the call-up for military service of the confidential courier in the Technical Department working on the He 162 project. Carl Francke's secretary wrote to the Hitler-Youth organisation in Wien from where the request originated advising that the member of staff in question, Erwin Mikysa, '... delivers secret mail between all our branch offices... This knowledge about our various offices is top secret and only privy to a small circle. In case of Erwin Mikysa's call-up, we would have to train another courier which would jeopardize the secret nature of our work.'[47]

On Friday, 1 December, a display of the latest German weapons, aircraft and equipment was held at the *E-Stelle* Rechlin for the benefit of Karl-Otto Saur, head of the *Jägerstab* and now a recipient of the *Ritterkreuz des Kriegsverdienstkreuzes mit Schwertern* since 29 October 1944. The event began at 0800 hrs, but the morning was taken up with a display of army and navy weapons. After lunch, Saur's party travelled to nearby Lärz airfield where they examined many of the latest types of German aircraft including the wooden model of the He 162.[48]

Meanwhile at the *E-Stelle* Tarnewitz, it was realised that the installation of the Revi 16 G gunsight into the He 162 was no longer possible and was abandoned, but research into the feasibility of using the EZ 42 was not affected at this stage.[49]

Finally, it seems EHAG was having to prepare itself to accept 'ethnic' Germans from the Sudetenland as assembly workers on the He 162. But as Francke's secretary commented, they would need to be 'good and reliable.' Furthermore he warned 'This has to be done as soon as possible, otherwise it will be too late.'[50]

Above and opposite page top: Two views of the He 162 V1 W.Nr. 200 001, VI+IA in its bare metal finish. The aircraft was completed and ready for take-off at Heidfeld on 1 December 1944, in less than 70 days following the authorization of the Volksjäger programme.

Side view of the prototype Heinkel He 162 V1.

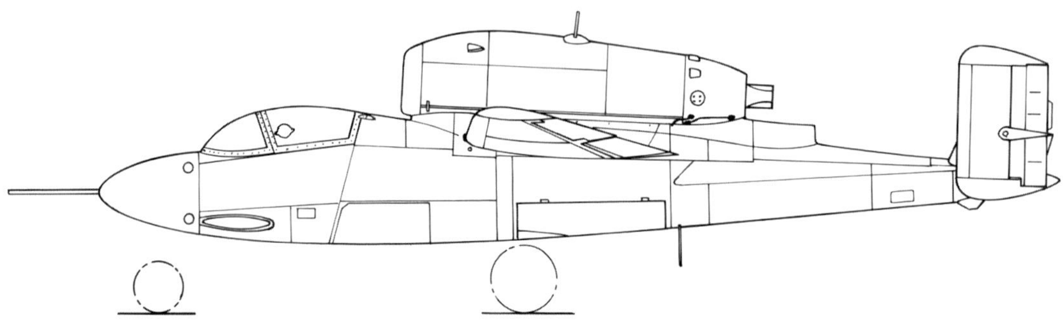

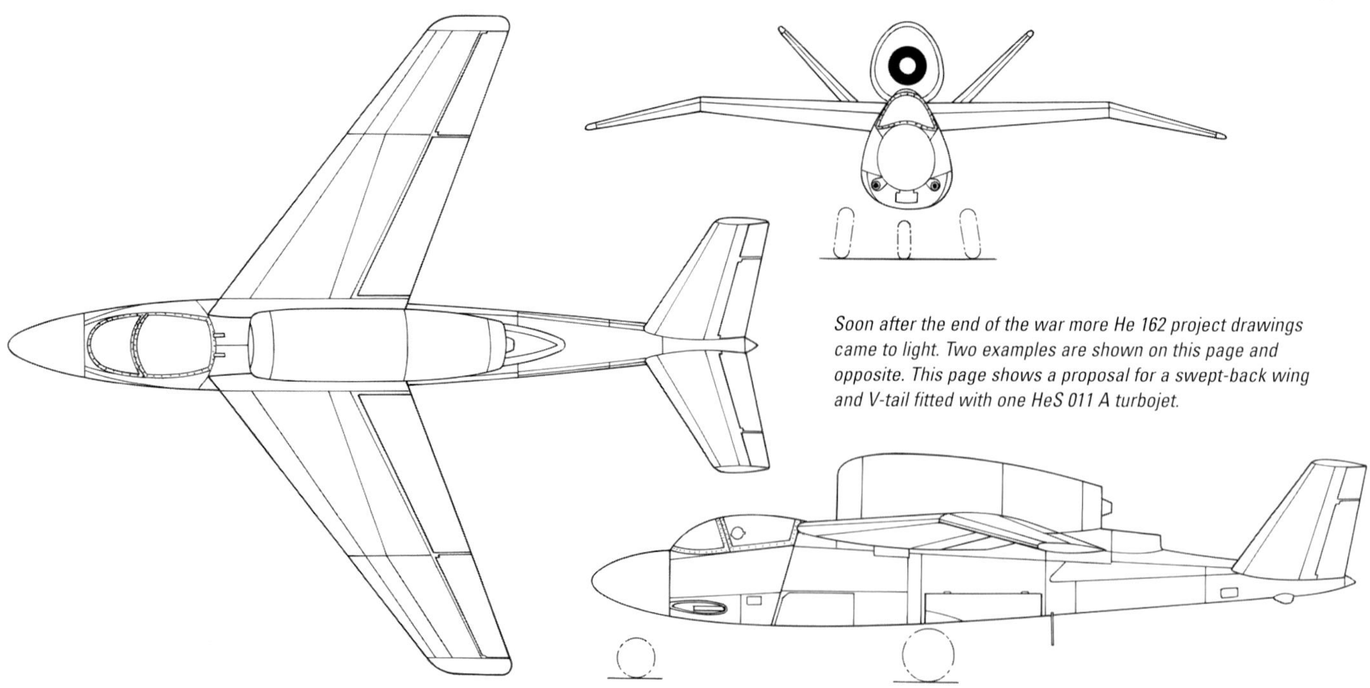

Soon after the end of the war more He 162 project drawings came to light. Two examples are shown on this page and opposite. This page shows a proposal for a swept-back wing and V-tail fitted with one HeS 011 A turbojet.

Left: A prototype He 162, but probably not the V1, since the finish is 'rougher' and the engine cowling is dark. It is possible that this could be the He 162 V2.

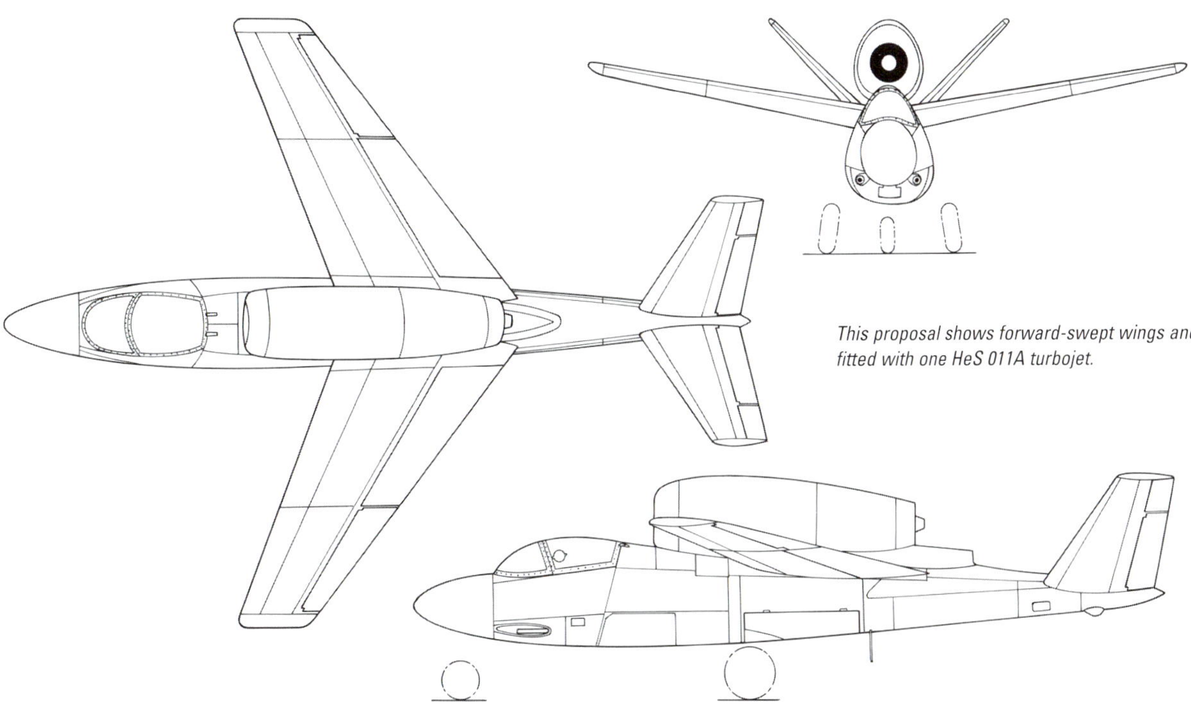

This proposal shows forward-swept wings and a V-tail fitted with one HeS 011A turbojet.

Monday, 4 December – Sunday, 17 December 1944

On 6 December, the He 162 V1 W.Nr. 200 001, VI+IA, was flown for some twenty minutes on its maiden flight by *Flugkapitän Dipl.-Ing.* Gotthold Peter, Heinkel's Chief Test Pilot, who reported that the engine ran 'beautifully', that control forces were very light, but that there was a tendency for the aircraft to turn to port. The aircraft had been fitted with two MK 108 cannon and during the flight, defective bonding resulted in an undercarriage door breaking away, but no other problems were encountered.

Carl Francke noted, presumably with some satisfaction, that the flight took place 'five days ahead of schedule'. Also: 'Decisions [re He 162V1]: No basic problems. Slight hang to the left, power altogether minimal, especially the rudder, stability of vertical axis good. But some bounce on landing. Engine ran beautifully. Undercarriage flap parts cracked. Reason: Bad glueing in the timber parts.'

Above: This British Interpretation Report No. L.273, dated 29 December 1944, appears to be the first time that the He 162 was spotted on a photograph after an RAF reconnaissance mission carried out over Schwechat on 6 December 1944. It is interesting to note that the first impression was that the 'Schwechat 25', the designation given by British Intelligence to the unidentified aircraft, was thought to be a smaller aircraft resembling the He 280. The photograph above is an enlargement of the image shown on the document. No doubt this discovery led to the bombing of the airfield on 18 February 1945 – shown opposite.

Elsewhere, the V2 had reached final assembly stage, although it, and the V1, had leaking wings while the V3 and V4 were reported on schedule.[51]

The presence of the He 162 V1 at Schwechat this day did not go unnoticed by the RAF's Central Interpretation Unit (CIU) at Medmenham in Buckinghamshire which issued an Interpretation Report on 29 December in which, following a reconnaissance flight over Schwechat, it revealed the first appearance of, '*An unidentified aircraft, with a span of only about 25 ft, and in some ways resembling a small edition of the He 280. This aircraft, which is light-coloured, was photographed at the end of the runway and a number of vehicles and personnel were seen nearby. Its design suggests it may possibly be jet-propelled, but there is at present no conclusive evidence of this.*' The CIU christened the mystery aircraft the 'Schwechat 25' about which it issued a reasonably accurate report.

The photo interpreters at Medmenham concluded that, in terms of its design characteristics the aircraft was '*... a mid-wing or low-wing monoplane of unusually low span-length ratio, and almost certainly has a tricycle undercarriage. The wing is of low aspect ratio; wing plan is not clearly seen, but the trailing edge is swept forward, and may be curved. The wing is set well back on the fuselage, giving the aircraft a very long nose, reminiscent of the He 280.*'

The report continued: '*No statement on tail unit design can be made, but twin fins and rudders may possibly be fitted. Activity at Schwechat, which for the past few months has been gradually increasing, appeared to be at a fairly high level on 6.12.44, and large numbers of personnel and vehicles were seen in movement near all the factory buildings.*'[52]

By this stage, the He 162 V2, with MK 108 cannon, was in its final stages of construction and would move from *Languste* to Heidfeld on 7 December, while the V3 and V4 were still in progress.[53] The wings and engines for the V3 and V4 arrived at Schwechat on 7 December under the code name '*Salamander*'[54], but there was still concern about the strength and leaking of the wings on the V1 and V2 which were judged by Francke as 'unsound'.

Later that day, Francke noted the contents of a telephone call he had received from *Frau* Bantow in the Construction Department: 'Re leaks in the first two wings. A soft shellac won't work as we had assumed! It will probably be impossible to achieve a 100 per cent leak-proof state in retrospect. The only quick fix would be 'Asplid putty'. (Studies were being undertaken with this product by the *Luftwaffe* at the *E-Stelle* Travemünde.)[55]

Furthermore, in weighing the He 162 V1 it was discovered that the aircraft's centre of gravity had never been calculated; 'Weight is 17 kg

The series of images on this page, opposite and page 46, show a sequence of still photographs extracted from a movie film possibly taken at the time of the first flight of the He 162 V1 and seen during take-off (note the crowd gathered to watch events in the images on page 46).

Flugkapitän Dipl.-Ing. Gotthold Peter

Gotthold Peter was born in Dresden on 23 June 1912. In 1932 he studied at the *Technische Hochschule* in Dresden and then two years later at the *Technische Hochschule* in Berlin-Charlottenburg and was a member of the *Akademischen Fliegergruppe* in both cities. Like many young men in Germany during the inter-war years, his interest was caught by the adventure of flight and he began flying gliders in 1930. In 1938 he became a *Dipl.-Ing.* in aircraft construction and won his Gold-C badge for glider flying. He went on to help design and develop the Akaflieg Berlin B5, B6 and B8 sailplanes and achieved an altitude of 7000 metres and two distance records before joining the *Luftwaffe*. In 1939, he trained at the DVL in aircraft construction. Following a period of employment with Arado, he joined Ernst Heinkel on 12 August 1940, with whom he conducted important test flights on the He 177 bomber and the first flight of the He 219 night fighter.

Flugkapitän Gotthold Peter, standing on the port wing, glances down into the cockpit of the He 280 V3 as it taxies past the camera following a test flight in the summer of 1942.

***Flugkapitän* Gotthold Peter (left) with his wife, Helga, and Arado test pilot, Adolf Frach. Frach flew both the He 162 and Ar 234 during his career.**

over,' noted Francke in his weekly report. 'This overweight needs to be stripped out.'[56]

Francke's concerns over timber and glueing proved well-founded when disaster struck on 10 December. That day, a large party had gathered in Wien to witness another flight by Gotthold Peter in the He 162V1. Included amongst the spectators were a number of TLR and Armaments Ministry officials, including *Generalkommissar* Kessler and 24 members of his staff, *Generalmajor* Diesing and *Oberst* Edgar Petersen, the *Kommandeur der Erprobungsstellen* (Test Centre Commander) – men whom Heinkel needed to both impress and assure. Also attending were *Major* Otto Behrens, *Oberstabsing.* Harry Böttcher, *Fliegerstabsing.* Paul Bader and *Fliegerstabsing.* Heinrich Beauvais from the *E-Stelle* Rechlin.[57]

During the demonstration, Peter attempted an unscheduled low-level, high-speed run over Schwechat airfield. At an estimated speed of 735 km/h the leading edge halfway along the starboard wing ripped away, causing the aircraft to go into a roll, which broke away the aileron and wing tip. At such a low altitude, Peter was unable to evacuate the aircraft, which crashed out of control beyond the airfield boundary, killing the pilot.

Dr. Baumann of Heinkel's *Flugabteilung* was curt in his subsequent report of the incident: 'Normal take-off, curve to the left, at an estimated speed of about 600-650 km/h, around 100 m above ground level. From where the guests were standing, it appeared that the left aileron suddenly dropped 90° opposite to the rudder. The application of the normal counter control to the right-side rudder and wing flaps caused damage to the fin and rudder through stress which, in turn, caused the break up of the leading edge of the other side wing.

'Further (around four) fast rolls to the right. Crashed into the ground some 400 m beyond the airfield perimeter near Fischamend.'[58]

Dramatic images of the aircraft as it went into its roll were provided from a cine-film shot by *Leutnant* Helmut Kudicke, an officer serving on the staff of the *General der Jagdflieger* who had been despatched to Schwechat by a curious Adolf Galland who wished to have events recorded for study. Kudicke was later congratulated officially for the value of his work. On 13 December, EHAG wrote to *Oberst* Kallab at the OKW *Filmstab* in Berlin:

'During a test flight of a new fighter aircraft on 10.12.1944 in Wien, a cameraman, *Leutnant* Helmut Kudicke took some important footage. Since this footage was of a fatal crash, it is of great importance to us so that we can evaluate it in order to determine the reason for the crash.

'*Leutnant* Kudicke, through his own initiative, made sure he was filming throughout all the phases of this extremely important test flight. He provided a great service to the *Luftwaffe* and Ernst Heinkel AG.

'At our request, and with the enthusiastic co-operation of *Leutnant* Kudicke, the film was developed and copied the same day. It was shown immediately to the designers and builders of this aircraft for their expert evaluation. Because of the film, the cause and result of the crash were easier to evaluate, and series production can begin on schedule. We therefore request that *Leutnant* Kudicke film the flight of the second prototype here in Wien. *Heil Hitler*!'[59]

Indeed, as a result of Kudicke's film, EHAG's Technical Department was able to determine the true speed of the aircraft at the moment of the wing collapse as being 680-700 km/h.[60]

Subsequent investigation of the accident by EHAG (which was conducted by representatives from Rechlin, the DVL, Focke-Wulf and Junkers) revealed that it had been caused by instability around the aircraft's lateral axis which, combined with a complete lack of glue bonding, resulted in the tearing away of the wing leading edge at rib number 2.[61] The quality of glue used in the rudder was also questioned. One source has stated that the destruction of Heinkel's planned glue supplier, the Goldschmitt Tego-Film factory, by Allied bombing compelled the company to seek alternative supply from other manufacturers who offered poorer quality glue which resulted in weaker joints.[62]

Following the crash, Kessler immediately ordered that the wings of the He 162 be strengthened – a task to be completed by 24 December – and also imposed a 500 km/h speed restriction on all subsequent test-flying, while Diesing set up a committee which was – over the following few days – to assess the cause or causes of the crash and to re-examine the design of the aircraft.[63]

In July 1945, Ernst Heinkel and Karl Frydag told Allied interrogators: 'In our opinion, the cause of the accident was down to a lack of stability around the transversal axis, until then unknown to the pilot. Apparently, weak points were also discovered in the design of the nose ribs of the wing.'[64]

The crash of the V1 was a blow to morale within Heinkel and to confidence within the RLM. For the next six to eight weeks, EHAG would work feverishly to rectify the faults and to introduce improvements to the construction of the aircraft. These were to centre on increasing the span of the horizontal stablizer, displacement of the centre of gravity by shortening the main fuel tank, the strengthening of wing ribs and their attachment to the main beam, the strengthening of wing coverings and curving down the rear end of the wing profile in the area of the landing flap.[65]

By 9 December, the *E-Stelle* Tarnewitz was still wrestling with problems associated with the installation of the Revi 16 gunsight into the He 162; the illumination of the sight and crosshairs had to be improved.[66] However, one item of good news was that He 162 V2 was reported ready for flight on 10 December.

Despite the difficulties of the first half of the month, the *Jägerstab* Production Programme No. 227 of December 1944 called for the following deliveries of He 162s:[67]

Heinkel He 162 V1 W.Nr. 200001, VI+IA built at *Languste Werk*

The construction of the fuselage was started on 13 November 1944 and on 2 December the aircraft arrived at Schwechat-Heidfeld where it was completed. On 6 December 1944 the aircraft was first flown by Heinkel test pilot, *Flugkapitän* Dipl.-Ing. Gotthold Peter. On its second flight, four days later, the aircraft was destroyed due to construction defects, killing Gotthold Peter. The machine was painted overall in RLM 02 with the only other marking being the Werk Nummer painted on the lower part of the fin, in black. The style of the '*Balkenkreuze*' is also unusual for that time.

The dramatic sequence of film of the He 162 V1 shot on 10 December 1944 by Leutnant Helmut Kudicke, of the Stab General der Jagdflieger, revealed to anxious EHAG designers and technicians how test pilot, Gotthold Peter, was killed. Subsequent investigation showed that the aircraft had suffered from instability around its lateral axis which, combined with a lack of glue bonding, resulted in the tearing away of the wing leading edge at rib number 2. Peter's crash would have severe ramifications for the He 162 programme.

Month	Units
1	50
2	100
3	200
4	310
5	430
6	555
7	750
8	1150
9	1150
10	1150

The big problem, however, was that because of the aforementioned necessary stability repairs, it was thought by Heinkel that no aircraft could be delivered in January or February. Besides, difficulties within the transport infrastructure of the Reich as a result of Allied bombing had become so acute and supply problems so serious that Programme No. 227 became untenable. For example, the transportation of wings and wing components by rail from sub-contractors required more time than usual to deliver. Smaller components had to be delivered by truck or, for urgent parts, by dispatch riders – but even they took up to five times longer than the usual duration.[68]

Programme No. 227 was subsequently replaced by Programme No. 228 which saw a significant reduction in projected production:

Month	Units
1	–
2	–
3	150
4	315
5	460
6	530
7	530
8	530
9	530
10	530

The planned *Werk Nummer* series blocks were as follows:

EHAG Nord Rostock-Marienehe	-	120 001
EHAG Süd Wien-Schwechat	-	200 001
Hinterbrühl ('*Languste*')	-	220 001
Bernburg (Junkers)	-	300 001
Mittelwerke Nordhausen	-	310 001

(Surviving documentation suggests that the *Mittelwerke* block was later assigned to Junkers Bernburg).

It was envisaged that fuselages were to be completed at '*Languste*' with final aircraft assembly and flight-readiness being completed at EHAG *Süd* at Wien-Heidfeld.[69]

One of the entrances to the cave complex which had been the site of a former chalk mine at Mödling in the Hinterbrühl in lower Austria. In late 1944, code-named 'Languste' ('Crayfish') by EHAG, the cave mines were adapted as a crude, but effective, underground assembly facility for He 162 jet fighters. Note the lighting and power cables fixed to the rock.

The ghostly figure of a worker can be made out attending to the stencilled fuselage in the foreground. Many airframes were delayed at Languste while awaiting deliveries of components from sub-contractors, a continual source of frustration for the EHAG management.

Right: Two partially assembled He 162 fuselages lie in moble gantries in the 'Languste' caves at Mödling, early 1945. Note the low height and closeness of the rock walls, which must have made for a somewhat claustrophobic and oppressive atmosphere.

Right: No fewer than five fitters can be seen working on this He 162 fuselage mounted on timber cradles. Evident is the poor lighting of the cave facility.

Below: Rear fuselage frames hang in mobile jigs at the Languste cave factory at Mödling in early 1945 awaiting skinning in dural as well as some plywood for inspection covers. To the right of this composite photograph – which has been cut to avoid including a pair of wooden doors in the brick wall! – is another partially complete fuselage resting on wooden trestles showing the bulkhead and cross-section.

On 7 December, however, Carl Francke sent a confidential memo to one of Heinkel's Directors, *Dr.* Schüngel, with an observation that the tooling machines at *Languste* were being used at 20 to 30 per cent less than their capacity. On the housekeeping front, Francke also commented that accommodation for 35 of the female auxiliary staff at the Laaer Berg Strasse facility was in poor condition, especially the washing facilities, while differing standards of food were being served, particularly at Heidfeld.[70]

A high-level meeting was hurriedly convened on Tuesday, 12 December to discuss the future of the He 162. At this meeting, which was attended by Göring, *Generalleutnant* Karl Koller, the Chief of the *Luftwaffe* General Staff, Diesing, Frydag and Saur, it was decided to let preparations for mass production proceed as planned, although in normal circumstances it would have been prudent to suspend these until the He 162's deficiencies had been thoroughly investigated by extensive flight-testing. But political considerations, combined with the consequences of cancellation, dictated otherwise, and nothing was allowed to delay the *Volksjäger* programme, on which so much had been staked.[71]

At the Heinkel offices on Fichtegasse in Wien another meeting took place that morning – on this occasion chaired by Carl Francke who had summoned representatives of the Hermann Wächter firm from Neustadt an der Orla to discuss changes to the wood components of the He 162.[72] Under discussion were the questions of the installation of the integral wing tank into the wing, the possible introduction of a wing with greater fuel capacity, fittings for control surfaces, the testing of wing tank leak-proofing, camouflage colour and surface preparation, wing installation for both Jumo 004 and HeS 011 engines and the schedule of deliveries.[73]

Two days later on the 14th, on instructions from *Generalkommisar* Kessler, discussions were held in Muldenstein between *Stabs.Ing.* Heinz Borsdorff of the *E-Stelle* Rechlin, *Stabs.Ing.* Waldmann and *Leutnant* Hünninghaus of *Chef* TLR/Fl.-E3 and *Herr* Böttger and Hertling of the Muldwerke engine component firm regarding the fitting of the Jumo 004 B and/or the HeS 011 into the He 162, probably because of continuing delays to the BMW 003.[74] However, it was recognised that investigation would be needed to assess whether the wing and fuselage of the He 162 would be capable of carrying the weight of either – heavier – engine. It was envisaged series production of He 162s powered by Jumo 004 Bs would have to take place no later than the summer of 1945. However, in view of recent technical problems being experienced with the Jumo 004 in the operational Me 262 units, Junkers was to clarify if it was able to conform. Heinkel-Hirth was also asked to investigate whether the HeS 011 could be used for series production and to submit its findings to Junkers.

EHAG was still struggling with suppliers on the 15th, when it was noted that technicians had reported that the sealing of the wing tanks on the He 162 was still considered inadequate. Leak tests with water had, apparently, already been conducted by the sub-contractors manufacturing the wings. One problem was that the recommended sealing compound could no longer be obtained.[75]

Hundreds of kilometres away in the snow-laden forests of the Ardennes, German forces launched their last great counter-offensive of the war, catching the Allies by surprise.

Monday, 18 December – Sunday, 31 December 1944

On Tuesday, 19 December, Carl Francke recorded that the Gotha company had built a '*Holzschalenflügel*' – a prototype timber shell wing for the He 162. In this regard, *Generalkommissar* Kessler ordered that in order to have more than one wing option and in the event that the glue adhesion problems on the existing wings were not resolved, Gotha be authorised to build a further 20 sets of wings.[76]

Following a detailed examination of drawings and documents, and having made relevant calculation checks, the *Materialprüfungskommission* in Wien – the investigative body comprised of engineers and

These tail cone sections have been completed and riveted with dural and await removal from their assembly jigs at Languste. The atmosphere in the underground caves was dusty, airless and dark – hardly perfect conditions for sophisticated assembly.

A fitter attends to wiring in the nose section of a He 162 under construction at Languste in early 1945.

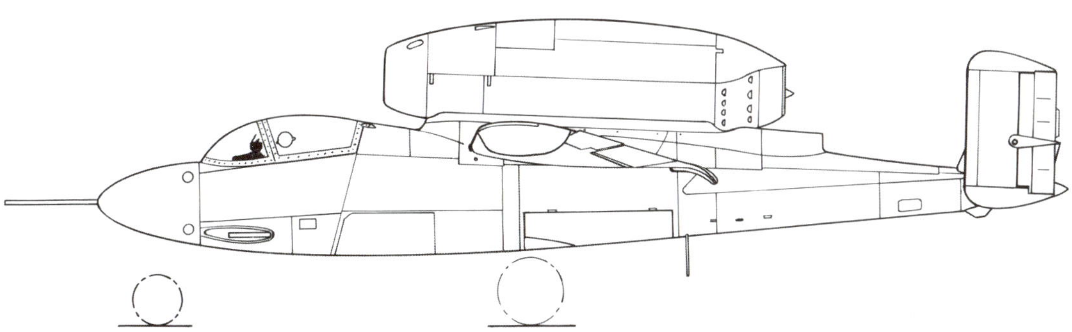

Side view of a Heinkel He 162 fitted with a Jumo 004 turbojet.

Fliegerstabsing. Paul Bader, an experienced jet test pilot at the Erprobungsstelle Rechlin flew the He 162 on several occasions and was eventually appointed 'Typenbegleiter' ('Project Leader' or 'Development Co-ordinator') for the He 162 programme.

technicians from the DVL, Junkers, Focke-Wulf and the *E-Stellen* led by *Oberstabsing.* Schwarz and set up by Diesing following the crash of the He 162 V1 – issued a report on 20 December. Despite still awaiting the official crash report, according to the *Kommission's* findings the workmanship on the V1's wing section appeared satisfactory, although it was recommended that the wing covering should be strengthened from 4 mm to 5 mm and the leading edge ribs should be strengthened from 1.5 mm to 3 mm. There was, however, some suspicion over the quality of adhesive being used. It was emphasised that, generally, much better quality control would need to be put in place over timber components and their fastenings.[77]

On 20 December, the He 162 M3, W.Nr. 200 003, VI+IC, was reported as flight-ready and was moved from *Languste* to Heidfeld.[78]

On 22 December the second prototype, the He 162 V2/M2 W.Nr. 200 002, VI+IB, made its first flight with Carl Francke at the controls. The aircraft had been assigned primarily to conduct testing with the 30 mm MK 108 cannon.[79] Readers may consider it somewhat unusual for a Technical Director to fly an untried prototype aircraft, but it should be remembered that *Dipl.-Ing.* Carl Francke was one of Germany's most experienced test pilots, having been head of *Abteilung* E2 (Airframe Testing) at the *E-Stelle* Rechlin until 1942. Because of the urgency of the *Volksjäger* Programme, he felt it necessary to demonstrate his confidence in the He 162 by undertaking the maiden flight of the second prototype. It is of interest to note here that when members of the Allied Farren Mission interviewed former EHAG employees in the immediate post-war period, they viewed Francke's decision to fly the V2 personally as indicative of '... the character of the man heading the team responsible for the development of the He 162.'[80]

The flight proceeded without mishap, and eight further prototypes and a batch of 20 pre-production aircraft would follow in rapid succession, most of them incorporating a host of modifications to rectify the He 162's inherent defects. These included reinforced wings with a thicker covering, down-turned wing tips to reduce the effective dihedral angle of the wing and thus improve lateral stability, modifications to the wing trailing edge where it joined the fuselage, displacement of the centre of gravity by shortening the main fuel tank, and an enlarged tail assembly.

At 1603 hrs the same day, *Fliegerstabsing.* Paul Bader of the *E-Stelle* Rechlin made a second flight in the V2 which lasted six minutes.[81] Apparently, Francke and Bader had tossed a coin to decide who would first be in the air and Francke had won. For his part, Bader had had considerable experience in test-flying jet aircraft, having flown the He 280 V1 and V2 as well as the Me 262 V1.

In accordance with Kessler's instructions, Bader kept to under 500 km/h and found that, loaded with 450 litres of fuel and a full complement of ammunition, the aircraft handled like a much larger jet, but there was some unpleasant 'snaking' experienced during take-off and landing. Bader also considered that forward visibility on the ground from the cockpit was so poor that the only clear way to see ahead was to 'snake' the aircraft manually. Furthermore, even with the canopy closed, he was aware of exhaust entering the cockpit. The flight itself was problem free.[82]

On the 23rd, *Professor* Heinkel suggested that the test-pilots now arriving to assist with the He 162 programme, including Bader and others such as *Dipl.-Ing.* Schuck, *Oblt.* Georg Weydemeyer and *Lt.* Huldreich Kemnitz, be insured for RM. 80,000.

At this point, EHAG mapped out a provisional forward plan for prototype flight-testing in which it was foreseen that the He 162 V2 would be used to trial take-offs and landings and testing of rudder stability; the V3 would test a modified nosewheel leg to prevent ground looping; it was envisaged that the V4 would fly at the end of the year, while the V6 was to be fitted with a strengthened wing, and to fly ten days after the new wing had been delivered. Wind tunnel tests showed that the critical Mach number for the He 162 was 0.72 and a top speed of 870 km/h was not to be exceeded.

The He 162 V4/M4, W.Nr. 200 004, VI+ID, fitted with MK 108s, was reported flight-ready at *Languste* on the 29th to assess general flight characteristics, but V5/M5, W.Nr. 200 005, VI+IE, had beaten it by five days and on the 28th, this aircraft engaged in static and vibration tests, but it would never fly and no weapons were fitted to the aircraft.[83] These aircraft had the new strengthened wings requested by Kessler and the downward hanging tips designed by *Dr.* Alexander Lippisch as described earlier.

On 27 December, Francke attended to the radical question of accommodating an ejector seat in the He 162. The whole idea had ground to a halt for a number of weeks and Francke pressed his design engineers for a solution to the fact that the proposed seat could not fit into the existing design. 'I have been waiting for an answer for several weeks,' Francke grumbled.[84]

Although there was a projected output of four V-series aircraft in December, with six following in January and ten in February, towards the end of December, Heinkel replaced its existing 'V' prefix (for '*Versuchs*' or prototype) designation with the more standard practice of using an 'M' – denoting '*Muster*' (Model) – prefix. As a result of this, the He 162 V2 became the M2 and the V6 became the M6 etc.[85] Reinforced and redesigned wings were listed as fitted to the He 162 'M4' – the first time the 'M' designation appeared in place of the 'V'.

The new strengthened wings featured a modified double skin structure consisting of the skins, a tapered pressure plate and lattice work, all of which was glued with a hardener known as Kaurit. Two shells were connected through a web which ran span-wise and there were four ribs of similar construction.[86]

Monday, 1 January – Sunday, 14 January 1945

On Wednesday, 3 January 1945, two days after the *Luftwaffe* had launched its last, 'do-or-die' fighter offensive against Allied tactical airfields in the West under the code name, Operation '*Bodenplatte*', the OKL described the '162 Assembly Programme' as being of the 'greatest importance in the fight to break the Allied air terror.' As such, every assistance was to be rendered to *Generalkommissar* Kessler in his efforts to push forward production of the He 162 with all speed.[87]

The following day, another *Volksjäger* was rolled out when the He 162 M4, W.Nr. 200 004, VI+ID, was officially declared flight-ready for Schuck to fly it to a maximum speed of 500 km/h. With reinforced wings, it would achieve a speed of 700 km/h during tests later in the month. Meanwhile the He 162 M2 (V2) W.Nr. 200 002, VI+IB, which had test-fired 1,000 rounds from its MK 108 cannon to date, was destined for an engine change and the He 162 M3, W.Nr. 200003, VI+IC was also ready to make take-off and landing, and vibration trials, piloted by Kemnitz.[88]

With the coming of the new year, on 10 January, *Fliegerstabsing.* Paul Bader of the *E-Stelle* Rechlin, who had flown the M2 on 22 December, was appointed '*Typenbegleiter*' ('Project Leader' or 'Development Co-ordinator') for the He 162 programme. One of his first tasks that day was to attend to a problem on the Heinkel fighter's fuel tanks, which, following pressure tests, showed that they were still inadequately sealed.

Also on the 10th, the He 162 M18 (as an A-2), W.Nr. 220 001, VI+IK, was reported flight-ready at '*Languste*' and moved to Heidfeld.[89] This aircraft was actually the A-01, intended as a pre-production machine for the planned A-2 series, though the Heinkel '*Muster-Übersicht*' of mid-February lists it as being an A-2. It was equipped with two 20 mm MG 151/20s and carried added ballast in its nose section with the aim of shifting its centre of gravity.[90] The aircraft would be used to test take-off, landing and endurance and also to undertake radio trials and a camera installation.[91]

On 14 January, EHAG at Rostock reported its first He 162 ready in the form of W.Nr. 120 001 which flew the same day, for the first time, for 14 minutes with unstrengthened wings. A number of further flights took place once a radio unit had been installed and no subsequent problems were encountered.[92]

Monday, 15 January – Sunday, 28 January 1945

Around 15 January, the airframe of He 162 M11, W.Nr. 220 017, (designated He 162 'A-017' – a prototype for the planned A-2 series of aircraft), which had been fitted with 30 mm MK 108 cannon, was set aside for the mounting of a Jumo 004 B-1 engine.

On the 16th, He 162 M4, W.Nr. 200 004, flew on its maiden flight. The aircraft, with ballast in its nose, would partake in stability tests and roll trials, and carry strengthened wings and fuselage.[93] Also this day, He 162 M3, W.Nr. 200 003, VI+IC, which had been completed on 20 December and was intended to assess general flight characteristics, flew with reinforced wings with 'Lippisch ears' and enlarged tail assembly, possibly with *Lt.* Kemnitz at the controls.[94] This aircraft would undergo a remarkable 13 test flights in one week and would ultimately reach a top speed of 880 km/h. Likewise this day, the He 162 M19 (as an A-2), W.Nr. 220 002, VI+IL, was declared flight-ready.[95]

At Rostock, He 162 W.Nr. 120 002 left final assembly without strengthened wings and missing a tail assembly, which was subsequently fitted. It was planned to flight test the aircraft on 22 January.[96]

The following day the He 162 M6, W.Nr. 200 006, VI+IF, which was to be the pre-series machine for the A-1 type, was reported flight-ready to assess stability, rudder functioning and weapons-testing, while other unidentified He 162s were involved in ground-firing weapons trials with both MG 151 and MK 108 cannon.[97]

Also on the 17th, *Dr.* Janzen of the Heinkel Engine Department wrote to *Dr.* Baumann of the Flight Test Department informing that fuel odour was penetrating the He 162's cockpit from the tank located behind section 5 of the fuselage. Janzen enquired whether this could be expected to be a regular occurrence and whether simple ventilation of the cockpit would solve the problem. If this was not possible, it was suggested that improved sealing at section 5 be considered.[98]

The second half of January 1945 would see an attempt at acceleration in activity in both He 162 production and the associated flight-testing programme, but this was thwarted to some extent by a delay in delivery of the strengthened wing sets, of which only 15 had been produced by 21 January – which, of course, affected prototype production. Tail assembly also became delayed, affecting output at Heidfeld. The catastrophic transportation bottlenecks within the Reich resulted in ever-increasing delays to deliveries in components and it was decided that the entire January production of 20 aircraft should be used for test purposes.

On the 18th, He 162 M3, W.Nr. 200 003, VI+IC, made its third flight, while the He 162 M20 (as an A-2), W.Nr. 220 003, VI+IM, became flight-ready and was designated as an A-03. Its principal feature was a simplified undercarriage and it was used to assess in-flight performance, centre of gravity, flaps and rudders.[99]

On Saturday, 20 January 1945, the He 162 M4, W.Nr. 200 004, VI+ID, made its fourth test flight. By the 22nd, the aircraft had achieved a total test-flying time of 2 hours 54 minutes, although it was damaged when it ran into deep snow and it was estimated that it would take two days for repairs. The M3 was also damaged on the 22nd when its port wing collapsed on landing.[100]

Meanwhile, on 21 January the He 162 M21 (as an A-2) 220 004, VI+IN, was delivered from *Languste* to Heidfeld.[101]

On the 23rd, the He 162 M6, W.Nr. 200 006, VI+IF, flew its maiden flight, having been completed five days earlier, and was assigned to conduct weapons trials with two 30 mm MK 108 cannon in readiness for the planned He 162 A-1.[102] Disappointment had surrounded the arrival at Heidfeld of the He 162 M18 (A-01), W.Nr 220 001, VI+IK, from *Languste*, when it was discovered that there were more than 50 deviations from the type drawings, all of which had to be rectified before the machine was able to make its maiden flight. However, with these faults eventually solved, the aircraft took to the skies on 24 January and was assigned to conduct roll tests, take-off and landing tests and – as a He 162 A-2, fitted with MG 151/20s – trials with a BMW 003 E-1 engine.[103] The same day the He 162 M7 200 007, VI+IG, was moved from *Languste* to Heidfeld, fitted with two MG 151s and the He 162 M22, W.Nr. 220 005, VI+IO, was delivered (as an A-2).[104]

At EHAG Rostock, He 162 W.Nr. 120 003 was still in final assembly, but unlike its local predecessors, this aircraft had strengthened wings. It was to be handed over for flight-testing on 23 January.[105]

Next day He 162 M23 (A-06 to an A-2) W.Nr. 220 006, VI+IP moved from *Languste* to Heidfeld to commence general flight-testing.[106]

On the 26th, Carl Francke enquired of his team whether three or four He 162s could be fitted out as '*Behelfs-Aufklärer*' – improvised or emergency reconnaissance variants – and whether such machines could be ready by February.[107]

By Saturday, 27 January 1945, the He 162 A-01 W.Nr. 220 001, VI+IK, (formerly the M18), made ten starts to assess general flight performance. However, it was observed that there was some play in the nosewheel strut and that the brakes were proving temperamental. The same day, the M6, W.Nr. 200 006 took off on a flight test which had to be abandoned due to engine failure when, at between 5000-7000 rpm, there was a 'grinding noise'. Heinkel was forced to concede that the engine would need to be examined and probably changed.

During a personal visit on 27 January, *Inspekteur Direktor* Meyer from EHAG Marienehe made an assessment of the production status of the He 162 at Rostock. Meyer discovered that the planned completion of thirty He 162s in January had not been possible due to the non-delivery of engines and wings. In fact, Meyer reported the following findings:

Transferred	-	0 aircraft
Handed over	-	0 aircraft
Flown	-	2 aircraft
Engine tests completed	-	12 aircraft
Completion	-	58 fuselages
Nearing completion	-	71 fuselages

In order to maintain the agreed production programme for January and February, and subject to confirmation from Kessler in Berlin, Meyer proposed to increase Heinkel's prevailing single working shift to two shifts per day by withdrawing personnel from the He 219 construction programme, since that aircraft was being phased out.

Only 16 machines with all parts – with the exception of rudders, which were being transported by road from Langenöls and Rostock – were ready.

A crated fuel tank intended for a He 162 undergoes a water pressure test in order to eliminate leakage due to poor construction. Note the area around the timber crate is soaked with water from previous experiments. EHAG struggled through the whole He 162 production programme to overcome leaking tanks.

An American serviceman crouches to inspect the abandoned airframes of He 162 M23 (A-2) W.Nr. 220 006, VI+IP (left) and He 162 A-2 M20, W.Nr. 220 003, VI+IM at München-Riem in the summer of 1945.

Meyer further proposed the following completion programme: for the first days of February, one aircraft, then gradually increasing so that by the end of the month, the previous total for January and February of 85 aircraft would be achieved. This, of course, would be dependent on all the necessary parts being delivered on time. 'It is imperative,' Meyer wrote, 'that to achieve this, the delivery firms must deliver punctually, so that by 18 February the last parts for the end of February delivery are available. It is down to Heinkel to make sure that they inform Berlin daily by telephone so that the personnel in the *Generalkommissar's* office are kept fully informed.'

However, it seemed that much of what Meyer proposed would be academic since, despite protest from local EHAG management, from 29 January for eight days the Heinkel works would be closed on a pre-planned basis due to lack of electricity! Meyer ventured to suggest that since only 750 kilowatts of power could be supplied to Rostock, the Me 262 and Ta 152 be halted in favour of the He 162.

Furthermore, high-speed flight-testing at Rostock had been hindered due to bad weather and a lack of fuel.[108]

Next day, the A-01, W.Nr. 220 001, made three good flights followed by the first two take-offs by the He 162 M19, A-02 W.Nr. 220 002, VI+IL, which was fitted with an extended trailing edge with which it was intended to test stability of the ailerons at high-altitude as well as stability across the lateral axis.[109] However, Heinkel observed that the rudder trimming was not working and that the aircraft was subject to excess stress. Furthermore, the fuel lever brake did not pull and it was recommended that before the aircraft fly again, ballast should be placed in the nose.[110] In later trials however, the M19 would attain a top speed of only 480 km/h due to poor stability around its lateral axis.

Monday, 29 January – Sunday, 11 February 1945

Monday, 29 January saw the He 162 M8 (an A-1) W.Nr. 200 008, VI+IH completed and armed with MK 108s. This aircraft was to be used for experiments with a lightened undercarriage and weapons trials as an He 162 A-2, while the M7 would be used to test vibration and a brake parachute, which weighed 25 kg. The He 162 M25 (A-08), W.Nr. 220 008, VI+IR, was declared flight-ready. M25's fuselage had been extended by 12 cm and ballast had been loaded into its nose section which carried MK 108 cannon. The plan was to conduct more centre of gravity tests as well as to assess performance in the climb.[111]

This day also saw the newly appointed *General der Jagdflieger, Oberst* Gordon Gollob, address a major staff conference in Berlin the aim of which was to address '... the current personnel and materials situation with a view to avoiding the *Reichsmarschall's* suggestions which cannot be realised.'

Gollob had been appointed successor to *Generalleutnant* Adolf Galland who had been dismissed by Göring following worsening disagreements, particularly over the deployment of the Me 262. Gollob wanted to achieve a smooth transition of two piston-engined fighter *Geschwader*, JG 300 and JG 301, which had been assigned to the *Reichsverteidigung*, over to the Me 262 to supplement the operations of JG 7. He also wanted to speed up the transition of former bomber units belonging to IX.(J) *Fliegerkorps* – KG(J) 54, III./KG(J) 6, KG(J) 55, KG(J) 27, and I. and II./KG(J) 6 – on to the jet fighter. Parallel to this was a plan to form a new *Jagdgeschwader*, JG 80, to train up on the He 162 *Volksjäger*. However this proposal was abandoned in the light of a downturn in production of the Fw 190. It was therefore proposed to cancel the planned establishment of I./JG 80 and to draw on existing Fw 190 units for conversion to the He 162. As a result, Gollob ordered the conversion of I./JG 1 to the *Volksjäger* (see Chapter Three).[112]

The next day, the 30th, EHAG reported that the He 162 M26 (an A-2 with MG 151/20 cannon) W.Nr. 220 009, VI+IS, built with an extended fuselage, was announced flight-ready which, with the He 162 M18 (A-01), W.Nr 220 001, VI+IK, made a total of nine starts. It was planned to use the aircraft to test the intended ejector seat. At Heidfeld the He 162 M2 W.Nr. 200 002, VI+IB had received an extra 3 mm of strengthening to its nose section, which had also been sprayed with a preservative. The He 162 M3, W.Nr. 200 003, VI+IC had the span of its horizontal tail surfaces increased and would be ready for flight on 1 February. After the first few test flights, ballast would be installed to assist with the centre of gravity. The He 162 M4, W.Nr. 200 004, VI+ID had been fitted with new wings with downward-pointing tips and would be ready for flight the next day. The He 162 M6, W.Nr. 200 006, VI+IF had been fitted with an extra 5 kg of weight to assist with rudder control and this was found to be reasonably satisfactory in its functioning to left and right, although a strong veer to the left was still evident. The He 162 M7 W.Nr. 200 007, VI+IG was undergoing compass alignment and stability tests on the 30th. The He 162 M19, A-02 W.Nr. 220 002, VI+IL would be ready for flight on the 31st after having ballast loaded into its nose. The He 162 M20, A-03 W.Nr. 220 003, VI+IM underwent engine tests and steering modifications and was fitted with 45-degree downward-pointing wing tips, so as to be ready for flight on 1 February. Francke also asked that the undercarriage as fitted to the A-02 should be installed in all other aircraft since the mechanism functioned without trouble.[113]

However, the end of the month saw a virtual standstill at Heinkel's Rostock plant because the required tail units were found to be faulty, though 10 aircraft were reported ready to be delivered. Furthermore, in Wien 12 Heinkels had been ready for some time but, again, unable to be delivered due to some faulty parts. The reality was that only fourteen machines had been completed by 31 January.

On Thursday, 1 February 1945, EHAG in Wien-Schwechat issued a major technical document – a '*Prüfmappe Flugzeug 162*' – intended as a general testing guide for any technicians working on the aircraft and which portrayed in great detail and with many drawings, the mechanical and electric functioning of the fuselage, wings, undercarriage, cockpit, fuel systems, weapons, engines, navigational instruments, radio equipment and access points (see page 81).[114]

That day, the He 162 M27 (A-010) W.Nr. 220 010, VI+IT, made its first flight with a strengthened airframe constructed at Heidfeld, while the He 162 M28 (A-011) W.Nr. 220 011, VI+IU, was completed, also with a strengthened airframe and armed with 30 mm MK 108 cannon.

So problematic was the wing quality situation proving that, on 2 February, Heinkel's erstwhile competitor in the *Volksjäger* project the previous year, Blohm und Voss, was approached with a view to the company manufacturing metal wings.

Meanwhile the lessons learned during the testing of the prototype aircraft to date resulted in desired amendments and enhancements to the design and build of the aircraft. As a result, on 2 February, representatives of the three main building groups, or 'licensed assembly companies' – Heinkel at Rostock (covering Ludwigslust and Oranienburg), Heinkel at Wien and Junkers (covering Dessau and Bernburg) – attended a meeting in Berlin at which extensive documents showing all planned modifications and revised drawings were presented to the licensees. It was agreed that the *Musterbau* – the

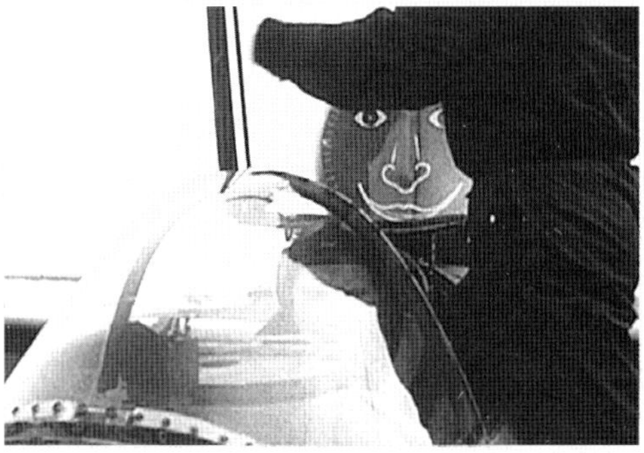

A test pilot, bearing a striking resemblence to Oberleutnant Georg Weydemeyer, conducts last minute instrument checks before take-off from Wien-Schwechat in He 162 M6 W.Nr. 200 006, VI+IF. Note the unusual depiction of a smiling face applied to the protection cover mounted on the intake of the BMW 003 engine (far left), as well as the Revi 16 b gunsight mounted on the rim of the instrument panel. The photograph above shows what appears to be another test pilot, closing the canopy of the aircraft, while in the photograph to right, the pilot locks the canopy down.

prototype construction section at Wien – would carry out the modifications for aircraft built in Wien.[115]

As of 2 February, the M6 W.Nr. 200 006 had made two flights piloted by *Feldwebel.* Gerhard Gleuwitz and *Flugbaumeister* Gerhard Full, while the A-02, W.Nr. 220 002, had made one flight piloted by *Dipl.-Ing.* Schuck. Further flying was prevented by fog. The nosewheel on the M6 suffered a collapse after 100 metres during its landing run and the aircraft continued to slide along the ground on its nose, damaging the undercarriage doors. After carrying out repairs the aircraft was ready for flight again at midday on the 3rd. The A-02 had its tail assembly strengthened and would also be ready for flying on the 3rd along with the M3 W.Nr. 200 003 and the M4 W.Nr. 200 004. The M7 W.Nr. 200 007 was fitted with a brake parachute and 'Lippisch ears', copied from the M3, as well as other, minor, adjustments connected mainly with steering. Four brake parachutes were to hand for He 162 testing with a further 15 due to be delivered.

This day, an instruction was issued by a *Herr* Scholl to paint the respective *Muster* – or 'M' – numbers on the noses of all prototype aircraft together with the preparation of a master document listing all such aircraft – the *8-162 Muster-Übersicht* (162 Prototype Overview).[116]

Next day, the He 162 M8 (an A-2) W.Nr. 200 008, VI+IH, was in the workshops receiving attention to its ailerons.[117]

On the 4th, another fatality struck the test programme when the experienced test pilot, *Oberleutnant* Georg Weydemeyer, crashed in the He 162 M6, W.Nr. 200 006, VI+IF, during its eleventh test flight. Weydemeyer had been born on 10 March 1910 in Westphalia and had flown in the *Luftwaffe* since 1934. That year he was posted to the *Fliegerschule* at Tutow as an instructor and from the end of the year served as a bomber pilot with KG 4 with whom he saw operations over Poland, Norway, England, Crete and Russia following which, in late 1941, he joined Heinkel and test-flew the He 177, He 219 and He 280. He had been awarded the Iron Cross First Class and was a married man with three children.[118]

Eye witnesses reported observing Weydemeyer's aircraft go into a right-hand curved dive, but the actual reason for the crash was not clear, although it was suspected a seized rudder was attributable. It was however considered certain that it had no connection to that of Gotthold Peter's crash in the M1.[119] Later it was discovered that some of the plywood covering on the ribs of Weydemeyer's tail unit had not been glued adequately. An angry Ernst Heinkel stressed that such crashes would not be tolerated and requested personally that the strongest of complaints be made to the appropriate party regarding the poor workmanship involved. The finger of blame was pointed at the firm of Albrecht, a sub-contractor at Weitramsdorf.

Dr. Heinkel further ordered that landing flaps and other wooden parts produced by all sub-contractors be subjected to the closest scrutiny before acceptance and that on any future occasion poor quality build from outside EHAG would not be an acceptable excuse. To this end, Heinkel proposed that a department from the construction office for the now abandoned He 219 be appointed as a controlling and instructing body to supervise all procedures in Wien.[120]

Oberleutnant Georg Weydemeyer, an experienced Luftwaffe pilot who had joined Heinkel in 1941, was killed when the He 162 M6 W.Nr. 200 006, VI+IF crashed on 4 February 1945. The pilot seen in the cockpit in the movie film stills at the bottom of the page could well be Weydemeyer.

The day of Weydemeyer's death also saw the end of a week in which there had been 29 take-offs in He 162s, spanning 7 hours 33 minutes of flying time. Seventeen starts had taken place on the 4th alone using the M3, M4, M6 and M18, with Francke, Bader, Weydemeyer, *Lt.* Kemnitz, *Hptm.* Geyer, *Flugkapitän* Bartels from DLH, *Dipl.-Ing.* Schuck, *Ing.* Meschkat and *Flugbaumeister* Full and *Fw.* Gleuwitz all flying. The M3 required the installation of radio equipment, ballast to compensate for a full tank of fuel, weights to ease stick control, improvements to the rudder trim, and 10 mm needed to be trimmed off the rear edge of the horizontal stabilizer. The aircraft would subsequently be flown by Gleuwitz, Full and Schuck on stability tests. The M4 would continue to conduct take-off, landing and stability tests, while the M18 was fitted with a camera to assess undercarriage functioning.[121]

To date, the entire test programme had accumulated a total of 86 take-offs with a flying time of 16 hours and 33 minutes, an indication of the extent to which testing of the He 162 was still in its infancy. The He 162s M4 and M19 were undergoing minor improvements to their stability, and following these improvements, *Hauptmann* Horst Geyer from the staff of the *Kommandeur der Erprobungsstellen*, and formerly commander of *Erprobungskommando* 25, the weapons testing and evaluation unit, had flown the former machine without problems.[122]

There was still little cheer from the Heinkel works at Rostock-Marienehe; by early February no completed aircraft had been delivered from the plant, though 12 machines had been signed off as far as engine serviceability was concerned. Seventy-one fuselages had been completed, with a further 58 in the early stages of construction.

On 4 February, '*Werk-Nr.* 009' was flown by both *Flugkapitän* Heinrich and *Flugkapitän* Sulzbacher, on each occasion with faultless performance. However, the two available airworthy aircraft at Rostock were subsequently dismantled and sent by rail to the *Lufthansa* facility at Oranienburg with some parts transferred to Ludwigslust where they were used to convert other aircraft to the latest specification.

Heinkel He 162 M20 (A-03) W.Nr. 220003 coded VI+IM built at *Languste Werk*

The third pre-production series aircraft, which was first flown by Gerhard Gleuwitz on 10 February 1945. At the end of March 1945 the aircraft was moved from Schwechat to Lechfeld and it was later found damaged at München-Riem. The aircraft was equipped with 2 x MG 151/20 cannon replacing the proposed MK 108s. The fuselage was painted in RLM 76/82 and the rear fuselage cone appeared as though it was left in its natural metal finish with the camouflage just being applied to the upper side. The BMW 003 engine cowling and covering was painted overall in RLM 81 with the wing upper surfaces painted in RLM 81/82.

The He 162 A-2 M20, W.Nr. 220 003, VI+IM, was discovered at München-Riem airport in May 1945 in a state of abandon, with its canopy and nosewheel missing. It was probably one of the ten machines flown out of Wien to Lechfeld in early April in the face of the Soviet advance on Wien. The 'M20' painted on the nose in black denoted the twentieth prototype. 'M' ('Muster' or model) numbers were used to identify He 162 prototypes rather than the more customary 'V' ('Versuch' or Experimental) numbers. The missing engine cowlings and its MG 151/20 cannon were probably removed as result of inquisitiveness on the part of Allied troops. At the time of its roll-out in mid-February 1945, it featured a simplified undercarriage and was used to assess in-flight performance, centre of gravity, flaps and rudders.

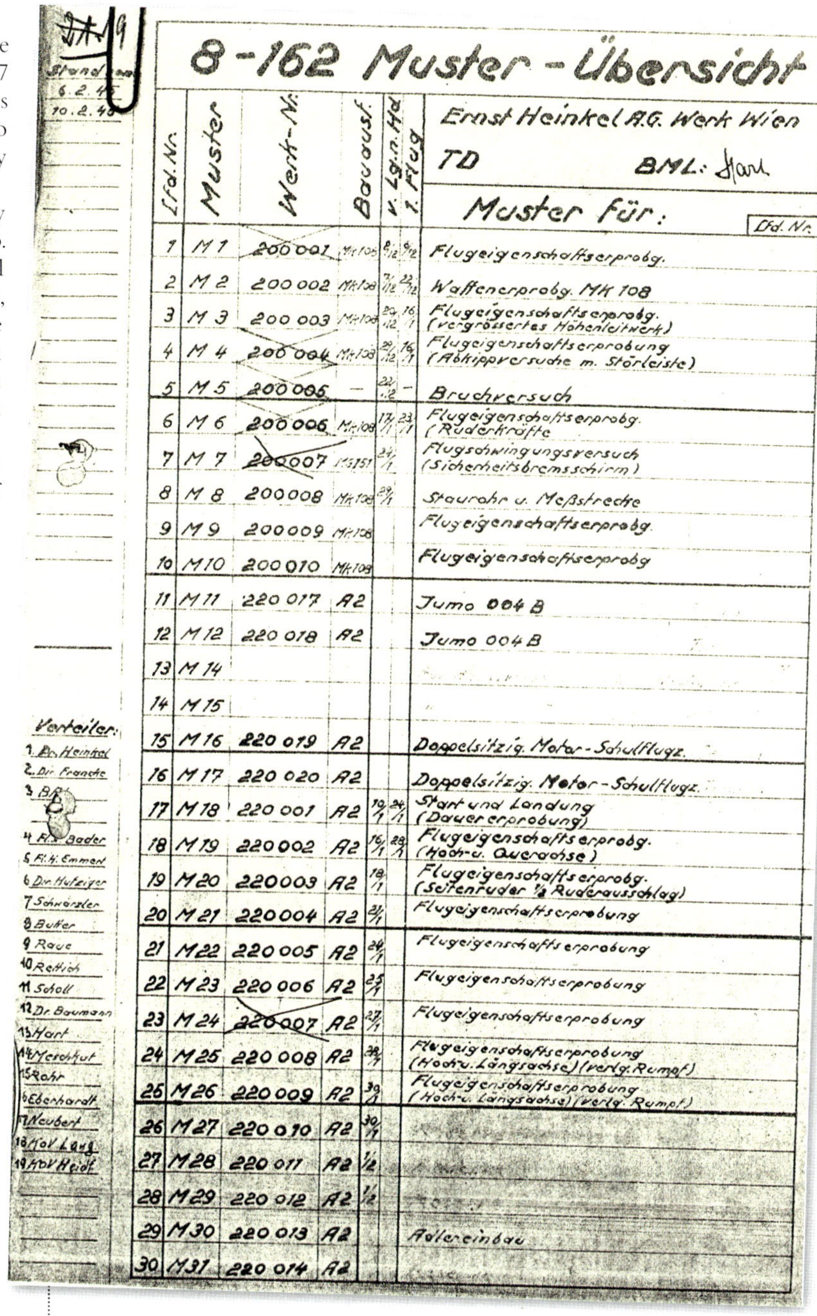

Stand vom 6.2.45 / 10.2.45

8-162 Muster-Übersicht

Ernst Heinkel A.G. Werk Wien

TD BML: Hart

Lfd. Nr.	Muster	Werk-Nr.	Bauausf.	v. Lg.n.Hd	1. Flug	Muster für:
1	M 1	200 001	Mk 108	8/12	9/12	Flugeigenschaftserprobg.
2	M 2	200 002	Mk 108	7/12	22/12	Waffenerprobg. MK 108
3	M 3	200 003	Mk 108	20/12	16/1	Flugeigenschaftserprobg. (vergrössertes Höhenleitwerk)
4	M 4	200 004	Mk 108	29/12	16/1	Flugeigenschaftserprobung (Abkippversuche m. Störleiste)
5	M 5	200 005	–	22/12	–	Bruchversuch
6	M 6	200 006	Mk 108	17/1	23/1	Flugeigenschaftserprobg. (Ruderkräfte
7	M 7	200 007	MG 151	24/1		Flugschwingungsversuch (Sicherheitsbremsschirm)
8	M 8	200 008	Mk 108	29/1		Staurohr u. Meßstrecke
9	M 9	200 009	Mk 108			Flugeigenschaftserprobg.
10	M 10	200 010	Mk 108			Flugeigenschaftserprobg
11	M 11	220 017	A2			Jumo 004 B
12	M 12	220 018	A2			Jumo 004 B
13	M 14					
14	M 15					
15	M 16	220 019	A2			Doppelsitzig. Motor-Schulflugz.
16	M 17	220 020	A2			Doppelsitzig. Motor-Schulflugz.
17	M 18	220 001	A2	19/1	24/1	Start und Landung (Dauererprobung)
18	M 19	220 002	A2	16/1	28/1	Flugeigenschaftserprobg. (Hoch-u. Querachse)
19	M 20	220 003	A2	18/1		Flugeigenschaftserprobg. (Seitenruder ½ Ruderausschlag)
20	M 21	220 004	A2	21/1		Flugeigenschaftserprobung
21	M 22	220 005	A2	24/1		Flugeigenschaftserprobung
22	M 23	220 006	A2	25/1		Flugeigenschaftserprobung
23	M 24	220 007	A2	27/1		Flugeigenschaftserprobung
24	M 25	220 008	A2	28/1		Flugeigenschaftserprobung (Hoch-u. Längsachse) (verlg. Rumpf)
25	M 26	220 009	A2	30/1		Flugeigenschaftserprobung (Hoch-u. Längsachse) (verlg. Rumpf)
26	M 27	220 010	A2	30/1		
27	M 28	220 011	A2	1/2		
28	M 29	220 012	A2	1/2		
29	M 30	220 013	A2			Adlereinbau
30	M 31	220 014	A2			

Verteiler:
1. Dr. Heinkel
2. Dir. Francke
3. BR
4. Fl.H. Bader
5. Fl.H. Emmert
6. Dir. Hutzeiger
7. Schwärzler
8. Butter
9. Raue
10. Rettich
11. Scholl
12. Dr. Baumann
13. Hart
14. Meschkut
15. Rohr
16. Eberhardt
17. Neubert
18. KdV Lang
19. KdV Heidt

A Heinkel document dated February 1945, detailing the current status and testing of the He 162 prototypes. Those machines crossed out had been destroyed by 10 February 1945.

The parts situation at Rostock was dire: only 36 sets of wings were available against a planned 47 sets; 42 engines against a planned 47; 67 undercarriage mechanisms against a planned 81; 24 sets of weapons bay access panels against a planned 67. The shortages also extended to landing- and nosewheel doors, rudders, nosewheels and other key parts.[123]

Meanwhile a total of 42 fuselages were on the Rostock assembly line, with a further 38 having been moved to the finishing shop. Thirty-four fuselages were completed. However, the plant was still missing major quantities of key components such as wings, tail units, nose cones, undercarriage doors and weapons access panels, all due from timber sub-contractors. Of the wings that had been delivered in consignments between 17-20 January, five sets had major faults such as leaking fuel tanks, poor glueing and wrongly-constructed components.

Furthermore, 20 engines plus nosewheels, canopies, and 27 FuG 24 radio sets were outstanding. 'The completion of further aircraft,' warned a senior engineer at Marienehe on 5 February, 'hangs in the balance pending the arrival of these missing parts.'

The Rostock plant was also labouring under problematic electricity supply and the local management was compelled to 'demand' 20 hours of power per day in order to function, with the four-hour shutdown period being between 1700-2100 hrs. On the plus side, Kessler had arranged for 100 student workers from Pomerania to be available at Rostock in February, who would each be assigned to an individual instructor. It was planned to assign 10 men to electrical training for a period of one week; a further 10 men to be trained as mechnics for one week; 30 men as aircraft fitters under two weeks training; and 20 men on aircraft maintenance for two weeks.[124]

In a somewhat surprising *Blitz! Blitz!* communication of 6 February, Francke cabled Kessler and *Gen.Stabs-Ing. Dipl.-Ing.* Lucht, the head of the Emergency Aircraft Commission, advising that, apparently, the He 162 was 'not in the Emergency Programme' unlike the Me 262, Ta 152, Ar 234 and Do 335. 'We have difficulties with matters of urgency with our suppliers,' Francke lamented, 'and ask you to place the 162 within the emergency programme accordingly.'[125]

By the 6th, the He 162 M3 W.Nr. 200 003, VI+IC was undergoing various modifications involving rudder, hydraulics and controls, while the M19 (A-02) W.Nr. 220 002, VI+IL remained ready for flight and the M4 W.Nr. 200 004, VI+ID was being used for taxying trials. There was also investigation into the installation of a night-vision camera into this aircraft.[126]

At last, on 8 February, another three machines were completed: the He 162 M29 (A-012) W.Nr. 220 012, VI+IV equipped with two MK 108s and a lengthened fuselage; the He 162 M30 (A-013) W.Nr. 220 013, VI+IW equipped with MG 151s and the He 162 M31 (built as an A-2 with two MG 151s) W.Nr. 220 014, VI+IX. None of these aircraft would fly for several days, but in any case, the M29 was slated as a reserve machine for weapons-testing, while the M30 was similarly assigned but was also installed with an EZ 42 gunsight – as was the M31 – and an *Adler* homing device.[127]

This day *Flugbaumeister* Full had to force-land off the airfield following an engine failure while flying the He 162 M4 W.Nr. 200 004 at 8000 m at a speed of 800 km/h to conduct stability and dive tests. The M4 was 40 per cent damaged and its strengthened wings carried the new, down-turned 'Lippisch ear' wing tips. It was also armed with MG 151s.[128]

In the light of Full's crash and the dangerous instability affecting the He 162's lateral axis, Francke ordered that speed limitations of 500 km/h at 0-1000 m, 400 km/h at 1000-5000 m and 300 km/h over 5000 m be imposed on test flights.[129]

The M3 W.Nr. 200 003 was fitted with an enlarged tail unit. It was also decreed that in order for the aircraft to conduct flight trials, the fuselage fuel tank should not contain less than 375 litres of fuel to maintain stability, and that test speeds should be carefully monitored. Similarly, in the case of the M20 W.Nr. 220 003, the aircraft was not to be flown with less than 300 litres in its fuselage tank. The M19 W.Nr. 220 002 was to be fitted with a 20-degree V-tail, but otherwise it was as per the M3 in configuration, although instructions were issued to weigh the aircraft after refitting to confirm the centre of gravity. It was planned to eventually fit enlarged, downward-pointing tail fins on the machine.

As a result of wind tunnel testing at the DVL Braunschweig and Heinkel's own test flying, it was realised that the wings of the He 162 were 'dangerously' unstable and could cause stalling! In this regard, small wooden wedges, 10 mm high and 450 mm long, were fixed with wooden screws to the leading edges of the wings of the M18 W.Nr. 220 001, VI+IK which was to be ready for testing on 10 February.

By 9 February, in Hangar 47, there were five series production aircraft ready, and on each day following, one additional aircraft was planned to be ready. These aircraft were to be further modified to bring them up to the latest specification with the aim of delivering 20 completed aircraft by the end of the month.[130]

Testing continued on the 10th when the He 162 M20 (A-03) W.Nr. 220 003, VI+IM, fitted with a simplified undercarriage, took off on its

The widely-used Revi 16b gunsight was proposed initially for installation in the He 162, and was to undergo trials for the aircraft at the Erprobungsstelle Tarnewitz in November 1944, but Carl Francke preferred the EZ 42 gyroscopic sight.

maiden flight. The aircraft would be used to test centre of gravity issues, flaps and rudders. Also flown this day for the first time was the M24 (A-07), W.Nr. 220 007, VI+IQ, which was fitted with two MG 151s and would be used for taxying trials and general flight-testing.[131] The He 162s M7, M9 and M10 were undergoing work to strengthen their ailerons.[132]

By this stage, EHAG was listing the He 162s M16 (W.Nr. 220 019) and M 17 (W.Nr. 220 020) – both A-2s – as '*Doppelsitzig Motor-Schulflugzeuge*' (two-seat, powered trainers).[133]

On Sunday, 11 February the *Luftwaffe* demonstrated its increasing interest in the He 162 programme in the form of a 'heavyweight' visit to Schwechat by the *General der Jagdflieger*, *Oberst* Gordon Gollob, who was accompanied to the city of his birth by *Oberstleutnant* Walter Dahl, the 93-victory *Ritterkreuzträger* who had recently commanded JG 300 in the Defence of the Reich but who was now serving on Gollob's staff as *Inspekteur der Tagjäger*, and *Stabs Ingenieur* Rauchensteiner.[134] They were joined by *Oberst* Edgar Petersen, the *Kommandeur der Erprobungsstellen*, and *Hauptmann* Horst Geyer from his staff.

According to Dahl's memoirs, under a cold downpour of rain he departed Staaken airfield near Berlin with Gollob at 0900 in a Siebel 204.[135] The two officers then flew a course over Dresden. As Dahl records: '... the rain develops into a true snowstorm... we continue flying on course over the Erzgebirge, then over Aussig in the Sudetenland in the direction of Prague, and everybody is lost in their own thoughts. The weather has become bad. The mountains are covered with clouds, and sometimes we have to turn to blind flying, using only the instruments.'

'About 1030 the weather clears up, a shaft of of bright rays shines through the clouds and shows us, for some moments, the undamaged city of Prague beneath us with its sparkling lights. We fly over the Moldau river with its magnificent bridges, pass the Hradschin, then to Wien, jumping over the Bohemian-Moravian mountains. At 1130 the Danube river emerges in front of us, and soon we have a very nice view: Wien – just ahead of us, bathed in bright sunshine. The *Stephansdom* (St Stephen's Cathedral) towers up out of the ocean of buildings like a giant. Automatically I remember the year 1683 when this town resisted the Turkish attacks from the east. Will it resist again this time [against the Soviets]?

'We land at Schwechat, the airfield to the south-east of the town. Some gentlemen from the Heinkel-Werke come to welcome us, and after the greeting procedure, *Flugkapitän* Francke, Chief Pilot of the Heinkel Werke at Schwechat takes us immediately to some He 162 aircraft parked along the runway.'

The EHAG team invited Gollob and Rauchensteiner to fly the He 162 M3 and both men took up the invitation, with Gollob recording a speed of around 650 km/h during a short flight. After their flights, both men remarked that there was no doubt that they were flying a true fighter aircraft – and, according to Heinkel, one that was 'really good'. Gollob was informed, politely, that he was welcome to return to Wien to fly the He 162 whenever he wished as long as he flew it within the recommended speed limits. However, the *General der Jagdflieger* commented to the EHAG representatives that Hitler had been informed in a recent report that thirty He 162s were ready in Wien for operations, whereas in reality, as of 10 February, there were no operational aircraft, and just four flyable, with a further 14 undergoing conversion and final assembly. Asked when these aircraft would be ready for operations, Francke advised Gollob the middle of April.[136]

There has been much speculation as to Dahl's graphic account in his post-war memoirs of his flight in the He 162. Certainly, surviving Heinkel and K.d.E documents refer only to the flights made by Gollob and Rauchensteiner in the He 162 M3. Nevertheless, Dahl recalled that apparently: '... After the masterly flight demonstration by *Flugkapitän* Francke, *Oberst* Gollob and then *Stabs Ingenieur* Rauchensteiner test the new aircraft; obviously both are impressed. My fingers are itching, but because I intend to test the machine a bit more seriously, I take off last. After some rolls, turns and fighter pilot-like aerobatics, I dive at high speed towards the airfield, aiming directly at the group. In low-level flight, I bring the aircraft close to the ground until, at about 20-30 metres, I pull up steeply rolling against the sky. All of a sudden there comes a strict order over the radio: '*Stop flying immediately! Come down immediately!*' I acknowledge receipt, prepare the landing, enter a normal circuit, lower the undercarriage and land. All runs well. The aircraft is easy to handle and also during the landing procedure.

'Having finished taxying and stopped the engine, Francke approaches, with an embarrassed expression on his face: '*This time, it was lucky*,' he said, '*but didn't you know in just the same aerobatic manoeuvre – a steep dive with following rolls – our test pilot, Peter, crashed to his death in December 1944?*' A bit confused, I accompany *Flugkapitän* Francke, who tells me the details of the fatal course of the tragic flight.'[137]

He 162 M6 W.Nr. 200 006, VI+IF streaks down the runway at Schwechat at the beginning of a test flight on a wintry day in early 1945. The aircraft was destroyed when it crashed on 4 February 1945 with Oberleutnant Georg Weydemeyer at the controls. Poor construction was blamed.

During Gollob's visit, Francke and Bader reassured the *Luftwaffe* delegation of the work being undertaken to improve the He 162's stability in flight and its flight characteristics as well as outlining the various modifications undertaken as described earlier in this chapter. In his summary of the *Luftwaffe's* visit to Wien, Petersen recorded that both Gollob and he concurred that full operational testing could not be considered until all EHAG's planned improvements had been incorporated and the He 162 was able to fly at full speed. This being said, Francke further commented that the earliest likely availability for operations would be the second half of April, thus it would be unlikely that any actual fighter operations could commence before mid-May, since the first test aircraft to incorporate all enhancements would not be ready until mid-March.

Oberst Gordon Gollob, the General der Jagdflieger, flew the He 162 on a short flight at Schwechat on 11 February 1945, recording a speed of around 650 km/h. While the fighter ace broadly welcomed the development of the Heinkel, he had concerns over various technical aspects of the aircraft. Gollob is seen here in September 1944 during a visit to JG 400 at Brandis at which time he was serving as the 'Typenbegleiter' for the Me 163 rocket interceptor.

Francke advised that it was projected that at least 50-60 initial aircraft would be fitted with the BMW 003 E-1 engine, which would require B4 fuel, not the J2 type as used by the Me 262 and Ar 234. From the start, Gollob asked that rocket-powered auxiliary take-off units be considered, presumably to enable operations from shorter runways.[138] In a later telephone conversation on 19 February between Frydag and Francke, Francke confirmed that the required runway and take-off distance for the He 162 was the same as the Me 262 due to the increased requirement for fuel and endurance, thus increasing weight.[139] Francke informed the *Luftwaffe* officers of this. 'Fundamentally important information for the General commanding the ground organisation!' recorded *Oberst* Petersen.

Gollob also agreed with the recommendations of the K.d.E that the He 162 should be fitted with an ejector seat in order, in an emergency, to throw a pilot clear of a jet engine located immediately behind his cockpit, while travelling at 1000 km/h.[140] Also a strengthened metal frame for the cockpit hood and windscreen was to be investigated so that the risk of metal debris breaking off during combat and being ingested into the engine was minimised.

As far as armament was concerned, for an operational environment, *Oberst* Gollob was of the view that an increase from 60 rpg to 80 rpg would be preferable for the He 162's two 30 mm MK 108 cannon. EHAG advised that it would investigate the ramifications of the increase in weight and the effect on the centre of gravity. However, events overtook this when Allied bombing of the Rheinmetall manufacturing plant halted supply of the MK 108 thus making the need for the installation of the MG 151 as an alternative (to create the He 162 A-2) a top urgent priority. However by 12 February, Gollob, based in Berlin, remained in favour of the MK 108, presumably because of experiences with the weapon in the Me 262, and was endeavouring to determine whether any other companies could manufacture the gun under licence.

The long-awaited EZ 42 gyroscopic gunsight to complement the proposed armament was finally ready and, according to Francke, all series aircraft from 1 May 1945 were to be fitted with the sight.

Under wider-ranging conversations between EHAG and Gollob during his visit to Schwechat, the possibility of fitting 55 mm R4M air-to-air rockets (as planned for the Me 262) was also to be examined by EHAG Wien and reported to the *General der Jagdflieger* by 20 February.

Accompanying Gollob to Schwechat on 11 February 1945 was Oberstleutnant Walter Dahl who was attached to Gollob's staff as Inspekteur der Tagjäger. According to his memoirs, Dahl also flew the He 162 but was chided by Carl Francke for the way in which he handled the aircraft.

Monday, 12 February – Sunday, 25 February 1945

The beginning of the new week saw a major meeting on the increasingly dire state of the He 162 programme held at Heinkel's offices on Angermayergasse in Wien. *Prof.* Heinkel chaired the meeting, which saw Francke, Karl Schwärzler and several members of the He 162 development team in attendance as well as a representative from *Generalkommissar* Kessler's department.

It was recognised that continual electrical power failures at Heidfeld – which were proving insurmountable – had caused major difficulties to the test programme, and would affect production and adversely extend the test programme. In the period 17 January to 10 February, Heidfeld was without power for 104 hours. The importance of keeping EHAG fully operational with power was stressed to the representative from Kessler's staff. Furthermore, EHAG was running short of fuel to function and requested that Kessler supply immediately 1500 litres of petrol and 4000 litres of diesel. In addition the company requested two lorry trailers in which to store gas for emergency power generators. One trailer would be connected while the other was being filled and so on. It was noted that this could be set up within three days.

At *Languste*, there were two petrol-powered generators and one diesel generator which would provide emergency power supply.

Despite massive challenges from power cuts, Allied bombing, and a failed transport system, EHAG strove to continue production against all odds, but often in the most appalling conditions. Here skilled, but probably forced, male and female labour assemble components for the He 162 under supervision at the 'Languste' cave factory at Mödling in the Hinterbrühl in early 1945. Workers laboured for long shifts with little food and light, and when they were finally released it was into a cold Austrian winter to travel on an unreliable transport system amidst an increasingly bomb-shattered environment.

A typical scene underground at Hinterbrühl in early 1945: the worker to the left fits a dural fuselage section intended for a He 162 over a mould, while to his right two carpenters use a power tool to work on timber components. In the background a lathe operator is at work. Note the dismal shafts of light from the overhead lamps.

A works foreman walks past men at work on pipes and cables deep within the Languste complex in early 1945. The facility's output was impressive given the conditions.

Transport was also a major problem: due to Allied bombing raids, local and regional train schedules were heavily disrupted and it was proposed that a member of the EHAG works management obtain a small bus with capacity for 10-12 persons which could be used to transport key personnel in an emergency (provided, of course, the bus itself was not bombed!). Stocks of food and drink would also be placed aside as safely as possible in case of need.[141]

Faced with the very likely prospect of more frequent Allied raids, a heavily disrupted transport system and supplies difficulties, the production figures now had to be reassessed on the basis of reality, not the wishful thinking upon which Production Programmes 227 and 228 and the target figures for May 1945 had been based. Consequently, series production plans were proposed as follows[142]:

Ex Heidfeld	-	10 machines by 2 March 1945
Ex Rostock	-	10 machines by 5 March 1945
Ex (Junkers) Bernburg	-	10 machines by 10 March 1945

Other problems affecting efficient output centred around the demand for retro-fitting, even aircraft which were perfectly functional, and the reliance upon prisoner labour which lacked motivation and often skill and which usually suffered from malnourishment while working in long shifts in cramped, poorly organised underground facilities. EHAG Heidfeld was awaiting confirmation of the transfer of 25 further men from *Lufthansa*, and another 20 personnel living near the EHAG facility at Zwölfaxing were to be transferred. A further 300 personnel from other sources were promised and were still awaited.

Despite these adversities, *Dr.* Heinkel requested that the plants do their utmost to keep to the production programme, particularly in view of the report given to the *Führer* to the effect that 30 aircraft were available in Wien – something that was clearly not the case.

According to EHAG's *Muster-Übersicht*, the 12th marked the targeted planned completion date of various items connected to ailerons, wing tips, flaps, nose sections, and tail assemblies on a number of aircraft – the M7, M9, M10, M19, M20, M25 – though to what extent this was accomplished is not known.[143]

In tandem with flight-testing at Wien, wind tunnel testing on a model of the He 162 with a 1.2 metre wingspan had been continuing at the DVL at Berlin-Adlershof to assess high speed characteristics. Testing took place in a 2.7-metre tunnel and was completed on 10 February. The results essentially told the aerodynamicists and engineers what they already knew: that lateral stability was a problem.

On 13 February, in the sixth such attack of 1945, heavy bombers from the US Fifteenth Air Force bombed depots and railway repair sheds in Wien; it was to be the first of three consecutive daylight raids targeting railway yards and oil refineries in and around the city. The He 162 M31, W.Nr. 220 014, VI+IX, a reserve aircraft which had – briefly – carried out trials with a gyroscopic gunsight, was damaged in the attack on the 13th, having been completed only five days earlier.

The next day, two Jumo 004 engines arrived at the *Languste* facility at Hinterbrühl intended to be fitted to the He 162 M11, W.Nr. 220 017, (A-017) and M12, W.Nr. 220 018.

On the 15th, the He 162 M9, W.Nr. 200 009, VI+II, an unarmed two-seater, was reported as complete.

Activity was underway at Junkers in Bernburg, where He 162s were now being built. *Flugkapitän Ing.* Hermann Steckhan, a Junkers pilot, flew the plant's first He 162, W.Nr. 310 001 for 20 minutes during the late afternoon of 15 February. There were apparently no problems. Steckhan was heavily involved in flight-testing *Mistel* composite aircraft at this time as well.[144]

Back in Wien, the fuselage of the M14, W.Nr. 220 015, equipped with MK 108 cannon, was set aside in readiness for mounting a Heinkel-Hirth HeS 011 power unit.

Francke was compelled to write to *Herr* Haberer of the EHAG building maintenance unit complaining over the condition of the access route for aircraft transiting from the hangars to the runway take-off point at Heidfeld. The route was grass which had deteriorated to a very muddy and rutted condition. So bad was it, that during a taxy run, the

He 162 M20 sank into mud between Hangar 50 and the runway, risking major damage. 'As you have 100 people at hand,' Francke wrote on the 15th, 'this would take only a few hours to rectify and repair.'[145]

The 15th also saw a reversal of what had been agreed earlier – at the meeting in Berlin on 2 February – concerning the incorporation of design and build amendments by the Wien prototype section to series machines. EHAG General Manager, Karl Frydag, instructed that all major manufacturing components – although to be built by the Heinkel *Musterbau* by 28 February – were to be delivered to the 'ALS *Umrüstbetrieb*'.† This was a reference to the Amme-Luther-Seck (ALS) *Werk* at Wien-Atzgersdorf which would now take charge of 'rebuilding' 12 aircraft as follows at Hangar 7 at Heidfeld as well as more widespread production at Atzgersdorf, Wiener Neustadt and Theresienfeld[146]:

He 162 M21 (A-04) W.Nr. 220 004,VI+IN
He 162 M22 (A-05) W.Nr. 220 005,VI+IO
He 162 M23 (A-06) W.Nr. 220 006,VI+IP
He 162 M24 (A-07) W.Nr. 220 007,VI+IQ
He 162 M26 (A-09) W.Nr. 220 009,VI+IS
He 162 M27 (A-010) W.Nr. 220 010,VI+IT
He 162 M28 (A-011) W.Nr. 220 011,VI+IU
He 162 M29 (A-012) W.Nr. 220 012,VI+IV
He 162 M30 (A-013) W.Nr. 220 013,VI+IW
He 162 M14 (A-015) W.Nr. 220 015,VI+IY
(code assigned, but never used)
He 162 M15 (A-016) W.Nr. 220 016,VI+IZ
(code assigned, but never used)
He 162 M11 (A-017) W.Nr. 220 017

Rebuilding was to commence on 20 February.

Meanwhile, the EHAG *Musterbau* would rebuild the following 13 machines:

He 162 M2 W.Nr. 200 002,VI+IB
He 162 M3 W.Nr. 200 003,VI+IC
He 162 M4 W.Nr. 200 004,VI+ID
He 162 M8 W.Nr. 200 008,VI+IH
He 162 M9 W.Nr. 200 009,VI+II
He 162 M10 W.Nr. 200 010,VI+IJ
(both M9 and M10 were trainers)
He 162 M11 (A-017)W.Nr. 220 017*
He 162 M12 (A-018) W.Nr. 220 018
(M11 and M12 fitted with Jumo 004 engines)
He 162 M18 (A-01)W.Nr. 220 001,VI+IK
He 162 M19 (A-02)W.Nr. 220 002,VI+IL
He 162 M20 (A-03)W.Nr. 220 003,VI+IM
He 162 M25 (A-08) W.Nr. 220 008,VI+IR

He 162 ? – to be second machine with lengthened fuselage from 0-series, but the *Muster* number had not yet been determined by the Technical Department by this date.

It was also agreed that the surplus German and 'detainee' assembly staff at Heidfeld's Hangar 7 would, as a result of some of the final assembly moving to the ALS *Umrüstbetrieb*, be transferred to the Flight Test Department. The collection and delivery of engines, fuselages and completed tail assemblies, including fins with unbalanced rudders, was to be handled by ALS which was to pick up from *Languste*. 'However,' Frydag directed, 'engines will remain in storage at *Languste* until actually required for the rebuilding programme to avoid losses to enemy action.'

Indeed, as Frydag's instructions were prepared, bombers from the US Fifteenth Air Force made their third successive attack on the Wien area, bombing an oil refinery, freight yards at five different locations, a goods depot and railway marshalling yards. Wiener-Neustadt was also targeted, along with the cities of Graz and Klagenfurt.[147] According to Carl Francke, by the 18th '80 per cent' of the Schwechat area lay in rubble.[148] If, EHAG and its associates did not have enough to contend with in the rush-development of a jet fighter, they now had to deal with a transport system that was virtually at a standstill. In his report for the week ending 18 February, Francke commented on the disruption caused by the bombing and the fact that the He 162 production programme was having to fight against power cuts, transport problems and up to five hours lost per day in flight-testing.[149]

Delivery of all outstanding components for the 30 prototype aircraft, from the V1 to the M30, was ready for Hangar 47 at Heidfeld which was to be cleared in readiness to be taken over by ALS. However, ALS planned to bring with them twenty '*Ostarbeiter*' (conscripted workers from the East) and for this '... translators will be required.' Further quarters were to be provided for additional ALS German workers.[150]

On the 16th an RAF reconnaissance flight had photographed an He 162 as it came in to land at Schwechat; 'although an exact calculation of landing speed cannot be made (owing to lack of data on the camera setting),' read the subsequent report, 'it is of interest to note that the aircraft covered about four-fifths of the 1725 yard runway before coming to rest.'[151]

The 17th February saw both the He 162 M25 (A-08) W.Nr. 220 008,VI+IR, and the He 162 M26 (A-09) W.Nr. 220 009,VI+IS take to the air for the first time, the former with *Fw.* Gleuwitz at the controls. The next day, the He 162 M28 (A-011) W.Nr. 220 011 and the He 162 M29 (A-012) W.Nr. 220 012 made their maiden flights, both with extended and strengthened airframes made at Heidfeld and fitted with MK 108 cannon. The M29 was assigned as a reserve aircraft used mostly for armaments trials.

That week, the enlarged tail unit fitted to the M3 improved the aircraft's stability and it achieved 880 km/h at 2500 m while being flown by *Flugbaumeister* Full. The total number of flights flown to date in the He 162 programme amounted to 134, with an accumulated flying time of 32 hrs 19 mins (the week 13-18 February saw 31 starts).[152]

The beginning of the following week, the 19th, was marred by an opinion expressed to Karl Frydag by *General der Flieger* Josef Kammhuber, the recently appointed *Kommissar für die Bekämpfung 4-motoriger Feindflugzeuge* (the 'Plenipotentiary for action against enemy four-engined bombers'), to the effect that the He 162 would prove unsuitable for combat. If this was not enough criticism, *Generalmajor* Eckhard Christian, Chief of the OKL *Führungsstab* commented to Frydag that the He 162 was '... extremely difficult to fly.' Francke's brief response was, 'I'll give *General* Christian a call!'[153]

'I'll give General Christian a call!' exclaimed Carl Francke, when he heard that Generalmajor Eckhard Christian, the Chief of the OKL Führungsstab (seen here), had expressed some concern about the He 162's airworthiness.

The same day, the *E-Stelle* Tarnewitz noted that firing trials using a He 162 A-2 with two

† According to Frydag's instructions, the firm of '...Hoffmann & Scherny, Wien, have been entrusted with the modification of wooden components by the *Flugzeugholzproduktionsleiter Niederdonau* [Aircraft Production Controller Lower Danube], *Herr* Schaffer. ALS will liaise directly with Hoffmann & Scherny as regards modifications of wooden components for the ALS rebuilding programme.'

* There is an anomaly here: on EHAG's original document, the '011' is shown as a machine slated for rebuild at Heidfeld. This can be assumed to be He 162 M11 (A-017) W.Nr. 220 017, but the 'M 11' is also listed as one of the 13 aircraft for rebuild by EHAG *Musterbau*.

MG 151/20 had been carried out at EHAG Rostock/Marienehe. The guns functioned without problem, but the results of similar tests using two MK 108s in Wien were not known by the *E-Stelle*. In any case, the Tarnewitz report stated, '… further flight trials (within five days) are necessary.'[154]

EHAG was apparently experiencing problems in locating skilled labour for work on the planned two-seat glider trainer version of the He 162 – a somewhat curious state of affairs given the surplus German and 'detainee' assembly staff at Heidfeld's Hangar 7 forecast by Frydag only a few days earlier. The He 162 trainer was to be designated the He 162 S 'Spatz' and it was planned to build the type at Schönhagen, near Hannover. A prototype was tested by *Ing.* Haase on 28 March 1945. The aircraft flew without any problems. Based on this performance, it was proposed to build further examples which were to be towed into the air. It was also proposed to fit dummy engines but the undercarriage would remain fixed.

On 21 February meanwhile, three more He 162s – the M35 W.Nr. 220 023, M36 W.Nr. 220 024 and M37 W.Nr. 220 025 – were being rebuilt at *Languste* to accommodate required changes to fuel tanks and weapons installations while at Junkers in Bernburg, *Flugkapitän Ing.* Hermann Steckhan flew He 162 W.Nr. 310 002 during the late afternoon for 10 minutes. All seems to have gone well.[155]

Steckhan, who would fly the He 162 on more that twenty occasions, recounted one astonishing incident at Bernburg in which, having started one aircraft, he decided the machine did not 'feel right'. During taxying, the He 162 persisted to veer off to one side. He aborted the flight and taxied the aircraft back to the hangar, whereupon he informed the engineers of the problem. The engineers shrugged their shoulders. Steckhan promptly grabbed a large saw, sawed off the wing tip and peered into the framework of the wing to observe that the timbers used were far larger than was specified.[156]

It was hoped that following some minor amendments to its wing fittings, the He 162 M19 (A-02) W.Nr. 220 002, VI+IL could be flight- ready by evening on Saturday, 24 February, while a second such '*Versuchsträger*' ('test platform/aircraft'), the M35, would hopefully be ready shortly at *Languste*. By Sunday, it was planned to have the He 162 M22 (A-05) W.Nr. 220 005, VI+IO, ready once some adjustments had been made to its wing joints, with the M36 as a back-up machine. Similarly, Heinkel projected that the He 162 M23 (A-06) W.Nr. 220 006, VI+IP would be ready by the 27th following similar changes to the M19, with the M37 as a back-up.[157]

The next day, *Fw.* Gerhard Gleuwitz flew the He 162 M21 220 004, VI+IN, up to a speed of 955 km/h in a performance test during its first flight. The aircraft had been fitted with MG 151/20 cannon, while the He 162 M22 W.Nr. 220 005, VI+IO, also flew this day to test redesigned wing root fillets.[158]

At Bernburg, flight-testing continued when Steckhan flew He 162 W.Nr. 310 004 in the early morning on a 20-minute flight, reaching a speed of 750 km/h. Then, just over an hour later at 1012 hrs, he took off in W.Nr. 310 008 for 23 minutes and, in the late afternoon, he flew W.Nr. 310 004 again.[159]

In a case of supreme irony, on 24 February the He 162 M30 (A-013) W.Nr. 220 013 took off on its maiden flight with the aim of,

In mid-February 1945, the He 162 attracted criticism from General der Flieger Josef Kammhuber, the recently appointed 'Plenipotentiary for action against enemy four-engined bombers', to the effect that it was unsuitable for combat. Kammhuber is seen here during a luncheon reception at Heinkel's plant at Rostock-Marienehe in January 1942 (third from left) while General der Nachtjäger, talking with Ernst Heinkel to his left. Also in this photograph are the night fighter aces, Wolfgang Falck and Helmut Lent (first and second from the left respectively), while to the left of Heinkel can be seen designer, Karl Schwärzler and test pilot, Gotthold Peter, both of whom would be deeply involved with the He 162.

The He 162 S ('Spatz') was the two-seat glider trainer version of the He 162 in which it was planned to train up NSFK candidate pilots for operations on the powered version. Just one prototype was completed, seen here, which was flown on at least one occasion at the Reichsegelflugschule at Trebbin in March 1945. Further production, however, did not occur before the end of the war.

Heinkel He 162 A-1 W.Nr. 310001 built by Junkers at Zweigwerk Bernburg

The first Bernburger 'Spatz' was first flown by chief test pilot, Hermann Steckhan, on 15 February 1945. On 27 March Steckhan crashed with the aircraft and sustained serious injury. The aircraft was fitted with similar wings as fitted on the early production aircraft from the Heinkel Süd factory, which were without 'Lippisch ears'. The fuselage was painted RLM 82/76.
Of note is the unique colour dividing line.

A test pilot prepares to settle into the cockpit of He 162, W.Nr. 310 001, at Bernburg. A number of test flights were conducted by this aircraft, including two by Flugkapitän Ing. Hermann Steckhan.

Junkers personnel watch as the test pilot straps himself in and carries out final instrument checks prior to the test flight.

Junkers engineers wait on the airfield at Bernburg by the first He 162 – W.Nr. 310 001 – to be produced by the Zweigwerk in February 1945.

W.Nr. 310 001 is pushed across the grass and mud by the Junkers flight-test team. The canopy is down.

Pedal power: in an image of supreme irony, a bicycle is used to tow He 162, W.Nr. 310 001 out towards the runway at Bernburg. Flugkapitän Ing. Hermann Steckhan recalled one acceptance flight in the aircraft on 27 March 1945: 'The machine lifted off quite quickly. At the edge of the airfield, the engine suddenly began to vibrate…'

Two photographs depicting what is believed to be the first He 162 A-1 to be completed by EHAG at Rostock, W.Nr. 120 001, preparing for its maiden flight at Marienehe on 14 January 1945. A small crowd has gathered around the aircraft to watch events and identifiable in the photograph at top is, from left to right, Otto Bütter and Carl Francke of EHAG and to the right, the stocky figure in a suit and boots is Herr Tiedemann, the Director of Junkers at Bernburg. In the photograph above, the aircraft has been moved to the runway for take-off and technicians await the arrival of the test pilot, with chocks placed against the mainwheels. Note the parachutes lying on the nose directly in front of the canopy.

Two further photographs showing the first He 162 A-1 to be completed by EHAG at Rostock, W.Nr. 120 001, on 14 January 1945. In the photograph (above right), the crowd has gathered around the aircraft to watch as the test pilot climbs into the cockpit, while below right the canopy has been closed and the aircraft is about to taxy for take-off. The aircraft enjoyed a relatively trouble-free flight-testing.

eventually, conducting weapons-testing and assessing the EZ 42 '*Adler*' gyroscopic gunsight. However, it had come to Carl Francke's attention that due to the Allied bombing of Dresden the previous week, production of the EZ 42 at the Carl Zeiss works at Jena had virtually stopped; the *E-Stelle* Tarnewitz had already complained that it had been asking since 21 January when it would be possible to inspect the '*Adler*' as fitted to a He 162.[160] 'We hear that for the next month,' Francke telegrammed Kessler, 'there is no question of having the EZ 42, especially since all stock is destined for the Me 262. I need, urgently, 20 to 50 sets to go into existing 162 production. I fear there is a risk, that putting the 162 into operations with two guns and the normal Revi as per the 262 will be a bad thing ...'[161]

Also on the 24th, take-off trials using the He 162 from the grass field at Heidfeld were ordered, but these could not take place until the craters left from the recent Allied air attacks had been filled in and levelled. Francke requested that this work be treated as a matter of urgency and be completed by, latest, 3 March.[162]

At Wien, stocks of B4 fuel had run out, but despite this, there was apparently sufficient supply to allow the He 162 M31 (A-14) W.Nr. 220 014 to make its first flight that day, while *Flugkapitän Ing.* Hermann Steckhan was airborne in He 162 310007 at Bernburg in the early morning for a 22-minute flight. Back at Schwechat however, the He 162 M20 W.Nr. 220 003, suffered damage to its right wing and rudder on landing, with Carl Francke at the controls.

Another blow struck the He 162 programme on the 25th when the He 162 M3 W.Nr. 200 003 crashed at 1455 hrs one kilometre east of Schwechat airfield while being flown by *Flugbaumeister* Full. Once again, the tragedy was blamed on instability around the aircraft's lateral axis. A witness on the ground reported that Full had attempted to bale out at about 215 m, but his parachute was on fire. Earlier, the M3 had achieved a speed of 880 km/h during flight-testing.[163]

Also during this week four more aircraft – the M35, M36, M37 and M41 – were slated to be fitted with lengthened fuselages.

Monday, 26 February – Sunday, 11 March 1945

By late February 1945, the once mighty Third Reich had crumbled almost to its core, but was still defiant. Neither the Rhine in the west nor the Oder in the east had been crossed, although the Russians had managed to get bridges across the latter river. Nevertheless, when Adolf Hitler addressed his *Gauleiters* in Berlin on the 24th, he told them: 'You may see my hand tremble sometimes today and perhaps even my head now and then; but my heart – never!'[164]

Yet far to the south in Wien, Heinkel was already making firm plans at least to move its Technical Department to Rostock, which presumably was considered a safer location.

Junkers reported that the first He 162 was ready to be ferried from Bernburg and the first *Luftwaffe* detachment – an '*Auffangsstaffel*' (Collection Squadron) – of ten pilots under *Oberleutnant* August Hachtel of 2./JG 1 arrived at Heidfeld in order to collect He 162s arriving off the production lines. The Heinkel technicians reported that: 'These men were incredibly impatient to take on the He 162s which had been cleared by our technicians. As soon as they were ready, the pilots took over the aircraft.'[165] Francke also noted on 2 March that Hachtel's men '... had an unbelievable will and do everything with great energy and they were overwhelmed by the He 162. These people must be given flyable aircraft as quickly as possible and introduced to the aircraft by our people at Heidfeld. The He 162 has been developed in an unbelievably short period of time and therefore must be made available in an unbelievably short time for front line use.'[166]

As a first step, the detachment was assigned He 162 M19 (A-02) W.Nr. 220 002, VI+IL, and was ordered not to fly the aircraft over 500 km/h, above 3000 m and for longer than 15 mins. (See Chapter Three).

By the 26th the He 162 M30 (A-013) W.Nr. 220 013 appears to have been back in the workshops with work being undertaken on its flaps and rudders, tail assembly, nose and a warm air heating system.[167]

By the end of the month, as projected, the He 162 M23 (A-06 to an A-2) W.Nr. 220 006, VI+IP (from *Languste* to Heidfeld on the 25th) and the He 162 M10, W.Nr. 200 010, VI+IJ, became flight-ready for general flight characteristics assessment.

It is believed that during February the M22 was forced to make an emergency landing when its engine cut out. Upon landing, its instruments indicated a high fuel level in the tanks. Later investigation revealed that negative *g*-forces incurred during the aircraft's manoeuvres, forced fuel to the top of the tanks and away from the pumps resulting in air locks which prevented the engine from being restarted. Heinkel would never overcome this problem before the end of the war.[168]

Some time during February, it is believed that the He 162 M11 W.Nr. 220 017 and He 162 M12 W.Nr. 220 018 were declared flight-ready for tests with Jumo 004 engines and 30 mm MK 108 and 20 mm MG 151 cannon respectively. Both aircraft were known to have been at Mödling/*Languste* on 14 February. The fuselage of the He 162 M15 (A-016) W.Nr. 220 016 (assigned the code VI+IZ), was set aside on 28 February and prepared for mounting with a Heinkel-Hirth HeS-011 engine but, ultimately, the aircraft would never fly.

Only nine FuG 24 sets were available by the end of the month, presumably as a result of disruption to supply and delivery by Allied bombing.

The beginning of the new month, March 1945, heralded the first flight of the He 162 M27 (A-010), W.Nr. 220 010, VI+IT, which, in configuration, was similar to the M25. This latter aircraft suffered 60 per cent damage during a test flight the following day, 2 March, but its very capable *Luftwaffe* pilot, Gerd Pawolka, managed to bale out and land safely.[169] As a result of this accident, it was proposed that another machine with an extended fuselage – the third of its kind – would be so converted to be assigned as the M41 and to be taken from the '0' series production line at *Languste*.[170]

The USAAF returned to bomb various targets in Austria on the 2nd and as a result, the He 162 M7 W.Nr. 200 007, VI+IG, which had been fitted with MG 151/20s and a brake parachute in its tail section, was damaged in a hangar in Wien.[171]

Above: The bomb-peppered runways and perimeter tracks of Schwechat airfield photographed by an Allied reconnaissance aircraft during February 1945. According to Carl Francke, by 18 February 80 per cent of the Schwechat area lay in rubble; under such circumstances, it was a miracle that EHAG was able to continue production at all.

On 2 March it was confirmed that three aircraft of the planned '0' series from *Languste* were to be assigned as the M35, M36 and M37 and to be delivered to Heidfeld on 3 and 4 March to be modified. These aircraft would feature the latest modified wings and landing flaps and were to be used for high-speed trials. The next completed machine, as yet not assigned a *Muster* number, was to be transferred from *Languste* to Heidfeld where EHAG and ALS would also conduct modifications.

Carl Francke's faith in the aircraft at this stage seems to have been unshakeable. In a report of 2 March he opined: 'When the He 162 is finally ready, then it will become the most economic aircraft in Germany in terms of material used and will be much sought after. No one else will be able to do this.'[172]

On 4 March, by which time the He 162 test programme had notched up a total flight time of 48 hrs and 12 mins in 191 flights, the second group of five *Luftwaffe* pilots arrived in Wien under the command of *Oberleutnant* Karl-Emil Demuth, *Staffelkapitän* of 3./JG 1, who had orders to defend the EHAG Rostock works with the *Volksjäger*. The problem was that there had been no aircraft available in Rostock, and it was the same story in Wien, with only the M19 available; but this aircraft, as mentioned previously, was being used by *Oblt*. Hachtel's group. Demuth had no option but to return to Parchim from whence he had come.[173] (see Chapter Three)

The same day, *Feldwebel* Denzin, who had joined the test programme, flying the He 162 M22 (A-05) W.Nr. 220 005, VI+IO, suffered 15 per cent damage during a flight to test wing root strength. The ever-active *Flugkapitän Ing.* Hermann Steckhan continued to test Junkers-built He 162s at Bernburg, flying He 162 W.Nr. 310 012 in the early morning of 6 March for 23 minutes and W.Nr. 310 014 in the late afternoon for 18 minutes. The following day, Steckhan was in the air again making four test flights in He 162s at Bernburg (W.Nr. 310 004, 310 008, 310 007 and 310 012) throughout the day as well as one in a *Mistel* composite! On the 8th, he flew W.Nr. 310 013 and 310 012 during the morning. He would continue to fly unidentified He 162s built at Bernburg on a regular basis through to 27 March.[174]

On 9 March it was decided to convert BMW engines to J2 fuel instead of B4. This day, *Fw*. Denzin reached a true airspeed of 955 km/h at 5000 m while flying an unidentified He 162, but upon landing his jet engine cut out, echoing the aforementioned problem experienced with the M22 in late February.

Two days later, Junkers reported 70 fuselages completed, but with no landing gear available or otherwise faulty, Francke ordered the installation of Bf 109 gear.

By this date, total He 162 flights amounted to 211, with a flight time of 51 hrs 13 mins. Jets cut out on several more test flights. Apparently still worried by risks to both machine and pilots, the *E-Stelle* Rechlin imposed the following speed limitations on all aircraft: 750 km/h at 0-5000 m, 600 km/h at 5000-7000 m and 400 km/h at 9000-11000 m.

Continued on page 70

Flying the He 162

Very soon after the end of hostilities, a former German test pilot advised the Allies on the correct procedures for conducting engine starts, trial runs on the ground, preparations for flight, take-offs, landings, overshooting and engine shut-offs on the He 162. The following description is based on that information.[175]

Instrument layout

There are four groups of controls/instruments in the cockpit:

a) Engine controls
- rpm indicator (for starter and turbine)
- Exhaust thermometer
- Differential pressure gauge
- Oil temperature gauge
- Fuel gauges

b) Flying instruments
- Airspeed indicator
- Compass
- Turn and bank indicator

c) Thrust nozzle control

d) Switches for:
- Master cut-out
- Fuel pump
- Instrument panel
- Riedel starter (two-way)
- Igniter and primer (on control column)

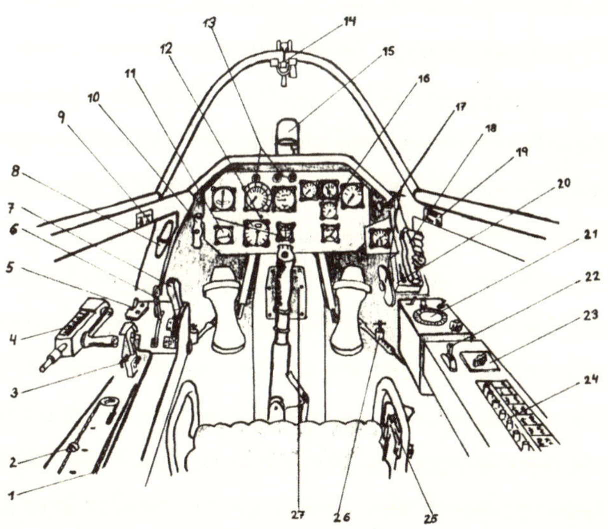

1. Abwurf der Starthilfen
2. Seitentrimmung
3. Fahrwerkschnappschalter
4. Höhentrimmung
5. Starthilfen-Auslösung
6. Brandhahnhebel
7. Leistunghebel
8. Fahrwerkentrastung
9. Fahrwerksanzeige links
10. Landeklappen-Handpumpe
11. Navigationsgeräte
12. Flugüberwachungsgeräte
13. Schauzeichen für Staurohr u. Waffen
14. Dachverschluss
15. Visier
16. Triebwerksüberwachung
17. Atemanlage
18. Leuchtpistole
19. Fahrwerksanzeige rechts
20. Bediengerät Fuss 25 a
21. Empfänger FuG 24
22. Anlasskippschalter
23. Verstelldüsenschalter
24. Selbstschalter
25. Katapultsitz-Auslösung
26. Pedalverstellung
27. Fenster am Bugrad

Selbstschalter :

Sammler
Kraftstoffpumpe
Waffen, Revi
Staurohr-Heizung
Anlass-und Messanlage
Wendezeiger, Starthilfe
Verstelldüse
FuG 24
FuG 25 a
Anlasser.

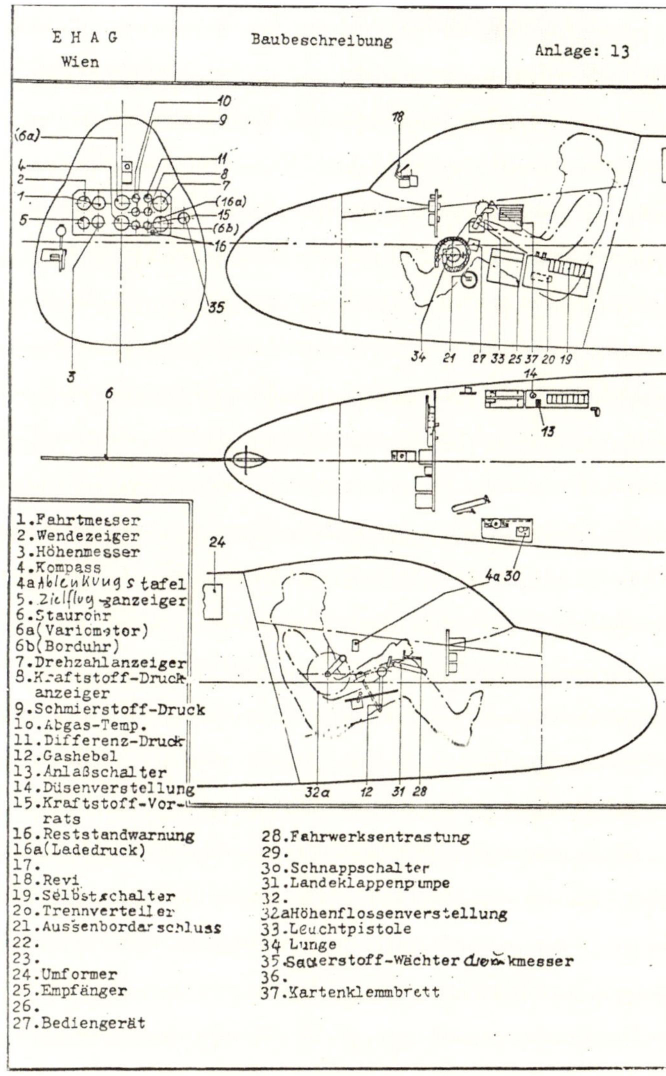

E H A G Wien	Baubeschreibung	Anlage: 13

1. Fahrtmesser
2. Wendezeiger
3. Höhenmesser
4. Kompass
4a Ablenkungstafel
5. Zielfluganzeiger
6. Staurohr
6a (Variometor)
6b (Borduhr)
7. Drehzahlanzeiger
8. Kraftstoff-Druckanzeiger
9. Schmierstoff-Druck
10. Abgas-Temp.
11. Differenz-Druck
12. Gashebel
13. Anlaßschalter
14. Düsenverstellung
15. Kraftstoff-Vorrats
16. Reststandwarnung
16a (Ladedruck)
17.
18. Revi
19. Selbstschalter
20. Trennverteiler
21. Aussenbordanschluss
22.
23.
24. Umformer
25. Empfänger
26.
27. Bediengerät
28. Fahrwerksentrastung
29.
30. Schnappschalter
31. Landeklappenpumpe
32.
32a Höhenflossenverstellung
33. Leuchtpistole
34 Lunge
35 Sauerstoff-Wächter Druckmesser
36.
37. Kartenklemmbrett

British Translation of the Above Document

1.	Air Speed Indicator	20.	Electric Connection Panel
2.	Turn Indicator	21.	External Connection
3.	Altimeter	22.	
4.	Compass	23.	
5.	Homing Device	24.	Transformer
6.	Pitot Tube	25.	Radio Receiver
6a.	Rate of Climb	26.	
6b.	Clock	27.	Radio Switches
7.	R.P.M. Indicator	28.	Landing Gear Release
8.	Fuel Press. Indicator	29.	
9.	Lubricant Pressure	30.	Snap Switch
10.	Exhaust Temp. Ind.	31.	Flap Hand Pump
11.	Differential Press. Indicator	32.	Tail Plane Trim
12.	Throttle	33.	Very Pistol
13.	Starter Switch	34.	Oxygen Equipment
14.	Nozzle Adjustment	35.	Oxygen Press. Gage
15.	Fuel Supply Ind.	36.	
16.	Fuel Warn. Signal	37.	Map Racks
16a.	Super charge Press.		
17.			
18.	Reflector Sight		
19.	Automatic Switch		

Left: Facsimile of Page 2 taken from a preliminary Heinkel 'Bedienungsvorschrift' (operating instructions) dated November 1944, showing the layout of the cockpit instruments.

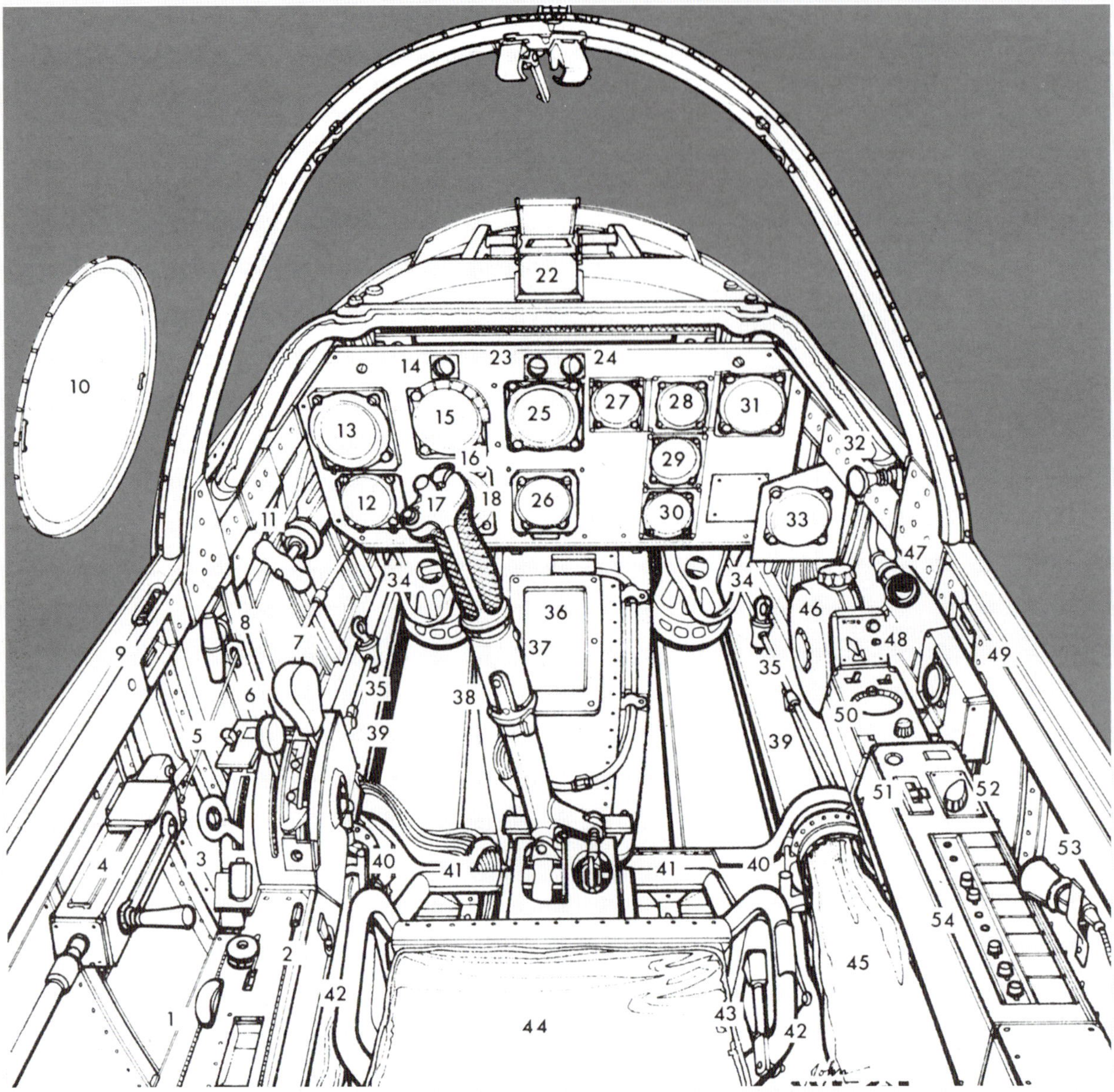

Heinkel He 162 A-2 cockpit

1 Rudder trim control
2 Take-off rocket jettison
3 Undercarriage selector
4 Elevator trim control
5 Take-off rocket activation switch
6 Fuel cock
7 Throttle lever
8 Undercarriage operating lever
9 Port undercarriage indicator
10 Ventilation/clear vision disc
11 Flap manual control pump
12 Flap indicator
13 Turn-and-bank indicator
14 Pitot indicator
15 Airspeed indicator
16 Firing button (A-Knopf)
17 Gun-charging button (B-Knopf)
18 Altimeter
19 One-piece windshield
20 Canopy release
21 Canopy lock
22 Revi gunsight
23 Port cannon indicator
24 Starboard cannon indicator
25 Rate of climb/descent
26 Compass
27 Oil pressure gauge
28 Jet pipe temperature
29 Fuel pressure gauge
30 Fuel contents
31 Revolution counter
32 Oxygen valve
33 Oxygen contents
34 Rudder pedals
35 Rudder pedal adjustment screws
36 Nosewheel well window (visual check)
37 FuG 24 transmit button (front of column)
38 Control column
39 Cannon blast tubes
40 Cannon forward mounts
41 Foot stirrups
42 Seat handles
43 Seat ejection trigger
44 Ejection seat
45 Canvas recoil-spring cuffs
46 Oxygen supply
47 Flare pistol holder/chute
48 FuG 25a control box
49 Starboard undercarriage indicator
50 FuG 24 (R/T) and AFN 2 (radio-navigation) control box
51 Starter switch
52 Engine setting
53 R/T socket
54 Electrics switch panel, reading from front: battery, fuel pump, weapons and gunsight, pitot heating, ignition, turn-and-bank/ rocket take-off, FuG 24, FuG 25a, starter

Starting the engine with an outboard battery

1. Aircraft battery set to 'off'
2. Connect outboard battery
3. Thrust nozzle, gauge system, starter, fuel pump – 'on'
4. Set thrust nozzle to 'A'
5. Riedel starter switch on for three seconds (warm engine for one second only). Then Riedel switch to 'start' in small graduations
6. Once Riedel starter is running, fuel cut-off 'on'
7. At 1,100 rpm (small scale) operate ignition and priming for the jet unit (via button on control column)
8. At 1,800-2,000 rpm (small scale) release Riedel starter switch. From now on, large-scale applies
9. At about 3,000 rpm throttle down to ground idling notch. Then allow engine to warm up by running at 4,000-5,000 rpm for 2 or 3 minutes
10. Aircraft battery 'on', outboard battery 'off'

The exhaust temperature should not exceed 650 deg. when the engine is being started up. If the engine is heard to hum, draw throttle back to ground-idling notch. Thrust nozzle check; set thrust nozzle between 'A' and 'S' and have the chief mechanic observe the 'adjustment skip' [British technical translator note: probably behaviour of control in nozzle] from the outside. If the Riedel starter is required again it should be used for a period exceeding 60 seconds irrespective of how many times it has been used within the last ten minutes.

Trial run on the ground

1. Idling on the ground at 3,000 ± 200 rpm. Switch thrust nozzle to 'S' at 6,000 rpm
2. Advance throttle smoothly to last notch (full throttle). The engine should then run at 9,500 ± 100 rpm; maximum for cold engine 7,900 rpm. The interval between idling and maximum power should not be less than 10 seconds on the ground
3. Observe following instruments carefully:
   Exhaust temperature 600 deg.

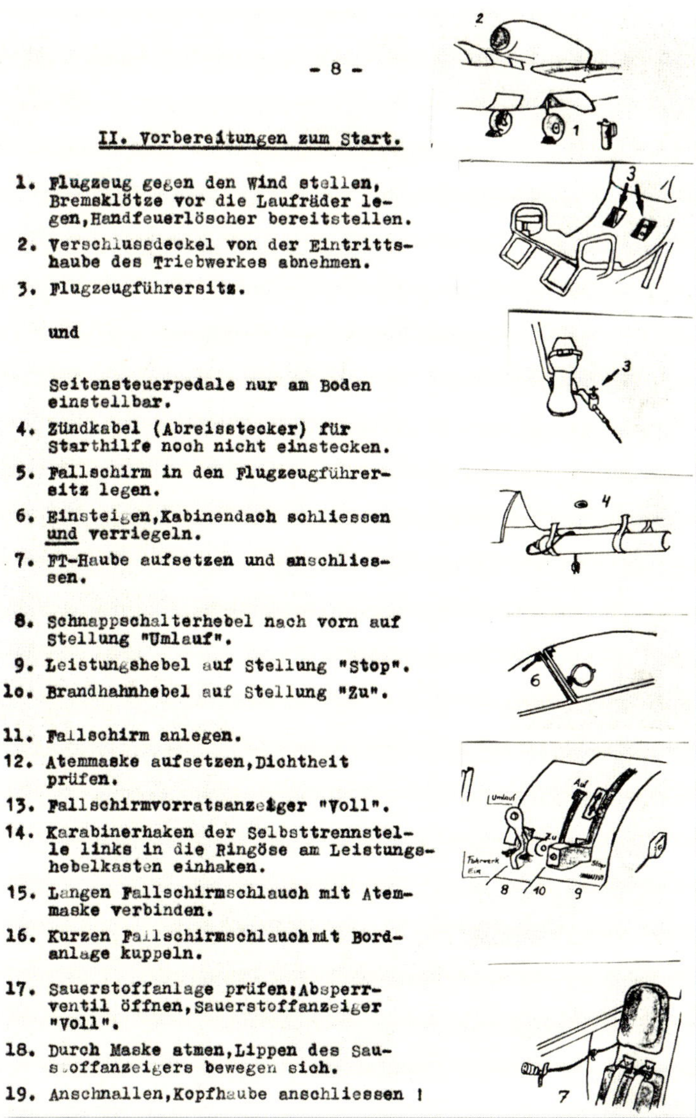

\- 8 -

II. Vorbereitungen zum Start.

1. Flugzeug gegen den Wind stellen, Bremsklötze vor die Laufräder legen, Handfeuerlöscher bereitstellen.
2. Verschlussdeckel von der Eintrittshaube des Triebwerkes abnehmen.
3. Flugzeugführersitz.

   und

   Seitensteuerpedale nur am Boden einstellbar.
4. Zündkabel (Abreissstecker) für Starthilfe noch nicht einstecken.
5. Fallschirm in den Flugzeugführersitz legen.
6. Einsteigen, Kabinendach schliessen und verriegeln.
7. FT-Haube aufsetzen und anschliessen.
8. Schnappschalterhebel nach vorn auf Stellung "Umlauf".
9. Leistungshebel auf Stellung "Stop".
10. Brandhahnhebel auf Stellung "Zu".
11. Fallschirm anlegen.
12. Atemmaske aufsetzen, Dichtheit prüfen.
13. Fallschirmvorratsanzeiger "Voll".
14. Karabinerhaken der Selbsttrennstelle links in die Ringöse am Leistungshebelkasten einhaken.
15. Langen Fallschirmschlauch mit Atemmaske verbinden.
16. Kurzen Fallschirmschlauch mit Bordanlage kuppeln.
17. Sauerstoffanlage prüfen: Absperrventil öffnen, Sauerstoffanzeiger "Voll".
18. Durch Maske atmen, Lippen des Sauerstoffanzeigers bewegen sich.
19. Anschnallen, Kopfhaube anschliessen !

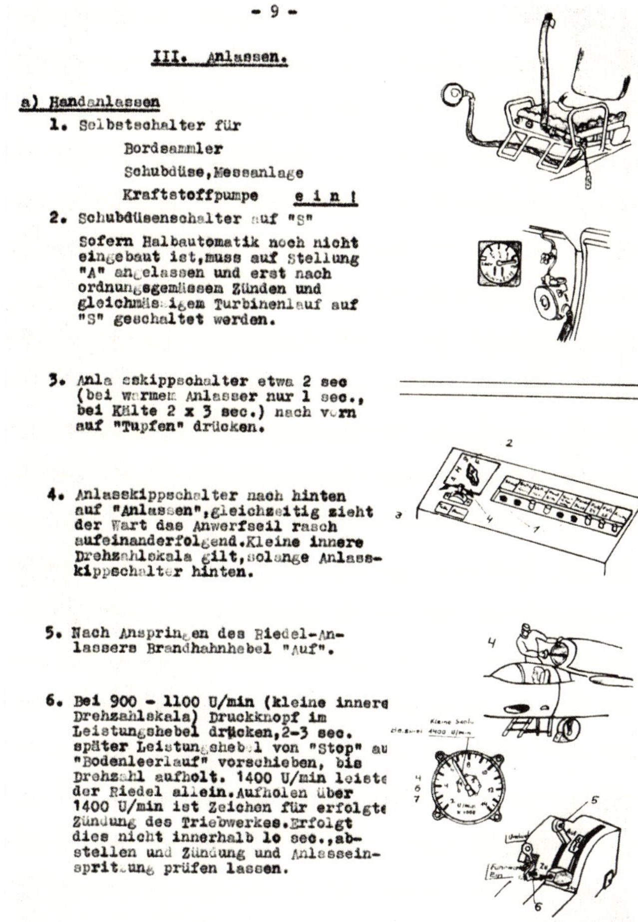

\- 9 -

III. Anlassen.

a) Handanlassen

1. Selbstschalter für
   Bordsammler
   Schubdüse, Messanlage
   Kraftstoffpumpe **e i n !**
2. Schubdüsenschalter auf "S"

   Sofern Halbautomatik noch nicht eingebaut ist, muss auf Stellung "A" angelassen und erst nach ordnungsgemässem Zünden und gleichmässigem Turbinenlauf auf "S" geschaltet werden.
3. Anlasskippschalter etwa 2 sec (bei warmem Anlasser nur 1 sec., bei Kälte 2 x 3 sec.) nach vorn auf "Tupfen" drücken.
4. Anlasskippschalter nach hinten auf "Anlassen", gleichzeitig zieht der Wart das Anwerfseil rasch aufeinanderfolgend. Kleine innere Drehzahlskala gilt, solange Anlasskippschalter hinten.
5. Nach Anspringen des Riedel-Anlassers Brandhahnhebel "Auf".
6. Bei 900 - 1100 U/min (kleine innere Drehzahlskala) Druckknopf im Leistungshebel drücken, 2-3 sec. später Leistungshebel von "Stop" auf "Bodenleerlauf" vorschieben, bis Drehzahl aufholt. 1400 U/min leistet der Riedel allein. Aufholen über 1400 U/min ist Zeichen für erfolgte Zündung des Triebwerkes. Erfolgt dies nicht innerhalb 10 sec., abstellen und Zündung und Anlasseinspritzung prüfen lassen.

Left and Above: Facsimiles of pages 8 and 9 taken from a preliminary Heinkel 'Bedienungsvorschrift', showing some hastily prepared free-hand sketches of various items of equipment.

Differential pressure 0.5 ± 0.05 atü
Fuel pressure 25 ± 3 atü
Oil pressure 6 ± 1 atü
Dynamo (cut in) 6,700 rpm

Preparation for flight

Brakes on. Undercarriage lever down
Start the turbines; run for 3 minutes and check revs at full power
Throttle back nozzle at 'A'
Taxi out. Brakes must not be used harshly
Line up with runway. Brakes on
Cockpit check
Trim control
Nozzle at 'H'
Flaps pump down until the trailing edge is clearly visible

Note: the airfield controller should check that the nozzle is correctly adjusted by reference to certain marks on the tail of the tube before signalling 'Go'. Check the instruments (exhaust temperature).

Take-off

Open up to about 6,000 rpm against the brakes and release them, opening up to full throttle very slowly. Ease the aircraft off the ground at about 200 km/h and let speed build up to 300 km/h before climbing away. Undercarriage up. Flaps up at 120 metres. The best climbing speed is 300 km/h.

Adjust the nozzles for the following conditions:

'A' = starting, taxying and idling
'H' = climb and high speed flight above 8 kilometres
'S' = high speed flight at altitudes from 4 to 8 kilometres
'F' = high speed flight above 700 km/h at altitudes between 0 and 4 kilometres

- 1o -

7. Bei 1800-2000 U/min Anlasskippschalter in Mittelstellung vorspringen lassen. Von jetzt ab gilt äussere Drehzahlskala. Triebwerk stellt sich auf Bodenleerlaufdrehzahl (3300 ± 200) ein.

8. Nach 2 - 3 Minuten abbremsen.

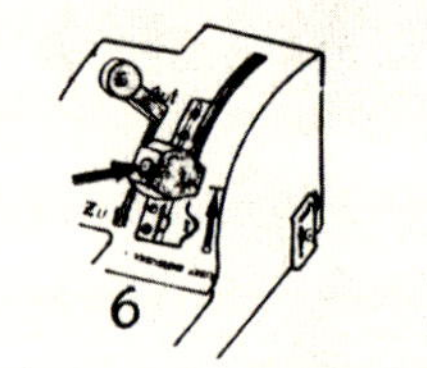

b) Anlassen mit Aussenbordstromquelle:

1. Stecker der Aussenbordstromquelle in den Aussenbordanschluss stecken und Aussenbordstromquelle einschalten.
2. Selbstschalter wie beim Handanlassen jedoch Sammler aus ! Anlasser ein !

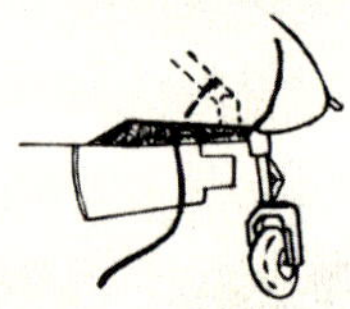

3. Verstelldüse und Anlasskippschalter wie beim Handanlassen bedienen.
4. Riedel-Anlasser wird auf "Anlassen" elektrisch angeworfen. Nach dem Anspringen alles weitere wie beim Handanlassen.
5. Aussenbordstromquelle ausschalten, Stecker von Aussenbordanschluss abziehen
6. Selbstschalter für Sammler " e i n ".

c) Anlassen mit Bordsammler.

Alle Vorgänge wie mit Aussenbordstromquelle, jedoch von Anfang an Sammler " e i n ".

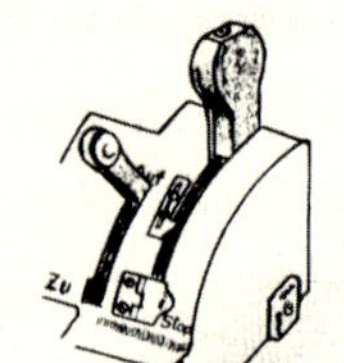

Die Abgastemperatur darf beim Anlassen 750° nicht überschreiten, sonst Überhitzung im Turbinenteil. Triebwerk abstellen. Beim Triebwerksbrummen Leistungshebel auf Bodenleerlaufraste zurücknehmen.
Riedelanlasser innerhalb 15 Min. höchstens 60 sec. betätigen.
Anlassvorgang dauert 20-30 sec.
Anlasseinspritzpumpe darf höchstens 5 Min. ununterbrochen laufen.

Page 10 from the Heinkel 'Bedienungsvorschrift' showing external electrical connections and controls.

- 13 -

Achtung : Gleitwinkel im Sackflug steiler, Abfangen nicht mehr möglich, Folge : Bruch !

Abflug :

Landeklappen in "Startstellung" anstellen (etwa 7 Pumpenhübe). Wenn diese Anstellung erreicht ist (vergl. weisse Strichmarkierung), Handpumpengriff durch Drehen nach rechts arretieren.

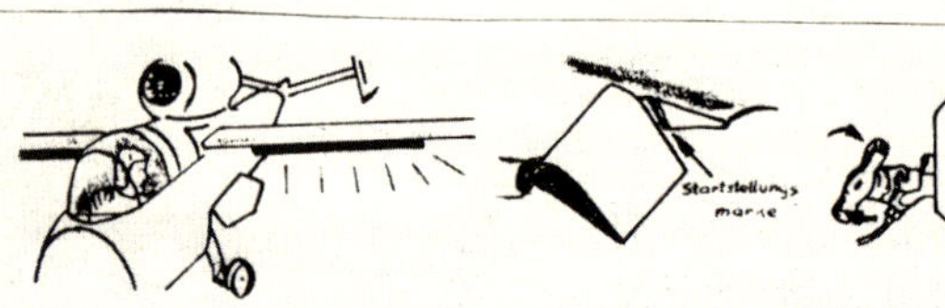

Page 13 from the Heinkel 'Bedienungsvorschrift' showing the layout of the wing flaps.

- 14 -

Start :

1. Schubdüsenschalter auf "S".
2. Drehzahl max. 9800 U/min, nach 2 min. 9500 ± 100 U/min.
3. Flugzeug in Startrichtung rollen, Bremsen betätigen.
4. Rollstrecke bei Windstille auf Betonbahn ca. 650 m, auf Grasnarbe etwa 10 % mehr. Für kurzen Start kann Höhensteuer ab V_a = 180 km/h stark gezogen werden.
5. Abhebegeschwindigkeit normal 190 km/h.
6. Nach dem Abheben Fahrwerk einfahren, Schnappschalterhebel nach hinten in Stellung "Fahrwerk ein". Hebel springt selbsttätig in Stellung "Umlauf" zurück.
7. Beim Einfahren V_a = 350 km/h nicht überschreiten.
8. Landeklappen zurückstellen, hierzu Handpumpengriff in tiefste Stellung drücken und nach links drehen. Bei alter Bauausführung Drehsinn umgekehrt.

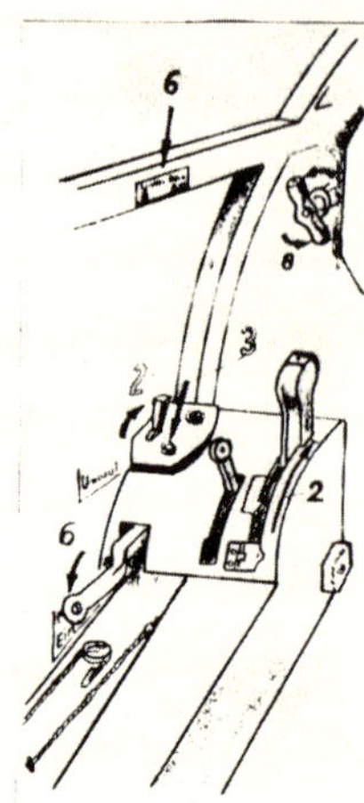

Mit Starthilfe :

1. Zeichen "fertig", Wart schliesst Zündkabel an.
2. Beim Anrollen Kippschalter auf dem Auslöseschaltkasten auf "Ein". Schaltzeichen zeigt weisses Feld.
3. Bei 100 bis 150 km/h Druckknopf drücken. Brenndauer 6 sec. bei 500 kg Schub je Gerät.
Lastigkeit des Starthilfenschuhes erleichtert das Abheben.
4. Nach dem Abbrennen Geräte durch Ziehen des Seilzuges (hinter dem linken Bedientisch) abwerfen.
5. Nach dem Abwerfen Kippschalter auf dem Auslöseschaltkasten auf "Aus", Schaltzeichen schwarz.

Above: Page 14 from the Heinkel 'Bedienungsvorschrift' showing instructions for the engine controls. Below: Page 15 showing the engine throttle controls and instructions for climbing and high speed settings.

- 15 -

VI. S t e i g f l u g .

Schubdüsenschalter bis 8 km Höhe auf "S".
über 8 km Höhe auf "H" schalten.
Drehzahl hierbei 9500 ± U/min.
Volleistungs-Geschwindigkeit des besten Steigens um V_a = 380 km/h.

VII. Reise- und Schnellflug.

1. Schubdüsenstellungen :

H = normal über 8 km Höhe.
S = normal unter 8 km Höhe.
F = Schnellflug von 0 bis 4 km Höhe bis $V_a > 650$ km/h.
Bei eingebauter Halbautomatik entfällt die Stellung "S" durch direkte Kupplung mit dem Leistungshebel.
Achtung: wenn V_a = 650 km/h unterschritten wird, Schubdüse wieder zurückschalten auf "S".

2. **Betriebsdrehzahl** normal 9500 U/min, Veränderung des Schubes durch Drehzahländerung. Drehzahl nicht unter 6500 U/min zurücknehmen, da Triebwerk sonst ausgeht.

3. **Triebwerksüberwachungsgeräte beobachten :**

Kraftstoffdruck in Bodennähe bei 9500 U/min 50 kg/cm²
Abgastemperatur 400 - 600° C
Steigt Temperatur über 600°C, Bedienungshebel zurücknehmen. Bei trotzdem weiter steigender Temperatur weiter drosseln und evtl. Triebwerk abstellen, besonders wenn Kraftstoff steigt und Drehzahl sinkt. Störung am Triebwerk.

\- 16 -

4. Behälterzuschaltung:

Einspritzpumpe des Triebwerks erhält durch eine Behälterpumpe den Kraftstoff aus dem Rumpfbehälter zugeführt. Kraftstoff aus dem Tragflügel fliesst in den Rumpfbehälter nach. Inhaltskontrolle des Rumpfbehälters: Vorratsanzeiger an der Flugzeugführergerätetafel. Flugzeiten überwachen, da Anzeige ungenau sein kann.

5. Durch Drosseln des Triebwerks wird an Reichweite wenig, an Flugzeit viel gewonnen.

Bordfunkanlage FuG 24

A. Sprechverkehr (FT -Betrieb):

1. Schalter am Empfänger auf "FT".

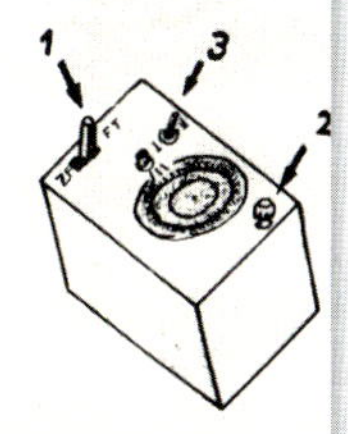

2. Empfangbetrieb nach Abstimmen auf markierte Frequenz. Hierbei Knopf für Skalenbeleuchtung auf schmalen oder breiten Leuchtsektor drehen.

3. Am Empfänger Sendefrequenz "I" (Betriebsfrequenz) oder "II" Ausweichfrequenz) wählen.

4. Zum Senden Sprechknopf vorn am Steuerknüppel drücken.

Above: Page 16 giving further instructions on engine control and for operating the FuG 24 radio equipment. Above Right: Instructions on high-altitude flight and operation of the oxygen supply controls through an Oxygen mask when flying at 4000 metres and above. Right: Instructions on setting the controls for approach flight and landing.

The controls are very light.

The aircraft is unstable about the vertical axis (snaky). There is a tendency to tighten up in steep turns. Flight should not be continued after the indicators show 300 litres of fuel.

Landing

Reduce speed to 350 km/h. Undercarriage down
Pump down flaps by hand, which requires much force and a lot of time
Reduce speed to 200 to 250 km/h, adjusting angle of approach so that the turbine still runs at about 6,000 rpm and close the throttle 10 seconds before the anticipated touchdown (power is still operative for this time). Aircraft should be wheeled on to the runway and brakes used as sparingly as possible.

Overshoot

Because of the long time necessary for opening the throttle (10 seconds), overshoot action must be taken very early.

To shut engine off

1. Throttle down to ground-idling notch. Switch thrust nozzle to 'A'
2. Throttle down to 'stop'. Fuel cut-off 'off'
3. Fuel pumps 'off'. Aircraft battery 'off'

\- 20 -

VIII. Höhenflug.

1. Sauerstoff-Absperrventil öffnen.
2. Spätestens ab 4000 m Flughöhe Atemmaske aufsetzen. Maske und Kleiderklammer müssen festsitzen. Zuführungsschläuche am Sitzfallschirm nicht abquetschen! Schnelltrennstellen auf festen Sitz prüfen.
3. O_2-Wächter beobachten. Anzeige im Rythmus der Atmung.
4. Bei erhöhtem Atemwiderstand Druckknopf am Höhenatmer einige Male kurzzeitig drücken ("Sauerstoffdusche").
5. Über 8 km Höhe Schubdüse auf "H",
6. Bei einem Sauerstoffrestdruck zwischen 1/4 und Leer Höhen unter 4000 m aufsuchen. Atemmaske bei vorübergehendem Aufenthalt in geringeren Höhen nicht absetzen, sie friert sonst ein und ist nicht mehr verwendungsfähig.
7. Nach Beendigung der Sauerstoffatmung Absperrventil schliessen.

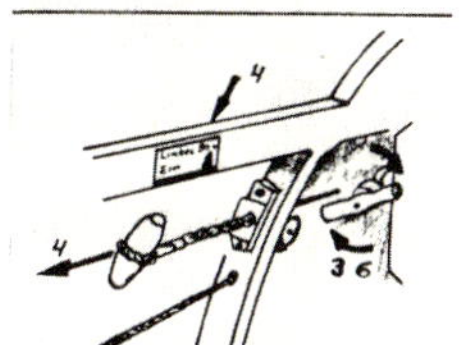

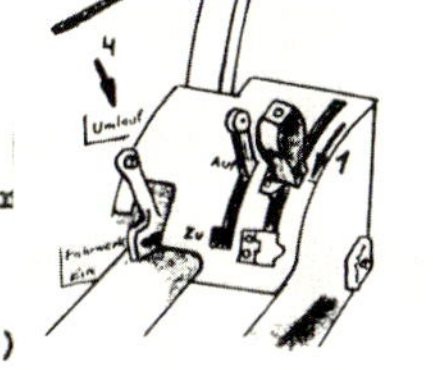

IX. Gleitflug u. Landung.

1. Zum Gleitflug Leistungshebel an Flugleerlaufraste (6500 U/min) zurückstellen. Erst beim Anschweben zur Landung unter 1 km darf auf Bodenleerlauf (3500 U/min) zurückgegangen werden.
2. Schubdüsenschalter in Stellung "S".
3. Landeklappen in "Startstellung" bei 250 bis 300 km/h anstellen. Ist Startstellung erreicht, Handpumpengriff durch Rechts drehen arretieren.
4. Fahrwerk ausfahren unter 350 km/h. Hierzu Fahrwerksentrastungsgriff ziehen. Schnappschalterhebel muss auf "Umlauf" stehen.

\- 21 -

5. Anfliegen mit etwa V_a = 250 km/h, Landeklappen noch in Startstellung.
6. Nach Eindrehen in Landerichtung Landeklappen bei 200 km/h in "Landestellung" anstellen. Nach erreichter Anstellung Handpumpengriff durch Drehen nach rechts arretieren.
7. Lastigkeitsänderungen durch Trimmung ausgleichen, Höhenflossentrimmung etwa -0.5°.
8. Vor dem Abfangen bei laufendem Triebwerk V_a = 190 km/h, bei stehendem Triebwerk V_a = 200 km/h nicht unterschreiten.

9. Flugzeug muss beim Aufsetzen voll abgefangen sein. Aufsetzen erfolgt nur auf dem Hauptfahrwerk.
10. Nach dem Aufsetzen möglichst lange mit angehobenem Bugrad ausrollen.
11. Bremsen erst nach Aufsetzen des Bugrades. Nicht mehr bremsen, als nötig.
    Achtung: Längsneigung steuern, damit Rumpfende nicht aufschlägt!

12. Schiesshebel in Ruhestellung.
13. Landeklappen nach dem Ausrollen einfahren.
14. FT - Geräte bleiben bis zum Ausrollen eingeschaltet.

By 11 March it is believed that the He 162 M6 W.Nr. 200 006, VI+IF; the M24, W.Nr. 220 007, VI+IQ; and the M27 W.Nr. 220 010, VI+IT were at Heidfeld, while the M11, W.Nr. 220 017 and the M12, W.Nr. 220 018, both fitted with Jumo 004B turbojets, were at Rostock-Theresienfeld, together with the M37, W.Nr. 220 025. The M27 is known to have had its tail strengthened by the 12th.

Monday, 12 March – Sunday, 25 March 1945

The 12th March was a bad day: firstly, He 162 M8 W.Nr. 200 008, VI+IH, armed with two MG 151s, crashed and was destroyed when, on the landing approach, the engine suddenly stopped functioning at a height of 100 m. As it came in to land, the aircraft somersaulted, smashed into a two-metre high embankment just short of the runway and caught fire. Despite the cockpit section being obliterated and most of the machine being burnt out, the pilot, *Feldwebel* Wanke, escaped through a hole in the fuselage with light burns and bruising.[176] The same day, in landing, *Fw.* Gleuwitz damaged the He 162 M26 220 009, VI+IS to a scale of 60 per cent.

On a more practical level, the He 162 M27 (A-010) W.Nr. 220 010, VI+IT, had its fuselage and cockpit area strengthened at Heidfeld.

Two days later, another aircraft was destroyed when *Unteroffizier* Tautz of 2./JG 1, having aborted a first attempt to land in He 162 M19 (A-02) W.Nr. 220 002, VI+IL, made another circuit and in landing, hit a pile of barrels near to the runway, somersaulted and caught fire. Tautz, making his first flight in the *Volksjäger*, was thrown out of the cockpit and killed. It was thought pilot error was the cause. This aircraft had been intended to test a 20-degree V-tail, in comparison flights with the M3.[177]

On the 14th, *Fw.* Gleuwitz, apparently recovered from his crash in the M26, took the He 162 M33 W.Nr. 220 021 on its first flight as a reserve aircraft.

On 16 March, EHAG issued a new and very detailed specification sheet for the '*Strahljäger 162*' as fitted with a Jumo 004 D/E engine and armed with two MK 108 cannon with 50 rpg – despite the apparent lack of availability of the weapon (see Appendix 1).

The following day, discussions took place at Heidfeld between *Dr.* Baumann of the EHAG *Flugabteilung* (Flight Department) and pilots Schuck and Kemnitz to discuss the ratio between speed and fuel consumption. The He 162 M32, which had just commenced flight-testing, had been fitted with a BMW 003 using B4 fuel and had undertaken tests to assess this. However, the resulting B4 fuel usage was not considered of relevance since subsequent production aircraft were to use J2.[178]

By 18 March 1945, the He 162 test programme had performed 255 flights, with a flying time of 55 hrs 10 mins.

In the second half of March there was considerable dialogue between EHAG and BMW over the need to accommodate an additional rocket booster motor (and fuel load) in order to provide the necessary additional thrust to enable the He 162 to increase speed during, for example, take-off and climb. Similar experiments were being carried out at Lechfeld with a BMW 003 TLR composite turbojet and rocket engine for use on the planned high-speed Me 262 C-2b *Heimatschützer* rocket-boosted fighter. In this engine a BMW P.3395 rocket engine was mated to a standard BMW 003 A turbojet, with the rocket fuelled by a combination of R-*Stoff* (*Tonka* – an organic amine mixture) and SV-*Stoff* (*Salbei* – a mixture of 90-98% concentrated nitric acid + 10-12% sulphuric acid) which resulted in spontaneous combustion upon contact with each other. This would give the Me 262 a thrust of 1000 kg for three minutes. The propellant pumps for the rocket engines were electro-hydraulically coupled via a 125 hp extension shaft to the turbojets. However problems were experienced, not least due to fuel volatility, but also because of tank-sealing, pressure difficulties and faulty electric wiring.[179]

In the case of the He 162, it was proposed to locate a rocket booster on the underside of the rear fuselage, offset to port. The dilemma that this posed centred around the potential danger of three different fuels. A drawing dated 12 March 1945 shows no fewer than three different types of fuel which would be needed to power both the main BMW 003 jet unit and the rocket booster. A tankage of 470 litres (428 kg) of '*TL-Kraftstoff*' (jet fuel) would be required to power the main engine, while another tank contained 560 litres (855 kg) of 'S-*Stoff*' and a further two tanks contained 380 litres (346 kg) of 'T-*Stoff*'. A note on the drawing states that the wing would have to be moved rearwards by 200 mm to compensate.

It was foreseen that such an arrangement would provide 1800 kg of thrust from a standing start. The rate of climb was calculated as 2 minutes 47 seconds to reach a height of 10 km, with a speed of 98 metres per second. A total flying time of 44 minutes could be achieved

The Me 262 C-2b Heimatschützer II, W.Nr. 170 074, seen during testing of its BMW 003 TLR composite turbojet/rocket engine at Lechfeld on 23 March 1945. At around the same time EHAG and BMW were exploring the possibility of incorporating a rocket-boost system in the He 162 to give the fighter the necessary additional thrust it needed during take-off and climb. However, the Lechfeld tests with the Me 262 revealed problems with pressure and wiring and plans were put on hold for both aircraft while BMW investigated.

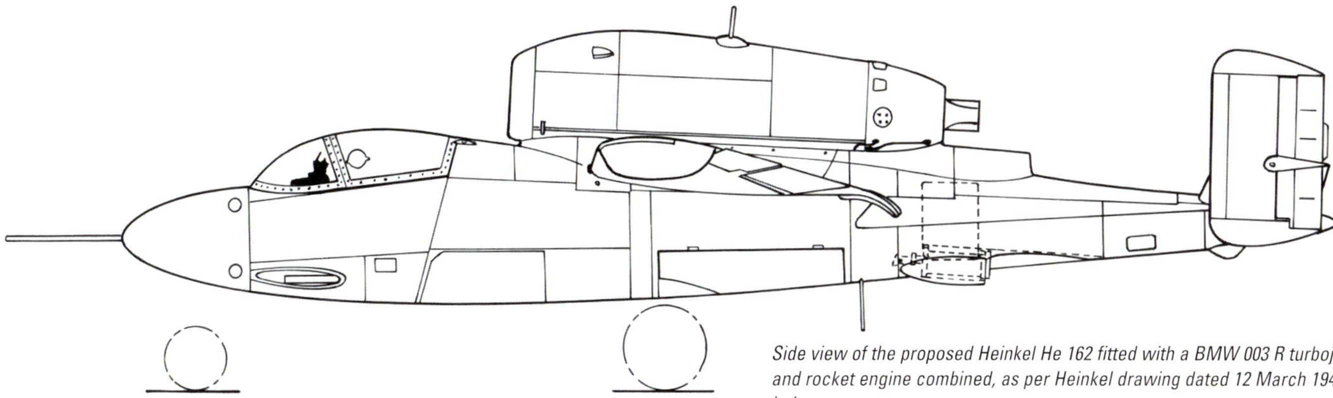

Side view of the proposed Heinkel He 162 fitted with a BMW 003 R turbojet and rocket engine combined, as per Heinkel drawing dated 12 March 1945 below.

The forlorn-looking He 162 M23 (A-2) W.Nr. 220 006, VI+IP, lies amidst the bomb-damaged hulk of a hangar at München-Riem after the cessation of hostilities in 1945. The aircraft is missing its nosewheel, its canopy has been shattered and its tail assembly has been damaged. The 'M23' painted on the nose in black on the bare primer finish denoted the twenty-third prototype. 'M' ('Muster' or model) numbers were used to identify He 162 prototypes rather than the more customary 'V' ('Versuch' or Experimental) numbers.

Below: An original Heinkel drawing number 162 01-42 dated 12 March 1945.

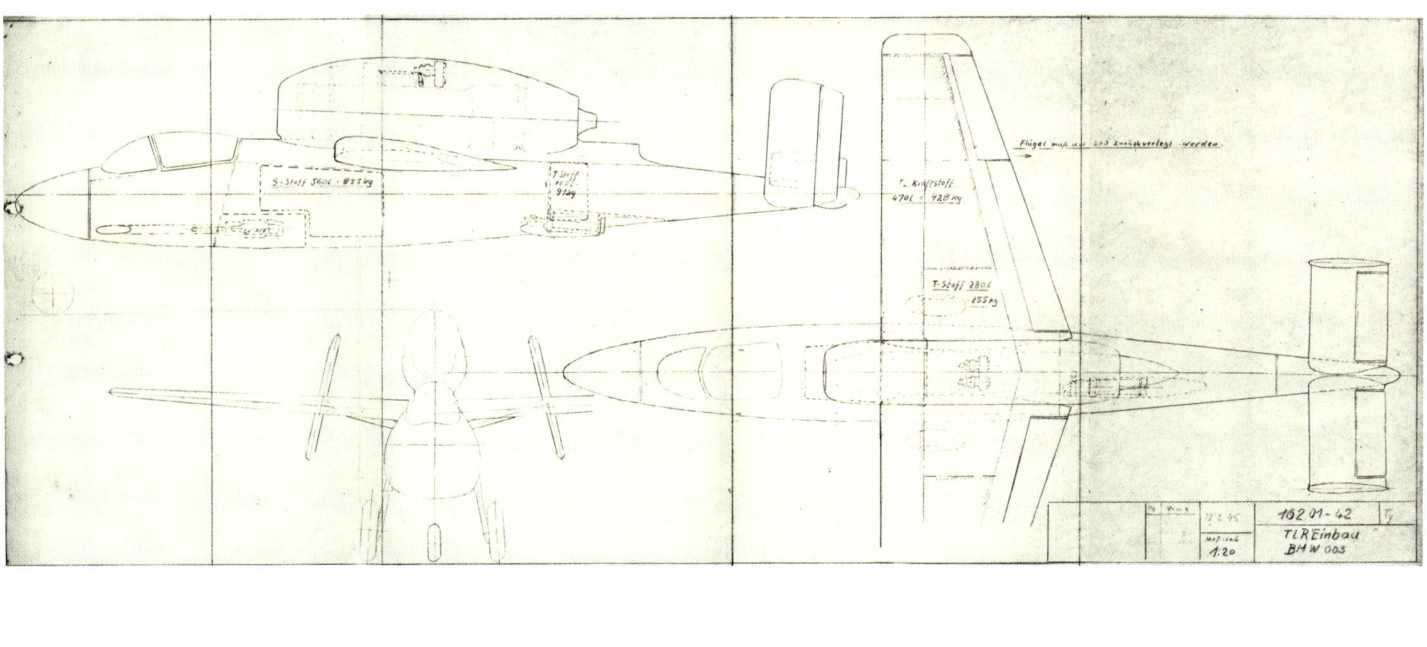

at a height of 10 km. It was further calculated that a high-speed performance of 985 km/h for 5 km and 965 km/h over 10 km could be attained.

Concern over fuel mix volatility was the subject of correspondence between Francke and *Dr.* Bruckmann of BMW in München on 19 March. On 27 March *Herr* Huber of BMW and *Herr* Reiniger of EHAG issued a joint report in which the conclusion was that it would be far more practical for BMW to investigate the possibility of increasing the performance of the BMW 003 from a thrust of 800 kg to 1000–1100 kg.[180]

At least one surviving EHAG document about components from 19 March testifies to the fact that the code name '*Salamander*' was beginning to be more generally adopted for the He 162 programme.[181] Also on the 19th, *Fw.* Gerhard Gleuwitz was airborne again, this time in He 162 M23, W.Nr. 220 006, on its first flight as a trial for new fuselage/wing root fairings with the wings of the M19.

On the 23rd, Carl Francke, accompanied by Heinkel designer, Karl-Otto Bütter, flew to Junkers at Bernburg to witness the first flight of a Junkers series aircraft and, shortly after, series machines took to the air at Rostock and Oranienburg.[182]

Monday, 26 March – Sunday, 8 April 1945

Despite EHAG's strenuous efforts to complete the test programme, military use of the He 162 remained a faltering exercise. At Heidfeld, *Oblt.* Hachtel and his fellow pilots of JG 1 had grown impatient with waiting for something to happen. Hachtel – who was distinctly unimpressed with the He 162 because of its limited endurance which he believed needed to be increased by at least 40 minutes – wanted to return to Berlin as the promised aircraft had not been delivered. In any case, it seems that at the beginning of the following week, on the 26th, a 'flight stop' order was issued to Hachtel effectively cancelling any activity by his detachment for the time being, since the *Bauaufsicht Luft*

In these three views, the He 162 M23 W.Nr. 220 006, VI+IP, is seen having been literally dragged out of the hangar into the sunlight at München-Riem where it, and He 162 A-2 M20, W.Nr. 220 003, VI+IM, no doubt attracted the attention of American personnel. Note the aircraft is in bare primer finish and has been marked on its engine unit as 'Off Limits' by its captors; it would have been a rare find.

Heinkel He 162 M23 (A-06) W.Nr. 220006, coded VI+IP was built at Werk Languste

This aircraft was first flown by Gerhard Gleuwitz on 19 March 1945. Like the M20, the M23 was also found at München-Riem in May 1945. The M23 was tested with a revised wing root and fuselage fairing. The aircraft was painted overall in RLM 02 with only the air intake of the jet engine being left in its original colour of RLM 81. The factory call sign VI+IP was painted in black on the fuselage sides and also in large letters on the underside of the wings. The *Balkenkreuze* and *Swastika* were painted in black in a very simplified way without any white outline. The *Werknummer* 220006 was painted on both the top and bottom of the fin.

The He 162 M23 W.Nr. 220 006, having been moved to a more accommodating hardstanding outside a hangar at München-Riem, now minus its BMW 003 engine, with its nosewheel fork propped up on a wooden crate, but its mainwheels evidently in need of some inflation. Amongst other things, the aircraft had been used to test the strength of wing joints.

Another view of He 162 M23 outside the hangar at München-Riem.

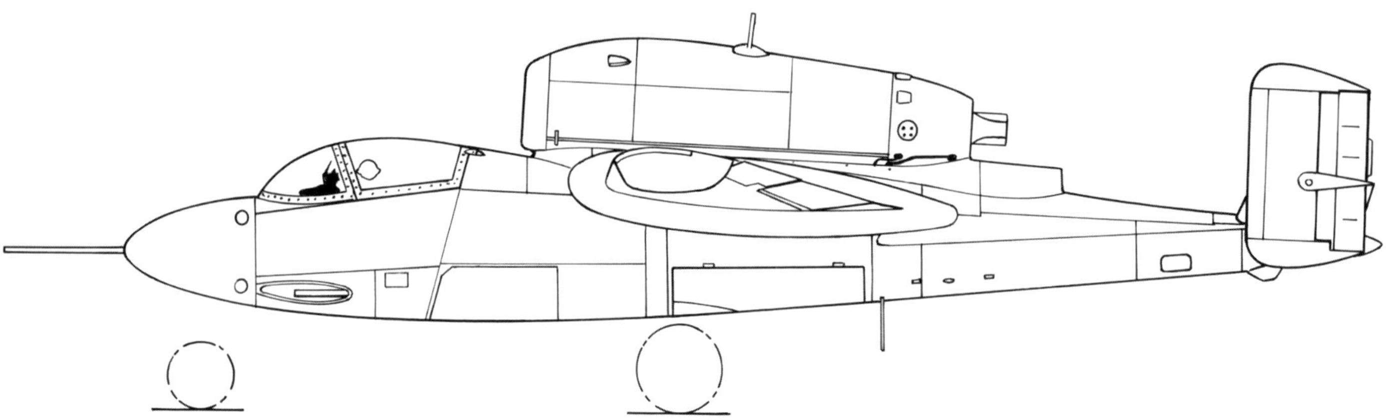

Side view of the Heinkel He 162 M23 fitted with smoothed fairings at the junction of the wings and fuselage.

As can be seen from these two views of M23, by this stage the damage to the right-hand horizontal stabiliser had been repaired, but the aircraft's BMW 003 engine had been removed leaving just the cowlings in place. Note the rotors of an Fa 223 helicopter in front of M23.

(BAL) ordered that all completed He 162s were to be used for test purposes only.

On the question of endurance, on the 27th EHAG issued a specification entitled '*Behälteranordnungen*' (fuel tank locations) in which two hastily sketched emergency fuel tanks were incorporated into the design of the He 162 – one (160 litres) forward of the main 470-litre fuselage tank, with an option to house a further 120-litre tank in the fuselage. By incorporating the 160-litre tank, total capacity increased to 630 litres in the fuselage, with a further 280, 680 or even 900 litres in the wing tanks depending on design. Endurance at 11000 m would then be 1 hr 32 mins, 2 hrs 16 mins and 2 hrs 35 mins respectively (the weight increasing from 2775 kg to 3115 kg to 3300 kg). Respective required take-off distances of 900 m, 1150 m and 1320 m would be required.

The sealing of fuel tanks by the Duco firm in Berlin-Spindlersfeld continued to present problems. On 12 March *Abt.*-E.10, handling the supply of materials for the OKL *Chef* TLR at Zeulenroda, commented that upon the issue of sealing the He 162's fuel tanks '... hangs the feasibility of using the aircraft for operations.'

Abt.-E.10 stressed that it was the utmost duty of all concerned in the production of the fuel tanks to ensure that they were sealed correctly and sufficiently. All materials used in the tank area should be of the highest quality; all areas were to be glued stringently and by means of pressure and the use of nails was forbidden. The use of P 600 glue gave the best sealing, and therefore EHAG was instructed to convert all existing glues used in the tank areas from the current Kaurit type to P 600.

It was also considered imperative that sealing lacquer was applied by hand using a brush to all areas of the tank including 'unseen corners'. Immediately prior to application, and with the aid of a magnifying glass, the lacquer was to be mixed with a hardening compound at a proportion of 9:1 and it was vital that this ratio was maintained. Before sealing, the area had to be cleaned meticulously, if necessary using a vacuum machine. Where holes had been made to accommodate feed pipes, such areas were to be filled with a special adhesive paste.

Above: The cannibalised cockpit of He 162 M23, W.Nr. 220 006, following Allied 'liberation'.

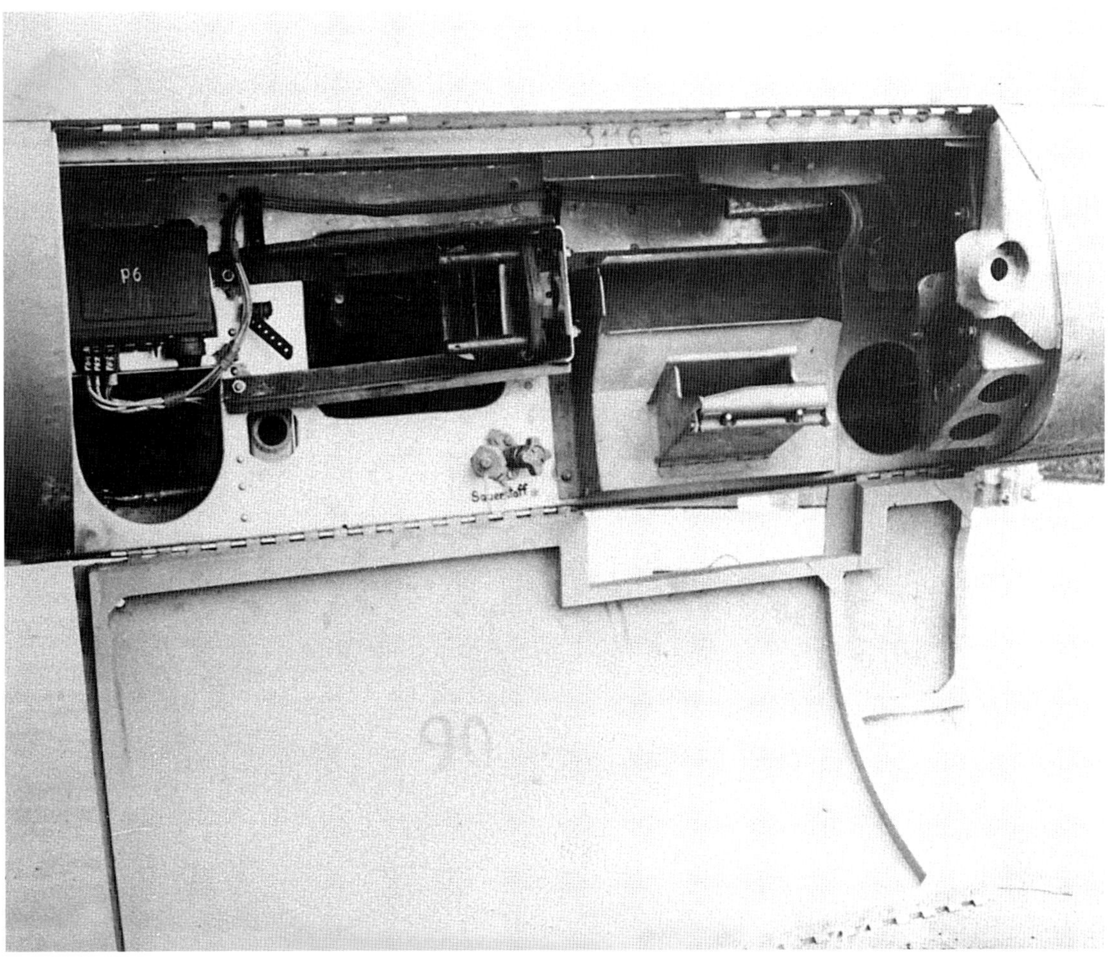

View of the open gun bay of M23, with the MG 151/20 cannon removed.

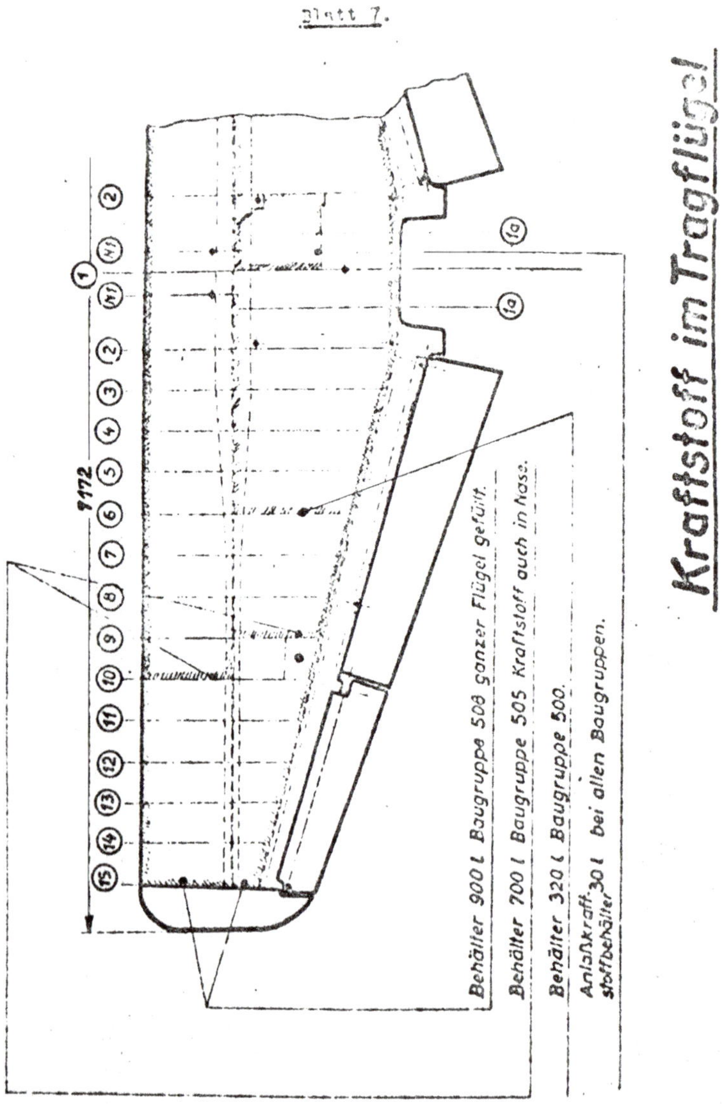

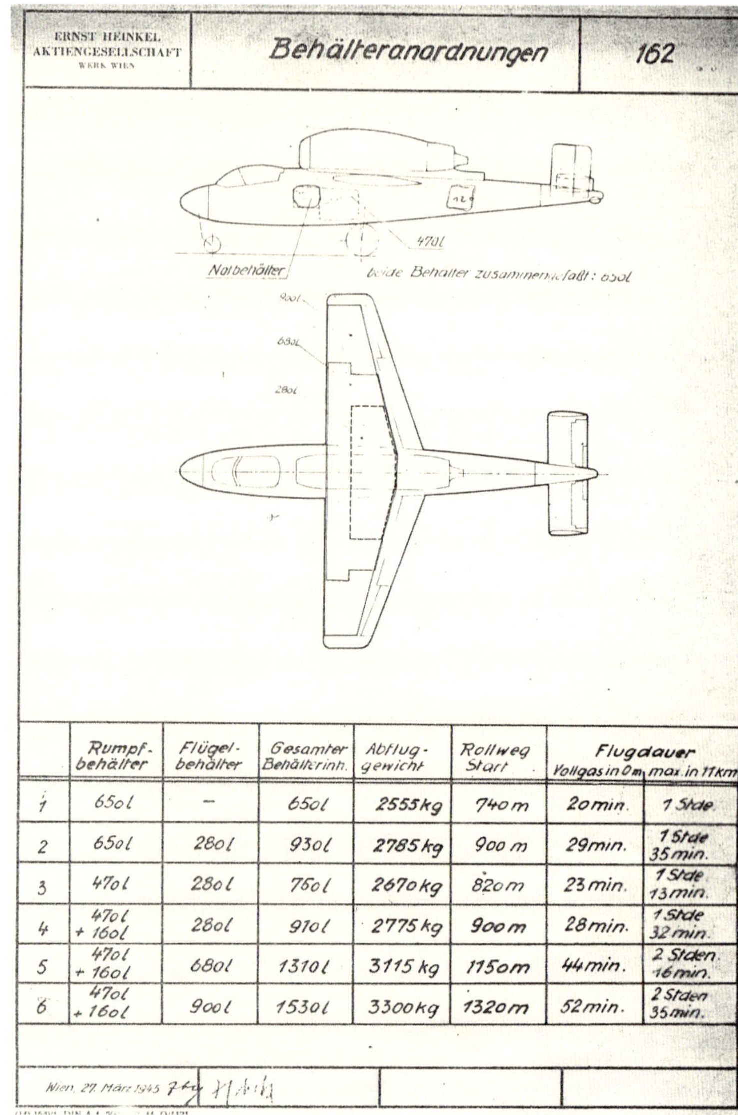

ERNST HEINKEL AKTIENGESELLSCHAFT WERK WIEN — Behälteranordnungen — 162

Notbehälter — beide Behälter zusammen(?) 470l

	Rumpf-behälter	Flügel-behälter	Gesamter Behälterinh.	Abflug-gewicht	Rollweg Start	Flugdauer Vollgas in 0m	Flugdauer max. in 11km
1	650l	–	650l	2555kg	740m	20min.	1 Stde.
2	650l	280l	930l	2785kg	900 m	29min.	1 Stde 35min.
3	470l	280l	750l	2670kg	820m	23min.	1 Stde. 13min.
4	470l + 160l	280l	910l	2775kg	900m	28min.	1 Stde 32min.
5	470l + 160l	680l	1310l	3115kg	1150m	44min.	2 Stden. 16min.
6	470l + 160l	900l	1530l	3300kg	1320m	52min.	2 Stden 35min.

Wien, 27. März 1945

Page 7 of the October 1944 'Beaubeschreibung' showing the layout of the fuel tanks in the wings of the He 162. The drawing (right) is a facsimile of the revised fuel tank layout dated 27 March 1945 which also shows the proposed emergency fuel tank behind the cockpit with an extra 120-litre fuel tank in the rear fuselage.

An unidentified early production He 162. From this angle, the proximity of the jet engine to the cockpit hood can be seen, as well as the Revi 16 b gunsight mounted on top of the instrument panel and the pronounced style of riveting along the canopy frame. Note also the gun troughs and the size of the nosewheel door. The small number just visible below the pitot tube ('92') is probably a component number.

Oberst Edgar Petersen, the Kommandeur der Erprobungsstellen, who was heavily involved in liaison between EHAG and the Luftwaffe over the He 162, identified a number of performance and construction weaknesses which afflicted the aircraft, but nevertheless conceded that Heinkel had produced the fighter with 'amazing speed'.

The highly experienced test pilot, Flugkapitän Hermann Steckhan (left), was seriously injured following his flight in He 162 W.Nr. 310 001 at Bernburg on 27 March 1945. To that point he had flown the He 162 on no fewer than fifteen occasions.

The working atmosphere was not to become cold and the whole wing section was to be kept in a constant temperature for at least 20 minutes. In order to prove that the sealing process had been successful, a test pressure was to be applied.[183]

Prying Allied reconnaissance aircraft had made a total of 16 photo sweeps over Schwechat since 6 December and had identified a total of 29 He 162s.'*There is no doubt that the small aircraft which has hitherto been known as the 'Schwechat 25' is the new German single-jet fighter, the Volksjäger or 162, and the provisional name will no longer be used. In most cases,*' recorded the RAF interpreter,'*the 162s have been photographed on the runway, sometimes at one end and sometimes the other, but on 16.2.1945, three of the five visible were seen (together with a He 219) outside the central hangar, and the 162 seen on 4.1.45 was in movement on the main taxi-track near the hangars.*'[184]

By the 27th, EHAG had performed 259 flights with the He 162, totalling 65 hrs 21 mins. It was hoped that the following output of aircraft would be completed in March:

18 at Bernburg
10 at Rostock
5 at Oranienburg
10 at Ludwigslust
15 at Wien

Junkers test pilot, Heinrich Osterwald, flew He 162 W.Nr. 310 018 over Bernburg for 14 minutes. His logbook decribes the flight as '*Salamander mit BMW*'.[185] Also, Hermann Steckhan flew He 162 W.Nr. 310 001 at 1658 hrs from the '*Industrieflughafen*' at Bernburg on a test flight. Observing Steckhan's flight was a group of pilots from I./JG 1, including *Oberleutnant* Wolfgang Wollenweber, who recounted: 'When Steckhan pressed the button of the Riedel two-stroke starter motor, the turbine caught immediately with a high-pitched whine. This gradually rose in pitch to a shrill whistle and then a long tongue of flame shot from the exhaust outlet. Steckhan taxied to the runway threshold. The hellish din of the jet engine reached a crescendo as he accelerated and lifted off. But at height of just 150 metres the turbine abruptly cut out. We heard Steckhan calmly report that he was doing 240 km/h and was having problems with the automatic thrust nozzle

Luftwaffe personnel, one holding a fire extinguisher, observe the BMW 003 engine start up on He 162 W.Nr. 310 001 with Hermann Steckhan at the controls.

A grainy glimpse of Flugkapitän Hermann Steckhan as he commences his take-off from Bernburg on 27 March 1945.

A civilian engineer peers into the cockpit of He 162 W.Nr. 310 001 as Flugkapitän Hermann Steckhan prepares to taxi out ahead of his fateful flight at Bernburg on 27 March 1945.

control settings. After completing a half circuit he came in at 50 metres for a deadstick landing. This was much too high, and he had too much speed. We watched as the tiny machine smashed down hard onto the runway. The turbine was ripped off upon impact and went sailing off to the right. Then the two wooden wings snapped off, the cockpit was squashed flat and the fuselage broke into several pieces.'[186]

Steckhan recalled the events in a more measured way: 'On 27 March at 16.58 hours, I took off in He 162 '1' on an acceptance flight. The take-off went smoothly. The machine lifted off quite quickly. At the edge of the airfield, the engine suddenly began to vibrate. Fuel pressure fell slowly. I switched the undercarriage from 'up' at which the gear unlocked. I closed the fuel cock and then drew to an abrupt stop. After a moment I came around and recovered from the shock.'[187]

From Wollenweber's account this was something of an understatement: 'It was little short of a miracle that Steckhan was able to extricate himself from the 95 per cent destroyed machine. He managed to stagger a few paces, but then collapsed in a heap. We immediately rushed to the site of the crash and found him lying unconscious and horrifically injured beside the wreckage of the Heinkel. He had been flung violently forward by the crash and his face had hit the control column. His teeth had been pushed through his upper lip, one incisor had been broken off and the other front teeth all pushed inwards. The right side of his upper jaw had been dislocated, his spine badly compressed, and his right leg was a bloody mess.'[188]

Officially, the aircraft was assessed as suffering 85 per cent damage.[189] As Steckhan was taken off to hospital one of Wollenweber's comrades commented that if the test pilots couldn't control the aircraft, then flying it operationally would be 'plain suicide'.

JG 1 was slated to receive the 18 aircraft from Bernburg and seven from Wien, but on the 28th *Oblt.* Hachtel received a telex informing him that He 162s were to be accepted only if the BMW engines had been converted to accept J2 fuel. In the meantime, when available, seven aircraft would be transferred to Lechfeld for flight-testing. Quite where Hachtel was to go at this point remains unclear.

However, the first of three He 162s was delivered (from where is unclear) to Fl.Ü.G 1 (*Flugzeugüberführungsgeschwader* – Aircraft Ferrying Wing) at Barth on 27 March, then one on the 31st and one on 3 April.[190]

On the 28th He 162 W.Nr. 120 082 was flight-tested over Rostock-Marienehe in the early afternoon.[191]

On 29 March the He 162 M42 W.Nr. 220 030 was reported ready for engine-testing purposes, while at Bernburg test pilot, Heinrich Osterwald, flew W.Nr. 310 015 for 18 minutes. His logbook decribes the flight as 'TL – *Kleinstjäger*. Test flight'.[192] He 162 W.Nr. 120 068 was flight-tested over Rostock-Marienehe in the morning and in the afternoon of the 31st it was the turn of W.Nr. 120 076 and W.Nr. 120 070.[193]

By Sunday, 1 April 1945, however, to use a British colloquialism – 'the writing was on the wall' as far as the German war effort was concerned. Adolf Hitler relocated his headquarters from the Chancellery building in Berlin to a deep bunker complex just behind it. It was a move redolent of defeat. In Moscow the same day, Josef Stalin enquired airily of his commanders: 'Well now, who is going to take Berlin, we or the Allies?'

In a touch of irony, in Hamburg the *Reichsführer*-SS, Heinrich Himmler, told local officials that it would be the disagreements between the Allied powers as well as the imminent appearance of new jet aircraft in large numbers that would save Germany. At this point, the SS began to 'move in'. In southern Germany, *Luftwaffe* motor transport was being put at the disposal of Hitler's personal Plenipotentiary for Jet Aircraft Production and Operational Deployment, SS-*Obergruppenführer und General der Waffen*-SS *Dr.-Ing.* Hans Kammler. Towards the end of March, Hitler had ordered that Kammler was to command all necessary development, testing and production of jet aircraft and to co-ordinate all necessary logistic operations previously handled by the Minister for Armaments and War Production. He was also to assume command of jet production through to operational deployment. According to Hitler's decree '… Kammler is placed under my personal command and has my fullest authority. All Commands of the *Wehrmacht*, Party and Reich organisations are to assist him in the execution of his duties and are to carry out his orders.'

At Wien, following *Hauptdienstleiter* Saur's authorisation to Francke on the 31st, the decision was taken, heavily and reluctantly, to evacuate the Heinkel works in the face of the threatening Soviet advance from the east and move the business and as much of its production as possible to hastily arranged provisional facilities in the Salzburg (Jenbach) and Klagenfurt areas.[194] A specially requisitioned train carrying Francke, Günter and approximately 35 key members of staff departed Wien bound for Gandersheim in the Harz Mountains.[195] However, due to the American advance, the party had to divert to the small Heinkel satellite facility at Jenbach in the Tyrol. In July 1945 *Dr.* Heinkel and Karl Frydag recorded events for their British interrogators:

'On April 1, 1945 our workshop in Wien had to close down. Complete machines were conveyed; larger fittings ready to be mounted at the Amme-Luther-Seck Werk, were transferred as far as possible. Drawings and documents were secured and transported to Jenbach where they were hidden in a cellar near the Achensee to protect them from being destroyed. At Rostock, meantime, production had begun with similar difficulties. The last news came from Rostock at the beginning of April. Then every communication ceased. From mid-April, communications were also lost with Junkers at Dessau. By the time we had to leave Wien, about 12 complete machines [aircraft] were ready there; they were to be flown to Hörseburg [sic – probably Hörsching] near Linz and to Lechfeld, but as we heard, not all of them arrived.'[196]

Indeed, the He 162 M 11 (fitted with a Jumo 004 engine) had been destroyed by bombing at *Languste*, while the M9, W.Nr. 200 009, VI+IH, and M10, W.Nr. 200 010, VI+IJ, were blown up to prevent capture by the Russians.

Ten aircraft were flown out of Schwechat and Heidfeld by the end of March via Langenlebarn and Hörsching to Lechfeld. One He 162 was abandoned at Hörsching during the transfer and another was destroyed when it crashed, not far from Langenlebarn during the subsequent leg from München to Lechfeld, killing its pilot, *Lt.* Huldreich Kemnitz.[197]

The Allied radio intercept service picked up a signal from Lechfeld airfield to SS-*Obergruppenführer* Kammler on 8 April stating that some eight He 162s were apparently at Hörsching, and enquiring as to whether the pilots of the aircraft should be posted for retraining on the Me 262 or be used for operations with the He 162 in the Memmingen area.[198]

Further machines were delivered to Rechlin, presumably from Junkers. *Oberst* Edgar Petersen, the *Kommandeur der Erprobungsstellen*, told his interrogators that the first ten He 162s were built with 'amazing speed'. According to Petersen, from the aircraft delivered to Rechlin for testing, which were also subsequently moved to Lechfeld, it became evident that:

> The maximum speed was 100 km/h less than that promised.
> The endurance, in practice, was never more than 30 minutes.
> The take-off run was between 1000 m and 1200 m
> The landing speed was between 170 km/h and 180 km/h
> The altitude performance of the BMW 003 jet engine precluded any attempt to discover the true ceiling performance of the aircraft.
>
> Furthermore, during tests, the following problem areas were noted:
>
> The jet engine could not deliver its full thrust
> The nosewheel was too weak
> The wing used as a fuel tank leaked
> Acceleration interfered with the fuel feed
> The flying qualities were poor, especially in rolls
> The rudder was too sensitive.

Modifications to the fin and rudder and mainplanes were undertaken to endeavour to rectify these faults, but Petersen's main criticism was that a series embodying the very components which required modification was already underway and in order to prevent a sharp fall in series output, it became necessary to set up a modification factory (Mödling).[199]

The gutted and bomb-blasted remains of hangars and outbuildings at EHAG's site at Rostock-Marienehe in 1945. It was planned to build 1,000 He 162s per month here, but by January 1945 the plant was suffering from regular power cuts and lack of functioning equipment, and local flight-testing was affected by bad weather and a lack of fuel. By early February 1945, the factory had still not produced any aircraft and on 2 May it fell to the Soviet Army.

On 3 April *Dr* Goebbels, the Reich Propaganda Minister, wrote in his diary: 'The *Führer* has had very prolonged discussions with *Obergruppenführer* Kammler, who now carries responsibility for the reform of the *Luftwaffe*. Kammler is doing excellently and great hopes are placed on him... At the daily briefing conferences, the *Luftwaffe* comes in for the sharpest criticism from the *Führer*. Day after day, Göring has to listen without being in a position to demur at all...'

The next day, Heinrich Osterwald had problems with two aircraft at Junkers Bernburg when, firstly, He 162 W.Nr. 310 079 was airborne for just over eight minutes when it developed a fault, and secondly in W.Nr. 310 081, when a fault occurred after just four minutes. Both flights were terminated and the aircraft inspected.[200] On 5 April an EHAG delegation comprising Francke, Meschkat, Reiniger, Hilber and Hohbach was asked to travel to Lechfeld where it met with *Dipl.-Ing.* Gerhard Caroli and *Herr* Kaiser of the so-called *Autobedarf Lechfeld*, the cover name for the local Messerschmitt flight-testing detachment working on the Me 262. Also in attendance were *Fl.Stabs.Ing.* Bader and *Fl.Ob.Ing.* Pangratz of the *Chef* TLR *Abt.*E3 (Engines), and *Fl.Stabs.Ing.* Dietrich and *Fl.Stabs.Ing.* Jachmann of *Abt.*E2 (Airframes).

Both sides compared notes on their respective experiences with the BMW 003 engine with a view to considering the practicalities of using a BMW 003 TLR composite turbojet and rocket engine as trialed on the Me 262 C-2b *Heimatschützer*. When Caroli put forward the relevant technical information with regard to the Me 262, the EHAG representatives realised that a similar installation in the He 162 would not be possible because the unit would have a higher constant thrust temperature in flight and, most importantly, the aircraft would be 20 per cent overloaded in such a composite configuration.[201]

At the end of October 1944 it had been proposed that all variants of the Me 262 should be fitted with the BMW 003 as an alternative powerplant to the Jumo 004. The problem with the BMW 003, however, was its need to be fuelled by B4, as opposed to the lower grade and more readily available J2 and the reality was that by early 1945 at least six Me 262s had been equipped with the BMW.[202] The Lechfeld discussions seem to have been inconclusive and without firm result.

To the north in Bernburg, flight-testing continued at Junkers: Heinrich Osterwald made a 17-minute flight in He 162, W.Nr. 310 080. Between 7-9 April flight-testing continued when Osterwald made three more flights: on the 7th in W.Nr. 310 021 for 6 minutes; on the 8th, in W.Nr. 310 010 for 16 minutes; and on the 9th in W.Nr. 310 021 for 6 minutes. At Rostock-Marienehe W.Nr. 120 076 was flight-tested in the late morning.[203] But by early April, moves were in place to halt further production of the He 162 in favour of the Me 262. So, in a sense, Willy Messerschmitt had won the day.

Monday, 9 April – Sunday, 22 April 1945

On 11 April, *Oblt.* Hachtel's detachment from 2./JG 1 at Heidfeld was ordered to transfer as *Stabsstaffel* JG 1 to Lechfeld (and/or Memmingen) for operations as part of '*Erprobungskommando Lechfeld*'.

On Tuesday, 10 April the following status report was issued on the He 162 programme: the M30 (A-013) W.Nr. 220 013, now coded 'WA+51', which had been assigned for trials with MG 151 cannon was still without sealed wing fuel tanks; the unpainted M11, W.Nr. 220 017, now coded 'E2+51' (a K.d.E code) had its wing tanks sealed and was used for engine and undercarriage tests; the M28 W.Nr. 220 011 had been assigned – in theory – to the '*Stabsstaffel Hachtel*', had its tank sealed and been fitted with an additional small fuselage tank; the M27 (A-010) W.Nr. 220 010, now coded 'E2+52' and which had been undertaking performance tests, was awaiting the installation of a large fuselage fuel tank; the W.Nr. 220 022, coded 'E3+51' was assigned to engine-testing for Rechlin and had had its tanks sealed; the M31 W.Nr. 220 014, re-coded VH+HC, had been assigned to Hachtel but could only accept B4 fuel; W.Nr. 220 018, W.Nr. 220 103 ('E5+E4'), and W.Nr. 220 102 ('E2+53') all had sealed tanks; while the M29 (A-012) W.Nr. 220 012, VI+IV had also been assigned to Hachtel's detachment but its tanks still required sealing.[204]

After this, it seems, there were no further aircraft available from Wien to be placed at the *Luftwaffe's* disposal.

On the 12th, Junkers test pilot, Heinrich Osterwald, flew He 162 W.Nr. 310 021 (again) from Bernburg to Ludwigslust, a flight which took 20 minutes, while He 162 W.Nr. 120 083 was flight-tested over Rostock-Marienehe that morning. Next day, W.Nr. 120 069 and W.Nr. 120 085 were both tested at Marienehe.[205]

On 16 April 1945, the Japanese embassy in Berlin cabled Tokyo with detailed information on the He 162 including dimensions, performance data, information on engines, weights and materials. A further, even more detailed message, followed four days later. However, as the Military Intelligence Service of the US War Department commented in a post-war report of August 1945, 'From the available evidence it seems quite clear that the Japanese did not possess information to allow construction of the He 162 in Japan.'[206]

At 1926 hrs the following evening, *Fliegerstabsing. Dipl.-Ing.* Heinz Borsdorff of *E-Stelle* Rechlin's powerplant testing department, E3, and a former transport pilot of KG zbV 101 and blind-flying instructor, commenced a series of engine test flights in He 162, W.Nr. 220 022, E3+51, which had been flown out of Wien, over Lechfeld. He was airborne again in this machine on the 20th (twice – 29 and 27 mins), the 21st (21 mins) and 22nd (15 mins).[207] Borsdorff had been sent to

Lechfeld from Rechlin as part of a small advance detachment of jet aircraft and jet engine testing personnel. Increasingly, flight-testing was taking place at manufacturer's premises, which involved lengthy and often dangerous train journies from one end of the Reich to the other. Lechfeld was geographically closer to the Messerschmitt, Heinkel Süd and Dornier firms than was Rechlin; it was also further away from the Soviet advance from the east. Borsdorff had been working on the installation of new Jumo 004 engines and instruments into the He 162s W.Nr. 220 022, E3+51 and E3+52 at Lechfeld in consultation with *Obst*. Petersen.[208]

Furthermore a team of three 'examiners' and nine '*Musterbauvorarbeiter*' (prototype charge hands) together with operational diagrams and sufficient disintegrating belt mechanisms from Heinkel Rostock were ordered to Lechfeld by He 111.[209]

On the 17th He 162 W.Nr. 120 092 was flight-tested over Rostock-Marienehe in the early afternoon.[210]

By the end of April, production of the He 162 had all but ceased at EHAG's plant at Rostock-Marienehe, due to the rapid advance of the Soviet Army.

On 20 April 1945, Adolf Hitler's 56th birthday, the Allies mounted a heavy daylight raid by more than 800 US bombers against rail targets in the Berlin area. The RAF would follow that night. That day, *Hauptdienstleiter Dipl.-Ing.* Karl-Otto Saur, who had done so much to push the He 162 programme forward, was awarded the *Goldenes Ritterkreuz des Kriegsverdienstkreuzes mit Schwertern* (Knight's Cross of the War Service Cross in Gold with Swords).

On 2 May, Rostock fell to the Russians. According to recent research, 171 He 162s were manufactured. *Luftwaffe*, *GenQ*. 6. *Abt*. Statistics list a total of 116 He 162s as being delivered by the various factories, of which 56 machines went to the *Luftwaffe*. By the cessation of hostilities, this broke down as follows:

From EHAG Süd Wien-Schwechat	ca 8 aircraft
From EHAG Süd Hinterbrühl (*Languste*)	ca 20 aircraft
From EHAG Nord Rostock-Marienehe /Rostock-Theresienfeld	ca 55 aircraft
From Junkers Bernburg	ca 15 aircraft
From Mittelwerke Nordhausen	ca 1-5 aircraft
From DLH Oranienburg	ca 1-5 aircraft
	116 aircraft

This total was streamed as follows:

To the *Chef* TLR	19 aircraft
To the *Kommando der Erprobungsstellen*	3 aircraft
For training purposes	5 aircraft
To *Jagdgeschwader* 1	29 aircraft
	56 aircraft

In summary – and in what are undeniable accomplishments – in the five months between November 1944 and March 1945, using whatever means were available, Heinkel built the first operationally ready single-engine jet fighter. This fighter was also the first of its kind to incorporate an ejection seat.

In response to *Professor* Messerschmitt's indictment of the *Volksjäger* concept, Karl Frydag offered a rational riposte shortly after the war. He told Allied Intelligence officers that it had been statistically proven that the He 162 could be built using 40 per cent fewer man-hours and 20 per cent less metal than the Me 262, and that in its final version the He 162 would perform exactly the same role as the Messerschmitt but in a more efficient manner. Moreover, Frydag claimed that it was an 'indisputable fact' that no impact on Me 262 production was suffered on account of a lack of metal, as Messerschmitt had claimed.[211]

Frydag further asserted that the great advantage of the He 162 over the Me 262 was its far superior manoeuvrability at all speeds, a factor which offset its lighter armament of two MK 108s as opposed to the four cannon installed in the Me 262. Furthermore, although earlier versions of the *Volksjäger* had a somewhat restricted range due to problems associated with developing the entire wing section to house a fuel tank, this had been overcome by the cessation of hostilities and a completed, improved machine was ready.

Indeed, so far as handling the *Volksjäger* in flight was concerned, in general engineering was not sub-standard: Carl Francke did consider the wing area to be too small, but flight trials proved landing characteristics better than expected and the wing area sufficient. According to Siegfried Günter, a number of *Luftwaffe* pilots who flew the He 162 straight from training aircraft found the landing characteristics of the He 162 to be 'easy', while more experienced pilots judged them to be superior to those of the Bf 109.[212]

To Messerschmitt's allegation that the decision to proceed with the He 162 had dealt his firm two 'mortifying blows' by robbing it of valuable manufacturing space and by exacerbating the difficulties of jigs by the appearance of a competing design, Frydag responded by pointing out that underground space assigned to the production of the He 162 would have been too confined for the Me 262. Additionally, Messerschmitt's jig difficulties had arisen in December 1943, a full seven months *before* the *Volksjäger* concept had even been contemplated. By the time the He 162 reached the drawing board in detail in September 1944, Messerschmitt's difficulties were not just founded on jigs, but also upon 'internal organisational difficulties' and the worsening national transport situation. Frydag stressed to his captors that, as he saw it, not one Me 262 was cancelled on account of the He 162 which was built largely of wood. In his view, in the long run it was fortunate for the Reich that certain individuals 'had the courage to press the He 162' since the Messerschmitt-controlled factory at Wüstegiersdorf, which was the sole manufacturer of the steel main spar of the Me 262, had been captured by the Russians in January 1945, with the result that had the war continued, the loss of supply of an essential component would have spelt disaster for the production of the Me 262.

In fact the *Luftwaffe's* position lends credence to Frydag's claims; the minutes of a meeting which took place at the headquarters of the *General der Jagdflieger*, *Oberst* Gollob, on 29 January 1945 record that: '... 60 per cent of the Me 262 spars have been lost in Silesia.'

The same minutes also comment: 'It should also be considered that in December 1944, industry produced 681 Me 262s. The OKL received 499 machines. The difference of almost 200 aircraft is due to the fact that the various parts for the aircraft were stored in different places and assembly of same was not achieved, therefore the sum of 681 aircraft is purely a theoretical one. Out of 499 aircraft destined for the new units, only 186 Me 262s were delivered, the others being lost partly as a result of bombing, partly during ferry flights and partly in railway transportation.'[213]

Perhaps the most fitting commentary on Heinkel's endeavours came – ironically – from Germany's erstwhile enemy. On 7 June 1945, the 'Farren Mission' comprising certain members of the British aircraft, aircraft engine and armament industries was invited to survey a cross-section of its corresponding German industries under the leadership of William S. Farren, director of the Royal Aircraft Establishment, with the following terms of reference: 'To find out how the Germans developed, introduced, and manufactured military types of aircraft.' In a subsequent report entitled '*He 162 – An achievement in Rapid Aircraft Development and Manufacture*', the Mission opined that construction of the He 162 represented '... an outstanding achievement from whatever aspect it may be considered... This remarkable result was achieved, once the general scheme had been agreed, mainly by eliminating all technical or other controls by the RLM, (which nevertheless gave the firm all the support and priorities it required), by flooding the job with the maximum practicable number of men working the maximum number of hours, and by a willingness on the part of everyone to take risks which, under anything like normal conditions, would not have been countenanced.'[214]

Anatomy of the *Volksjäger*

The following description is based on documents produced by EHAG Wien and Allied post-war inspections from late 1944/early 1945.

The He 162 was a small, shoulder-wing monoplane of mixed construction. The all-wood wing has a straight leading edge, the trailing edge being swept forward to square cut wing tips with rounded corners and a pronounced anhedral angle.

Fuselage

The aerodynamically clean fuselage of the He 162 was constructed of the following materials:

Formers and skin	-	dural
Fittings	-	part steel
Glazing	-	Plexiglas
Inspection covers	-	dural or wood

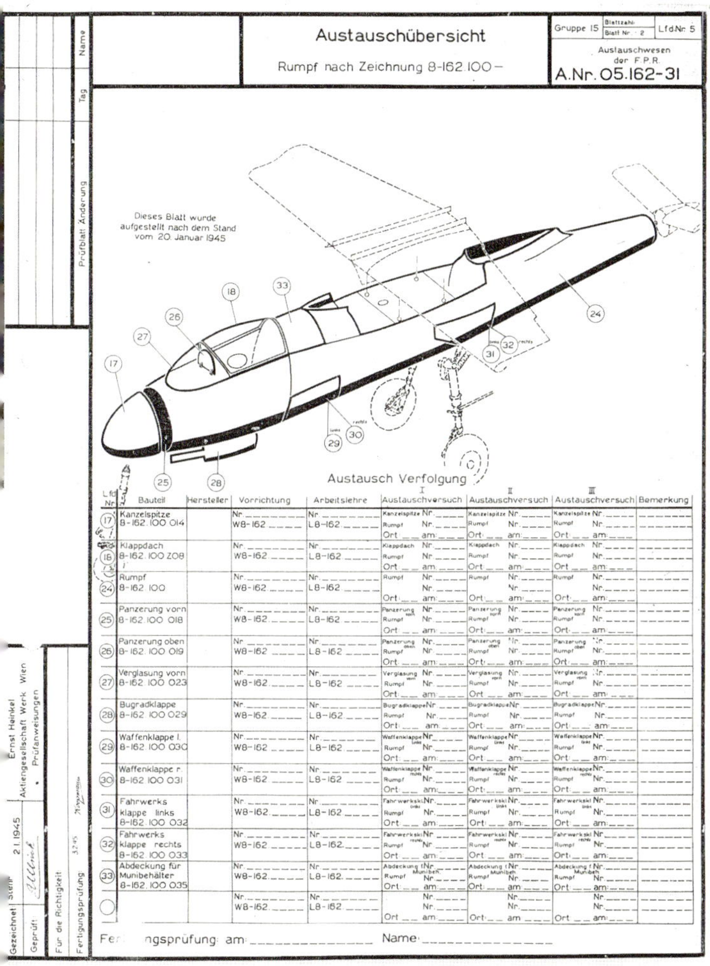

It was of semi-monocoque construction. From the conical tail fairing to the trailing edge of the wing, it was circular, blending to pear-shaped in cross section with a flattened underside as far as the cockpit. From there, it gradually changed to oval at the nose which was constructed of plywood.

The fuselage as a whole was made up of the following sections:

Nose cap	-	forward of former 1
Section port	-	from former 1-11
Section starboard	-	from former 1-11
Under section	-	from former 1-13
Centre section	-	from former 11-15
Rear section	-	from former 15-22
Cockpit enclosure	-	from former 1-5

The individual sections were supported by cross formers and longitudinal stringers to which the dural sheet was riveted. The fuselage was compartmentalised as follows:

- Fuselage cap
- Cockpit compartment
- Undercarriage compartment
- Fuselage tubes

The fuselage end section which carried the tail unit was attached to the fuselage in such a way that it could be adjusted. Flush riveting was employed throughout.

Jacking up:
There were three points on the fuselage suitable for the smallest type of jack.

Lifting:

1. Fuselage, without power unit or wings - three points
2. Engine - lifting lugs were fitted at three points
3. Wing with power unit attached - engine lugs were to be used
4. Wing without power unit - the three engine attachment points were to be used

Transportation:
Transportation could be effected on standard rail wagons or motor lorries.

Left: An 'Austauschübersicht' (Amendment Overview) from February 1945 showing numeric annotations referring to manufacturing drawing numbers which are listed below. The number 17 on the drawing relates to drawing number '8-162.100 014 Kanzelspitze', for the manufacture of the nose cone. Provision has also been made next to each drawing number for the insertion of amendment proposals for modification or alterations put forward by manufacturers. The aim was to circulate this updated information to all the factories involved in production.

The external construction of the He 162 A-1

Fuselage made of dural and steel parts, with panels riveted and panel lines pasted. Nose cap and key access panels of wood. Wings of wood, steel and aluminium alloy. Tail unit, duralumin, steel and wood. Engine housing, dural.

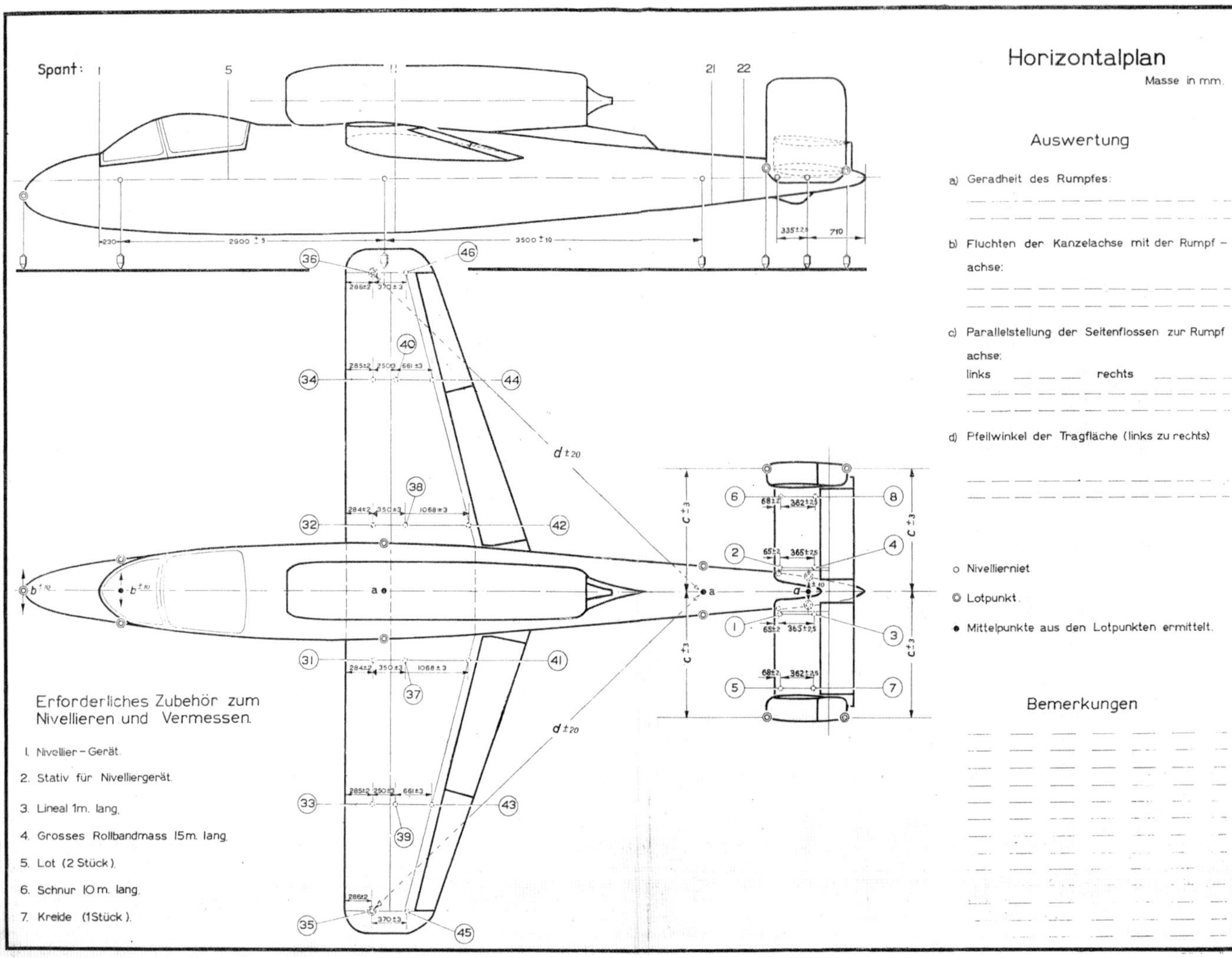
Horizontalplan
Masse in mm.
Spant: 1 5 11 21 22
Auswertung
a) Geradheit des Rumpfes:
b) Fluchten der Kanzelachse mit der Rumpf-achse:
c) Parallelstellung der Seitenflossen zur Rumpfachse:
links rechts
d) Pfeilwinkel der Tragfläche (links zu rechts)
○ Nivellierniet
◎ Lotpunkt.
● Mittelpunkte aus den Lotpunkten ermittelt.
Bemerkungen
Erforderliches Zubehör zum Nivellieren und Vermessen.
1. Nivellier-Gerät.
2. Stativ für Nivelliergerät.
3. Lineal 1m. lang.
4. Grosses Rollbandmass 15m. lang.
5. Lot (2 Stück).
6. Schnur 10 m. lang.
7. Kreide (1Stück).

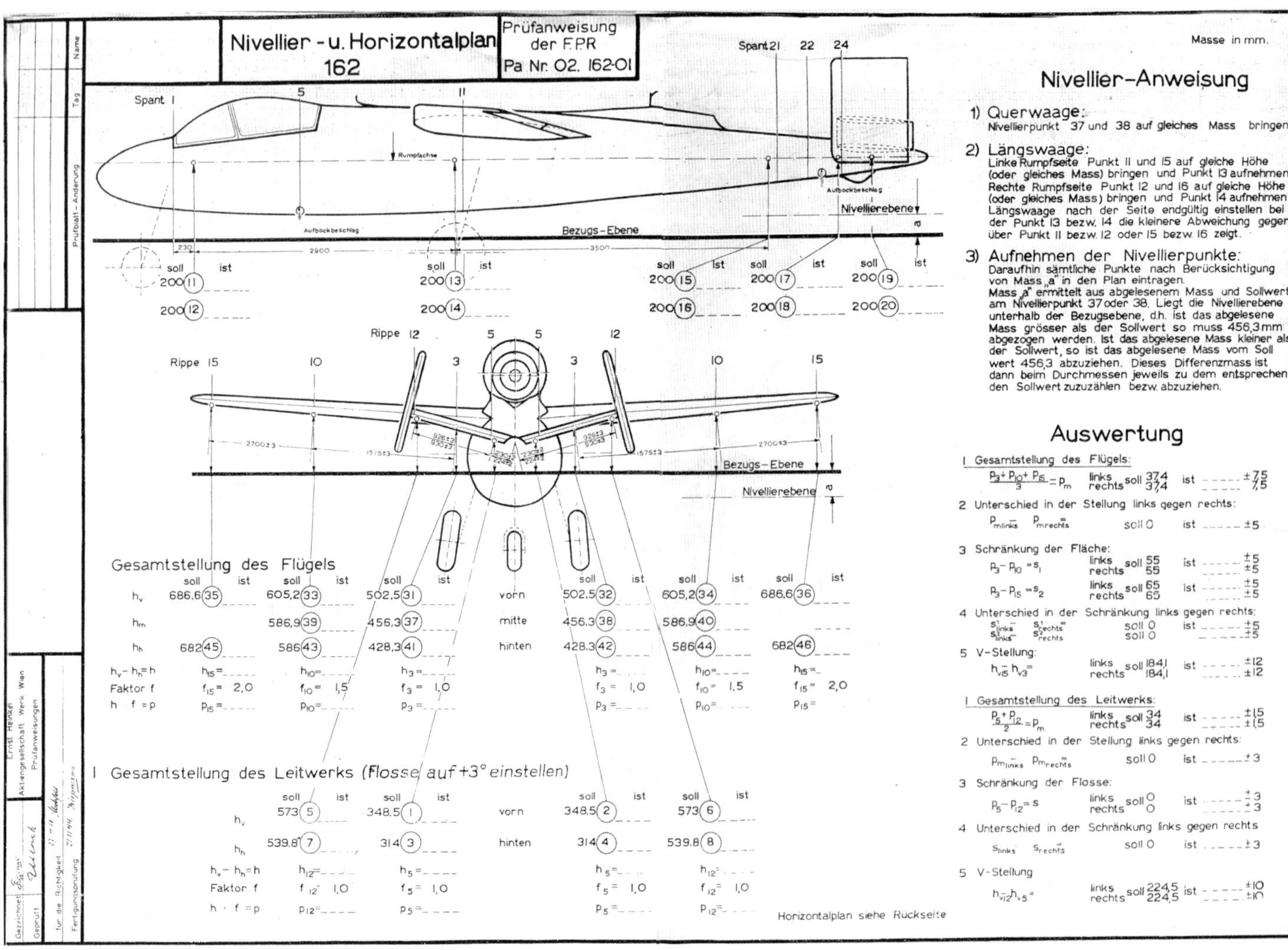
Nivellier - u. Horizontalplan 162
Prüfanweisung der F.P.R
Pa Nr. 02. 162-01
Masse in mm.
Nivellier-Anweisung
1) Querwaage:
Nivellierpunkt 37 und 38 auf gleiches Mass bringen.
2) Längswaage:
Linke Rumpfseite Punkt 11 und 15 auf gleiche Höhe (oder gleiches Mass) bringen und Punkt 13 aufnehmen. Rechte Rumpfseite Punkt 12 und 16 auf gleiche Höhe (oder gleiches Mass) bringen und Punkt 14 aufnehmen. Längswaage nach der Seite endgültig einstellen bei der Punkt 13 bezw. 14 die kleinere Abweichung gegenüber Punkt 11 bezw. 12 oder 15 bezw. 16 zeigt.
3) Aufnehmen der Nivellierpunkte:
Daraufhin sämtliche Punkte nach Berücksichtigung von Mass „a" in den Plan eintragen.
Mass „a" ermittelt aus abgelesenem Mass und Sollwert am Nivellierpunkt 37 oder 38. Liegt die Nivellierebene unterhalb der Bezugsebene, d.h. ist das abgelesene Mass grösser als der Sollwert so muss 456,3 mm abgezogen werden. Ist das abgelesene Mass kleiner als der Sollwert, so ist das abgelesene Mass vom Sollwert 456,3 abzuziehen. Dieses Differenzmass ist dann beim Durchmessen jeweils zu dem entsprechenden Sollwert zuzuzählen bezw. abzuziehen.
Auswertung
1 Gesamtstellung des Flügels:
2 Unterschied in der Stellung links gegen rechts:
3 Schränkung der Fläche:
4 Unterschied in der Schränkung links gegen rechts:
5 V-Stellung:
1 Gesamtstellung des Leitwerks:
2 Unterschied in der Stellung links gegen rechts:
3 Schränkung der Flosse:
4 Unterschied in der Schränkung links gegen rechts
5 V-Stellung
Spant 1 5 11 Spant 21 22 24
Bezugs-Ebene
Nivellierebene
Rippe 15 10 12 3 5 5 3 12 10 15
Gesamtstellung des Flügels
soll ist
vorn mitte hinten
1 Gesamtstellung des Leitwerks (Flosse auf +3° einstellen)
Horizontalplan siehe Rückseite
Ernst Heinkel Aktiengesellschaft Werk Wien Prüfanweisungen

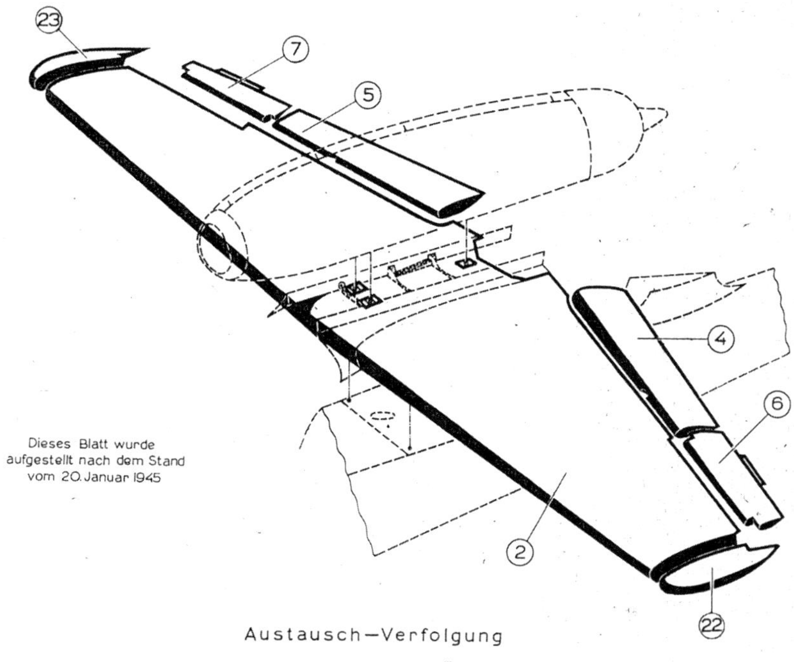

Wings

The wings of the He 162 were constructed of the following materials:

Wing spar boom	-	TBu 20
Webs and skin	-	Beech plywood
Wing ribs	-	Pine booms with plywood webs
Fittings and connecting bolts	-	Steel
End caps	-	Aluminium alloy

The wing section was fully cantilevered with approximately 3° dihedral. The main and auxiliary spars were T-shaped. The ribs were fully webbed. The skin was made up of 4 mm plywood which was thickened on the upper surface between the main and the auxiliary spar to 5 mm between ribs 2 and 6. The skin was also stiffened by means of longitudinal stringers.

The space between the main and the auxiliary spar and rib 6 on port and starboard sides was used as a fuel tank and was protected accordingly.

Servicing was performed by means of special equipment and a mirror after removing the end caps.

The upper surface included the filling point for fuel, whilst the connection between wing tank and fuselage tank came from the under surface.

The wing was connected to the fuselage by means of four vertical bolts. There were three further connection fittings for the power unit on the upper surface.

On the auxiliary spar there were two fittings for each aileron and landing flaps on either side.

The wing tips were of metal and were screwed to the wing with wood screws. They have an anhedral angle of about 128° to the under surface of the wing. This was not a design feature, but a modification to prevent turbulence and improve stability.

Ailerons:

These were constructed of wood and/or metal with two bearings on the wing rear spar and were dynamically and statically balanced. The design was that of a 'Keulen' aileron. Movements were limited to 18° upwards and 18° downwards. They projected 5 cm beyond the trailing edge of the flaps and were hinged at either end. The trailing edge line was broken in the centre for a fixed trim tab.

Landing Flaps:

There was one landing flap on each side of the wing and they were connected by means of a shaft. They were lowered by hydraulic pressure. As with the ailerons, the landing flaps were made of wood, with two bearings on the rear spar of the mainplane. A mechanical stop prevented them being lowered more than 45°.

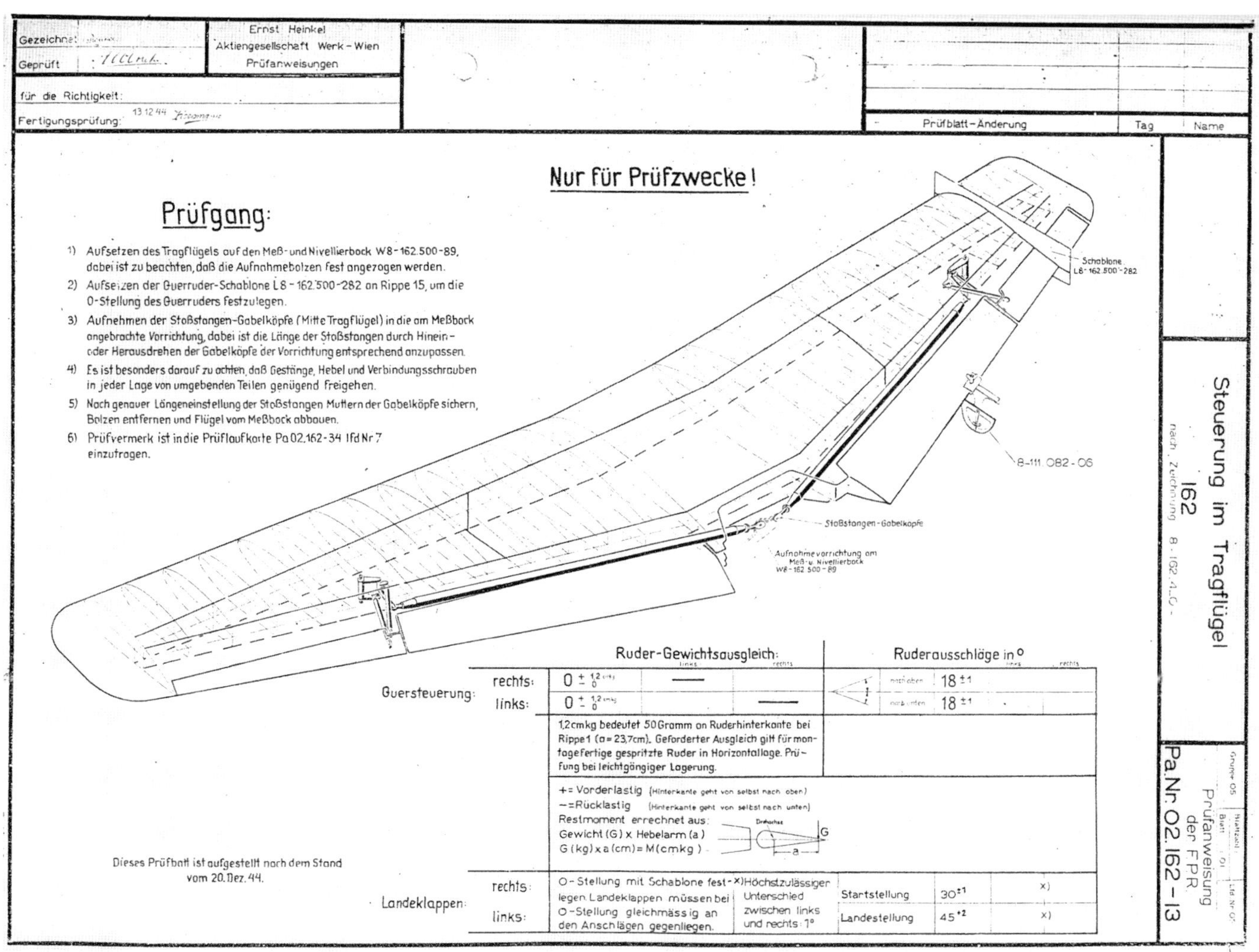

Tail unit

The cantilever tailplane had a dihedral of 14° and was of duralumin construction with steel fittings. The elevator was likewise of metal construction. A range of tailplane adjustment of + 3° to -2° was possible.

The wooden fins were rectangular and were attached to the ends of the tailplane by three bolts. Each rudder was carried on three bearings, the centre one being fixed and the two outer ones adjustable. The rudders were fully mass-balanced and their movement was limited by fixed stops to 25° on either side.

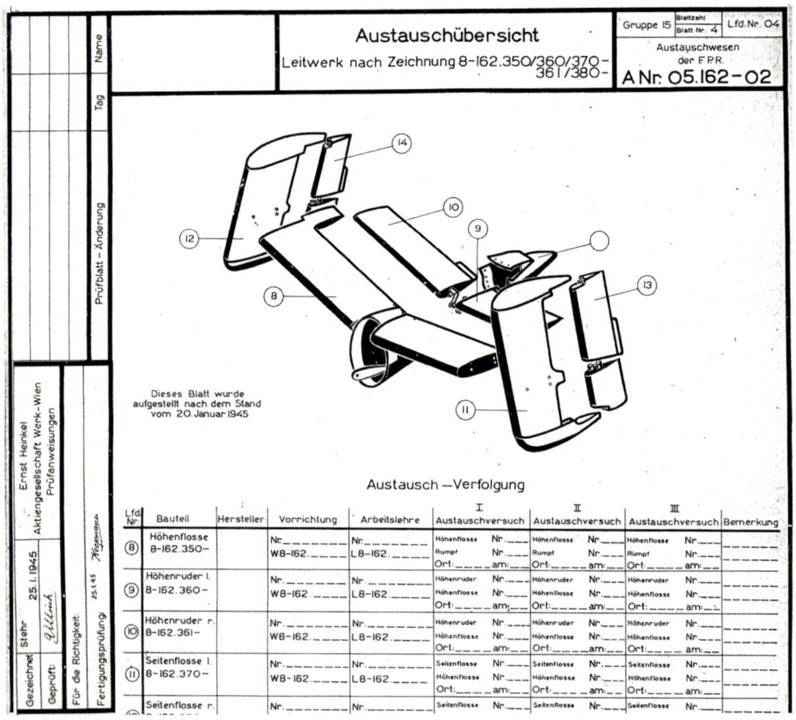

Controls

The controls of the He 162 were constructed of the following materials:

Tubes	-	Dural and steel
Shafts	-	Dural and steel
Lever	-	Elektron, Hydroalium and steel

Mounting of controls:
Despite the use of plain bearings, the controls were very light.

Operation of elevator:
Effected from the control column through push/pull rods, etc.

Aileron operation:
Effected from the control column through push/pull rods, etc.

Rudder operation:
From pedals, via cable and push/pull rods.

Tailplane trimming:
Mechanically by means of a wheel on the port side of the cockpit. 20 turns for 5° change. The highest force required for 1,000 km/h and pull-out 9.5 kg.

Undercarriage

The undercarriage of the He 162 was constructed of the following materials:

Oleo leg	-	Steel
Knee-jointed strut	-	Steel

Construction
The main undercarriage was retracted by hydraulic pressure. It was lowered by means of a spring which was compressed during retraction.

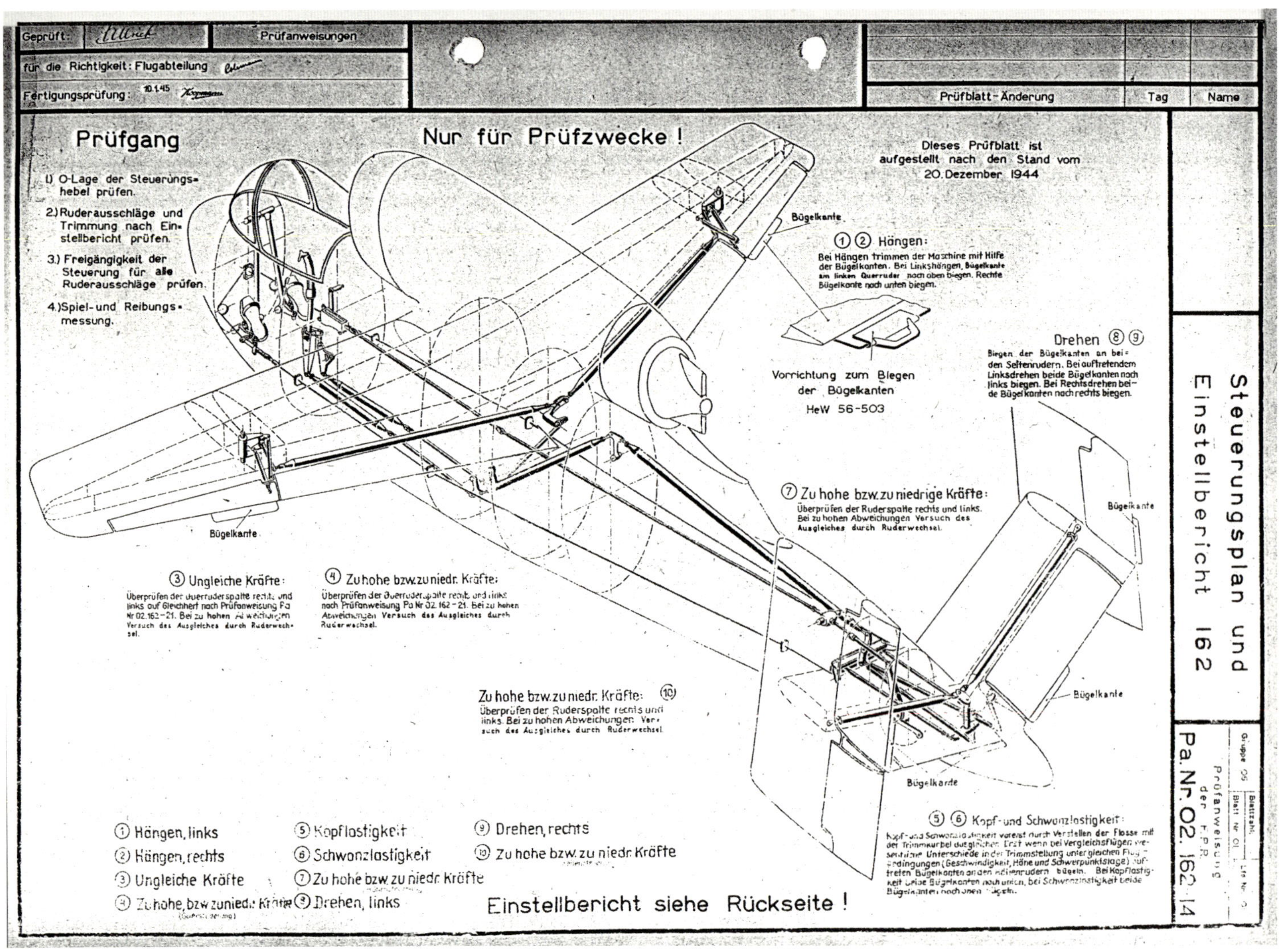

The undercarriage was locked in the 'up' position by means of a bolt which was released by means of a cable when the undercarriage was to be lowered.
The undercarriage was locked in the 'down' position by means of the knee joint which had gone past the 'dead' position. The position of the main undercarriage was shown by a mechanical indicator in the cockpit. When the nosewheel was retracted, it could be seen through a special window.

Construction of main undercarriage

General:

Each undercarriage consisted of one brake wheel and one oleo pneumatic leg, one knee joint with spring and one retraction cylinder.

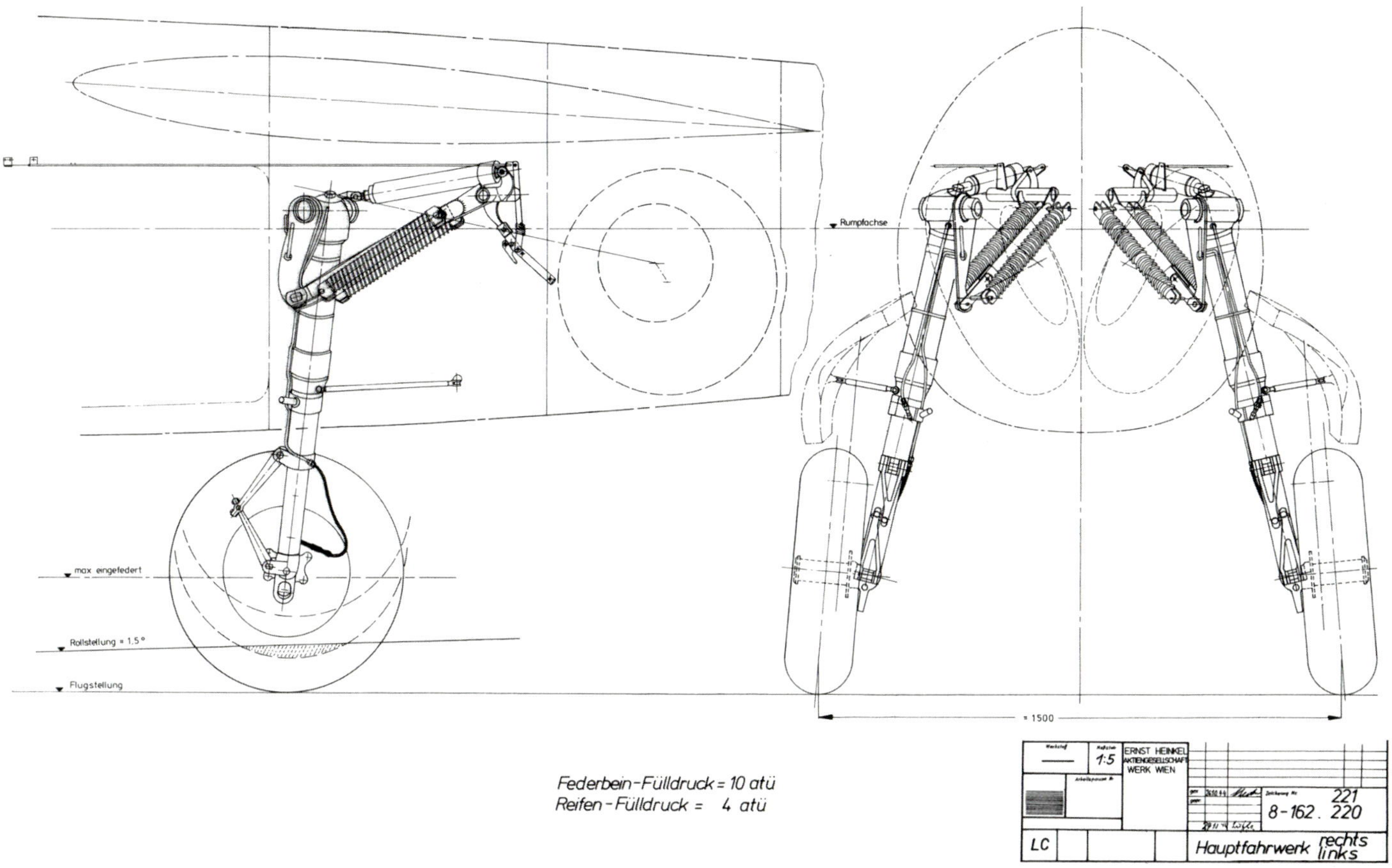

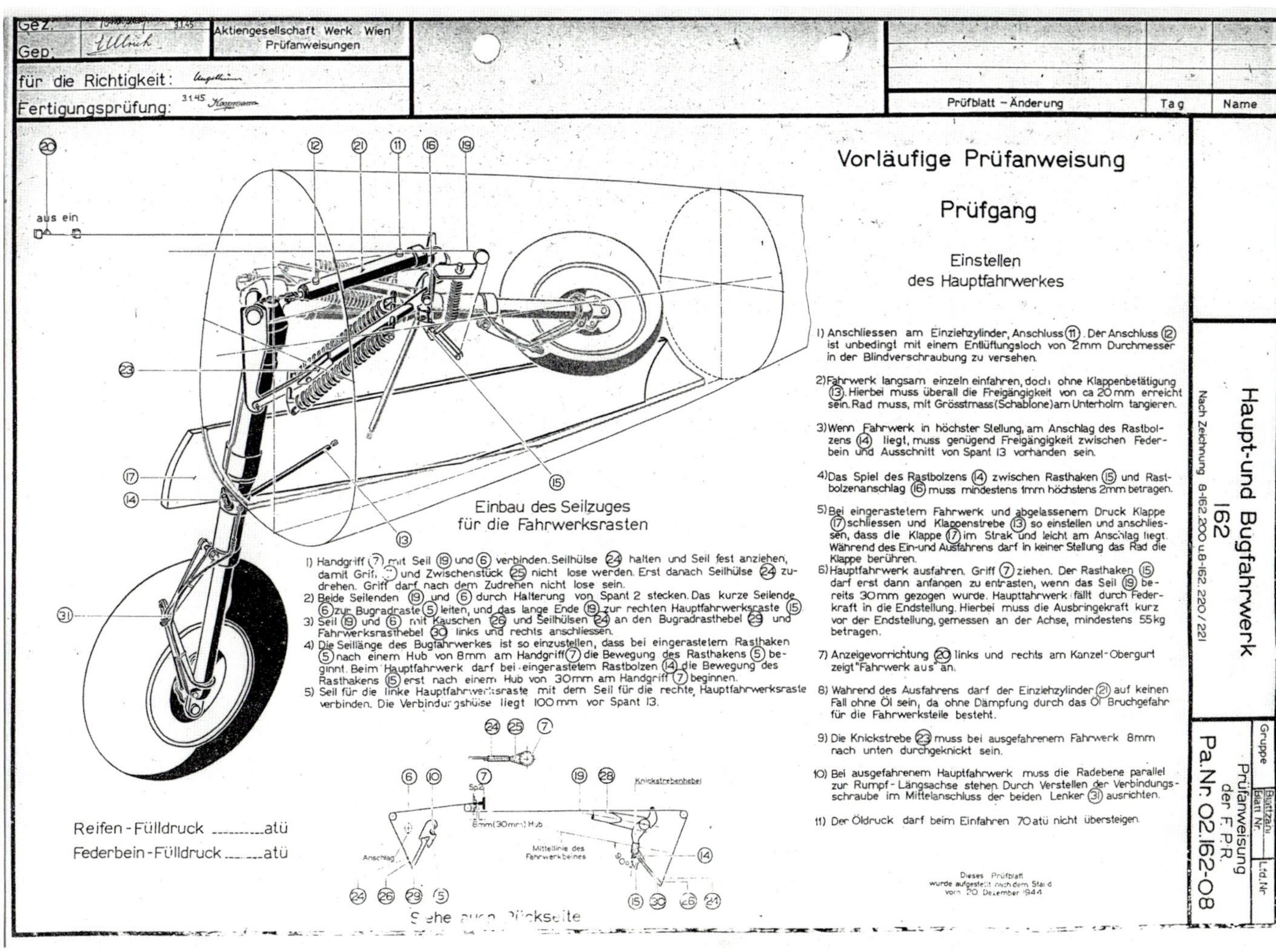

Main Wheels
The wheels were 660 mm x 190 mm. The brakes were operated by means of foot pumps on the rudder pedals.

Oleo leg:
The Bf 109 K oleo pneumatic leg was used.

Undercarriage doors:
The stowage space for the undercarriage in the fuselage was covered by doors which opened and shut automatically as the undercarriage was raised or lowered.

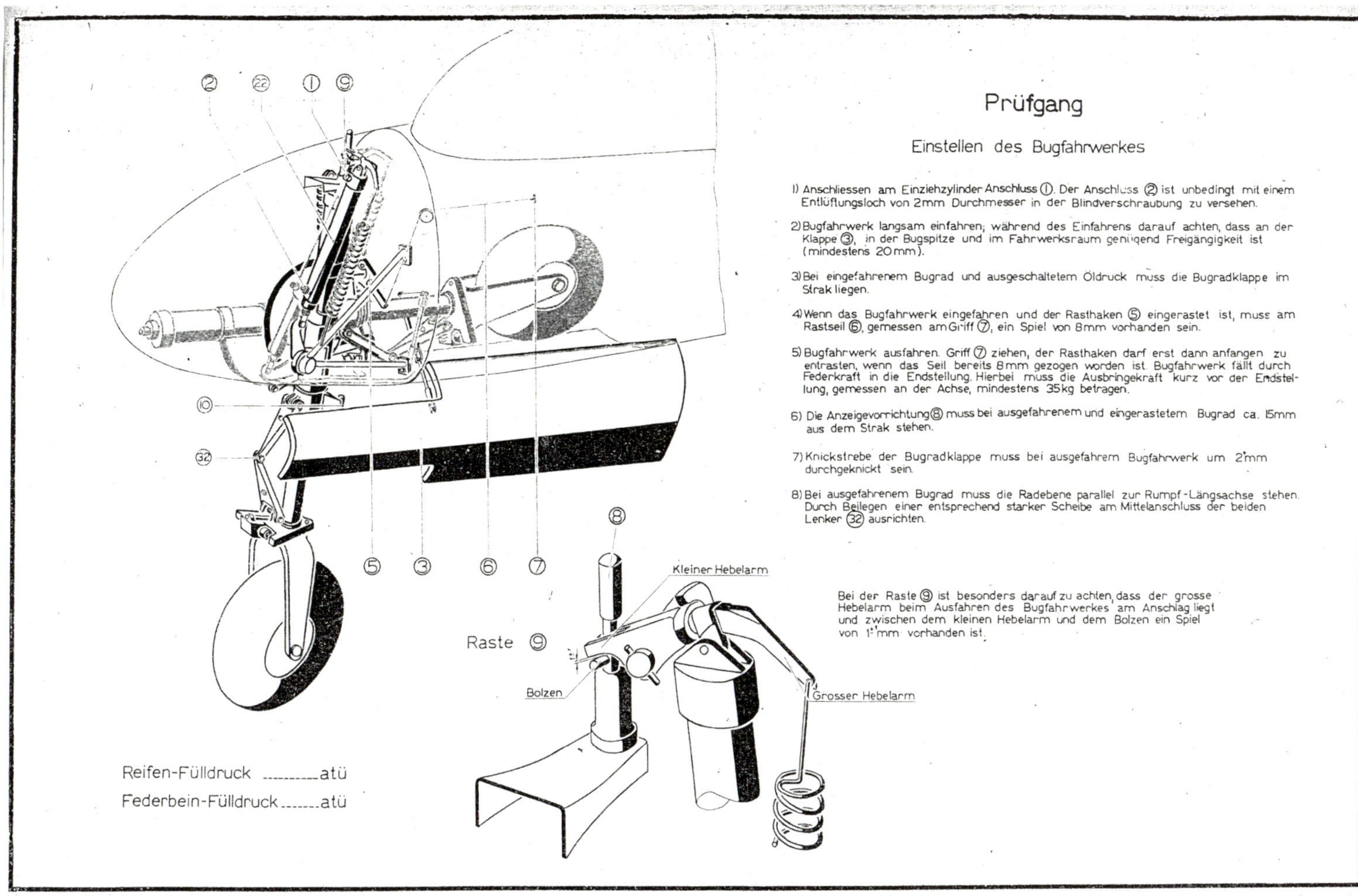

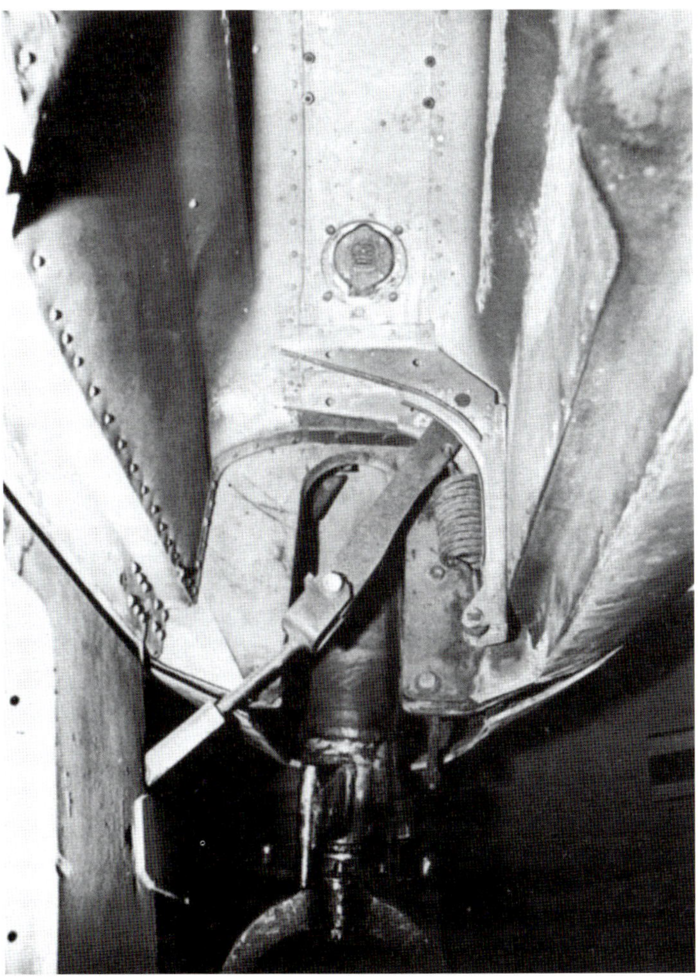

Close-up view of the nosewheel undercarriage bay looking towards the nose of the aircraft.

Nosewheel

General:

The main parts of the nosewheel were the wheel, shock absorber with wheel fork, retraction cylinder and lowering spring.

Wheel:

The size was 380 mm x 150 mm and there was no brake. The wheel fork could be turned left or right. There was space in the fuselage for a larger nosewheel, if necessary.

Shock absorber:

The oleo pneumatic shock absorber was made by VDM.

Nosewheel doors:

The stowage space for the nosewheel in the fuselage was covered by means of doors, which opened and shut automatically as the nosewheel was raised or lowered.

Hydraulic Installation

General:

The hydraulic system operated the undercarriage retraction, lowering of flaps and wheel brakes.

Undercarriage retraction mechanism:

The associated equipment comprised the hydraulic header tank, oil filter, hydraulic pump, automatic switch and pressure relief valve.

Oil was circulated by means of an engine-driven pump made by BAMAG, having a capacity of 11.8 ltrs per minute at 5,300 rpm through a filter and the automatic switch back to the header tank. When the automatic switch was depressed, the return flow of oil was prevented and it was led to the retraction cylinder of the undercarriage. At a pressure of 80 atü, the automatic switch cut out and the oil again returned to the tank. If the pressure rose above 80 atü without the switch cutting out, then the oil was returned to the tank via the pressure relief valve.

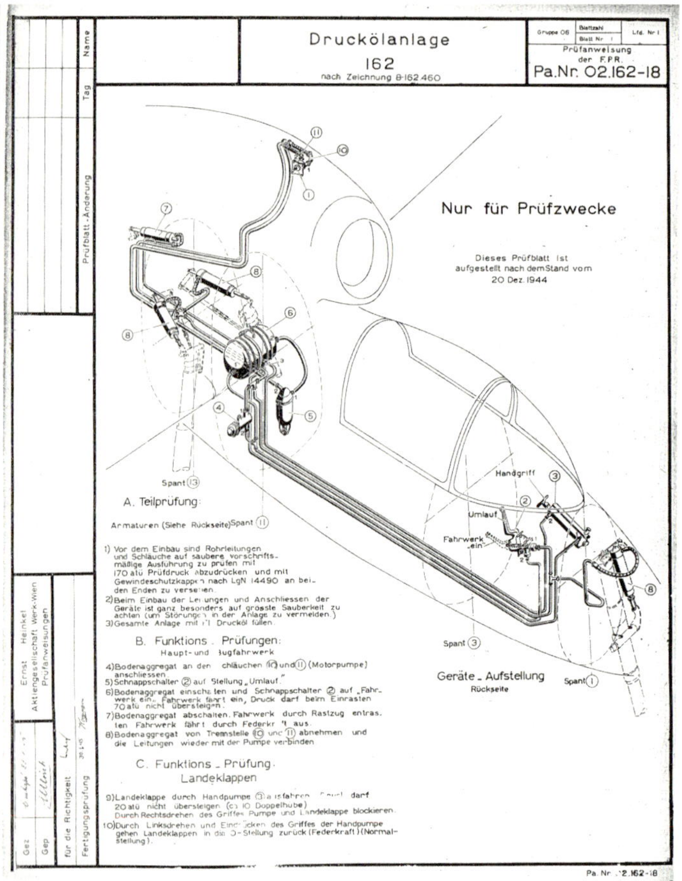

After unlocking, the undercarriage was lowered by its own weight and the power of the spring.

Landing flap operating installation:

The hydraulic oil came from the same tank. Pressure was built up by means of a hand pump having a capacity of 2.27 litres at double strokes per minute. The flaps were raised by means of a spring which was compressed whilst the flaps were being lowered.

Brake installation:

This was not connected to the main hydraulic installation. The brakes were operated by means of pumps attached to the rudder pedals. The brake fluid was stored in small tanks on the foot pumps.

BMW 003 E-1 Powerplant

The BMW 003 E-1 had a sea-level static thrust of 800 kg at 9500 rpm. At 11000 m and at a speed of 805 km/h, the thrust was 265 kg. The specific fuel consumption was high at 0.73 kg per hour per kg of thrust.

The jet unit was fitted above the fuselage on the upper surface of the wing. At the forward end it was attached by two vertical bolts and at the rear by one horizontal bolt. The front and rear cowlings were fixed to the power unit and were delivered with it; the centre cowling consisted of two large flaps which could be opened sideways and were normally held shut by a quick-release fastening.
If necessary, these flaps could be removed entirely. There was a detachable fillet between the jet unit and the wing.

With special lifting tackle, a quick powerplant change was possible by virtue of the fact that the engine could be suspended from two points and that all joins in the pipelines and leads were close together.

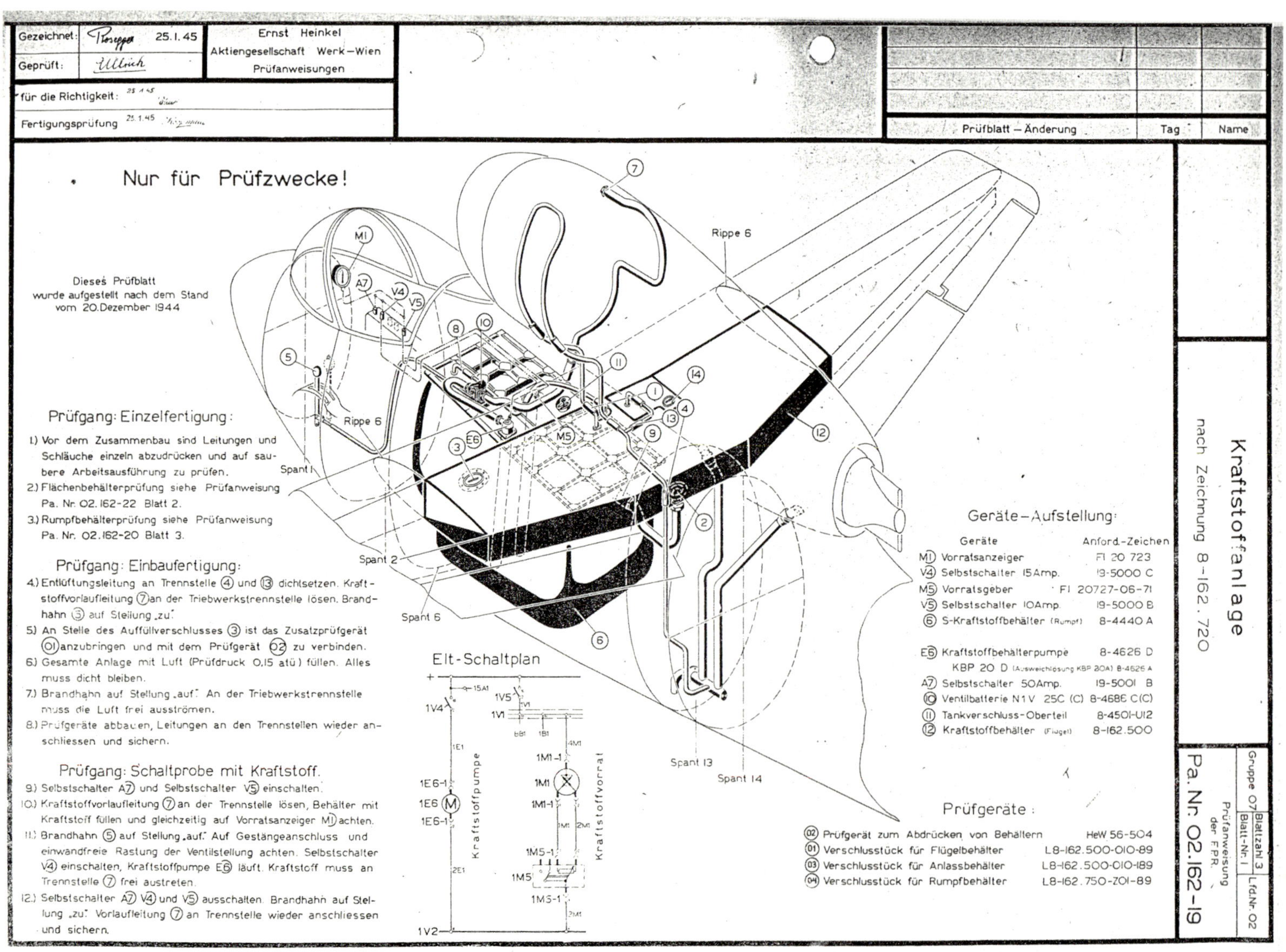

The following controls were fitted:

Throttle lever with switch for ignition and fuel injection
Clamp for throttle lever
Lever for fuel cock
(All above located on port-side fuselage wall)

Main electrical cut-out
Starter switch
Main switch for jet unit
Switch for tank pump

The jet unit was started by a Riedel two-stroke starter unit which was, in turn, started electrically by a switch on the starboard side of the cockpit. The ignition was switched on when a button on the throttle lever was pressed. Fuel was injected by means of an electrical injection pump.

Fuel tankage

In standard configuration, fuel was supplied from a single, flexible, self-sealing tank in the fuselage located behind the ammunition tanks to the rear of the pilot. This tank had a capacity of between 400-570 litres for normal flight, with an additional 127 litres for warming up, take-off and initial acceleration. For the maximum fuel load, the capacity of the fuel tank was increased to 763 litres (including the 127 litres allowance) and an additional 300-500 litres could be carried in the fuel-tight wing compartment.

Both the main tank and the specially prepared wing compartment were filled from a single point on the upper surface of the wing. Fuel was delivered to the jet unit from the fuselage tank, into which the wing tank fed, by an electric immersion pump via a fuel cock and filter.

The fuel lines between the wing and fuselage tank, as well as between fuselage tank and power unit, were pipes with 'muff' joints. There were electrical contents gauges. Fuel pressure was shown on a pneumatic indicator in the cockpit.

Cockpit

Entry and exit was through the hood, which was double-strengthened for very high speed operation, and which opened rearwards. It could be jettisoned in an emergency. The pilot had a catapult seat to which a parachute was attached. The seat was mounted in channel sections riveted to a bulkhead and ejected by means of an explosive cartridge which was fired by pulling a handle, with a safety catch to the right of the seat. Emergency oxygen equipment was stored in the seat cavity. A chain clipped to the airframe operated an oxygen cock to supply oxygen from a flat container in the parachute pack when the pilot was ejected. A small clip in the parachute harness prevented the harness release being pressed in until the clip was removed.

The seat was adjustable on the ground for the pilot's height. Control instruments were in the panel in front of the pilot. On the port side were the controls for the power unit, throttle, fuel cocks, undercarriage control lever, tailplane incidence, rudder trim, and, on a level with the instrument panel, the flap hand pump. On the starboard side were automatic switches for the electrical installation and FuG 25a and FuG 24 radio control, plus combined oxygen pressure and visual indicator, oxygen economiser, fixed signal pistol firing through the cockpit side and the main switch box. The pilot was protected by means of armour plates above the instrument panel and movable shutters.

The nosewheel cover was under the instrument panel and had a window in it as a visual 'nosewheel retracted' indicator. A further indicator took the form of a red-painted rod which projected about 7.5 cm forward.

Operating Instruments

The instrument panel was made of plywood and had two rows of instruments. The engine instruments consisted of fuel pressure gauge, oil pressure gauge, exhaust temperature indicator, indicator for thrust, and fuel contents gauge.

The flight instruments consisted of airspeed indicator, turn indicator and pitot head heating indicator, while navigation was controlled by a FK 38 magnetic compass.

The control column was short and had a Bf 109-type grip.

The rudder pedals hung on tubes which were hinged on the 12 mm armour plate forward of the gunsight. They were equipped with toe-operated brakes and were adjustable for length. Cables for the pedals ran back on either side of the pilot's seat, although to the rear the motion was conveyed by a rod. The elevators and ailerons were rod-operated.

Continued on page 92

Internal view of part of an incomplete metal wing fuel tank. Many problems were encountered with the fuel tanks due to leakage, causing fuel seepage into the cockpit. Special attention had to be given to seal the tanks with an appropriate sealant compound.

Right: Wartime photograph of a He 162 instrument panel, showing basic flight instruments and the window in the nosewheel leg fairing, which showed the pilot that the nosewheel had retracted.

Above and below: Two views of a restored cockpit of a He 162, showing the Bf 109 type-grip on a shortened control column.

Two views of the ejector seat as installed in the He 162. The safety catch is visible on the left-hand side of the seat frame, above the foot rest. In the photograph to lower right showing the rear of the seat, the hollow piston head with cartridge and firing pin is at the top of the cylinder. At the bottom of the cylinder is the cylinder head and plunger spring-loaded against gas pressure.

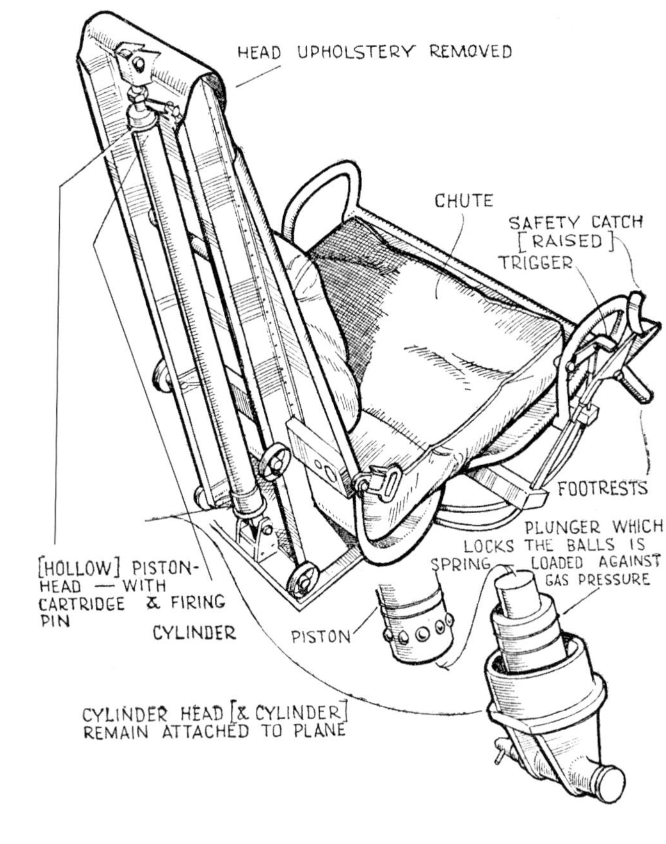

Allied drawing showing the components of the ejector seat.

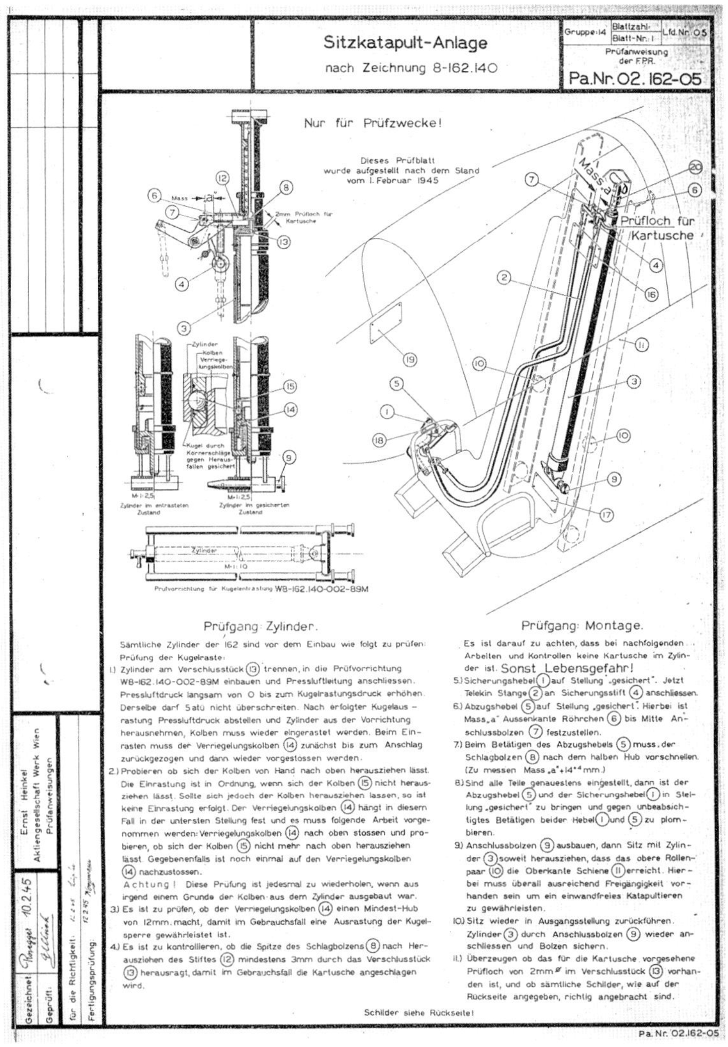

Sitzkatapult-Anlage
nach Zeichnung 8-162.140

Gruppe 14 | Blattzahl | Lfd.Nr. 05 | Blatt-Nr. 1
Prüfanweisung der F.P.R.
Pa.Nr. 02.162-05

Nur für Prüfzwecke!

Dieses Prüfblatt wurde aufgestellt nach dem Stand vom 1. Februar 1945

Prüfloch für Kartusche

Zylinder im entrasteten Zustand — Zylinder im gesicherten Zustand

Prüfvorrichtung für Kugelentrastung W8-162.140-002-89M

Prüfgang: Zylinder.

Sämtliche Zylinder der 162 sind vor dem Einbau wie folgt zu prüfen:
Prüfung der Kugelraste:

1.) Zylinder am Verschlusstück (13) trennen, in die Prüfvorrichtung W8-162.140-002-89M einbauen und Pressluftleitung anschliessen. Pressluftdruck langsam von 0 bis zum Kugelrastungsdruck erhöhen. Derselbe darf 5atü nicht überschreiten. Nach erfolgter Kugelausrastung Pressluftdruck abstellen und Zylinder aus der Vorrichtung herausnehmen, Kolben muss wieder eingerastet werden. Beim Einrasten muss der Verriegelungskolben (14) zunächst bis zum Anschlag zurückgezogen und dann wieder vorgestossen werden.
2.) Probieren ob sich der Kolben von Hand nach oben herausziehen lässt. Die Einrastung ist in Ordnung, wenn sich der Kolben (15) nicht herausziehen lässt. Sollte sich jedoch der Kolben herausziehen lassen, so ist keine Einrastung erfolgt. Der Verriegelungskolben (14) hängt in diesem Fall in der untersten Stellung fest und es muss folgende Arbeit vorgenommen werden: Verriegelungskolben (14) nach oben stossen und probieren, ob sich der Kolben (15) nicht mehr nach oben herausziehen lässt. Gegebenenfalls ist noch einmal auf den Verriegelungskolben (14) nachzustossen.
Achtung! Diese Prüfung ist jedesmal zu wiederholen, wenn aus irgend einem Grunde der Kolben aus dem Zylinder ausgebaut war.
3.) Es ist zu prüfen, ob der Verriegelungskolben (14) einen Mindest-Hub von 12mm. macht, damit im Gebrauchsfall eine Ausrastung der Kugelsperre gewährleistet ist.
4.) Es ist zu kontrollieren, ob die Spitze des Schlagbolzens (8) nach Herausziehen des Stiftes (12) mindestens 3mm durch das Verschlusstück (13) herausragt, damit im Gebrauchsfall die Kartusche angeschlagen wird.

Prüfgang: Montage.

Es ist darauf zu achten, dass bei nachfolgenden Arbeiten und Kontrollen keine Kartusche im Zylinder ist. Sonst Lebensgefahr!
5.) Sicherungshebel (1) auf Stellung „gesichert". Jetzt Telekin Stange (2) an Sicherungsstift (4) anschliessen.
6.) Abzugshebel (5) auf Stellung „gesichert". Hierbei ist Mass „a" Aussenkante Röhrchen (6) bis Mitte Anschlussbolzen (7) festzustellen.
7.) Beim Betätigen des Abzugshebels (5) muss der Schlagbolzen (8) nach dem halben Hub vorschnellen. (Zu messen Mass „a"+14+4 mm.)
8.) Sind alle Teile genauestens eingestellt, dann ist der Abzugshebel (5) und der Sicherungshebel (1) in Stellung „gesichert" zu bringen und gegen unbeabsichtigtes Betätigen beider Hebel (1) und (5) zu plombieren.
9.) Anschlussbolzen (9) ausbauen, dann Sitz mit Zylinder (3) soweit herausziehen, dass das obere Rollenpaar (10) die Oberkante Schiene (11) erreicht. Hierbei muss überall ausreichend Freigängigkeit vorhanden sein um ein einwandfreies Katapultieren zu gewährleisten.
10.) Sitz wieder in Ausgangsstellung zurückführen. Zylinder (3) durch Anschlussbolzen (9) wieder anschliessen und Bolzen sichern.
11.) Überzeugen ob das für die Kartusche vorgesehene Prüfloch von 2mm ø im Verschlusstück (13) vorhanden ist, und ob sämtliche Schilder, wie auf der Rückseite angegeben, richtig angebracht sind.

Schilder siehe Rückseite!

Ernst Heinkel Aktiengesellschaft Werk Wien Prüfanweisungen

Gezeichnet: 10.2.45 | Geprüft: | für die Richtigkeit: 12.2.45 | Fertigungsprüfung: 12.2.45

Pa. Nr. 02.162-05

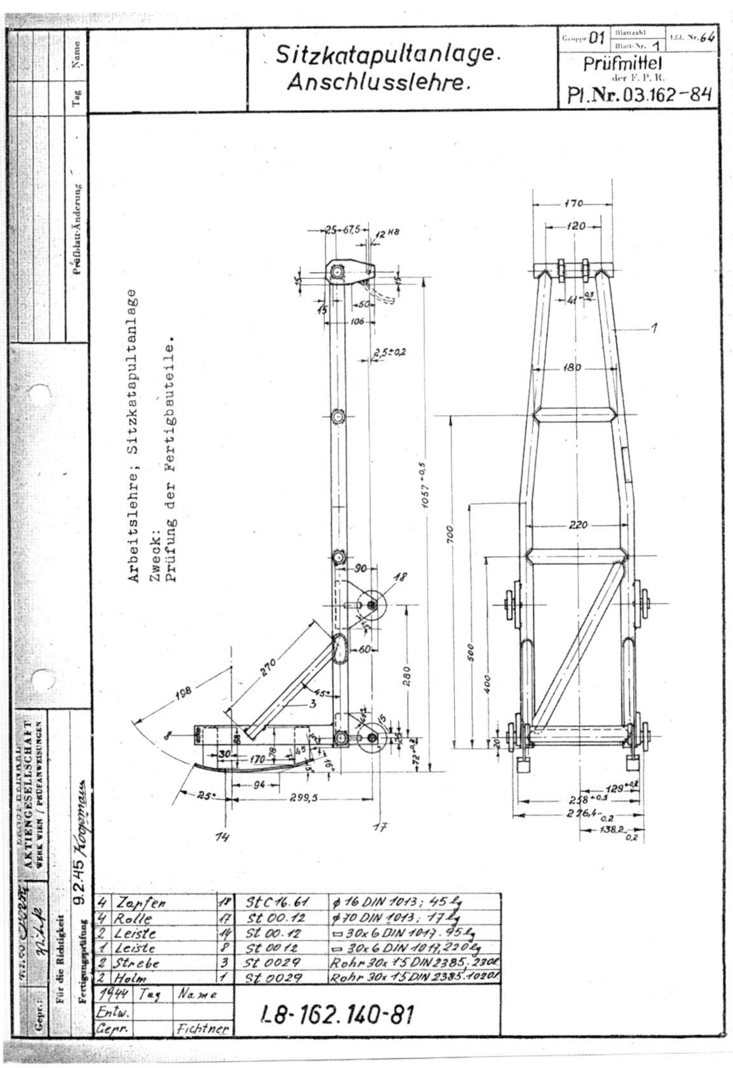

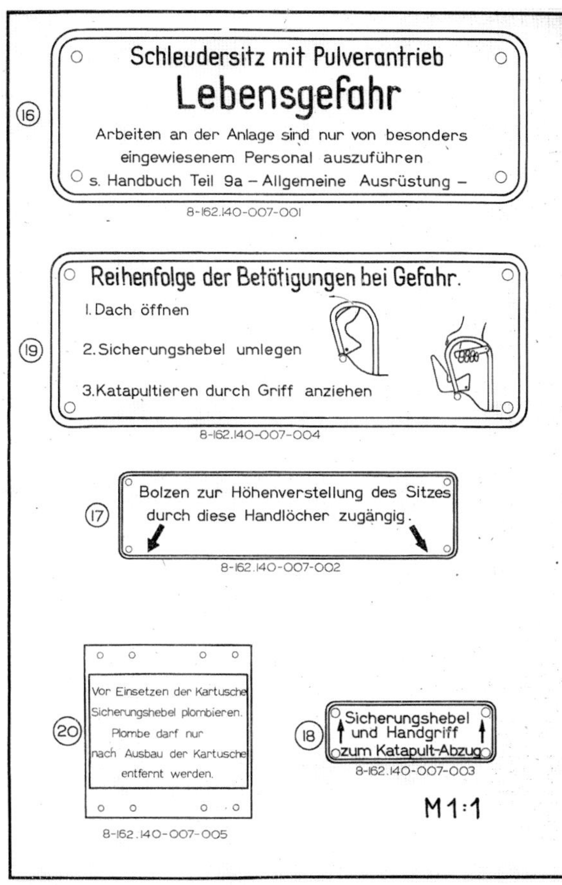

ABOVE: Instruction plates to be fixed at appropriate positions as per instructions provided in the 'Prüfmappe Flugzeug 162'. They were produced at 1:1 scale in the manual.

Safety Equipment

For high-altitude flight, oxygen equipment was located on the port side of the fuselage, with the indicator and pressure gauge in front of the pilot. Oxygen was supplied from a two-litre bottle. The shut-off valve could be operated in flight. The bottle was topped up from an external connection in the port gun compartment.

Communication Equipment

Apart from radio, communication could be made through light signals using a short-barrelled flare pistol. It was fired through an opening in the starboard fuselage wall near the pilot.

Radio equipment comprised FuG 24 (R/T and homing) and FuG 25a (IFF). The BG 25a and E24 receiver and automatic switch for the whole radio installation were on the right-hand side of the cockpit. The AFN2 indicator was on the pilot's instrument panel. The 'speak' button was on the control column. The U15 transformer and the ZVG5 homing equipment was located on the fuselage above the fuel tank. The D/F loop was on the power unit cowling.

The FuG 25a was fitted in the rear fuselage, the S24 transmitter and the AAG 24E aerial matching unit were *in* the starboard fin, while the receiver aerial was *on* the starboard fin. The AAG 25A aerial matching unit was *in* the port fin while the transmitter aerial was *on* the port fin.

Armament

Armament sets consisted of either 2 x 30 mm MK 108 cannon or 2 x MG 151/20 20 mm cannon. The guns were mounted low in the forward part of the fuselage, one on each side of the cockpit, with the mountings sufficiently far back to accommodate the long barrels of the MG 151/20s in the fuselage. If MK 108s were installed, blast tubes were attached to the muzzles.

Ammunition boxes fitted above the guns held 2 x 120 rounds for the MG 151/20s or 2 x 50 rounds for the MK 108s. Empty cases were ejected into the airstream.

The gun mountings were accessible for installation and removal of the guns was effected through large doors in the fuselage sides.

The standard gunsight was intended as the Revi 16 G, although the Revi 16 B was eventually accommodated. The gunsight was mounted behind the windscreen, immediately in front of the pilot.

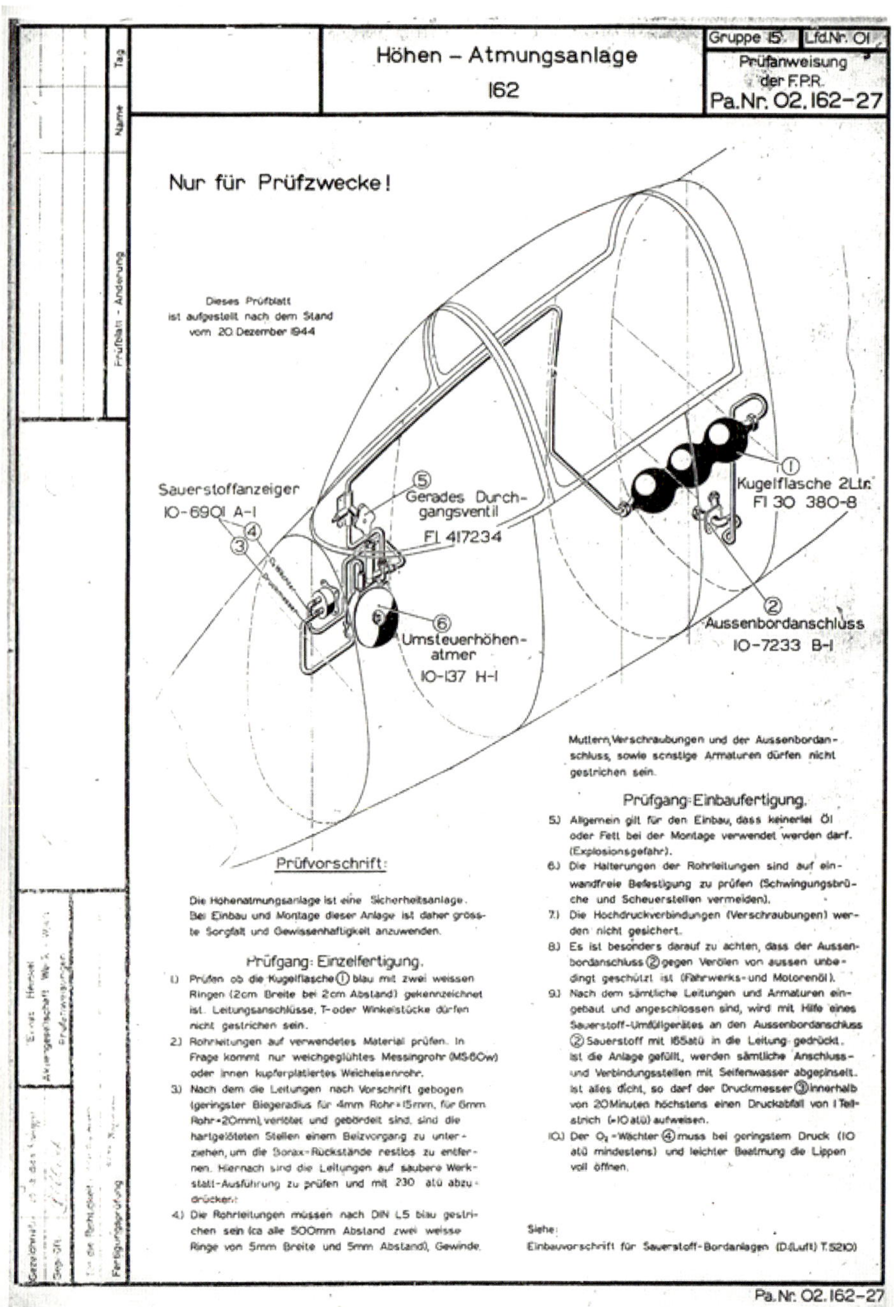

Höhen – Atmungsanlage 162

Gruppe 15 | Lfd.Nr. 01

Prüfanweisung der F.P.R.

Pa.Nr. 02.162–27

Nur für Prüfzwecke!

Dieses Prüfblatt ist aufgestellt nach dem Stand vom 20. Dezember 1944

Sauerstoffanzeiger 10-6901 A-1

(5) Gerades Durchgangsventil Fl 417234

(1) Kugelflasche 2Ltr. Fl 30 380-8

(6) Umsteuerhöhenatmer 10-137 H-1

(2) Aussenbordanschluss 10-7233 B-1

Prüfvorschrift:

Die Höhenatmungsanlage ist eine Sicherheitsanlage. Bei Einbau und Montage dieser Anlage ist daher grösste Sorgfalt und Gewissenhaftigkeit anzuwenden.

Prüfgang: Einzelfertigung.

1.) Prüfen ob die Kugelflasche (1) blau mit zwei weissen Ringen (2cm Breite bei 2cm Abstand) gekennzeichnet ist. Leitungsanschlüsse, T-oder Winkelstücke dürfen nicht gestrichen sein.

2.) Rohrleitungen auf verwendetes Material prüfen. In Frage kommt nur weichgeglühtes Messingrohr (MS-60w) oder innen kupferplattiertes Weicheisenrohr.

3.) Nach dem die Leitungen nach Vorschrift gebogen (geringster Biegeradius für 4mm Rohr = 15mm, für 6mm Rohr = 20mm), verlötet und gebördelt sind, sind die hartgelöteten Stellen einem Beizvorgang zu unterziehen, um die Borax-Rückstände restlos zu entfernen. Hiernach sind die Leitungen auf saubere Werkstatt-Ausführung zu prüfen und mit 230 atü abzudrücken.

4.) Die Rohrleitungen müssen nach DIN L5 blau gestrichen sein (ca alle 500mm Abstand zwei weisse Ringe von 5mm Breite und 5mm Abstand), Gewinde, Muttern, Verschraubungen und der Aussenbordanschluss, sowie sonstige Armaturen dürfen nicht gestrichen sein.

Prüfgang: Einbaufertigung.

5.) Allgemein gilt für den Einbau, dass keinerlei Öl oder Fett bei der Montage verwendet werden darf. (Explosionsgefahr).

6.) Die Halterungen der Rohrleitungen sind auf einwandfreie Befestigung zu prüfen (Schwingungsbrüche und Scheuerstellen vermeiden).

7.) Die Hochdruckverbindungen (Verschraubungen) werden nicht gesichert.

8.) Es ist besonders darauf zu achten, dass der Aussenbordanschluss (2) gegen Verölen von aussen unbedingt geschützt ist (Fahrwerks- und Motorenöl).

9.) Nach dem sämtliche Leitungen und Armaturen eingebaut und angeschlossen sind, wird mit Hilfe eines Sauerstoff-Umfüllgerätes an den Aussenbordanschluss (2) Sauerstoff mit 165atü in die Leitung gedrückt. Ist die Anlage gefüllt, werden sämtliche Anschluss- und Verbindungsstellen mit Seifenwasser abgepinselt. Ist alles dicht, so darf der Druckmesser (3) innerhalb von 20 Minuten höchstens einen Druckabfall von 1 Teilstrich (=10 atü) aufweisen.

10.) Der O_2-Wächter (4) muss bei geringstem Druck (10 atü mindestens) und leichter Beatmung die Lippen voll öffnen.

Siehe:
Einbauvorschrift für Sauerstoff-Bordanlagen (D.(Luft) T.5210)

Pa.Nr. 02.162–27

The oxygen regulator on the starboard side of the cockpit and, above right, the flare port tube.

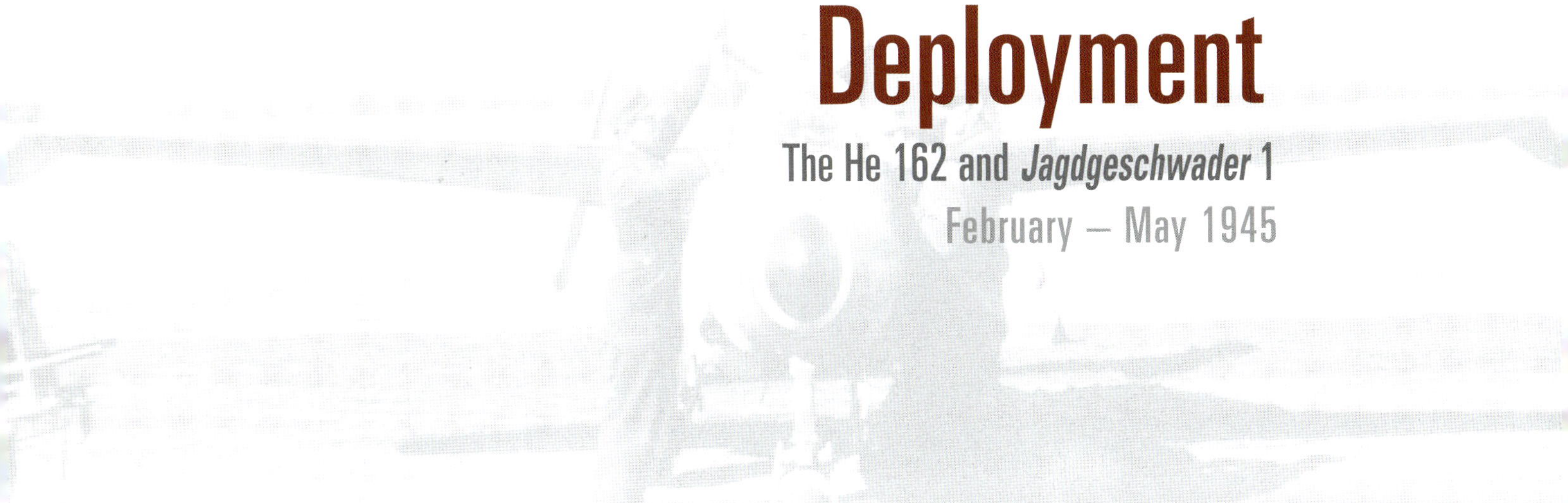

Deployment

The He 162 and *Jagdgeschwader* 1

February – May 1945

BY February 1945, the noise of guns rumbling on the Eastern Front was clearly audible at *Reichsmarschall* Göring's country residence on the Schorfheide, for by this time the Soviet winter offensive had formed a critical gap between the two German armies assigned to defend East Prussia. Increasingly desperate, Adolf Hitler could only bank on loyalty and tenacity. He therefore gave the task of defending East Prussia to *Reichsführer*-SS Heinrich Himmler, and his specially-created Army Group Vistula. But already, German troops had evacuated Tannenburg. With nothing to stop it, the Red Army had swept across the Oder and successfully established a bridgehead on the western bank. Its advance units were now only 400 km from Berlin.

Allied bombs continued to fall on the Reich; since the New Year, the US Eighth Air Force working in co-operation with RAF Bomber Command, which was now bombing regularly by day as well, had been systematically targeting the oil refineries. In attempting to intercept the American raids against industrial and fuel targets in northern and central Germany on the 14th, the *Luftwaffe* fighter force lost 107 pilots killed or missing with another 32 wounded. Tank and aircraft factories, benzol plants and the railway network – marshalling yards, repair shops, junctions, bridges – and also road traffic bottlenecks were subjected to ceaseless attacks by the US tactical air forces.

In the West, over 22 and 23 January alone, Allied aircraft destroyed 6,000 vehicles as von Rundstedt's battered armies retreated from the Ardennes.

For the *Jagdwaffe*, losses amongst the four *Jagdgeschwader* left for Reich defence following a massive transfer of units to the East, were rising to nearly 30 per cent of sorties flown, while victories gained amounted to less than 0.2 per cent of Allied strength. The existing resources were simply not enough, as is illustrated in a situation report issued by the OKL Operations Staff for 3 February 1945 following an attack by 937 USAAF bombers on the Tempelhof marshalling yards:

'During today's heavy air raid on Berlin, the *Reichsmarschall* asked the Chief of the Operations Staff why no German fighters were sent up. Owing to the difficulties on the Oder, OKL had ordered that all fighter formations, including those of *Luftflotte Reich*, be employed on the Eastern Front. These formations were engaged on bombing operations. When the enemy attack on Berlin commenced, JG 301 had already carried out one operation on the Oder Front and JG 300 was bombed-up and ready for a sortie. The Chief of the Operations Staff suggested to the *Reichsmarschall* that after the enemy bridgehead across the Oder had been eliminated, the fighter formations previously engaged in the *Reichsverteidigung* as well as further fighter *Geschwader* used to reinforce *Luftflotte* 6, be reassigned to the defence of the *Reichsverteidigung*. The *Reichsmarschall* agreed with this proposal. The Chief of Operations Staff will discuss this matter by telephone with the *Führer's Luftwaffe* adjutant.'

Such were the odds against the *Luftwaffe* by this stage that in reviewing German fighter response on 9 February, and following a raid by more than 1,200 Eighth Air Force heavy bombers on a range of oil and rail targets across central Germany, against which only 67 single-engine fighters were deployed, the Chief of the *Luftwaffe* Operations Staff lamented '...that the employment of such a small number of aircraft is purposeless and must be regarded as a mistake.'

It was against a background of almost total Allied air superiority over its homeland and with its supply infrastructure severely interdicted that, in an extraordinary paradox, the *Luftwaffe* took delivery of its third – and final – jet-powered aircraft (the Me 262 and Ar 234 having been operational since the autumn of 1944).

As has been related in Chapter Two, the first *Luftwaffe* officer to fly the He 162 was the new *General der Jagdflieger*, *Oberst* Gordon Gollob, who did so in a move which echoed that of his predecessor, *Generalleutnant* Adolf Galland when he had flown an Me 262 prototype just under two years earlier in May 1943. But while Galland had been rapturous in his enthusiasm for Messerschmitt's revolutionary new jet, Gollob had expressed only cautious optimism about Heinkel's little cheap-to-build fighter.

But even before Gollob flew the *Volksjäger* in February 1945, moves had been made to form a dedicated *Luftwaffe* detachment with which to test the aircraft for operational use. The precise details of this detachment's formation remain unclear, but it is believed that an order was issued by Galland – who was imminently to be sacked from his post as commander of the *Jagdwaffe* by Göring – at the end of 1944 to establish a unit of *Gruppe* strength comprising three *Staffeln*, each of 12 aircraft, together with a *Gruppenstab* of four aircraft. The unit was to be known as '*Erprobungskommando* 162' and it was envisaged that it would be in existence for only some six months, after which the He 162 was foreseen to have entered full operational service. Galland instructed that the *Kommando* was to be based in the vicinity of the *E-Stelle* Rechlin – to which it would report, probably at Lärz airfield. The *E-Stelle* Rechlin was notified formally of this proposal on 1 January 1945, with the official establishment order being issued to *Oberst* Petersen, the *Kommandeur der Erprobungsstellen*, on 9 January – by which stage, however, Galland had been usurped as *General der Jagdflieger*.[1]

Hauptmann Horst Geyer, formerly commander of E.Kdo 25, was assigned by Rechlin to oversee the establishment of E.Kdo 162, but it is believed he worked with an *Oberst* von Helden, who, on 14 January, was ordered to assign a group of 26 men, led by an NCO, for training and familiarisation to EHAG Rostock-Marienehe. This group arrived at Rostock on 15 January, with a further four men arriving on the 18th.[2]

After that, events moved quickly: on 23 January, the *Reichsmarschall* officially announced Galland's dismissal and *Oberst* Gollob as his successor. Gollob immediately revoked the instruction to form an '*Erprobungskommando*' and instead assigned the planned unit a new designation, I./JG 200, as well as a *Stabsstaffel*, to reflect its *Gruppe* status, with 40 aircraft and with ground crews being sourced from the embryonic II./JG 7 (which was actually slated for equipping on the Me 262 under the command of the sacked Galland!).[3]

Within days, it seems, and as mentioned in the preceding chapter, plans for the formation of I./JG 200 were abandoned in favour of yet another designation, 'I./JG 80.' This plan itself did not last long, however, when on 29 January, Gollob ordered the I./JG 80 designation to be

Once Oberst Gordon Gollob (left) had replaced Generalleutnant Adolf Galland as General der Jagdflieger on 23 January 1945, he set about undertaking a reorganisation of the Luftwaffe's jet fighter units, including the proposed establishment of new units and the conversion of existing units on to the He 162. Gollob is seen here in September 1944 during a visit to JG 400 at Brandis at which time he was serving as the 'Typenbegleiter' for the Me 163 rocket interceptor. To the right is Hauptmann Robert Olejnik, a former Gruppenkommandeur of II. and III./JG 1, who later flew the Me 163 with Erprobungskommando 16 and 1./JG 400. His earlier II./JG 1 would eventually convert to the He 162.

Fw 190 A-8s of I./JG 1, probably of 2.Staffel, on the mud-caked airfield at Greifswald in November 1944. By early 1945, JG 1 had fought a long, hard war, conducting aerial operations with the Bf 109 and Fw 190 over Normandy and in the Reichsverteidigung, during which it suffered heavy attrition. The unit also took part in the infamous Operation Bodenplatte, after which its combat effectiveness never fully recovered. The aircraft seen here carry the Geschwader's red defence of the Reich fuselage band and the aircraft to centre left has the unusual feature of extended spiral markings on its propeller blades. The semi-tracked Kettenkrad has just towed up a mobile starter cart.

Hauptmann Horst Geyer, formerly commander of the air weapons testing and evaluation unit, Erprobungskommando 25, was assigned by the Erprobungsstelle Rechlin to monitor progress and work on the He 162 during the early stages of its development. He was assigned by Galland, during his last days as General der Jagdflieger, to set up a new 'Erprobungskommando 162' to assess the Volksjäger and is believed to have flown the aircraft on one occasion in Wien in early February 1945.

cancelled and, as he decreed: '... in its place convert I./JG 1 to the He 162. The creation of new *Gruppen* for the He 162 must be set aside due to the considerable production loss in Fw 190s. Therefore it should be possible to convert Fw 190 units to the He 162.'[4]

The *Geschwader* emblem of JG 1 'Oesau'.

Gollob swiftly instructed his staff officers to repeal the formation of I./JG 80 and to arrange the conversion of the whole of JG 1, one of the *Luftwaffe's* oldest fighter units, to the He 162, beginning with I. *Gruppe* which was to include three *Staffeln*, each of twelve aircraft together with a four-aircraft *Gruppenstab* and the same signals and technical back-up as an Me 262 *Gruppe*. The unit was to form-up at Parchim.

JG 1 was to be placed under the tactical control of *Luftflotte Reich* and the implementation was to be carried out in consultation with the *Stab General der Jagdflieger*.[5]

Like so many of the *Luftwaffe's* fighter units based in the West in late 1944, all three *Gruppen* of *Jagdgeschwader* I had been depleted in strength ever since the intense air combat over France in the summer of 1944.

Lt. Hans Berger, of 3./JG 1 offers a revealing insight into conditions within I./JG 1 at this time: 'At the end of 1944, I returned to I./JG 1, the unit which I had left following the fighting over the Invasion Front. By now, everything had changed. Most of my comrades had disappeared; some had been posted to other units, but the great majority had been killed in action. I could feel that the mood had changed. The fact that we, the officers, were quartered separately from the soldiers had become normal since our departure from Schiphol, and certainly did nothing to strengthen the link between the men in the *Staffel*; but now a deep fracture appeared in the Officer Corps itself... While, in peacetime, to become an officer required high quality attributes, in time of war several brave soldiers were promoted to higher rank due only to their courage in battle. So, several fighter *Gruppen* were placed under the command of good pilots, but very poor leaders. These men were often unable to psychologically handle the extremely difficult situation in which we fought, to assume their authority in a skilful manner, and above all, to help their men avoid unnecessary losses in action. On the contrary, often chasing after awards and promotion, the only important thing for them was to claim the maximum of victories, even if the cost was high in wingmen or inexperienced pilots. Discovering their incapacity in their role, these wartime officers often used a blind authoritarianism, and nearly all of them were alcoholics. I saw them nearly daily drinking in officers' messes. Some drank an entire bottle of Cognac every day. When some young *Leutnante*, such as me, refused to drink in such an ill-considered manner, I had to withstand constant taunting. Many of the German aces, about whom one hears so much, were not, in truth, such good examples of leadership.'[6]

JG 1 had taken part in the massed, surprise fighter attack launched by the *Luftwaffe* against Allied tactical airfields across France, Belgium and Holland on the morning of 1 January 1945, known under the code name, 'Operation *Bodenplatte*'. Amidst conditions of great secrecy, the *Luftwaffe* committed 41 *Gruppen* to the operation drawn from ten *Jagdgeschwader* and one *Schlachtgeschwader* as well as Me 262 and Ar 234 jet bombers from KG 51 and KG 76 – in all a force of more than 900 aircraft. It was a bold and monumental effort for the *Luftwaffe* to mount such an operation at this stage of the war.

Since May 1944, the *Kommodore* of JG 1 had been the illustrious veteran fighter ace, *Oberst* Herbert Ihlefeld, who had first seen action as an NCO pilot during the Spanish Civil War. By the end of the fighting over the English Channel in the summer of 1940 where he served as *Kommandeur* of I./JG 77, Ihlefeld had achieved 25 victories. He went on to become the fifth fighter pilot to reach 100 kills and would lead a number of *Jagdgeschwader* – JG 52, JG 103, JGr 25, JG 11 and JG 1. He was awarded the *Ritterkreuz* in September 1940, following his 21st victory and then the *Eichenlaube* on 27 June 1941 in recognition of 40 victories. He would later become the ninth recipient of the coveted *Schwertern* to the *Ritterkreuz* on 24 April 1942 upon scoring 101 victories. He would end the war having flown more than 1,000 combat missions and having been accredited with 130 victories, including some 15 four-engined bombers.[7] He joined JG 1 from a staff post with a *Jagddivision*.

Oberstleutnant Herbert Ihlefeld, a veteran fighter ace and Ritterkreuzträger credited with 130 victories achieved over more than 1,000 combat missions, was appointed Kommodore of Jagdgeschwader 1 in May 1944 and would oversee the unit's operations until the end of the war. By all accounts a demanding commander, his involvement with the He 162, however, seems to have been mainly administrative.

The Focke-Wulf Fw 190-equipped I./JG 1, comprising 1., 2., 3. and 4. *Staffeln*, was under the command of *Hauptmann* Georg Hackbarth, who had previously served as *Kommandeur* of I./JG 108 and I./JG 103 before being appointed as Ia in the *Stab* I./JG 1 in October 1944. He had been ill during the first week of December and had rejoined the *Gruppe* at Twente from Greifswald, where the unit had been re-equipping and retraining for operations in the defence of the Reich. For the New Year's Day strike, the *Gruppe* had been assigned to attack Maldegem airfield, 15 km east of Bruges in north-west Belgium. The airfield was home to the three Spitfire squadrons of No. 135 Wing of the British 2nd Tactical Air Force.

Shortly after 0800 hrs on New Year's morning, the 22 Fw 190s of I./JG 1 took off from their airfield at Twente on a course that would take them, guided by a Ju 88 pathfinder, via Den Haag on the Dutch coast, south to Bruges where the unit would turn east to strike at Maldegem. Unfortunately, several of the *Gruppe's* pilots strayed from their course, including Hackbarth, and ended up attacking II. *Gruppe's* target at St. Denis Westrem, where they clashed with a number of Spitfires flown by Polish pilots. By the time I./JG 1 returned to Twente mid-morning, it had claimed 30 Spitfires destroyed on the ground with a further two claimed shot down during the operation. However, the *Gruppe* and *Stab* had suffered thirteen Fw 190s and nine pilots lost, representing an unacceptably high 56 per cent loss in aircraft and a 39 per cent loss in pilots.[8] Among the losses was Georg Hackbarth whose Fw 190 had been shot down by one of the Polish Spitfires over St. Denis. His body was recovered from the wreckage of his aircraft, which had crashed into a local florist's shop.

A seasonal greeting presented to Karl-Emil Demuth, Staffelkapitän of 3./JG 1, by his men for the wartime Christmas of 1944. The card bears the hand-drawn emblems of the winged '1' of JG 1, the demon emerging from the clouds of I./JG 1 and the Lion of Danzig of 3./JG 1.

The *Gruppe* emblem of I./JG 1.

Despite inflicting considerable damage at Maldegem (I./JG 1's claims were quite accurate), *Obstlt.* Ihlefeld was furious with Hackbarth for what he perceived to be navigational confusion over the target area and blamed him, to a great extent, for the high number of casualties.[9]

Leutnant Karl-Emil Demuth, although Staffelkapitän of 3./JG 1, effectively led the I. Gruppe of JG 1 from a tactical point of view. He is credited with 16 aerial victories and would lead I./JG 1 throughout its period of operations with the He 162.

Upon Hackbarth's death, the responsibility for leading the *Gruppe* in the air fell to the highly experienced *Staffelkapitän* of 3./JG 1, *Leutnant* Karl-Emil Demuth. Karl-Emil Demuth was born on 22 December 1916 in Affaltrach, near Heilbronn. His *Luftwaffe* service had commenced on 29 October 1935 when he joined 4./*Flieger Ersatz Abteilung* 15 in Neubiberg for basic service training, followed by preliminary flight training with *Flieger-ausbildungsregiment* 23 at Kaufbeuren from 1 November 1938 to 3 September 1939. After a short spell at the *Fluglehrerschule der Luftwaffe* at Brandenburg-Briest to the end of November 1939, Demuth returned to Kaufbeuren as a flying instructor where he remained until 18 August 1942. He then served for a year with the *Luftkriegsschule* 2 at Werder/Havel, during which time he spent six weeks on the Eastern Front flying supply missions in an old Junkers W 34 from Warsaw to Dnjepropetrowsk, as well as embarking upon supply missions to the trapped German forces at Stalingrad. He subsequently joined 2./JG 102 with whom he learned to fly the Bf 109. Via a short spell at 3./*Jagdgruppe West* at Casseau in France, Demuth joined 3./JG 1 on 19 August 1943 at Deelen and remained with that unit from that point on. Karl-Emil Demuth was credited with 16 aerial victories, all scored in the West and all thought to be over the USAAF.[10]

However on 3 January, *Major* Günther Capito, a former bomber pilot, who, in the meanwhile had been assigned to take over I./JG 1, arrived at Twente. He recalled: 'During the night of 3-4 January, following a bad train journey, I presented myself to *Oberstleutnant* Ihlefeld. He appointed me to the leadership of I. *Gruppe*, but immediately stated one condition; in the air, the chief of 3. *Staffel*, *Lt.* Demuth, was to lead the *Gruppe*. This restriction to my duties was made with the best of intentions for I lacked the experience of both being a fighter pilot as well as l eading a *Gruppe*. During the early days, fresh young pilots arrived from the training schools, together with new machines. Around 11 January, we were back up to strength again, although experience was cruelly lacking. We carried out our first formation flight under Demuth's direction.'[11]

The Lion of Danzig emblem of 3./JG 1. This emblem was carried on at least two He 162s of the *Staffel*.

In the East, the German military situation was deteriorating fast. The Russians could field 6,000,000 men and women, the *Reich* half that number. In material terms, German strength was about one-fifth of that of the Soviets. The Red Army was fighting in the streets of Budapest and it had reopened its offensive in central Poland. In all, 180 Soviet divisions were committed to the drive west; the Germans could only call upon 75. On the northern front, Army Group North, and other forces, had been isolated in Kurland since mid-October 1944 and it would be Kurland which would be JG 1's new theatre of operations. As Capito remembered: 'On the 12th, following the Russian offensive and the establishment of the bridgehead at Baranow, we were ordered to leave for the East. The *Kommodore* left the same evening to discuss matters with his superiors. We were due to leave on the morning of the 14th, but an intense fog enveloped the region so that a take-off with 'green' pilots was too dangerous. A message arrived; a large formation of enemy aircraft was reported over the North Sea.'

In Ihlefeld's absence, Capito had to deal with the threat, but the weather was against him. Ordering virtually the entire *Gruppe* into the air resulted in dire consequences, as the young, inexperienced fighter pilots tried to fly their way through the fog, in either an attempt to locate the enemy or to make emergency landings. No contact was made with the enemy bomber formation on the first attempt and after a mere 15 minutes in the air, I./JG 1 landed, scattered at airfields all over northern Germany. Worse still, some of the Focke-Wulfs had been bounced by RAF Spitfires and at least two pilots were lost, including one flying one of the new, and much-vaunted, 'long-nosed' Fw 190 D-9s.

Upon his return, Ihlefeld, once again, was furious with his subordinate officer. Capito remembered: 'Ihlefeld threatened me with arrest and court-martial. I avoided having to present myself before him on the airfield at Königsberg due to a transfer which had been arranged for me three days before. The threats were dropped and I learned later that the I. *Gruppe* pilots were able to reassemble on 15 January at Werneuchen, from where they reached their destination.'

Eventually, on Tuesday, 16 January 1945, two trains left Holland to head east carrying the ground crews of I./JG 1, and loaded with the necessary support equipment required for use at the unit's new base on the Eastern Front. One of the trains was diverted to Heiligenbeil, where pilots who had earlier evacuated Jürgenfelde were awaited. Heiligenbeil was reached at 1600 hrs on 22 January. Shortly after, a new transfer order arrived because the Russians continued to break through. At Heiligenbeil large numbers of refugees streamed westwards, trying to stay ahead of the Red Army which was rolling up everything before it. Four field kitchens belonging to I. *Gruppe* arrived in the nick of time. On 24 January, a move by rail to Königsberg was possible, but two days later the train had to be abandoned, and some personnel managed to reach an airfield near Neukuhren. At minus 22 degrees, the weather was bitter.

On 30 January, fresh information arrived to the effect that the Russians were barely 20 km away. After further moves, at 2230 hrs on 4 February the column, numbering 65 wagons laden with I./JG 1's personnel and equipment, finally arrived at Rahmel airfield, near Danzig, where it was once again at the disposal of the *Gruppenkommandeur* and the flying personnel. The men were not to know that a further transfer order awaited them the following day. But what happened to JG 1 was just one example of what was happening across the ever-shrinking German-held territory. Nearly every unit moving from west to east encountered similar difficulties.

The worries of the pilots moving east were of a completely different order. Their duties were to escort maritime convoys in the Baltic Sea, the only hope for troops and civilians encircled in the Kurland pocket. These pilots knew that they were up against not just Russian tanks, but also anti-aircraft batteries.

After its disastrous departure from the West in mid-January, I. *Gruppe* could muster only ten pilots. The first five arrived at Jürgenfelde four days later under *Oblt.* Demuth; the rest, led by *Lt.* Luepke, arrived the following day. On 20 January, operations began for these ten pilots when they had to 'clear' the airspace around Insterburg. Two pilots went missing following an engagement with Russian fighters. Jürgenfelde soon had to be evacuated in the face of the advancing Soviets and a move to Gutenfelde followed on 23 January, then Neukuhren on 26 January, Heiligenbeil later on 26 January and Danzig on 2 February. These continuing changes of base left little time for combat operations which should have taken the form of ground-attack sorties and escort to transport aircraft. On 30 January, *Oblt.* Demuth recorded his last victory, a Yak-9.

'Missions on the Eastern Front were difficult to fly because of weather conditions more than enemy opposition,' Demuth recalled. 'Snow covered everything and the mist was always so intense that it was almost impossible to find something on the ground to help orientation. My experience in blind-flying – experience that I gained on the Stalingrad front two years earlier as a *Transportflieger* evacuating wounded soldiers – was very precious to everyone. As a consequence of these chaotic operations in the East in January-February 1945, I nearly lost eight mechanics from my *Gruppe*. Indeed, when the greatest part of our ground personnel evacuated with trucks towards the west, we eight pilots, with our best ground crews, stayed on at Heiligenbeil in order to get our last eight Fw 190s serviceable. We could already hear the sounds of battle – explosions, approaching Russian tanks and so on – when we were advised by radio that no more Ju 52s would land at Heiligenbeil to pick up our mechanics. On 2 February, just after having been ordered to evacuate towards Danzig, I ordered the First Aid boxes and radios removed from all the Fw 190s so as to accommodate one mechanic in each fuselage behind the cockpit. I gave orders to my pilots to avoid combat and we took off. After a short flight, we landed without problem on the icy strip at Danzig. This way, our ground crew escaped capture by the Russians.'

On Tuesday, 6 February, while Demuth and his weary men were at Garz on the Island of Usedom, in Berlin, no less a figure than *Reichsmarschall* Hermann Göring gave his authorisation to *Luftflotte* 6 to move I./JG 1 west, to Parchim, 70 km south of Rostock, in northern central Germany '... for training and re-equipment with the He 162.'[12] It was further ordered that any of the *Gruppe's* 23 Fw 190 A-8s and A-9s, together with a small number of F-3s, which 'became surplus' were to be used to replenish II./JG 1 which would continue to conduct operations against Soviet troop concentrations. I. *Gruppe* was to stage from Garz via Anklam and Neubrandenburg and was to arrange movement as soon as possible.[13]

The order to transfer there and meet with engineers and technicians from EHAG Rostock reached Demuth the following day.[14] On the 8th, I./JG 1 handed over its aircraft to II. *Gruppe* and departed Usedom in a convoy of 65 vehicles, reaching Parchim at 0200 hrs on the 9th having managed to evade bombing attacks along the way.

Parchim would be home to I./JG 1 for the next two months, where – in the absence of any fully completed He 162s – it would receive theoretical training on the aircraft from technicians and test pilots from EHAG *Nord*. Eventually the *Gruppe* would be joined by the *Geschwaderstab*, while 4./JG 1, under *Leutnant* Gerhard Hanf, was disbanded and its pilots distributed among the other three *Staffeln*.[15]

Following his test flight in a He 162 at Schwechat on the 11th, *Oberst* Gollob stated his plans for the deployment of the *Volksjäger*:

> Trials with series type at Rechlin from March 1945.
> The first operational aircraft to be available from mid-April 1945.
> The first operational *Gruppe* to be ready from mid-May 1945, with commencement of pilot and ground crew training from the beginning of March 1945.

Furthermore, two '*Auffangstaffeln*' ('collection squadrons') would be assigned to accept and collect aircraft arriving off the production lines in Wien, Marienehe and Bernburg. In this regard, it was planned that 2./JG 1 would eventually transfer to Wien, while 3./JG 1 would transfer to Marienehe and Bernburg. Additionally, Gollob wanted one *Staffel* from II./JG 1 to be sent to Wien at the end of February. Until that time, the technical personnel from the allocated *Staffel* were to be instructed by technical personnel from EHAG using the prototypes for instruction so that the unit would be ready to take over the new aircraft when they were delivered. Gollob believed that it was important that personnel from this *Gruppe* should be included as part of the test programme in order for them to obtain a good understanding of the machine well in advance and so a mass transition to the He 162 would be facilitated.[16] By the 12th, I./JG 1 had commenced its familiarisation on the He 162 with ground-training for both pilots and ground crews under the supervision of *Major* Richter and three engineers from *E-Stelle* Rechlin.[17]

Meanwhile, on 14 February 1945, the Me 163 testing and evaluation unit, *Erprobungskommando* 16, was disbanded at Brandis and a small number of its pilots, including *Leutnant* August Hachtel and *Oberfeldwebel* Friedrich Oeltjen, received orders to report to the EHAG works at Wien-Heidfeld where they would form the leadership of the first *Auffangstaffel* and they too would undergo familiarisation on the He 162.[18]

Hachtel and Oeltjen were extremely experienced airmen. August Hachtel was born on 6 March 1916 in Stuttgart. He had joined the *Luftwaffe* in November 1935 and on completion of pilot training in August 1939 was posted to the Stuka unit, 7./St.G 51 (later 4./St.G 1). Apart from a brief spell with St.G 3 in 1940, he remained with 4./St.G 1 until November 1942. A very accomplished NCO ground-attack pilot, he was credited with destruction of 32 enemy tanks, and shipping totalling 32,000 tons. By the autumn of 1942 he had flown 500 sorties over Russia. He was awarded the *Ritterkreuz* on 6 January 1942 (having also received the *Ehrenpokal* from Göring in September 1941 and the *Deutsches Kreuz* the following month). From November 1942 until April 1944 he served as a flying instructor with the *Ergänzungsstaffel* St.G 1 and 2./St.G 103 during which time he was promoted to *Leutnant* in August 1943. He was then posted to E.Kdo 16 at Bad Zwischenahn in April 1944 where he was involved in trials using the Me 163 rocket-powered interceptor. In December 1944 he carried out experiments with the SG 500 '*Jägerfaust*' 30 mm automatic upward-firing weapon, but suffered severe back injuries and concussion on 24 December 1944 when the SG 500 installation in the Me 163 BV 45 in which he was flying, fired prematurely. The shock from the muzzles of the barrels shattered the aircraft's canopy and Hachtel received a strong blow to his head. He managed to land the rocket fighter while still dazed and with the sun in his eyes, but the aircraft was 40 per cent damaged.

Friedrich Oeltjen was born on 7 April 1913 in Astederfeld, Oldenburg. He started his flying career in 1937 at Darmstadt flying transport gliders. A year later he underwent training at the A/B flying school in Magdeburg and in 1939 he was posted to JG 54. From 1941 to 1943 he served as an instructor at the *Jagdfliegerschule* at Zerbst, afterwards returning to JG 54. In September 1943 he was posted to E.Kdo 16 and remained with that unit until it was disbanded. Awarded the Iron Cross First Class and *Frontflug-Spange* in Silver, he made a total of 58 sharp take-offs in the Me 163 B, but did not fly any operational sorties.[19]

The decision to send Hachtel and Oeltjen to Wien may have been linked to Gollob's orders in early February to the effect that the Me 163-equipped I. and II./JG 400 were to re-equip with the He 162 'later'.[20] This seems to have been a revision of his directive of 30 January, in which it was stated that JG 400 was to retain the Me 163 and then make the transition to the planned Me 263.[21]

Either way, and as has been recounted in Chapter Two, Hachtel and his small group of nine pilots arrived at Heidfeld on 27 February expecting to take delivery of the first He 162s. They were to be disappointed. Despite the *Luftwaffe* men being 'incredibly impatient to take on the He 162s', things moved very slowly while EHAG continued to grapple with the prototype development programme.

Eventually, a solitary machine, the He 162 M19 (A-02) W.Nr. 220 002, VI+IL, was handed over to Hachtel, but the *Auffangstaffel* was ordered not to fly the aircraft over 500 km/h, above 3000 m and for longer than 15 minutes.

Meanwhile, on 24 February pilots from I./JG 1 climbed aboard a train at the Baltic seaside resort of Warnemünde, where they had been billeted in a hotel, and made the short journey to Rostock-Marienehe, running parallel along the Warnow estuary. The train pulled to a stop directly outside the bomb-damaged Heinkel works and the pilots disembarked. They were given a hurried briefing on the He 162 before being taken on a tour of the factory and then shown into the final assembly shop for the *Volksjäger*. *Oberleutnant* Wolfgang Wollenweber was a pilot with 3./JG 1 and recalled his first impressions of the new fighter:

'Truth be told, we knew precious little about the He 162 and were all naturally eager to get our first glimpse of this new secret weapon. One thing that confused us was the plethora of names that had been bestowed upon the machine. Because of its small size and limited weight, its manufacturers referred to it as the 'Spatz', or 'Sparrow'. Another of its titles, the 'Salamander', was derived from the codename of the original lightweight jet fighter programme that had resulted in the He 162. Not surprisingly, perhaps, the regime preferred the much more bombastic '*Volksjäger*'...

'When we entered the hangar-like shed we saw a row of machines all carefully covered by tarpaulins. The scene somehow reminded me of my childhood Christmases when, as a boy, I had gazed at my presents piled under the tree, wondering what was hidden underneath all that wrapping. When the tarpaulins were removed, our group's reactions were mixed. Faces at first reflected surprise, and then either enthusiasm or scepticism. My initial thought: if that clumsy, almost misshapen great lump of a turbine hadn't been stuck on top of its neat little fuselage, this could have been the most beautiful and elegant aircraft I had ever clapped eyes on. I was also hugely impressed by the manner in which the most basic of materials – due to the shortage of metals, the wings and part of the tail unit were, after all, simply made of glued wood – had been combined with such a revolutionary concept.'

Leutnant August Hachtel was a very experienced operational pilot who had flown hundreds of dive-bomber and ground-attack missions over the Russian Front with St.G 1 where he had been credited with 32 enemy tanks destroyed. He later flew the Me 163 rocket interceptor with Erprobungskommando 16, but was subsequently transferred to Wien where he was ordered to conduct an assessment of the He 162. He was to experience profound disappointment and frustration at what he discovered there.

Two days later, *Flugkapitän* Heinrich briefed the still sceptical Luftwaffe pilots and informed them that although there would be no two-seat trainer versions of the He 162, 'You will be given a set of pilot's handling notes. These you will have to read and learn thoroughly. You will also receive instructions on the ground. One of our works pilots will explain all the controls to you. He will show you how to handle the throttle, and point out which instruments you need to keep a special eye on. He'll talk you through what you have to do at take-off, after lift-off, while in the air, and when landing. When the He 162 is demonstrated, fix firmly in your minds the exact point of lift-off, watch how the pilot handles the approach when he comes back in, and note precisely where he touches down.'[22]

Yet with no aircraft delivered from Rostock, *Oblt.* Demuth left Parchim to journey south, to Wien, with another five pilots, this time drawn from 2. and 3./JG 1 and believed to have included *Fw.* Friedrich Enderle, *Uffz.* Josef Rieder and *Uffz.* Tautz.[23] Demuth's group arrived on 4 March to be

Oberfeldwebel Friedrich Oeltjen joined August Hachtel at Wien but little is known about his experiences with the He 162. He seems to have left Wien with Hachtel, probably equally disgruntled.

Hauptmann Paul-Heinrich Dähne, Ritterkreuzträger and Gruppenkommandeur of II./JG 1. Despite being a very experienced combat pilot, he would lose his life while flying the He 162.

greeted with the deflating news that they would have to share the only available aircraft, the M19, with Hachtel, although more machines were promised. Furthermore, there were strict airspeed and flight time restrictions imposed.[24]

Three days later, however, Hachtel telexed Gollob to advise that eight pilots had completed their conversion courses, but that no ground personnel had arrived for training. Nevertheless, despite Hachtel's best endeavours, a dark shadow fell across the detachment's activities: as has been recounted in Chapter Two, on 12 March *Fw.* Wanke miraculously escaped with his life when the engine of He 162 M8 W.Nr. 200 008, VI+IH, suddenly stopped functioning and the aircraft somersaulted just short of the runway and caught fire. The same day, during landing, *Fw.* Gleuwitz badly damaged the He 162 M26 220 009, VI+IS.

There was no point to Demuth staying in Wien. Before departing for Parchim, probably with a considerable feeling of spiritlessness, Demuth's detachment witnessed the death of one of their number when *Uffz.* Tautz of 2./JG 1 crashed on the runway in the M19 on the 14th, his aircraft somersaulting and bursting into flames. Tautz was thrown out of the cockpit and killed.

In the meantime, as planned, another group of pilots, this time from 3./JG 1, were despatched to Rostock-Marienehe in late March in the hope that they could familiarise themselves on the He 162. The *Luftwaffe* pilots were given the rare privilege of being booked into a luxury hotel in Warnemünde on the Baltic coast while awaiting the aircraft. Eventually, at the very end of the month, some of the pilots made their first flights of between 10 and 20 minutes duration. *Lt.* Hans Berger had joined 3./JG 1 from 4./JGr. West and was among the first to fly the *Volksjäger*; he recalled: 'We viewed this little aircraft, with its wooden wings and large turbine on its back behind the cockpit, with a degree of scepticism. Accustomed to the protection of the Fw 190's massive engine, we felt exposed and unprotected behind the thin leaf of the cockpit Plexiglas. Even more importantly, there were several weaknesses which caused us concern, such as the fragile join between the wings and the fuselage. In flight, you had to pilot it with an incredible sensitivity, because the aircraft reacted to every smallest touch on the stick; she was that soft. It was especially at low speeds that the aircraft became most dangerous for it skidded easily. In just a few days, three pilots, including *Uffz.* Friedrich Enderle, were killed just after take-off. *Fw.* Rolf Ackermann lost his life while landing. Once again, and even more so than in the past, the lack of training amongst the new pilots was evident. With a machine so sensitive, intuitive flying was vital.

Leutnant Hans Berger (right) of 3./JG 1: 'We viewed this little aircraft [the He 162]... with a degree of scepticism...' Berger is seen here with his mechanic on 6 March 1944 following combat with B-17s over Berlin during which he shot down one 'Viermot' but suffered severe damage to the rudder of his Fw 190 A-7.

'In order to start the engine, it was necessary to use an electric starter coupled to the turbine, by pressing on a red button. There was a loud noise often accompanied by a jet of small, spitting flames. But if the noise was loud outside the aircraft, one was aware of it only slightly in the cockpit, and even less so after take-off. You couldn't hear the slipstream, just as with a glider. The most impressive thing without doubt was the speed; 750... 800... 850... 900... km/ h. I remember several exciting flights where I reached nearly 1,000 km/h at low altitude over the sandy beaches above the island of Amrum. The short range was the only handicap; 35 to 40 minutes flying duration at high altitude and by drastic economy, you could stretch it to 50 minutes. If you encountered the enemy, the order was to attack from a more elevated position. We regretted the lack of opportunities of measuring our new aircraft against enemy fighters.'[25]

On 20 March 1945, OKL issued its plans for the overall conversion of JG 1 on to the He 162 A-2 as follows:

Stabsstaffel:	establishment of 16 He 162
I./JG 1:	establishment of 52 He 162
II./JG 1:	to convert to the He 162 from existing Fw 190 A-8/9, with establishment with 52 He 162
III./JG 1:	to convert to the He 162 from existing Bf 109 G-10/G-14 in April and May 1945, with establishment of 52 He 162

For the time being, II./JG 1 remained in Garz under the command of *Hauptmann* Paul-Heinrich Dähne, a native of Frankfurt/Oder, who had replaced *Major* Hermann Staiger as *Kommandeur* at the end of February. Dähne, known by his nickname of 'Sarotti', had accumulated 100 victories, achieved whilst serving with 2./JG 52 in Russia and then 12./JG 11 in the *Reichsverteidigung*. He had been awarded the *Ritterkreuz* on 6 April 1944 in recognition of his 74th victory, and by the war's end would be accredited with at least 98 victories scored over an operational career which involved some 600 missions.

Back in Wien, by 21 March, *Lt.* Hachtel, who remained distinctly unimpressed with the He 162 because of its limited endurance which he believed needed to be increased by at least 40 minutes, was becoming increasingly impatient with the lack of any progress – or aircraft, and had threatened to return to Berlin to advise the senior command of his annoyance. Carl Francke evidently dissuaded him however, and pursuaded him stay on a for a little while longer.[26] It is possible that Francke told Hachtel of the new delivery plan for the series aircraft, namely that the first five series machines would go to his *Auffangstaffel*, the following eight aircraft would be allocated to an *Erprobungs-kommando* at Lechfeld, with a further seven machines to another *Erprobungskommando* at Rechlin-Roggenthin.

On 26 March, however, orders were issued by the *Bauaufsicht Luft* (BAL) to the effect that all completed He 162s were to be used for test purposes only, thus confounding any imminent chance of relieving Hachtel's boredom and impatience. The same day, new orders were issued by OKL relocating the *Gruppen* of JG 1 in readiness for the first He 162s arriving off the production lines at Junkers Bernburg (23 March) and EHAG Oranienburg and Rostock (24 and 25 March respectively): *Stab* and I./JG 1 were to relocate to Köthen, II./JG 1 to Wien-Schwechat and III./JG 1 to Lüneburg.[27]

In accordance with this, a detachment of 15 pilots under *Oberleutnant* Wolfgang Wollenweber of 3./JG 1, which included *Lt.* Büttner, *Uffz.* Dobrath, *Uffz.* Hartung, Fw. Strauss, *Uffz.* Franz Mann and *Uffz.* Josef Rieder, together with Finner, Stenschke, Köttgen, Seeling, and Häusel, was ordered to transfer to Bernburg where it would take delivery of He 162s and then ferry them to Parchim.

Meanwhile, Wollenweber's detachment left Rostock and travelled through the night to Bernburg, 230 km away, in a small truck and two trailers in order to avoid enemy air attack. Each man carried only one item of baggage – all that was possible to accommodate behind the seat of a He 162. Wollenweber and his men arrived at the Bernburg works in the early hours of the morning. After 'hammering on the gates for

Unteroffizier Wolfgang Wollenweber waits for his Bf 110 to be bombed up while serving with 13.(Z)/JG 5 'Eismeer' in Norway in 1943. After flying as a Zerstörer pilot in the Far North, Wollenweber would be assigned for training on the Me 163 rocket interceptor and later the He 162.

some time' they were eventually let in by a blind, half-asleep civilian night watchman. At daylight the next morning, the Luftwaffe pilots made their own tour of the works but found the assembly halls locked. Then, over breakfast, an engineer broke the news to them that no Volksjäger were ready for them and that it would be some time before they would be.

As if conditions were not bad enough, at midday an RAF Hawker Tempest fighter made a strafing run over the flight control building, but the airfeld Flak gunners did not seem capable of hitting it.

On the morning of the 26th, Dipl-Ing. Pankratz arrived at Bernburg from the *Erprobungsstelle* at Rechlin bringing orders for Wollenweber to transfer no fewer than fifteen He 162s, not to Parchim, but to Lechfeld, making an interim stop at Unterschlauersbach. Wollenweber recalled: '

Dumbfounded, I asked Pankratz how on earth we were supposed to fly 15 machines to Bavaria with just ten pilots. He could do no more than shrug helplessly, but he did say that we would be getting two of the works' own test pilots, *Oberfeldwebel* Strauss and *Feldwebel* Seeling. He also gave me a code number that would enable me to make priority phone calls in the case of dire emergencies. I immediately gave this a try and asked to be put through to the OKL in Berlin, hoping that they could shed some light on this now totally different situation. Amazingly, I was connected within seconds and a voice on the other end of the line announced itself to be an *Oberst* Eschenauer. When I expressed my misgivings about our new orders, explaining that not one of us had yet flown the He 162, that we didn't know the airfield at Unterschlauersbach and that, even if we did manage by some miracle to land safely at Lechfeld, there was still the problem of how we were to get back to our unit at Parchim, I was totally unprepared for the violent reaction my words provoked. Eschenauer started ranting and raving down the phone at the top of his voice. The tongue lashing I was getting seemed never ending, but he did eventually run out of steam and concluded by yelling that if I didn't follow the flight orders to the letter, immediate action would be taken and I would find myself facing a drumhead court-martial.'[28]

Notwithstanding this, at Lechfeld, Wollenweber was to report to a newly-formed '*Einsatzerprobungs-kommando He 162*' which was supposedly being organised under the command of *Oberstleutnant* Heinz Bär. In reality, Bär, one of the *Jagdwaffe's* most experienced and accomplished combat pilots who had been appointed commander of the Me 262 training unit, III./EJG 2 in mid-February, had essentially become 'overseer' at Lechfeld with umbrella responsibility for a range of tactical and technical training. Quite frankly, the Me 262 was his priority – the He 162 was not. It is unlikely that Bär took little more than a passing – and at most, curious – interest in the He 162. In any case, it seems Wollenweber never reached Lechfeld and remained in Bernburg until 11 April. A small number of his pilots, however, did manage to get there on 31 March routing in an aircraft via Unterschlauersbach.

On 27 March, OKL and the *General der Jagdflieger* optimistically forecast that 2./JG 1 would receive 18 He 162s, based on the projected deliveries from Junkers with a further seven machines expected to arrive from *Languste* (see Chapter Two). The following day, Hachtel received a telex informing him that He 162s were to be accepted from EHAG only if the BMW engines had been converted to accept J2 fuel. Hachtel was also told to prepare seven aircraft – as and when they became available – for transfer to Lechfeld for flight-testing, presumably by Wollenweber's expected detachment.

By the 30th however, no aircraft had been delivered to either Lechfeld or the *E-Stelle* Rechlin which was also awaiting them. At Bernburg, Wollenweber and his pilots were still kicking their heels: '...there was still no sign of the 15 machines we were supposed to ferry down to Lechfeld. We were told that they were not yet ready to fly, although I was, in fact, later to discover that there were at this time 20 operational He 162s tucked away in the sheds which, for some reason or other, were to be kept out of our sight.'[29]

That day, Hachtel signalled Gollob that he was in a position to begin ferrying aircraft from Schwechat to Lechfeld 'in a few days'. According to Hachtel, '...the pilots need a few more practice take-offs before then. The pilots must return by aircraft.'

He added: 'I request immediate information.'[30] However, by the time the first He 162s did reach the *Luftwaffe* in the south, Hachtel was not at all impressed since performance was way below the widely promoted expectations. He had left Wien by 11 April and would play no further part in subsequent developments with the *Volksjäger*.

By this stage of the war, the air war in the skies over Germany had adopted a familiar, but grim and depressing, trend as the outnumbered *Jagdwaffe* fought – as best it could – to defend the Homeland against the formidable combined might of the USAAF Eighth and Fifteenth Air Forces as well as RAF Bomber Command. On 30 March, it was the turn of the north German ports – U-boat yards and oil storage tanks at Hamburg, Bremen, Wilhelmshaven and Farge were bombed by a colossal USAAF armada of 1,320 bombers, protected by 852 fighters. That day, in a reflection of the prevailing conditions, *Luftflotte Reich* issued orders to the effect that to maintain operational serviceability of its Me 262 units, '... no alterations in personnel to be made. No training for ground fighting or other duties to be carried out. No women to be employed.'

On 31 March, I./JG 1 received orders to prepare to transfer from Köthen to Leck airfield in far northern Germany, close to the Danish border, staging via Parchim and Ludwigslust.[31] The last day of March

He 162 A-1, W.Nr. 310 003, the third machine to be built by Junkers at Bernburg, seen parked in a wood-walled revetment at an unknown location. The aircraft appears factory-fresh and may well have been taken prior to, or immediately after, delivery to JG 1 since it is awaiting tactical markings.

This photograph is contentious: some sources claim that it shows a relatively rare He 162 A-1, fitted with 30 mm MK 108 cannon, and was among the first aircraft delivered to I./JG 1 at Parchim in March 1945; others that this is Bernburg-built W.Nr. 310 012, of the same Gruppe seen at Leck on 4 May 1945.

Ground crew almost dwarf the diminutive fuselage of a He 162 of 3./JG 1 under the spring sunshine at Ludwigslust in April 1945. The aircraft is adorned with the twin red arrows on either side of the nose and the black/white/red nose tip associated with such aircraft of JG 1 at this time. Visible through the open canopy, the BMW 003 appears to have a dual-coloured protection plate fitted to its intake.

1945 would see another major effort in the relentless Allied strategic bombing offensive. While the US Eighth Air Force struck at oil refineries at Zeitz and Bad Berka and other targets at Brandenburg, Gotha, Stendal, Salzwedel, Braunschweig and Halle, RAF Bomber Command aimed for the Blohm und Voss shipyards in Hamburg. A force of 469 Lancasters, Halifaxes and Mosquitoes arrived over a cloud-covered target area, but still bombed, inflicting considerable damage to the southern districts of the port city.

Finally, and despite the bombing, it seems, at this point He 162s began to get through to the *Gruppe* from the Junkers plant and the *Luftwaffe* pilots were able to take to the air. At just after 18.00 hrs at Bernburg, *Oblt.* Wollenweber was airborne in the unarmed He 162 W.Nr. 310 006 for his first 15 minute flight. Within moments, Wollenweber had reached 2,000 m, climbing at 700 km/h. He later recalled: 'I reversed course, went down low and thundered across the rooftops of Bernburg at 800 km/h. I would have given a lot to hear the comments of those pilots who had opted to go into town. They would doubtless be staring up at the machine flashing past above their heads, not having a clue who was piloting it. I was filled with elation. I would never have believed that the He 162 could be flown so easily, and at speeds that no enemy fighter could possibly match. With this little beauty we need no longer worry about what sort of opposition we were up against: be they Mustangs, Thunderbolts, Lightnings, Mosquitoes, Spitfires, Typhoons or Tempests, all they would see of us would be our backsides as we shot past them. And if we did run into trouble, we could always use our superior speed to climb or dive away.'[32]

Leutnant Gerhard Hanf (left) was an experienced fighter pilot who made the transition to the He 162. He found the handling of the Volksjäger to be generally good. He is seen here while with 9./JG 77 in Rumania having just scored his second victory – a P 38.

There was also activity at Parchim that evening when *Lt.* Berger flew He 162 'White 1' for a 12-minute flight between 1823-1835 hrs, while former transport pilot, *Hauptmann* Heinz Künnecke, who was, ostensibly at least, the *Kapitän* of 1./JG 1, made two airfield circuit flights of 15 and 6 minutes duration respectively in an unknown He 162 during the late afternoon. Künnecke had transitioned from flying transporters with 4./TG 30 to fighters, serving with I./JG 103 and 15./EJG 1 before moving to JG 1.[33]

Leutnant Gerhard Hanf also flew an unidentified He 162 for the first time the same evening. Hanf had served with 4./JG 1 since that *Staffel* had evolved from 9./JG 77 in August 1944. Born on 16 May 1924, Hanf had joined the *Luftwaffe* in December 1941, graduating from the *Luftkriegschule* 5 in Breslau to train as a fighter pilot with 2./JG 102, *Jagdfliegerschule* 2 and 2./Erg.JGr. Ost between 1942-43. In June 1943 he was promoted to *Leutnant* and assigned to III./JG 77 which was then operating over Italy and Rumania where he flew the Bf 109 G-6 and claimed two victories. In August 1944, he acted as *Staffelführer* and was awarded the *Frontflug-Spange* in Silver in September. Fighting over Normandy and the Western Front with JG 1 in Fw 190s from June 1944, he claimed two P-47s shot down and also accounted for a tank destroyed in France in early August.[34]

Hanf recalled his first flight in the *Volksjäger*: 'On 31 March 1945, I took off at 1830 hrs on my first flight from the airfield at Parchim. Before take-off I was informed that performance was not to exceed 600 km/h, that there was a danger of a break-up in the air. Not surprisingly, that was not much of a recommendation for the aircraft. Of course, prior to take-off, I had no idea of the performance of the engine. Fully loaded the machine took a long time to take-off, but finally at 180 km/h it lifted off. The take-off distance was at least double that of an Fw 190. In flight, the machine demonstrated good characteristics, and the rudders reacted very precisely to pressure; however the controls were very basic. Following a quick half hour, my first flight ended without incident.'

On Sunday, 1 April 1945, the day EHAG's Wien plants and offices were evacuated in the face of the approaching Soviet advance from the East and elements moved off to Salzburg and Klagenfurt for safety, four He 162s were handed over to 2./JG 1 and by 7 April, two more aircraft had been delivered to the unit. Of all these aircraft, just 2-3 were reported serviceable, however, by mid-April. But II./JG 1 still had no He 162s at its disposal.

Also on 1 April, three of *Oblt.* Wollenweber's Bernburg detachment managed to secure aircraft and took off from the Junkers plant en route to Lechfeld via Unterschlauersbach with *Lt.* Büttner piloting He 162 W.Nr. 310 006, *Fw.* Strauss in He 162 W.Nr. 310 002 and *Uffz.* Dobrath in He 162 W.Nr. 310 018. The success or failure of these flights is not known, but *Uffz.* Dobrath was not able to land at Unterschlauersbach because the airfield had fallen to the Americans. He was forced to make an emergency landing east of Nürnberg, but eventually managed to return to Bernburg.[35]

The same day, Lt. Hanf flew a 10-minute test flight in an unknown He 162 over Parchim.[36]

On 3 April *Leutnant* Rudolf Schmitt of 1./JG 1 made a 20-minute training flight in He 162 'White 1' at Parchim in the early morning. Schmitt, who was known within JG 1 by the nickname '*Toni-Toni*' on account of the two 't's in his name, had joined the *Luftwaffe* at 18 years of age as a *Fahnenjunker* at *Luftkriegschule* 2 at Berlin-Gatow in August 1943. He was moved to the *Flugzeugführerschule* C 6 at Kolberg where he remained until May 1944 when he transferred to 2./JG 107 in Hungary until September. Then followed a spell with 5. and 6./JG 108 at Wiener-Neustadt until 16 February 1945 when he was posted to 1./JG 1.[37]

Comparatively, the factories were turning out quite satisfactory numbers of Me 262s: 120 machines had been delivered to the various jet units during March, with 89 going to JG 7, the main fighter

Geschwader operating in northern and central Germany and defending the route to Berlin – but it was a paltry amount compared to Allied resources. Furthermore, the first seeds of decay in any form of coherent fighter defence leadership were being sown. Command was already fragmented and competitive. In one quarter, from the headquarters of the IX.(J) *Fliegerkorps* at Treuenbrietzen, the former bomber commander, *Generalmajor* Dietrich Peltz, was consolidating his position as commander of all of the defunct bomber units now struggling to familiarise themselves with the Me 262 fighter, directing these units in the aerial defence of parts of Holland and Denmark, as well as Austria and Bohemia-Moravia. Peltz's attitude at this time is made clear from an intercepted radio message dated 3 April:

'Peltz... reports work on many airfields not being carried out with necessary energy. Half of the working day of 12 hours is wasted as a result of Allied air raids. Work is to be started before first light, any rest to be taken during main raid period and work resumed at night. Divisional commanders to report if this arrangement not practical or if repair of runways and tracks takes too long. Unit commanders to report to the Division or to Peltz personally if work is not carried out by the station commander in the spirit of this order.'

Over the next three days, the pilots of JG 1 pressed on – in generally small measure (by 12 April, I./JG 1 reported no more than 16 He 162s on strength) – with their familiarisation process at Parchim. The number of He 162s on JG 1's strength continued to grow – though slowly. While some pilots continued to make ferry flights from the EHAG plants, others carried out assessment and familiarisation flights, sometimes in small formations. Progressively, they began to understand their new aircraft and learned to appreciate it despite a few early teething problems. On the 4th, *Hptm.* Künnecke was in the air in 'White 1' shortly after dawn at 0655 hrs for just eight minutes, while *Lt.* Hans Berger followed in He 162 'White 2' for eight minutes at 0725 hrs.[38] During the afternoon, *Uffz.* Helmut Riehl of 2./JG 1 made two seven-minute training flights in 'White 1' over Parchim in the early afternoon. Riehl had flown Fw 190s with 2. *Staffel* since early 1944. He had been wounded in action, baled out and survived and had lodged claims against two B-17s.[39]

During the afternoon, *Lt.* Schmitt, of 2./JG 1, ferried He 162 W.Nr. 120 013 from Ludwigslust – known to He 162 pilots as 'Lulu' – (1745 hrs), to Parchim (1755 hrs).[40]

Fhj.Fw. Günther Kirchner undertook his first flights in the Heinkel fighter when he made three conversion flights during the fading evening light in 'White 3' between 1936-1943 hrs, 1948-1955 hrs and 2000-2004 hrs. Kirchner was a veteran of 5./JG 1, but had been wounded in action on 11 January 1944 when he had claimed two B-17s shot down during a USAAF raid over central Germany. Following recovery, he spent some time as an instructor with *Jagdgruppe West* in the summer of 1944 before transferring to I./JG 1 in mid-February 1945.[41]

Early on the morning of the 5th, at 0449 hrs, *Lt.* Berger flew He 162 'White 5' over Parchim on a 12 minute flight. Later that day, commencing at 1818 hrs, he flew 'White 3' twice – on each occasion for a duration of six minutes. *Hptm.* Künnecke took off in 'White 2' at 0704 hrs, remaining airborne for 11 minutes, while *Fhj.Fw.* Kirchner ferried the newly completed W.Nr. 120 028 from Ludwigslust (1840) to Parchim (1850) that evening.[42]

The following morning, *Lt.* Berger continued flying in 'White 2', making the first of two flights from Parchim at 0704 hrs for 14 minutes. The trend for early morning and evening training flights was broken when *Lt.* Adalbert Schlarb made three brief circuit flights in He 162 '2' (probably 'White 2') over Parchim between midday and 1225 hrs.[43] Berger made his second flight between 1759 and 1822 hrs, followed by *Oblt.* Wollenweber who flew He 162 W.Nr. 310 078 over Bernburg airfield for 10 minutes, taking off at 1825 hrs.[44]

Uffz. Alvo von Alvensleben, of 1./JG 1 also trained on the *Volksjäger* and remembered: 'When the engine was started up, an unusually loud noise came from the turbine. The aircraft, small and light, with a huge engine on its back, made such a din rolling on the runway that one was relieved when the aircraft lifted off. The wheels left the ground at a speed of 220 km/h. Acceleration was good and a normal runway sufficed. In flight, the aircraft was stable and quiet. It responded easily to the controls. In general, training speeds were between 500 and 700 km/h. In the dive, according to factory information, we could reach the speed of sound. As for myself, I was able to reach 1,000 km/h once. We did not have the opportunity to try aerobatics with it though. Lacking experience on the type, and having doubts as to the solidity of the undercarriage, I always touched down as gently as possible. After a very short flight, it would land, and once again the noise became appalling. I flew the aircraft on ten occasions.'[45]

The 6 April also brought losses: some sources state that *Uffz.* Helmut Rechenbach of 2./JG 1 crashed and was killed during a He 162 ferry flight but the reasons remain unknown.[46] It is further believed that *Lt.* Finner, *Fw.* Seeling, *Fw.* Häusel and *Uffz.* Dobrath, all from JG 1 took off in He 162s from the north on a ferry flight to Lechfeld. They never reached their destination and their fates remain unknown.[47]

Next day, *Hptm.* Künnecke made an unusually long flight over Parchim in He 162 'White 1' lasting for 40 minutes mid-morning.[48] This was a timely flight, for that very day the US Eighth Air Force despatched a formation of 1,261 heavy bombers to attack jet airfields and marshalling yards across northern and central Germany, including the airfield at Parchim. The airfield was left heavily cratered and the runway became unusable, and so that night all effort was made to conduct repairs ready for a transfer to Ludwigslust at the soonest moment in order to continue with training.[49]

It seems Rudolf Schmitt was lucky enough to escape the raid since he is recorded as ferrying He 162 W.Nr. 120 068 from EHAG Rostock-Marienehe to Ludwigslust that afternoon between 1500-1530 hrs.[50]

That evening of the 7th, a 'Secret' teleprint signal was issued by OKL amending a previous order of 26 March, and ordering on the grounds of a 'conversion', the following transfers[51]:

Stab JG 1 to transfer from Garz to Ludwigslust
I./JG 1 from Parchim to Ludwigslust
II./JG 1 from Garz to Warnemünde

Leutnant Gerhard Stiemer, who had shot down a B-17 and a P-51 while flying with 3./JG 1, but who had experienced emergency landings in Fw 190s twice in December 1944, remembered: 'On 8 April 1945, *Lt.* Köttgen and I picked

Unteroffizier Helmut Rechenbach of 2./JG 1 was killed when he crashed in his He 162 during a ferry flight in April 1945.

Leutnant Adalbert Schlarb of 4./JG 1, seen here, first left in the front row, at Greifswald in November 1944, would make the transition to the He 162 and flew the aircraft on several occasions. However, he crash-landed on 30 April 1945. Third from left in the front row is Unteroffizier Helmut Rechenbach of 2./JG 1, and at centre of the back row, Unteroffizier Anton Riemer of I. Gruppe, both of whom experienced crashes in the He 162, Rechenbach's being fatal.

Following the Allied bombing of Parchim in early April 1945, I./JG 1 relocated briefly to Ludwigslust, where conditions were more primitive, with no concrete runways. In an almost peaceful scene (bearing in mind the constant threat of Allied 'Jabos' at this time), pilots and ground crew relax in the sun around three of the unit's He 162s – including 'White 21' in the foreground, which is a different aircraft to the '21' seen in the series of photographs of the JG 1 'line-up' at Leck, JG 1's base after Ludwigslust.

Left: An enlarged view of 'White 21' at Ludwigslust, showing ground crew communicating with the pilot of the aircraft in the cockpit, the starter cart in position and what appears to be a cloud of efflux at the rear of the BMW 003, suggesting possible preparations for take-off.

up two 162s in Marienehe. Before take-off we learned that Parchim had been badly attacked and, due to damage on the runway, it would not be possible to land there. We had received enough fuel for only 30 minutes flying time and flew in the afternoon to Ludwigslust. Over Parchim we saw the destruction on the airfield and the runway. We returned to Parchim during the evening in a lorry.' [52]

In fact, II./JG 1 had already begun preparations for its move to Warnemünde from where it would embark on its conversion to the He 162 at nearby Rostock-Marienehe. On 5 April, 8./JG 1 had been disbanded and its pilots and Fw 190 A-8s assigned to a *Schlachtgeschwader*.

With the skeletal backdrop of a ruined hangar, pilots of 3./JG 1 gather on the airfield at Parchim shortly after it was bombed by the USAAF on 8 April 1945. Second from left is Feldwebel Rolf Ackermann who would fly the He 162 on a number of occasions and who would be killed in the process.

The *Staffelkapitän* of 8./JG 1, *Hauptmann* Wolfgang Ludewig, was reassigned to take command of 7./JG 1, whose *Kapitän*, *Leutnant* Günther Heckmann, had transferred to 10./JG 7 in March. This left the following command structure for II. *Gruppe* at the time of its transfer:

Kommandeur:	*Hauptmann* Paul-Heinrich Dähne
5. *Staffel*:	No commander since the death of *Lt*. Hubert Swoboda on 11 March 1945
6. *Staffel*:	No commander since previous *Kapitän*, *Oblt*. Fritz Wegener, transferred to JG 7 in March.
7. *Staffel*:	*Hauptmann* Wolfgang Ludewig

Those pilots of II./JG 1 who transferred to Warnemünde by rail included *Ofhr*. Feldt, *Fw*. Willi Gehrlein, *Fw*. Josef Gold, *Fw*. Erwin Steeb, *Fw*. 'Sepp' Kreutz, *Fw*. Christlieb Fenger, *Uffz*. Brück, *Uffz*. Emmel, *Uffz*. Konrad Augner, *Uffz*. Willo Widnmann and *Uffz*. Wilhelm Harder.

When the men of II./JG 1 arrived at Rostock-Marienehe on 11 April 1945 they were greeted by Carl Francke and other EHAG technical personnel, designers and engineers in a short welcoming ceremony.[53]

Uffz. Konrad Augner of 8./JG 1 recalled II. *Gruppe's* initial experiences with the He 162: 'The officers were lodged in a hotel at Warnemünde, and the other pilots on the airfield. Each morning, as workers headed for work, a bus or wagon collected us and took us to Marienehe airfield. It was an unusual place with three runways set out in a triangle in the middle of marsh land. First of all, we received theoretical training on the aircraft we would be flying. Then we learned to start the engine, increase the throttle progressively, and move onto the runway. We sat in this aircraft as if in a glider. Starting the engine was a completely different procedure to that of the Bf 109. The revs had to be increased slowly, while holding the aircraft still with the help of the brakes, up to the moment when one decided that there was sufficient power for take-off. Releasing the brakes, take-off was achieved at around 180 km/h. After retracting the undercarriage, we also retracted the flaps. We climbed at around 450-500 km/h. This aircraft had a mortal fault; at less than 300 km/h you had to be on your guard against tight turns. In this case, the aileron constrained the circulation of air around the

Unteroffizier Wilhelm Harder joined II./JG 1 from 15./EJG 1 in late December 1944, but found learning to master the He 162 a tough challenge.

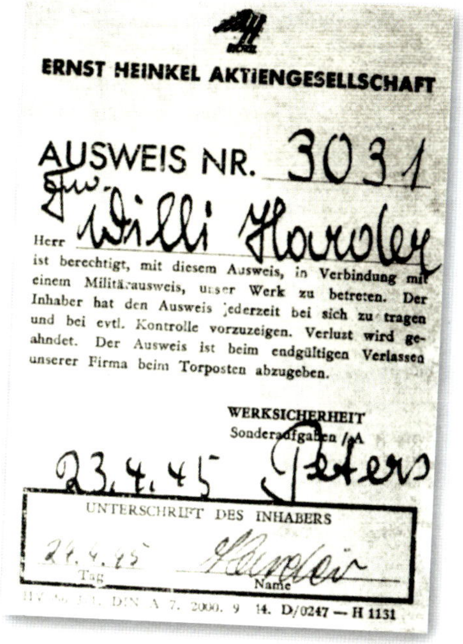

ERNST HEINKEL AKTIENGESELLSCHAFT

AUSWEIS NR. 3031

Herr Uffz. Willi Harder

ist berechtigt, mit diesem Ausweis, in Verbindung mit einem Militärausweis, unser Werk zu betreten. Der Inhaber hat den Ausweis jederzeit bei sich zu tragen und bei evtl. Kontrolle vorzuzeigen. Verlust wird geahndet. Der Ausweis ist beim endgültigen Verlassen unserer Firma beim Torposten abzugeben.

WERKSICHERHEIT
Sonderaufgaben /A

23.4.45 Peters

UNTERSCHRIFT DES INHABERS

24.4.45 Harder
Tag Name

DIN A 7. 2000. 9 44. D/0247 — H 1131

The pass issued by the Works Security Department at EHAG Rostock-Marienehe on 24 April 1945 to Unteroffizier Wilhelm Harder of II./JG 1 in order to allow him access to the plant to undertake training on the He 162.

Leutnant Gerhard Stiemer of 3./JG 1. He would fly the Volksjäger on a number of occasions but would suffer a crash-landing in the aircraft on 9 April 1945.

turbine, the He 162 skidded and fell like a leaf without any possibility of correcting it. Generally, we only flew for about 35 minutes at fairly low level. However we also made several flights at 8,000 metres. We would then be in the air for over an hour. The manoeuvrability of the aircraft was good. For landing, we approached the runway at about 250-260 km/h, and touched down at 200. It was a totally new flying sensation.'[54]

Another pilot to fly for the first time in a He 162 was *Unteroffizier* Wilhelm Harder who had joined II./JG 1 from 15./EJG 1 in late December 1944. He would make his first flight on the 24th. He recalled conditions at Marienehe: 'The single intact runway was barely 1000 m long and it was bordered to the east by the Breitling [a stretch of water at the mouth of the Warnow] and to the west by the Rostock-Warnemünde railway line. Of course the take-off distance for such a bird was a real tough one, especially due to the railway line with its obligatory telegraph cables.

'The He 162 was also so placed that the take-off was very close to the Breitling – *Herr* Francke took steps to sort that out. Initial acceleration was very sluggish. The thing rolled along the runway like a lit-up toy mouse and used up almost the length of the runway and at the end, literally had to pull up sharp so as to avoid the telegraph cables, and there it would hang in the air like a ripe plum… [Francke] landed so coolly as if it was a Klemm 35 and not a jet fighter, but in doing so he used the whole of the runway to the last metre.

'Over the next few days there was further instruction in technical aspects, servicing and eventually flight control, on a practical basis in the machine, and finally the engine was started.

'All this practising took up a lot of time – and eventually, after every run-up, the engine had to be left to cool down. During this period we were constantly given further instruction and advice. Now and again, the 'blow torch' didn't light up, and if it didn't start, we had to clean all the pipes out before we could start up again. Then the tail would have to be pushed down so that the fuel 'brew' would drain out and the rest of the interior workings had to be cleaned out with a rag and washed down, and then the bird would be ready for another take-off.

'Around 20 April 1945 training was put into practice. We each had to make a flight of about 20 minutes in the He 162. 'Around', because I believe I made my first flight on 24 April 1945 – and because I was then an *Unteroffizier* I was well back in the ranks.'[55]

For the period 8-11 April, I./JG 1 reported 13-16 He 162s on strength, of which 10-12 were flight-ready with 40 pilots on hand for conversion training. The *Gruppe* was making at most ten flights per day. II./JG 1 was still waiting for its own He 162s and had only 19 pilots to hand.

Feldwebel Christlieb Fenger of II./JG 1 underwent training on the He 162 at Warnemünde. Pilots found the airfield conditions there difficult.

On 9 April, *Lt.* Gerhard Stiemer, of 3./JG 1, crashed on take-off in a He 162 at Parchim due to hydraulic problems – as he recalled: 'During the night, the runway was repaired. The unit could now transfer to Ludwigslust (which had no runway, as it was only a grass field). During the afternoon I flew with a 162 to Ludwigslust. Because of a defect in the hydraulics for the flaps, the runway wasn't long enough, so I ended up 'standing on my head' in a ditch on the airfield perimeter.'[56]

The next day, *Oblt.* Wollenweber conducted, in his own terms, an '*Aufklärung*' (a 'reconnaissance') for 35 minutes in He 162 W.Nr. 210 011 having taken off from Bernburg in the early afternoon. He noted in his logbook: '*Nordhausen, Mühlhausen. Flak over Langensalza airfield.*' Meanwhile, Günther Kirchner undertook a ferry flight in He 162 W.Nr. 120 072 from Marienehe to Ludwigslust which took 25 minutes between 1350-1415 hrs.[57]

By now, it is believed the *Luftwaffe* had taken delivery of some 60 He 162s.[58]

On the 11th, what remained of *Oblt.* Hachtel's detachment at Heidfeld from 2./JG 1 was ordered to transfer as *Stabsstaffel* JG 1 to Lechfeld (and/or Memmingen) for operations as part of '*Erprobungskommando Lechfeld*'. Indeed, the state of affairs at Wien was dire. The Allied radio intercept services picked up the weekly report from *Fliegerstabsing.* Paul Bader to *E-Stelle* Rechlin; 'Beginning [Commencement] of testing is made difficult without spare parts.

A Hanomag truck tows a pristine, probably factory-fresh He 162 of JG 1, believed to be the machine assigned to Fähnrich Oskar Köhler of 3. Staffel, through the rutted grass at Ludwigslust in April 1945, with a starter cart coupled between the truck and the aircraft. The aircraft, with its tail assembly draped in camouflage netting, has not yet been assigned a tactical number.

The Austrian Ritterkreuzträger, Major Bernd Gallowitsch, joined I./JG 1 in February 1945. On paper, he was Staffelkapitän of 4./JG 1, but in reality this was probably more of an administrative role and it is not believed that Gallowitsch, a 64-victory ace, ever flew the He 162.

Preparation in Vienna area has been lost. Performance measuring, power unit testing, air-firing continue. Still no results. Power unit difficulties when starting and during flight owing to addition of the jets. Of 12 aircraft, 10 have been delivered with a leak-proof wing tank and still without ... [word or so illegible for deciphering] ... The weather as yet has no effect on parts constructed of wood. R/T receivers are lacking. Air safety is endangered owing to enemy situation. Support is requested by means of deliveries from Rostock... Number of take-offs = 25. Flying time = 7 hours 40 mins. Pilots who have completed conversion = 9.'[59]

That afternoon in the north, *Oblt.* Wollenweber, piloting W.Nr. 310 023, led a formation of He 162s from Bernburg to Ludwigslust, taking off at 1755 hrs and reaching their destination 40 minutes later. With Wollenweber were *Ofhr.* Stenschke, *Ofhr.* Köttgen, *Uffz.* Hartung, and *Uffz.* Riemer, but *Fhr.* Franz Mann of 3./JG 1 was was last seen in the Magdeburg area where his aircraft was observed to bank steeply, trailing white smoke. He was forced to make an emergency landing but his fate is not known.[60]

Next day, Wollenweber was in the air again, this time in He 162 W.Nr. 120 078 on a test flight over Ludwigslust in the mid-afternoon for 20 minutes.[61]

The 13th saw the last He 162s which remained at Parchim ferried to Ludwigslust. *Hptm.* Künnecke continued to master the He 162 at 'LuLu' when he took up 'White 5', while *Uffz.* Helmut Riehl of 2./JG 1, made a ferry flight in He 162 'White 6' from Marienehe to Ludwigslust.[62] Tragedy struck I. *Gruppe,* however, on the 14th, when one of its most experienced pilots, *Feldwebel* Friedrich Enderle of 3. *Staffel*, who had a personal tally of three B-17s shot down, crashed moments after take-off from Ludwigslust. '*The 162 did not climb,*' Gerhard Stiemer noted in his diary, '*and exploded on the airfield boundary. (We suspect automatic retraction of the flaps).*'[63]

Fähnrich Franz Mann of 3./JG 1 went missing while flying a He 162 in the Magdeburg area on 11 April 1945.

The military situation facing Germany on the Western Front had become almost hopeless. In the Ruhr, *Generalfeldmarschall* Walter Model's Army Group B struggled to retain any sense of operational cohesion. The tough Model refused his Chief of Staff's recommendation to surrender in order to spare further loss of soldiers' and civilians' lives. But by 15 April, stocks of ammunition had all but run out and the troops began to surrender to the British in numbers.[64] Late on the afternoon of 11 April, a US armoured unit reached the Elbe, having advanced sixty miles in just one day. Fighting its way through the village of Schönebeck, south-east of Magdeburg, a bridge was laid across the river a few hours later.[65]

With the Allied armies drawing ever nearer, on 15 April, I./JG 1 began its journey north, under the command of *Oblt.* Karl-Emil Demuth, in an attempt to stave off the British 21st Army Group for as long as it could – relocating from Ludwigslust to Leck close to the Danish border, from where it was envisaged combat operations with the He 162 would commence.[66] An interim refuelling stop would be made at Husum due to the limited range of the *Volksjäger* and pilots were ordered not to engage in combat and to evade, under all circumstances, using speed to escape.[67]

Hauptmann Ludwig Siegfried, the *Gruppe* supply officer for I./JG 1 recalled of this time: 'Since January 1945, the war could be summed up for us as a succession of road and rail journeys. At the beginning of April we were at Ludwigslust. We then received the order to move to Husum. Having waited for nightfall, we set off. We were four officers in one car; *Oberleutnant* Wilhelm Krebs (Technical Officer of I. *Gruppe*); *Major* Bernd Gallowitsch (an Austrian *Ritterkreuzträger* with 64 victories from JG 51 and recently posted to the unit by the *General der Jagdflieger*); *Hauptmann* Hans Bleser (HQ Company Chief); and myself, *Hauptmann* Ludwig Siegfried, supply officer of I. *Gruppe*. We travelled for an hour before we were hit head-on by another car. This happened frequently due to the poor headlights in the darkness. Krebs and Gallowitsch were slightly injured and, more through good luck than judgement, we made it to Husum. It was crowded with troops retreating from northern Germany. We could only spend the rest of the night there. The following day, at midday, we finally reached Leck, where the remainder of the *Gruppe* were established.'[68]

The *Geschwaderkommodore*, *Obstlt.* Ihlefeld, would not follow until 2 May.[69]

One by one, JG 1's He 162s had made their way north: *Oblt.* Wollenweber, flying W.Nr. 120 074, left Ludwigslust at 1755 hrs and touched down in Husum at 1835 hrs. He would continue to Leck on the 16th in 'White 22'. Gerhard Hanf took 'White 1', leaving Ludwigslust at 1500 hrs and arriving at Husum 40 minutes later. Hans Berger managed to fly direct to Leck, arriving there in 'Yellow 5' at 1750 hrs. Adalbert Schlarb left Ludwigslust at 1650 hrs flying He 162 '7'; he staged via Husum but did not move on to Leck until the following day, reaching his destination in the same aircraft at 1645 hrs on the 16th. He may have experienced technical problems. Günther Kirchner must have travelled to Leck via other means, for his logbook records no flight there via He 162 on the 15th, but he did conduct a '*Wetterflug*' (meteorological flight) from Leck that day at 1150 hrs in 'Yellow 2' returning at 1216 hrs. This may have been a general reconnaissance for the rest of the *Gruppe*. Whatever the case, he must have returned to

Feldwebel Friedrich Enderle of 3./JG 1 photographed in the cockpit of his He 162 at Ludwigslust, moments before taking off on what would be his last flight, on 14 April 1945. Many Luftwaffe aircrew considered it to be a bad omen to be photographed immediately prior to a mission.

At 1222 hrs, a *Rotte* from 3./JG 1, comprising *Lt.* Gerhard Stiemer and *Fhj.Fw.* Günther Kirchner, was sent off on an '*Alarmstart*' ('scramble') from Leck to intercept enemy fighters reported in the vicinity. Stiemer led the take-off, with Kirchner following about 30 metres behind and to the right as the two Heinkels lifted into the air. Only a few metres above the ground, two 'P-47 Thunderbolts' suddenly flew across their line of sight from behind. Stiemer glanced over his shoulder just in time to see the canopy of Kirchner's aircraft blow away and the pilot's ejection seat shoot into the air. Stiemer recalled: 'On 19 April, I took-off ahead of *Fw.* Günther Kirchner to intercept some P-47s. We had hardly reached an altitude of 50 metres, when we were attacked from the rear. Though Kirchner succeeded in ejecting his seat, the lack of altitude was not sufficient to allow his parachute to open and my comrade fell to his death. I was much luckier and managed to escape, but then I could not lower my undercarriage! I approached the airfield flying at the lowest altitude and landed as quickly as I could.'

Husum, for his logbook records that he took off from there on the morning of the 16th, again in 'Yellow 2'. This must either be an error in his *Flugbuch* or another pilot flew the aircraft back to Husum.

Heinz Künnecke did not leave Ludwigslust until the 17th, reaching Husum in 'White 4' at 1835 hrs. He landed at Leck the next day in the same machine some time after 1600 hrs.[70]

Lt. Gerhard Stiemer of 3./JG 1 remembered: 'On 15 April, I prepared to take-off in order to go to Leck. In readiness for a long journey, my He 162 was equipped with a 1,300 litre tank. The runway proved too short for my aircraft, burdened as it was by the additional fuel. At the very moment when my wheels finally got off the ground, the left wing collided with a radio mast. All my strength was necessary to keep control of the now very damaged aircraft. I did a U-turn and landed. On 16 April, I took off again for Leck, this time with *Uffz.* Rieder. Heavy *Flak* welcomed us over Hamburg. In traversing the *Flak*-belt, we consumed too much fuel and had to land back on the concrete runway at Husum.'[71]

Lt. Rudolf Schmitt of 2./JG 1 flew 'White 7' from Ludwigslust to Husum at 1540 hrs on the 15th and came into contact with a Spitfire south of Hamburg, but, as per orders, he did not attempt to engage.[72]

On the 17th, Stiemer and Rieder attempted to reach Leck once again. Stiemer took off and had a trouble-free flight, but Josef Rieder failed to lift off the runway sufficiently due to a problem with his aircraft's flaps and he crash-landed, suffering injuries to his spine. He was hospitalised.[73]

The next day, the casualty list increased when *Uffz.* Wolfgang Hartung of 2./JG 1 was killed in a crash during his transfer flight to Leck.[74] Helmut Riehl flew in He 162 'White 5' from Ludwigslust to Husum in the mid-afternoon, then from Husum to Leck, landing at 1830 after a 15-minute flight. He had contact with six Spitfires but there was no engagement.[75]

On 19 April the He 162 finally went to war. I./JG 1 had been briefed to patrol the airspace over Schleswig-Holstein and to act as a counter to the many RAF fighters and fighter-bombers which were operating, almost at will, against German troop movements and conducting general, low-level interdiction missions in the area. The problem facing the *Gruppe,* however, was one of numbers: firstly the small number of machines available, and secondly, within that number, the number of aircraft actually serviceable for operations. The reality was that I./JG 1 could only mount operations at little more than *Rotte* strength.

Smoke from the crash site of Feldwebel Friedrich Enderle's He 162 curls towards the sky on the horizon not far from Ludwigslust airfield, 14 April 1945.

The overturned wreckage of Feldwebel Friedrich Enderle's He 162, photographed near Ludwigslust following his fateful crash. 'We suspect automatic retraction of the flaps...' wrote fellow pilot Gerhard Stiemer. Note the rounds of MG 151/20 ammunition to the bottom right of the photograph.

Mechanics attend to the starter cart for He 162 'Yellow 5' W.Nr. 310 005 of JG 1 at Ludwigslust, early April 1945. This aircraft may have been flown by Leutnant Hans Berger of 3. Staffel.

He 162 'Yellow 5' taxies out across the grass at Ludwigslust.

This was the first known incident of a pilot deploying the catapult seat installed in the He 162. However, as Stiemer states, the parachute failed. Kirchner's abandoned aircraft, 'Yellow 2' crashed near the village of Klintum, 4 km south of Leck.[76]

Operating in the same area, at the same time, as part of the British 2nd Tactical Air Force's wide-ranging fighter sweeps against German airfields that morning, was a formation of eight Hawker Tempest Vs of 135 Wing's 222 (Natal) Squadron. The Squadron strafed the airfields at Schlisburg and Husum claiming one enemy aircraft destroyed and eight damaged.[77] The Tempests were over the latter target at 1220 hrs and at 1,000 ft, when one of their pilots, Flg. Off. Geoffrey Walkington, spotted an aircraft flying away from the airfield at 500 ft. In his subsequent combat report Walkington recorded:

'I was flying as Blue 1 strafing Husum Airfield when I sighted an aircraft flying in a northerly direction away from the aerodrome. I immediately broke off my attack on the airfield and chased this aircraft which was camouflaged mottled green with a yellow underside and appeared to have twin fins and rudders and one engine. The nose of the aircraft had a drooping appearance and the wings (plan view) resembled those of an Me 109. Due to my loss of speed on turning the enemy aircraft pulled away to about 1,500 yards. Having recognised this aircraft as hostile by its camouflage, I gave chase, but was unable to close, my IAS being 360 mph. The enemy aircraft did a 360 degrees turn to starboard which I followed, turning inside. During my turn I managed to close to 1,000 yards. Being unable to gain further I trimmed my aircraft carefully and, allowing about three quarters of a ring above enemy aircraft, I fired short bursts. Enemy aircraft then pulled up through cloud which was 8/10ths at 3,000 feet; I followed through a gap and passed enemy aircraft spinning down out of control from approx 3,500 feet. I then watched enemy aircraft explode on the ground near Husum aerodrome.'[78]

Heinkel He 162 A-2 W.Nr. 120072, 'Yellow 3', *Lt.* Gerhard Stiemer, 3./JG 1, Ludwigslust and Leck, April/May 1945

The emblem of 3. *Staffel, Jagdgeschwader* 1 was painted directly under the cockpit and was introduced by *Lt.* Gerhard Stiemer. The fuselage and tail fin were painted in RLM 82 with sides and undersides in RLM 76. The colour demarcation line on the fuselage is typical for aircraft built by Heinkel Rostock. The engine cover was painted in RLM 81 with the front of the air intake in RLM 02. The red arrow normally painted on both sides of the nose, which was common for He 162s flown by JG 1, has not been applied, which may be due to the fact that the nose was changed after being damaged. The aircraft was captured at Leck in May 1945.

The He 162 A-2, W.Nr. 120 072, 'Yellow 3' of Leutnant Gerhard Stiemer at Leck. The aircraft carries the Lion of Danzig emblem of 3./JG 1 and the pilot's parachute has been placed on the nose. In the background is Red or Yellow '7'.

Feldwebel Günther Kirchner of 3./JG 1: Geoffrey Walkington's victim on 19 April 1945?

Walkington claimed 'one unidentified enemy aircraft destroyed' having expended 150 rounds of semi armour-piercing ammunition and 150 rounds of high-explosive ammunition.

To consider that Flg. Off. Walkington was the assailant of *Fhj.Fw.* Günther Kirchner is understandable, given the time recorded in Kirchner's *Flugbuch* (1222 hrs) and the time stated on Walkington's combat report (1220 hrs). Indeed, as 2nd TAF historians, Christopher Shores and Chris Thomas, point out: 'The time of take-off was given as 1222. In combat it was not unknown for the Tempest, with its blunt nose and semi-elliptical wings, to be misidentified as a Thunderbolt and there can be little doubt that

Unteroffizier Herbert Dosch (centre) of 5./JG 1 would make several flights in the He 162 and on one occasion encountered six enemy fighters, but did not engage.

On 19 April 1945, Flying Officer Geoffrey Walkington (right), a Tempest pilot of 222 (Natal) Squadron, 2nd Tactical Air Force, claimed an aircraft that 'appeared to have twin fins and rudders and one engine' shot down over Husum. Walkington has been generally regarded as the pilot responsible for shooting down Feldwebel Günther Kirchner of 3./JG 1, but geographical factors serve to question this.

Walkington's victim was a He 162 (especially when it is considered that the twin-finned aircraft was able to keep its distance from a Tempest at low level). The times and heights of initial contact closely match in both accounts. The evidence is persuasive but for the fact that the accounts refer to different airfields; Husum and Leck, though both in Schleswig-Holstein, are about 15 miles apart. Even so the authors, in the absence of any other matching claims or losses, feel that these two accounts refer to the same incident – the first loss of Heinkel's diminutive jet fighter in combat.'[79]

There is a mystery to this. The distance by road between Leck and Husum is 35.1 km. The problem with the above hypothesis is that if, as Stiemer recalls, Kirchner was attacked by 'P-47s' *over the runway* at Leck, moments after take-off (ie ca. 1222 hrs) and if Walkington was accurate in both the identity of the airfield his squadron attacked (Husum), and the time he was over that airfield (1220 hrs), it is questionable whether such a distance of 35.1 km (nearly 22 miles) can be ignored even taking into account the speeds of a He 162 and Tempest V. Furthermore, Walkington states he 'chased' the enemy aircraft and that it '…pulled up through cloud which was 8/10ths at 3,000 feet; I followed through a gap and passed enemy aircraft spinning down out of control from approx 3,500 feet.'

Again, comparison with Stiemer's account provides a conflicting record, in as much that the Germans had only just taken off and were not at the altitude mentioned by Walkington. The story takes another turn when it is considered that the only American fighters that could possibly have been in the area that day were P-51s, as the US Eighth Air Force, officially, did not fly Thunderbolts to Germany that day and the Ninth Air Force was operating much further south. Of the 546 P-51s of the Eighth AF despatched that day, two were lost.[80] One plausible explanation is that Kirchner was attacked by another 2nd TAF pilot, perhaps even from another squadron. In their detailed history of the 2nd TAF, Shores and Thomas state: 'The day saw much more airfield strafing, particularly by the Tempest Wings…'

It is also possible that Walkington shot down another type of aircraft. The day's events may remain a mystery, but the *Luftwaffe* nevertheless had suffered its first He 162 combat loss on the first day the aircraft went into action.

Heinkel He 162 A-2 W.Nr. 120231, 'White 6', 1./JG 1, Leck, May 1945

In the last few weeks of the war many completed He 162s remained unpainted on the forward part of their fuselages. Only the rear sections were painted in RLM 82/76 with the timber parts being painted in different colour shades of RLM 65, 76, 02 and 22. The engine air intake on this machine, as seen on many other He 162s, was painted in RLM 02 with the covering being painted in RLM 81. The aircraft was captured at Leck in May 1945. A profile of the starboard side of this aircraft can be seen on the full title pages of this book (pgs 2-3).

Left: He 162 A-2, W.Nr. 120 231, 'White 6' photographed having been moved into a hangar at Leck for inspection by British technical personnel at the end of hostilities. The engine cowlings appear to have been removed.

Below: He 162 A-2, W.Nr. 120 231, 'White 6' at Leck in May 1945. The aircraft fuselage lacks paint in all its forward and lower areas, having been left in primer with bare paste around the panel joins. The nose cone appears to be a replacement, having been marked with the red arrows of JG 1. The wing tips carry unusual striped markings.

Meanwhile, flight training continued on the 19th both at I./JG 1's new base as well as at Rostock-Marienehe. *Oblt.* Wollenweber was airborne over Leck in He 162 'Yellow 11' while at Marienehe, *Unteroffizier* Herbert Dosch, who had joined 5./JG 1 from J.Gr West, flew the He 162 for the first time at Rostock between 0910 and 0925 hrs followed by another flight between 1012 and 1026 hrs. Likewise, *Fw.* Erwin Steeb – who had been with II./JG 1 since December 1943 and who was known to his fellow pilots as 'Sepp' – made his introductory flight in a Heinkel, number '5', between 1058 and 1110 hrs.[81]

During the day, OKL signalled various commands that I. and II./JG 1 together with III./JG 301 were to be placed under *Luftflottenkommando Reich* and were to operate in the 'north area' to be ready to deploy with the He 162 and Ta 152. The *Stabsstaffeln* of JG 1 and JG 301 were placed with immediate effect under *Luftwaffenkommando West.*[82] In reality, throughout April 1945, fighter operations were generally limited to relatively successful support operations for ground forces in western Germany, with JG 4, JG 26, JG 27, JG 53 and JG 300 conducting strafing and bombing missions against enemy troop concentrations, vehicle columns and bridges, unusually in formations of some 20 or so aircraft, around Lüneburg, Magdeburg, Bamberg, and Rastatt but on an increasingly less frequent basis.

By 20 April the Soviet Army was only some 16 kilometres from the north-eastern outskirts of Berlin and the city shook with the impact of continuous Russian shelling. The men of I./JG 1 went on with their work as word came through that II./JG 1 could expect delivery of ten He 162s by the end of April. *Lt.* Schlarb took off from Leck at 1012 hrs and embarked on an 8400 m '*Höhenflug*' (high-altitude flight) in He 162 '7'.

At some point during the day, JG 1 launched four aircraft to engage British Typhoons reported to be in the Leck area attacking ground targets. The pilots had spent their time, as usual, sitting on the grass by the edge of the airfield close to the Heinkels which had the starter carts connected. When the '*Start*' order came through, He 162s Yellow '1', '3' '7' and '11' were prepared for operation, but 'Yellow 1' and *Oblt.* Wollenweber's 'Yellow 3' (W.Nr. 120 074) both had problems starting up. After three unsuccessful attempts to start 'Yellow 3', Wollenweber told the other three pilots to go ahead without him. Wollenweber then waited another ten minutes, tried a fourth time, and the turbine spun into life. He took off immediately.

Over the radio, Wollenweber heard that the other three pilots had failed to locate the enemy and, due to the limits of endurance, had turned back. 'I climbed alone to 3000 metres and flew in the direction of Husum,' Wollenweber recalled in 1993.[83] 'I soon saw a burning bus and knew that I was on the right track. At this point I had to make some checks on my machine.'

Wollenweber released the safety switch to his cannon, but then discovered that his Revi 16 gunsight was malfunctioning and he resorted to the fold-out manual sight which was working. 'In front of me I saw Husum airfield from which I could see smoke rising from the ground defences. I pushed on and at 900 km/h, I came straight into the flight path of the attacking British, who were were concentrating on the ground targets. I took the last aircraft in my sight and at around 100 metres range pushed the firing button, but it was 'silence in the woods'. The weapons did nothing. I flew to the next Typhoon and overflew his cockpit canopy by just 5 metres and then pushed the throttle through to full power and flew into the heavens and that was a bit of a shock and a surprise for the British. They immediately broke off their ground-attack and tried to follow me which was like someone on a moped trying to catch a Porsche.'

In frustration, Wollenweber thumped the Revi sight but to no avail. At that point however, the British fighters took off over the coast back to their base. 'I then had the problem of trying to find Leck, where there would be waiting fighters… I was not reassured by the report that there was now a low-level attack on the airfield. I then solved the problem by making a low-level flight from Niebull, along the road to Leck at 300 km/h, and landed on the concrete runway where the last bits of rubber were stripped away, but nevertheless I managed to get back in one piece.'

On landing, Wollenweber erroneously described the British fighters in his logbook as 'Thunderbolts'.

Shortly after 1115 hours another *Alarmstart* order was given and *Lt.* Hans Berger took off in *Lt.* Stiemer's usual aircraft, He 162 'Red 1', at 1128 hrs. He landed back at Leck at 1207 hrs, apparently without incident.[84]

Meanwhile, another patrol was ordered that afternoon. In the first of two '*Rotteneinsatz*' from Leck, *Lt.* Hanf scrambled in He 162 A-2, W.Nr. 120 077, 'Red 1'. This was probably the often-photographed aircraft which became very well known because of its distinctive personal emblem, as Hanf explained: 'I flew 'Red 1' with the inscription '*Nervenklau*' (Nerve Claw). The unusual white '*Nervenklau*' marking suddenly appeared one day on the left-hand fuselage of my He 162. This was the creation of our technicians, whose rest in their quarters I often disturbed with my motorcycle, which was always honking. Since I didn't want to be a killjoy, I accepted the emblem with a smile.' [85]

Also that afternoon, *Lt.* Rudolf Schmitt baled out, apparently using his ejection seat, near Leck following a technical problem with his aircraft while on a familiarisation flight. *Unteroffizier* Gerhard Fendler, of 2./JG 1, was killed in a crash at a place unknown during a ferry flight. Two precious aircraft were lost.[86]

Hanf flew his second operational patrol that day at 1617 hrs, returning at 1637 hrs. Neither patrol was eventful.

At Rostock-Marienehe, Erwin Steeb flew another training flight in He 162 '5' in the early afternoon. The following day, 'Sepp' did not fare so well; at 1552 hrs, he took off on his third training flight of the day in '5', but was forced to bale out when the aircraft malfunctioned near Dierkow. Whether he actually ejected is not known.[87]

Uffz. Herbert Dosch was airborne for two training flights in an unidentified He 162 over Rostock-Marienehe for 7 minutes and then 6 minutes respectively on the 21st.[88]

Heinkel He 162 A-2 W.Nr. 120223, 'Yellow 1', 3./JG 1, Leck, May 1945

This aircraft was captured at Leck in May 1945 and was later transported to France where it was tested as 'Number 1'. The fuselage was painted in RLM 82/76 and tail in RLM 76. Whether the wings were painted in RLM 81/82 has not been confirmed.

He 162 A-2, W.Nr. 120 223, 'Yellow 1' of JG 1 parked on the grass at Leck in late April or May 1945. There appears to be heavy blast staining at the end of the barrel trough for the MG 151/20 cannon and the intake ring panel of the BMW 003 is in a different colour to the engine unit cover, probably RLM 02. Note also the unusual loop paint patterns on the 'Lippisch ear' wing tips.

Heinkel He 162 A-2 W.Nr. 120077, 'Red 1', *Lt.* Gerhard Hanf, 2./JG 1, Leck, April 1945

This aircraft was flown by *Staffelkapitän, Lt.* Gerhard Hanf, who made his last flight on 29 April 1945. The camouflage scheme was the same as all Heinkel Rostock mid-production aircraft, with the exception of the RLM 76 tail fins. The former emblem of III./JG 77 was applied on both sides of the nose, with the name 'Nervenklau' ('nerve claw' or 'jangler') painted in white on the port side only. However, it is uncertain whether this was a post-war addition, since no evidence as to its authenticity has been found.

Left: He 162 A-2, W.Nr. 120 077, 'Red 1', dispersed to the edge of Leck airfield in April 1945. This was the aircraft flown by Leutnant Gerhard Hanf of 2./JG 1. It carried the name 'Nervenklau' on the port side as a humorous reference to the pilot's motorcycle and was also adorned with the wolf's head emblem of III./JG 77 with whom Hanf flew before joining JG 1.

Below: An enlargement of the starboard forward fuselage of W.Nr. 120 077, 'Red 1' showing the wolf's head emblem of III./JG 77. The aircraft also carries the red arrows of JG 1. Note the capped barrel of the MG 151/20 20 mm cannon and the blast staining at the end of the barrel trough, the communication panel in the canopy hood and the Revi 16 B gunsight on top of the instrument panel, visible through the windshield. The intake of the BMW 003 has been protected by a tarpaulin.

The 22nd brought more *Alarmstarts*. In the morning *Hptm.* Heinz Künnecke took off in a small formation from Leck in He 162 'White 7' at 0955 hrs followed a minute later by his wingman, *Uffz.* Helmut Riehl, in 'White 4', while a minute after him came *Lt.* Gerhard Hanf in 'Red 1'. Hanf was first back, at 1022 hrs, while Künnecke returned safely at 1028 hrs, followed by Riehl who landed a minute later.

In the afternoon, Hanf was on another patrol in '+1' at 1445 hrs, accompanied by *Lt.* Hans Berger in He 162 'White 4' who took off five minutes later. Both pilots returned safely at 1510 and 1511 hrs respectively. During the day, *Oblt.* Wollenweber was also airborne in He 162 W.Nr. 120 223 'Yellow 1'.[89]

On the 23rd, the last remaining pilots of Hachtel's detachment were given instructions to blow up the 'unflightworthy He 162s at Memmingen' in the face of the Allied advance, although there is no firm evidence to suggest that there were any such aircraft at Memmingen. The detachment was then to transfer to 'fields in the Munich area.'

In the north, *Lt.* Hanf was despatched on an *Alarmstart* in He 162 '+ 1' from Leck between 0912-0940 and again from 1020-1047 hrs. Both flights were ultimately without incident.[90]

Uffz. Dosch of 5./JG 1 made a 15-minute transfer flight in an unidentified He 162 from Rostock-Marienehe to Warnemünde between 1503-1518 hrs, but there was more bad news when *Feldwebel* Rolf Ackermann of 3./JG 1 was killed in a crash on landing at Leck from a ferry flight at 1403 hrs.[91] There was growing evidence that either pilots were still not adequately trained or that the He 162 was proving a difficult machine to master – or both.

Hptm. Heinz Künnecke was airborne over Leck in He 162 'White 5' during the early evening.[92]

Feldwebel Rolf Ackermann, seen here second from left in this group of pilots of 3./JG 1, was killed when his He 162 crashed at Leck on landing from a ferry flight on 23 April 1945. Also seen here is Feldwebel Günther Kirchner, (second from right), who was killed over Leck airfield on 19 April when his He 162 was attacked by enemy fighters.

Feldwebel Erwin 'Sepp' Steeb of II./JG 1 smiles from the cockpit of his Fw 190 in 1944. During the afternoon of 21 April 1945, while serving with the same Gruppe, he was forced to bale out of a He 162.

Disaster struck on 24 April when the *Gruppenkommandeur* of II./JG 1, the *Ritterkreuzträger Hptm*. Paul-Heinrich Dähne, lost his life at the controls of a He 162. Konrad Augner of 8./JG 1 witnessed what happened: 'On 24 April, I was on the airfield looking skywards when a catastrophe occurred. Our *Gruppenkommandeur, Hptm*. Dähne, did not seem to have confidence in this machine, and I think he neglected his training. That day, at about 1600, he took off. We followed his manoeuvres – he was not flying higher than 500 metres. He started to turn, and the aircraft began to skid. I then saw the aircraft somersault. Small pieces of glass shone in the sun, and a trail of white smoke came from the turbine. The He 162 began to lose height. It fell like a dead leaf and crashed in the marsh at the mouth of the Warne. Our *Gruppenkommandeur* had probably tried to bale out without first having jettisoned the canopy, and had smashed his skull. That would explain the splinters of glass. We immediately jumped into boats to go to his aid. We searched in vain …'

'The He 162 had a very evil habit,' recalled *Uffz*. Wilhelm Harder. 'When you accelerated to the side, the jet from the engine forced the rudder to stick, which meant you couldn't control the machine. It then made a downward movement like a falling leaf from a tree. Once the He 162 went into this movement, there was only one thing to do – jettison the hood, pull up your feet and get out with the catapult seat. This was how our *Gruppenkommandeur, Hptm*. Dähne, crashed to his death on his first flight. At that point, *Major* Zober came from Rechlin, although he had already been assigned to our *Jagdgruppe*, and was appointed *Gruppenkommandeur* of II./JG 1.'[93]

Major Werner Zober was a former bomber pilot, a veteran of the *Legion Condor* and a holder of the *Spanienkreuz mit Brillanten* (Spanish Cross with Diamonds). He had suffered heavy wounds during combat and had had a leg amputated. He later served with the *E-Stelle* Rechlin and was then appointed the first commander of the *E-Stelle* Udetfeld. He had joined JG 1 a few days earlier, but it is doubtful whether he ever flew the He 162 while with JG 1.[94]

Another very seasoned officer who joined JG 1 a few days earlier (as mentioned in the account by *Hauptmann* Ludwig Siegfried), was Austrian, *Major* Bernd Gallowitsch. Born in Wien in February 1918, Gallowitsch entered an Austrian pilot school in 1936, but in 1939 transferred to the *Luftwaffe* to serve as a bomber pilot in KG 100 with whom he flew 'pathfinder missions'. He converted to fighters and joined IV./JG 51 in June 1940 with whom he fought over the English Channel where he scored his first victory. He then served on the Russian Front with 12./JG 51, but was heavily wounded. When he left the front, he had accounted for 64 enemy aircraft shot down and 23 tanks destroyed in 840 combat misions, during the course of which he was shot down five times himself. He was awarded the *Ritterkreuz* on 24 January 1942 on the occasion of his 42nd victory and later that year was transferred to the Staff of the OKL embarking on training for the Me 262 at Lechfeld before being assigned to I./JG 1 in February 1945.[95]

From now to the end of the war, the 'I./*Einsatzgruppe* JG 1' was given 'freedom of operations' by OKL to operate in the ground-attack role. Only a few operations were flown in an attempt to strafe enemy columns in the area Leck-Husum/Heide-Schleswig-Flensburg-Leck.[96]

On the 25th, *Lt*. Rudolf Schmitt of 1./JG 1, airborne from Leck at 1120 hrs in 'White 5' on a *Rotteneinsatz* apparently to conduct a ground-attack patrol, noted in his *Flugbuch*, '*Freie Jagd Mosquito*'. It is understood that the two aircraft were scrambled to engage low-flying British Mosquitos reported near Flensburg, but there was no engagement.[97]

That afternoon, on the last occasion he would fly the He 162, *Lt*. Hans Berger took off from Leck in 'Yellow 3' at 1315 hrs on an *Alarmstart*, together with *Lt*. Gerhard Stiemer, to engage 'P-47s'. 'I took off with *Lt*. Berger when we saw P-47s,' recalled Stiemer. 'Upon landing, lack of fuel forced me to come down on the runway at a bad angle.

Oberleutnant Karl-Emil Demuth (right), Staffelkapitän of 3./JG 1 (but commander in the air of I./JG 1 while flying the He 162 in 1945), saved the life of Leutnant Gerhard Stiemer, following his crash in a He 162 at Leck on 25 April 1945. Demuth is seen here with Leutnant Gottfried Just of I./JG 1, who was killed in action over the Ardennes on 27 December 1944.

I crashed my 162 and the shock made me lose consciousness. *Oblt.* Demuth was the first to arrive at the scene of the crash and smashed in the canopy with an axe. A puff of oxygen brought me back to consciousness. Suffering injuries to my legs, I was taken away to the hospital in Leck where I joined my friend Rieder. It was in that bed that I would hear about the surrender.'[98]

No combat ensued between Berger and the P-47s due to his *Volksjäger* being at the limit of its endurance. When he landed after 43 minutes, Berger's tanks must have been near empty.[99]

On 26 April, I./JG 1 deployed a small number of He 162s to engage RAF ground-attack aircraft operating over Schleswig-Holstein. Lt. Hanf took off on two *Alarmstarts* in He 162 '+ 1' from Leck around midday and again, as a *Rotteneinsatz* from 1695-1635 hrs.[100]

Unteroffizier Helmut Rechenbach and *Fähnrich* Emil Halmel, both from 2./JG 1, are believed to have crashed near Leck on the 26th from unknown causes while on ferry flights.[101] However, one source states that *Uffz.* Rechenbach is credited with the first victory in a He 162 this day. The unspecified 'kill' was supported by the testimonies of *Stabsintendant Hptm.* Siegfried and *Oblt.* Demuth but, at least with the 2nd TAF, there are no corresponding losses for this day.[102]

Next day, Gerhard Hanf was in the air again on an *Alarmstart* in He 162 '+ 1' from Leck at 0910 hrs for 25 minutes followed by a further such flight in the same machine on the 28th at 1555 hrs for 25 minutes.[103]

Meanwhile, *Leutnant* Alfred Dürr of II./JG 1 embarked on a training flight at Rostock-Marienehe in He 162 W.Nr. 120 108 for 17 minutes in the afternoon of 28 April.[104] A formation of between eight and twelve He 162s from his *Gruppe* transferred that day to Leck via Kaltenkirchen, but those pilots without aircraft had to make the move by road.[105]

On 29 April, *Lt.* Hanf took off on an *Alarmstart* in He 162 '+ 1' from Leck at 1000 hrs for 25 minutes. It was uneventful, but it would be his final flight.[106]

On the 30th, elements of II./JG 1 which were reported in Mecklenburg on their journey by road to Leck were warned that they would now have to move to their destination 'under enemy pressure'.

There was pressure in the air as the attrition in aircraft and pilots grew: *Leutnant* Hans Rechenberg of II./JG 1 was shot at by a Spitfire on the 30th while on a ferry flight from Rostock to Leck and his He 162 crashed near Wismar, but he was fortunate enough to escape unhurt. *Fw.* Erwin Steeb crash-landed near Kaltenkirchen and *Oberfeldwebel* Karl Beck of II./JG 1, crashed near Klintum, while flying to Leck, due to fuel exhaustion.[107] At 1100 hrs that morning, *Lt.* Schlarb took off in He 162 W.Nr. 120 099 on a ferry flight from Rostock, but crash-landed 15 minutes later near 'Lütjenburg' (this may have been Lutjenbüttel).[108]

Lt. Dürr, took off from Rostock-Marienehe to ferry He 162 W.Nr. 120 086 in the afternoon to Leck but had to make a forced-landing on the Autobahn north of Dänischburg near Lübeck due to a lack of fuel. He had been airborne for 30 minutes. Next day, 1 May, at 1315 hrs, he took off from the Autobahn and flew for 15 minutes to Blankensee. He carried out a ten minute test flight there the same day in the dusk of the evening. On 2 May he took off again to fly to Leck via Husum, reaching his final destination at 1845 hrs. It was his last flight.[109]

On 1 May, British forces under Field Marshal Montgomery continued their drive across northern Germany and advanced from the Elbe towards Berlin virtually unopposed. Russian forces had almost reached the Heinkel works at Rostock-Marienehe.

Adolf Hitler had just committed suicide in Berlin, where there was now street-fighting with the Russians, and Hermann Göring was under house arrest in southern Germany for attempting to seize control of what remained of the Third Reich as a result of the *Führer's* self-imposed incarceration. In the air, the *Jagdwaffe* continued its last, spasmodic but defiant defensive operations on both the Western and Eastern fronts. The ominous news from the capital reached Leck, as *Uffz.* Konrad Augner of 2./JG 1 recalled: 'Our commanding officer, Ihlefeld, advised us of Hitler's death and told us to stay together until the Allies captured our airfield. By so doing, no harm could come to us. He also told us that he no longer had the right to retain us. Everyone was free to go. I don't believe a single person left.'[110]

At Rostock-Marienehe, *Uffz.* Helmut Riehl crashed in a He 162 due to technical problems, while *Uffz.* Anton Riemer of I./JG 1 also crashed but at a place unknown.[111] *Oblt.* Wolfgang Wollenweber of 3./JG 1 recalled: 'I remember perfectly the last ferry flight of He 162s taking off from Marienehe. I assumed command. We had to get the aircraft out by ourselves from the jigs and bring them to the runway. I had to organise everything personally, eventually finding a tractor for the task. As we lacked two He 162s, I had prepared a Fieseler Storch in which I planned to escape the Russians. I put my leather coat and some provisions into the cockpit. After having accompanied *Uffz.* Riehl to the take-off point, I rejoined an NCO. We were quickly joined again by Riehl who had had to land back with his deficient Heinkel. Fortunately, despite the fact he had landed in a bomb crater, he was unhurt. In the meantime, someone had stolen my leather coat and the provisions. Before Riehl's take-off, I had offered the third seat in the Fieseler to the engineer, Gundermann. But with Riehl back (we were now four), an attempt to take-off in the small plane only designed for two or three occupants was almost collective suicide. We gave it a shot, despite everything, and we rushed down the runway – well, quite slowly really – in order to take-off. At the moment the wheels began to lift off, a *Nachkommando* (rear unit) exploded the fuel tanks near the runway. The blast pushed us into the air! We landed at Leck on 1 May at 1330, not without having been mistaken as a target by the *Flak* for our shipping in Lübeck Bay.'[112]

The *Stab* and II./JG 1 finally arrived at Leck with very little equipment, having endured 'enemy pressure' since Mecklenburg. The *Stab* was assigned to *Obstlt.* Ihlefeld while II. *Gruppe* was placed under the command of *Major* Zober. A general reorganisation of the unit's commanders took place, although it was very fluid with responsibilities being split between flying and non-flying officers and some degree of interchange in *Staffel* leadership taking place as well.[113]

Accidents do happen: Rostock-built He 162 W.Nr. 120 029 lies in a heavily damaged state having made a wheels-up landing at Parchim. It is unlikely the airframe could have been salvaged, but every effort would have been made to remove the BMW 003 engine for assignment to another aircraft.

Geschwader Stab	***Oberst* Herbert Ihlefeld**
Adjutant	*Oblt.* Wind
Ia.	*Hptm.* Reinbrecht
Ic.	*Hptm.* Liebrecht
NO	*Hptm.* Kootz
Kfz.O	*techn.Ob.Insp.* Mirbach
TO	*Fl.Ing.* Pfeiffer
zbV.	*Lt.* Nitschke
I. Gruppe	***Major* Werner Zober**
Adjutant	*Oblt.* Stärk
Ia.	*Oblt.* Vogt
TO	*Fl.O.Ing.* Hansen
	WO W.Insp. Weigelt
	Fl.Ing. Hansen
	Meteor *Reg.Rat.* Lopsien
NO	*Lt.* Suchy
Kfz.O.	*t.Insp.* Heese
IVa	*Stabsint.* Siegfried
IVb	*Stabsarzt.* Dr Seebach
Stabskompanie I./JG 1	
Chef	*Hptm.* Hans Bleser
zbV.	*Lt.* Hans Bittern
Spies	*Hptfw.*Heinz Irmisch
Plus 64 *Unteroffizier* and 125 Men	
1. *Staffel*	poss. Lt. Rudolf Schmitt (flying)
	Hptm. Heinz Künnecke (non-flying)
TO	*Lt.* Dörr
Pilots:	*Lt.* Dolderer
	Lt. Erlat
	Lt. Schröder
	Fw. Gudrath
	Fw. Horny
	Fw. Steeb
	Uffz. von Alvensleben
	Uffz. Dosch
	Uffz. Nieswohl
	Uffz. Riehl
2. *Staffel*	poss. *Lt.* Gerhard Hanf & *Oblt.* W. Wollenweber (flying)
	Hptm. Wolfgang Ludewig (non-flying)
TO	*Lt.* Heinen
Pilots:	*Lt.* Feldt
	Lt. Deppe
	Lt. Rechenberg
	Lt. Rodatz
	Lt. Hofmann
	Lt. Langer
	Fw. Schücking
	Fw. Gold
	Fw. Gehrlein
	Fw. Kreutz
	Fw. Schlösser
	Uffz. Cranz
	Uffz. Fenger
	Uffz. Augner
	Uffz. Widnemann
	Uffz. Harder
3. *Staffel*	poss. *Lt* Hans Berger & *Oblt.* W. Wollenweber (flying)
	Oblt. Karl-Emil Demuth (poss. non-flying)
TO	*Oblt.* Krebs
Pilots:	*Lt.* Hanf
	Lt. Stenschke
	Lt. Stiemer
	Lt. Köttgen
	Lt. Kriete
	Lt. Friese
	Lt. Lange
	Lt. Klein
	Fhr. Köhler
	Fw. Bartzen
	Uffz. Rieder
	Uffz. Brüne
	Uffz. Brandt
	Uffz. Schaumburg
	Uffz. Bauch
II. (Sammel) *Gruppe*	***Hptm.* Rahe (non-flying)**
Adjutant	*Oblt.* Beugler
4. *Staffel*	*Hptm.* Bernd Gallowitsch (non-flying)
	poss. *Lt.* 'Schmidt' (Schmitt?)
	Fl.Oberstabsing. Neuner
	Fl.Stabsing. Müller
	Tech.Oberinsp. Talinski
	Tech.Oberinsp. Müller
	Fl.Ing. Radomicki
5. *Staffel*	*Hptm.* Bergholz (non-flying)
zbV.	*Oblt.* Pilz
6. *Staffel*	*Oblt.* Zipprecht (non-flying)
zbV.	*Lt.* Werth

Ultimately, the *Geschwader* is believed to have had some 45 He 162s at Leck by this date.[114]

In the air, on 2 May, *Uffz.* Herbert Dosch of 5./JG 1 made a 26-minute transfer flight in an unidentified He 162 from Neumünster to Leck. He observed 'six Thunderbolts'.[115]

By 3 May, Leck had become an increasingly crowded assembly area for a number of the remaining *Luftwaffe* fighter units still able to operate freely and with fuel. In addition to I. and II./JG 1, elements of JG 2, II. and III./JG 3, *Geschwaderstab* and III./JG 4, *Geschwaderstab* and II./JG 301, III./KG 76, KG 3 and NJG 2 were arriving there – bringing a bewildering assortment of Bf 109s, Fw 190 As and D-9s, Ar 234s, He 162s, He 111s, Ju 88s and He 219 night fighters all being marshalled – somehow – under the composite command of *Oberstleutnant* Karl-Gottfried Nordmann, the *Inspekteur der Jagdflieger Ost* and *Jafü Nord Ost*. However, as the war diary of JG 4 recorded at this time: 'Fighter-bomber activity has now reached the most northerly part of Germany – several times during the day we have had to dive for cover...'

A further insight into the conditions at Leck early on 4 May is offered by the war diary: 'Orders arrive at 0200 – the serviceable aircraft must fly on, either to Norway or the Protectorate, to avoid being captured by British troops. Take-offs should be completed by 0600. The three Bf 109s of the former III./JG 4 are to remain at Leck. German forces in north Germany have signed a surrender, capitulating to Montgomery. It is forbidden to fire at any low-flying aircraft. At the same time no further take-offs are authorised. A lone Spitfire circled over the airfield. The war is over! The *Helferinnen* (female auxiliaries) Dobner and Augsen arrived on the airfield after an incredible journey. They are the only two service-women from their convoy that have been able to reach us here in Leck.'[116]

Yet even now, at the 'eleventh hour', the pilots of I./JG 1 soldiered on. At 1138 hrs on Friday, 4 May, just a few hours before *Admiral* Hans-Georg von Friedeburg, the German Chief of Naval Staff, and *General* Hans Kinzel, Chief of the North West Army Command signed the instrument of surrender of the German forces currently

Above and right: Two views of He 162 A-2, W.Nr. 120 095, 'White 20' of JG 1 at Leck in May 1945. The aircraft carries the Geschwader's red arrow symbols on its nose section and the intake ring panel of the BMW 003 is also red. Note the Fieseler Storch and Siebel Si 204 parked behind. The Heinkel next to 'White 20' could be W.Nr. 120 321.

Right: He 162 A-2, W.Nr. 120 095, 'White 20' of JG 1 having been moved by British troops into a hangar for protection and inspection, Leck, May 1945.

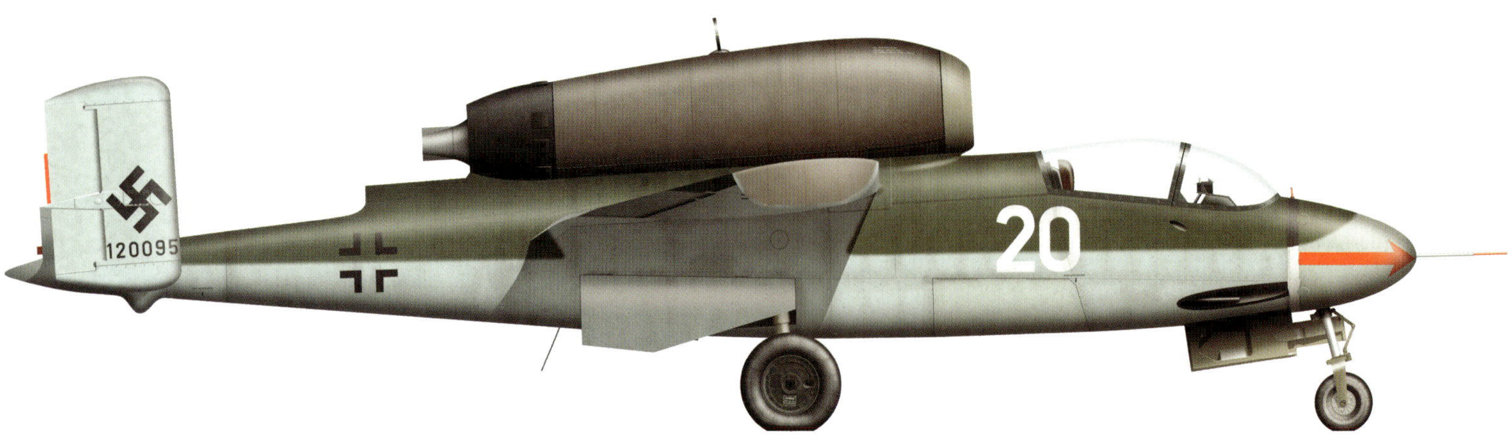

Heinkel He 162 A-2 W.Nr. 120095, 'White 20', Stab I./JG 1, Leck, May 1945

This aircraft was captured at Leck by British forces in May 1945. It was eventually shipped to the United Kingdom and given the British Air Ministry number 'AirMin 63'. The machine was camouflaged in the same way as all the Heinkel Rostock aircraft from mid-production batch that were captured at Leck. Note the wing tip in the same colour as the engine enclosure.

facing Montgomery's 21st Army Group, and in what would become one of the most controversial episodes in the He 162's very brief operational history, *Lt.* Rudolf Schmitt took off in 'White 1' from Leck to engage RAF Typhoons. Schmitt subsequently noted in his *Flugbuch*, '*1145 hrs: Typhoon wirksam beschossen*' following an encounter south-east of Husum.[117]

This has proved worthy of much analysis – and speculation – in the post-war period, primarily because no Allied loss appears to 'fit' Schmitt's claim. Probably the most careful investigation to date has been led by British researcher A.R. ('Rick') Chapman in 1989 who, in this writer's view, has correctly placed emphasis on the aforementioned choice of words used by Schmitt in his *Flugbuch*. As Rick Chapman wrote in an article in *Flugzeug* magazine in early 1989: 'One of the first things to surprise me while reading the entry in *Lt.* Schmitt's log was the use of the expression '*wirksam beschossen*' (fired upon with effect), an expression pilots normally use to describe the successful destruction of a ground target. Could it have been the personal habit of the pilot to express the fact that he had not been able to see his opponent's crash? If it had been like this, there would be no reason to doubt the pilot's conviction of having hit the opponent so badly that the crash would have been inevitable.'[118]

The possibility of a USAAF aircraft being Schmitt's victim can be discounted quite safely. An assessment of British losses that day, however, reveals four possibilities. Firstly, New Zealander Sqn Ldr J.R. Cullen, DFC, of 183 'Gold Coast' Squadron, who was leading a formation of eight Typhoon 1Bs from Celle that morning against shipping targets off Fehmarn Island. Cullen's aircraft was hit by the explosion from an enemy vessel's ammunition and he was forced to land on the island, being taken POW but released shortly after.

Secondly, a Typhoon of 245 'Northern Rhodesia' Squadron was badly damaged during another shipping sortie over the Flensburger Förde and was forced to land near Lüneburg while, thirdly, a Typhoon flown by W/O Swales of 175 Squadron was hit by *Flak* during a shipping strike over the Howachter Bight. Swales made it back to base, but had to belly-land due to damage to his undercarriage. The possibility also exists that what Schmitt took for a Typhoon was actually a Tempest, in which case the only loss of such an aircraft that day was one belonging to 486 Squadron, RNZAF, flown by Lt. Tom Austin which force-landed following a mechanical problem during an armed reconnaissance mission in the Rodecke-Hadersleben area. The pilot was taken prisoner.

'Officially' the RAF listed the loss of three fighter-bombers in the Leck area that day: Cullen's Typhoon, Austin's Tempest and a third unidentified machine, though not a single-engined one. Whilst it is therefore unlikely that Schmitt actually shot down an aircraft, he cannot be denied the likelihood that he opened fire 'with effect' on an enemy

Above and below: He 162 A-2, W.Nr. 120 095, 'White 20' of JG 1 photographed having been moved for initial inspection by British technical troops at Leck, May 1945.

A good view of the cockpit and instrument panel of He 162 A-2, W.Nr. 120 095, 'White 20' of JG 1 as found by British troops at Leck in May 1945. The top row of instruments from left includes the turn and bank indicator, airspeed indicator, turbine temperature and rpm; the bottom row includes the hand pump, homing gauge, altimeter, compass, fuel pressure and fuel gauge, ammunition counters, and oxygen pressure indicator. The panel to the left contains starter buttons, the ignition switch and throttle. To the centre is the control column and glass nosewheel retraction indicator panel, while mounted on top of the panel is the Revi 16 B gunsight.

single-engined fighter or fighter-bomber south-east of Husum on 4 May and assumed he had damaged the aircraft, perhaps even sufficiently to cause it to go down.

Interestingly, *Oblt.* Demuth remembers that: 'I had heard by telephone of the crash of a British aircraft in our sector so we went by car to look for the pilot and invited him to dinner in our mess. As some of us spoke some English, we discussed aeronautical matters and our lost war, and about the qualities and shortcomings of our respective aircraft. The following morning, we were sad to see him taken away to a POW camp.'[119]

Quite who the British pilot was remains unknown.

Also on the 4th, the under-strength I. and II./JG 1 were ordered to merge as 'I.(*Einsatz*)/JG 1' under *Obstlt.* Ihlefeld, with '1.(*Einsatz*) *Staffel*' under *Major* Zober and '2.(*Einsatz*) *Staffel*' under *Hptm.* Ludewig. However, soon after this, disconcerting and demoralising orders arrived for JG 1 from *Luftflottenkommando Mitte* to make ready to hand all its aircraft over to the British and Americans as and when they arrived at Leck.[120]

The following morning, Saturday, 5 May, *Luftflottenkommando Mitte* issued the order to 'cease action'. *Hptm.* Ludwig Siegfried of *Stab*, I. *Gruppe* remembered: 'On 5 May, at around 0800 hours we received the order from HQ *Luftwaffe Mitte*, to cease action. We each placed one or two kilos of explosives in our aircraft. In the evening we received a new order; we were to leave our aircraft intact and to deliver them to the enemy. During the night we removed the explosives. On 6 May, the British reached the aerodrome, which we had by then evacuated. We were on the way to Flensburg, to a camp at Schmörholm. Arms were collected and only the officers retained their pistols. On 8 May, the Allies took over the airfield and shared out our He 162s. They also took the technical personnel, who were required to keep the aircraft in flying condition. On 25 May, our 25 female auxiliaries were released. Myself, I was set free on 13 July. Five days later, at 2200 hours, I reached my family home at Wesermünde.'[121]

Elsewhere at Leck, the situation was bleak; according to the war diary of JG 4: 'At 0600 all officers and men must attend the execution of a *Leutnant* in JG 11 condemned to face a firing squad by a military tribunal for an act of high treason (desertion)... Today the airfield has been occupied by various detachments of the RAF and all fighting against enemy forces in the West is now at an end.'[122]

On 6 May 1945, a car and an armoured car carrying a party of four British Air Disarmament Officers and personnel from the RAF Regiment journeyed from the headquarters of Montgomery's 21st Army Group at Lüneburg to Schleswig to accept the surrender of *Luftflotte Reich* from *Generaloberst* Hans-Jürgen Stumpff. The British later recorded that: 'The Headquarters of *Luftflotte Reich* was situated in the middle of the thick, dark pine wood at Missunde, about six-and-a-half miles east of Schleswig town, and in this wood the various caravans and trailers were scattered, very heavily camouflaged, notwithstanding the fact that it was quite impossible to see anything through a wood of such density. We were led to a very comfortable caravan and found Colonel General Stumpff waiting outside to receive us. He made no attempt to shake hands, but saluted and the salute was returned; we were led very courteously and correctly into the caravan where the various senior officers of the staff were presented. Fortunately only one of them, the Chief of Staff, offered to shake hands – a very difficult gesture to refuse, but this hurdle was successfully avoided. The C-in-C pleaded lack of communications – a fact which was well understood – and said that he hoped to have news of the whereabouts of all his units within the next 48 hours. We had the impression that he was somewhat ashamed at being so disorganised, and it was quite clear that he wished to straighten out his difficulty and get his units under control as soon as possible.'[123] At Leck, there was a dramatic event when, in what must have been one of the final operational flights made by the He 162, *Fähnrich* Oskar Köhler of 3./JG 1 crashed. Köhler was a very experienced flying instructor who had joined the *Geschwader* from JG 105 where he had flown the Fw 190, but even for someone with Köhler's experience the hurried transition from piston-engined aircraft to the jet-powered Heinkel could be challenging. Köhler's aircraft landed on the runway at full speed and crashed on the airfield boundary. It was known that the 1200 m runway at Leck was barely long enough to allow safe operations of the He 162. Köhler suffered injuries to his legs and was removed from the wreckage of his aircraft by *Oblt.* Demuth and the *Geschwader* medical officer, *Dr.* Seebach.[124]

During the late afternoon, British tanks rumbled onto the airfield. Confined to their barracks, the Germans were obliged, initially, to give up all their weapons. The diarist of JG 4 recorded: 'Our aircraft, vehicles and other equipment is lined up as if for one last parade. The sight is an impressive one and will certainly give the British food for thought. We are proud to show off more than one hundred of our aircraft like this – from the ultra-modern Me 262 and He 162 that have flown only limited numbers of combat sorties – to the Bf 109 and Fw 190 fighters that have returned victories in thousands of successful air battles. All will pass into enemy hands. This afternoon several light tanks and trucks bring RAF ground forces onto the airfield. *Oberst* Nordmann, then the *Kommodore* and *Kommandeure*, have to go before the Colonel commanding the RAF forces. To our great surprise they receive a handshake by way of greeting! However we are airmen together – we remain sceptical as to what may follow the courtesies that are extended to us: what will happen when the other occupation forces arrive? The first orders are to draw up an inventory of all our matériel. All weapons must be handed in apart from the officers' sidearms.'[125]

It has been suggested during the post-war years that JG 1 arranged its He 162s to be parked in neat rows to wait for the arrival of British forces. This, evidently, has no basis in fact. One German historian was informed quite emphatically that the He 162s had been left dispersed and scattered across Leck airfield in the standard way to minimise the impact of enemy ground-strafing. They were only assembled into a line-up *after* the British arrived and at their request.[126]

Those He 162s believed to have been assembled at Leck included:[127]

W.Nr. 120 002	White 1	1./JG 1
W.Nr. 120 015	White 21	1./JG 1
W.Nr. 120 017	Yellow 6	3./JG 1
W.Nr. 120 028	White 3	1./JG 1
W.Nr. 120 067	White 4	1./JG 1
W.Nr. 120 072	Yellow 3	2./JG 1
W.Nr. 120 074	Yellow 11	3./JG 1
W.Nr. 120 076	Yellow 4	3./JG 1
W.Nr. 120 077	Red 1	2./JG 1
W.Nr. 120 086	none	?
W.Nr. 120 091	Red 5(?)	2./JG 1(?)
W.Nr. 120 095	White 20(?)	1./JG 1(?)
W.Nr. 120 097	Red 3(?)	1./JG 1(?)
W.Nr. 120 098	White 2(?)	1./JG 1(?)
W.Nr. 120 221	White 21(?)	?
W.Nr. 120 222	White or Yellow 7(?)	
W.Nr. 120 223	Yellow 1	3./JG 1
W.Nr. 120 227	Red 2	2./JG 1
W.Nr. 120 230	White 23	1./JG 1
W.Nr. 120 231	White 6	1./JG 1
W.Nr. 120 233	unknown	?
W.Nr. 120 235	Yellow 6(?)	2./JG 1(?)
W.Nr. 120 ???	Yellow 5	3./JG 1
W.Nr. 310 003	Yellow 5	2./JG 1
W.Nr. 310 012(?)	Yellow 5	3./JG 1(?)
W.Nr. 300 018	White 5	1./JG 1

In summary, while it may be true that the pace and accomplishment of *Luftwaffe* operations with the He 162 did not – perhaps could not – mirror that of EHAG's spirited and tenacious attempts at development and production of the aircraft under Carl Francke, *Jagdgeschwader* 1 nevertheless proved, against all odds, that the technology and build-standard that EHAG had produced in such little time was, in contemporary parlance, 'fit for purpose' – just.

In the early hours of 7 May, in a small schoolhouse at General Eisenhower's headquarters in Reims, *Admiral* Hans-Georg von Friedeburg and *Generaloberst* Alfred Jodl, representing *Admiral* Karl Dönitz, Hitler's successor, signed the terms of the German capitulation.

Line-up at Leck - *May 1945*

The solitary figure of Hauptmann Heinz Künnecke walks past the right-hand row of He 162s at Leck having just taken photographs of his units aircraft. Note the absence of the Allied jeep at the end of the taxi track, which appears in other photographs taken at the time.

IN accordance with a directive from British forces at the cessation of hostilities, *Oberst* Herbert Ihlefeld, *Geschwaderkommodore* of *Jagdgeschwader* 1, arranged to present the He 162s of his unit at Leck for surrender to- and inspection by Allied air/technical intelligence. The aircraft were lined up in two, neat rows of nine and thirteen aircraft, with noses facing each other along one of the taxi tracks.

This was the occasion for a sequence of photographs to be taken which have become very well-known to aviation historians and enthusiasts in the post-war years and which no study of the He 162 can overlook. The pages that follow showcase what is hopefully the most comprehensive assembly of this sequence, as well as offering the reader a fascinating and detailed-rich glimpse of what awaited British forces at Leck in early May 1945.

In order to avoid repetition in the captions, the last known ranks and positions of those personnel depicted in the photographs are appended opposite:

Oberst Herbert Ihlefeld	*Geschwaderkommodore* JG 1
Hauptmann Reinbrecht	*Geschwader* Ia (Operations Officer)
Major Werner Zober	*Gruppenkommandeur* I./JG 1
Hauptmann Heinz Künnecke	*Staffelkapitän* 1./JG 1
Leutnant Rudolf Schmitt	*Staffelführer* 1./JG 1 (Operations)
Hauptmann Wolfgang Ludewig	*Staffelkapitän* 2./JG 1
Oberleutnant Wolfgang Wollenweber	*Staffelkapitän* 3./JG 1
Oberleutnant Karl-Emil Demuth	*Staffelführer* 3./JG 1 (Operations)
Hauptmann Rahe	*Gruppenkommandeur* II./JG 1
Hauptmann Bernd Gallowitsch	*Staffelkapitän* 4./JG 1
Strasen?	Unknown

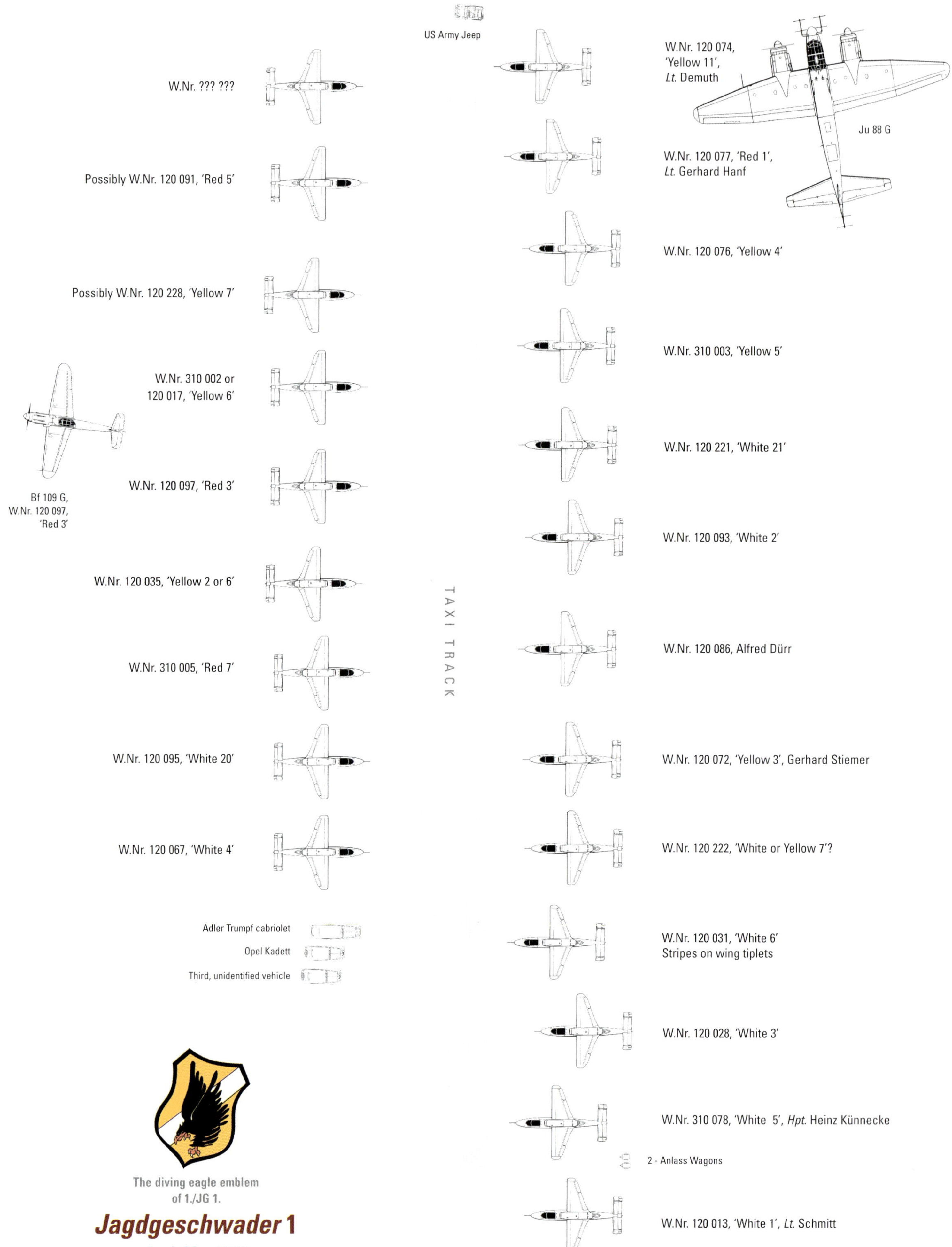

The diving eagle emblem of 1./JG 1.

Jagdgeschwader 1

Leck May 1945

Three views looking across the taxi track to the north-west and towards the right-hand row of He 162s with, in the photograph top, from right to left, Gerhard Stiemer's W.Nr. 120 072 'Yellow 3', Alfred Dürr's W.Nr. 120 086, W.Nr. 120 98 'White 2', W.Nr. 120 221 'White 21' and 'Yellow 5' in view with a Ju 88 behind. The photograph to centre shows W.Nr 120 028 'White 3' with the diving eagle emblem of 1./JG 1, the crudely finished W.Nr. 120 231, 'White 6', then W.Nr. 120 222 White or Yellow '7', followed by Gerhard Stiemer's W.Nr. 120 072 'Yellow 3'. In the picture at left is seen W.Nr. 120 013 'White 1' also adorned with the emblem of 1./JG 1 and believed to be the aircraft of Leutnant Rudolf Schmitt, with Bernburg-built W.Nr. 310 078, 'Yellow 5' next to it believed to be the aircraft of Hauptmann Heinz Künnecke.

Heinkel He 162 A-2 *Werknummer* probably 120013, 'White 1', *Lt* Rudolf Schmitt, 1./JG 1, Leck, May 1945

This aircraft was twice flown by *Lt.* Rudolf Schmitt. On the second flight on 4 March 1945, he claimed an aerial victory which has, however, never been confirmed. The fuselage was painted in an RLM 76 variation that appeared more cream than blue. The area behind the cockpit was painted in RLM 82 with the wings in RLM 70/65. This was unusual, but it also appeared on other early Heinkel-Rostock production aircraft. The front of the cowling was painted in RLM 81, as were the fins. The *Werknummer* is a matter of some speculation, but recent research favours 120013. The aircraft carries the diving eagle emblem of 1./JG 1 which is depicted showing a yellow background based on recent research.

The view looking from the eastern end of the left-hand row of He 162s at Leck with an unidentified Luftwaffe serviceman standing between an Opel Kadett and a camouflaged military Adler Trumpf 2.0-litre cabriolet staff car. The aircraft closest to the Adler Trumpf is W.Nr. 120 067 'White 4'.

The cameraman captures a relaxed moment: from left, Hauptmann Heinz Künnecke and Leutnant Rudolf Schmitt, while in discussion behind, Hauptmann Reinbrecht and Hauptmann Wolfgang Ludewig. Note there is now a third car parked immediately behind Künnecke and Schmitt, possibly another Opel Kadett..

A view from behind the right-hand row of He 162s, with, from left, the aircraft in the foreground being W.Nr. 120 013 'White 1', believed to be the aircraft of Lt. Rudolf Schmitt, then W.Nr. 310 078, 'Yellow 5' believed to be the aircraft of Hauptmann Heinz Künnecke with a starter cart positioned between the two machines. Moving to the right is W.Nr 120 028 'White 3'. Note the different styles in fuselage Balkenkreuz.

The view looking along the left-hand row of He 162s with W.Nr. 120 067 'White 4' in the foreground. It is possible that the cameraman has stood on top of the hard roof of the small car to take this photograph.

He 162, A-2, W.Nr. 120 097, 'White 3' was parked in the centre of the left-hand row.

Heinkel He 162 A-2 W.Nr. 120028, 'White 3', 1./JG 1, Leck, May 1945

An early production machine built by Heinkel-Rostock, which was captured at Leck in May 1945. The aircraft later moved to Kassel where it was probably scrapped. The camouflage is the same as seen on the 'White 1' on the opposite page and other early aircraft. The diving eagle was only painted on the port side of the fuselage and is depicted showing a yellow background based on recent research. Early style *Balkenkreuze* were applied on the fuselage sides.

Heinkel He 162 A-2 W.Nr. 120074, 'Yellow 11', *Oblt.* Karl-Emil Demuth, Stab I./JG 1, Leck, May 1945

This machine was the personal aircraft of *Oblt.* Karl-Emil Demuth with the camouflage being typical of the Heinkel-Rostock production line. The nose was painted in red-white-black with the arrow painted in red on both sides of the nose. The aircraft also carried the 'Devil in the Clouds' emblem of I./JG 1 painted below the cockpit. It is depicted showing a yellow background based on recent research. The tactical number '11' was painted in yellow followed immediately by a small number '20' in white. On the fin were painted sixteen white victory bars representing victories which Demuth had claimed before flying the He 162, as well as the aircraft's *Werknummer,* 120074, in white.

He 162, A-2, W.Nr. 120 074, 'Yellow 11', the aircraft of Oberleutnant Karl-Emil Demuth, was parked at the far (western) end of the right-hand row. The aircraft has a red, white and black nose tip and the emblem of I./JG 1. Note the variation in red arrow head on this machine, the small '20' next to the main tactical number. In the photograph below, the protective tarpaulins over the cockpit and BMW 003 engine have been removed presumably for photographic purposes, while Demuth poses next to the aircraft's port-side rudder. Note also the dual-coloured protection plate inserted into the engine intake bearing the number '21' or '24'.

Right: Oberleutnant Karl-Emil Demuth stands next to the fin of his W.Nr. 120 074, 'Yellow 11' which has been marked up with his sixteen victories.

From left to right: Hauptmann Wolfgang Ludewig, Hauptmann Heinz Künnecke and Oberleutnant Karl-Emil Demuth

Set of four photographs (from left to right) Ludewig, Künnecke and Demuth are joined by Major Werner Zober (second from left).

Top right and above: the collective attention of Ludewig, Zober, Demuth and Künnecke is attracted by movement beyond the row of parked He 162s.

Above: The bare metal and filler paste finish of He 162 W.Nr. 120 231, 'White 6' is clearly visible behind the group of officers.

Ludewig, Demuth and Künnecke are joined by Hauptmann Rahe (second from left) and Leutnant Rudolf Schmitt (far right).

Possibly taken from the roof of the small car parked on the other side of the taxi track, these three photographs show Künnecke, Demuth and Zober, (all to the left of the pictures) together with Rahe and Ludewig, who are looking at W.Nr. 120 231, 'White 6'.

The view from western end of the right-hand row of aircraft, with nearest, Oberleutnant Karl-Emil Demuth's He 162, A-2, W.Nr. 120 074, 'Yellow 11', followed by Leutnant Gerhard Hanf's W.Nr. 120 077 'Red 1' 'Nervenklau' (applied to the port side of the fuselage only) and bearing the wolf's head emblem of III./JG 77 which had been adopted by 2./JG 1. Then, following from left to right along the row, W.Nr. 120 076, 'Yellow 4', W.Nr. 120 221 'White 21', W.Nr. 120 093 'White 2', W.Nr. 120 086 and W.Nr. 120 072 'Yellow 3'.

Above: Heinz Künnecke (far left) winds on the film in his camera watched by Karl-Emil Demuth while Wolfgang Ludewig glances at the aircraft in the opposite row. Behind them are, from left to right, He 162s W.Nr. 120 067 'White 4', W.Nr. 120 095 'White 20' and Bernburg-built W.Nr. 310 005 'Red 7'. Note the different styles of red arrow on the aircrafts' noses.

Right and below: The photographer seems to have captured Künnecke, Zober and Demuth perhaps contemplating an unbcertain future while Ludewig and Rahe continue with their discussion in front of Künnecke's 'Yellow 5'.

The Kommodore arrives: Rahe (back to the camera) welcomes Herbert Ihlefeld. Seen here from left: Ludewig, Rahe, Ihlefeld, Zober (back to camera), Künnecke (just visible) Strasen, Demuth and Gallowitsch.

Ihlefeld addresses his officers. From left to right: Zober, Ihlefeld, Künnecke, Demuth, Gallowitsch, Strasen, Rahe and Ludewig.

Below: As Strasen moves off to attend to other matters, Ihlefeld continues his relaxed conversation with his pilots, close W.Nr. 120 028 'White 3'. Note the small '3' on the tarpaulin draped over the aircraft's cockpit hood.

Heinkel He 162 A-1 possibly W.Nr. 310078, 'White 5', 1./JG 1, Leck, May 1945

'White 5' has previously been identified as W.Nr. 310018, but current research indicates that this aircraft was flown by *Uffz.* Dobrat from Bernburg to the Nürnberg area on 6 April 1945 and it is not certain whether it ever reached JG 1 at Leck. The machine had the typical Bernburg fuselage camouflage finish of RLM 82/76. The upper surface of the wings were painted in RLM81/82. Of note are the different painted tail fins also showing two styles of *Hakenkreuz*. It may be possible that the starboard fin was replaced due to damage. The diving eagle badge was only painted on the port side of the fuselage and is depicted showing a yellow background based on recent research.

At the eastern end of the right-hand row of aircraft, Hauptmann Heinz Künnecke poses for a photograph standing next to his Junkers-built He 162, W.Nr. 310 078, 'White 5'. The aircraft carries the diving eagle emblem of 1./JG 1 and the red arrow nose marking of the Geschwader. Note the number '11' on the tarpaulin covering the cockpit – evidently purloined from another machine.

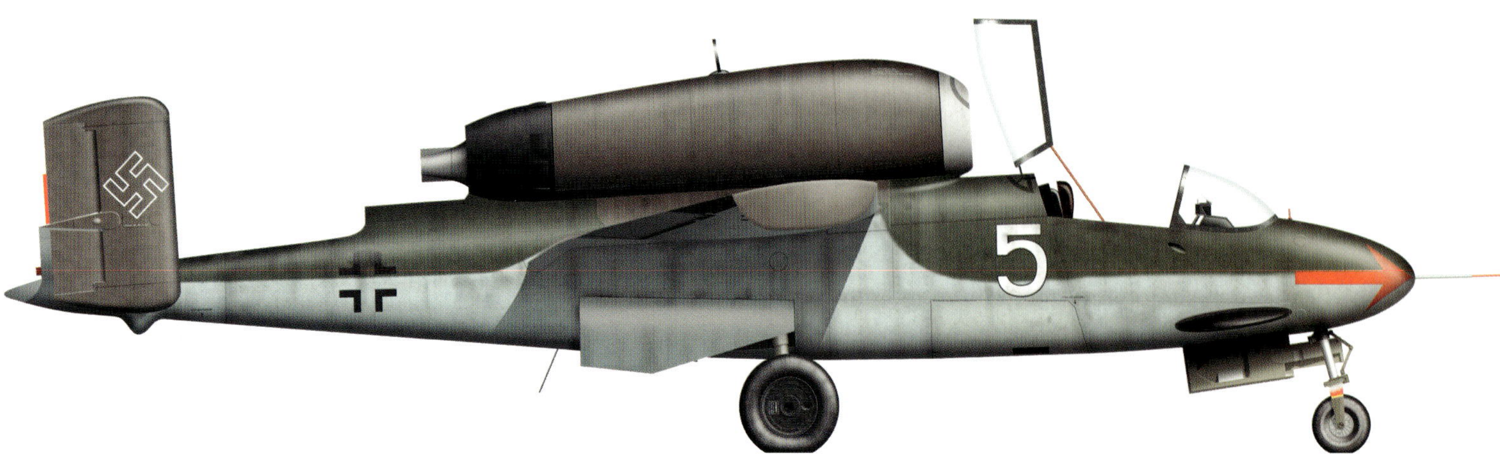

Eleventh Hour Exotica

Pulsejet Engines, Special Weapons and Mistel projects

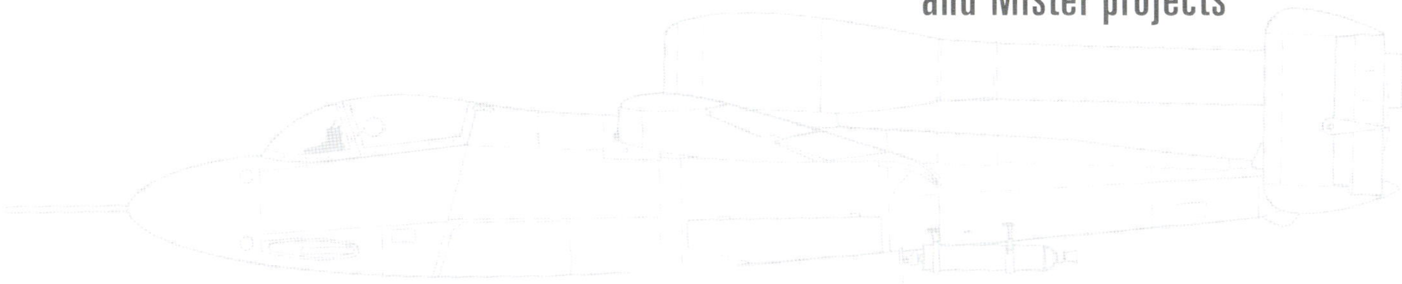

He 162 with Argus Pulsejet Engines

BY the end of March 1945, EHAG technicians were very much aware of both the fiscal and material cost, as well as the cost in terms of time, involved in the manufacture of jet engines for the He 162 – be it from BMW (BMW 003), Junkers (Jumo 004) or Heinkel-Hirth (HeS 011). From these three viewpoints at least, a lower cost alternative lay in the Argus As 014 and As 044 Pulsejet engines. The former had been developed originally to power the Fi 103 (V-1) flying bomb and worked by pressurising a fuel tank. From a tank, fuel flowed through a fuel control system and was delivered to the combustion chamber through atomising nozzles. The control system required careful design since correct fuel pressure at the nozzles was an essential factor in successful tube operation. In the case of the Fi 103/V-1 this had proved difficult due to its fluctuating operating conditions.

The As 014 was a comparatively crude but structurally simple powerplant. To start it, an initial quantity of air had to be suddenly admitted into the combustion chamber by means of a jet of compressed air which mixed there with the continually-injected fuel under pressure, the air/fuel mixture ignited by a spark plug. The initial explosion caused the hot gases to move to the rear to the open end of the cylindrical duct and generated a thrust. The sub-pressure thus resulting in the combustion chamber caused the front flexible flap valves to open, whereupon a fresh quantity of air sucked-in mixed in the chamber with the fuel, which upon ignition, closed the flap valves and projected the combustion gases once more to the rear. This air/fuel combustion cycle, no longer needing an igniter each time, repeated itself automatically and resulted in continuous periodic combustion. Although cheap and easy to build and of light weight, disadvantages of the pulsejet were its low thrust, high fuel consumption and limitation to low altitude operation, as well as causing severe damage through vibration to aircraft structures such as to the DFS 230 and Bf 109 flying test-beds, and resulted in the pulsejet exhaust nozzle being placed well clear of the aircraft's wing and tail control surfaces (as on the Bf 110 and Fw 190 flying test-beds) – a feature that was adopted on the Me 328 and other drawing-board projects.

As an alternative to possible bottlenecks in BMW 003 production in 1945, two pulsejet-powered variants of the He 162 were proposed, each of 7.2 m span and a wing area 11 m², both requiring a fuselage lengthened by 20 cm (to overall length 9.25 m) to accommodate the extra fuel needed. One variant, the He 162.01-43, featured a single 500 kg thrust As 044 mounted above the fuselage, the He 162.01-44 having two 335 kg thrust As 014s mounted side by side such that the pulsejet exhaust ducts in both proposals projected beyond the empennage control surfaces.

Due to the pulsejet's disadvantages mentioned above, plus the need for a rocket-assisted take-off in each case, EHAG preferred the single-duct arrangement because of its higher thrust and the better rearward vision than was offered by the two-duct arrangement (the He 162 was too small to support two As 044s and their 2,200 kg fuel load). A comparative performance between the single- and twin-duct proposals can be seen in the data table overleaf.

In an assessment dated 30 March 1945, EHAG reported: 'As a result of the pronounced falling-off in the power unit's thrust with altitude (more than with air density), the maximum speed is attained at ground level. For the same reason flight performance is poor at greater altitudes, so that operational flight can only be considered at low altitudes.

'Take-off must be effected by having recourse to auxiliary starting aids. If the take-off position is not to be betrayed by the smoke of the starting rockets, it will be necessary to employ a catapulting device. The amount of fuel required for above duration may be completely disposed of in fuselage and wing, making external tanks superfluous.

'The supply of auxiliary power for fuel and hydraulic systems is provided by a generating set on board the aircraft.'[1]

During the development of its pulsejet, the Argus Motoren Gesellschaft in Berlin carried out experiments using various aircraft to test its engines. The first pulsejet flight tests were made with an Argus unit giving a static thrust of 120 kp fitted beneath a Gotha Go 145 with the civil code D-IIWS. The unit was fitted in a balance that was swivelled to allow for ground clearance during take-off and landing. The first flight took place on 30 April 1941.

EHAG issued the following comparative specifications for a He 162 fitted with Argus As 014/044 Pulsejets:

	He 162.01-44	He 162.01-43
Powerplant	2 x As 014	1 x As 044
Thrust (kg) static, sea-level	2 x 335	1 x 500
Thrust (kg) at 700 km/h at 0 km	2 x 355	1 x 530
Thrust (kg) at 700 km/h at 6 km	2 x 160	1 x 250
Fuel cons. (kg/hr) at 700 km/h at 0 km	2 x 1,760	1 x 2,650
Fuel cons. (kg/hr) at 700 km/h at 6 km	2 x 830	1 x 1,250
Weights (kg)		
Airframe (clean)	930	930
Military load, made up of:		
Armament (2 x MK 108 with 70 rpg)*	155	155
Armour plating	170	170
Ammunition	80	80
Other equipment	85	85
Crew (1)	100	100
Pulsejet/s + fuel tanks	380	280
Fuel	1,400	1,100
Take-off wt (without RATO)	3,300	2,900
Take-off wing loading (kg/m²)	300.0	263.6
Landing wt (kg), 20% rest fuel	2,180	2,020
Landing wing loading (kg/m²)	198.2	183.6

Performance		
Max. speed (km/h), full power at 0 km	810	710
Max. speed (km/h), full power at 3 km	780	660
Max. speed (km/h), full power at 0 km (50% fuel)	710	590
Climb rate (m/sec), mean flying wt at 0 km	18.5	12.0
Climb rate (m/sec), mean flying wt at 3 km	11.5	6.5
Climb rate (m/sec), mean flying wt at 6 km	5.0	1.5
Range (km), full power at 0 km	270	250
Range (km), full power at 3 km	350	320
Range (km), full power at 6 km	410	380
Endurance (mins), full power at 0 km	20	21
Endurance (mins), full power at 3 km	29	32
Endurance (mins), throttled, at 0 km	40	45
Endurance (mins), throttled, at 3 km	40	45
Endurance (mins), throttled, at 6 km	40	45
Service ceiling (km), at climb rate I m/sec	8.0	6.5
Take-off run (m), with 1,000 kg RATO thrust	550	550

*2 x MK 103 could be fitted, or two triple-barrel SG 118

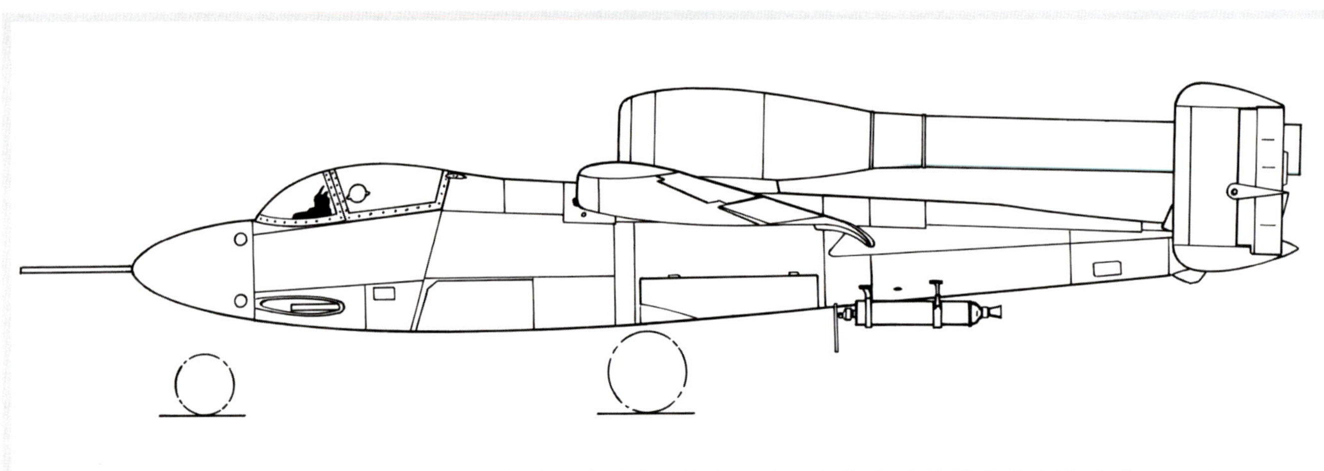

Side view of the Heinkel He 162 project dated 31 March 1945 fitted with one Argus As 014 pulsejet and RATO engines.

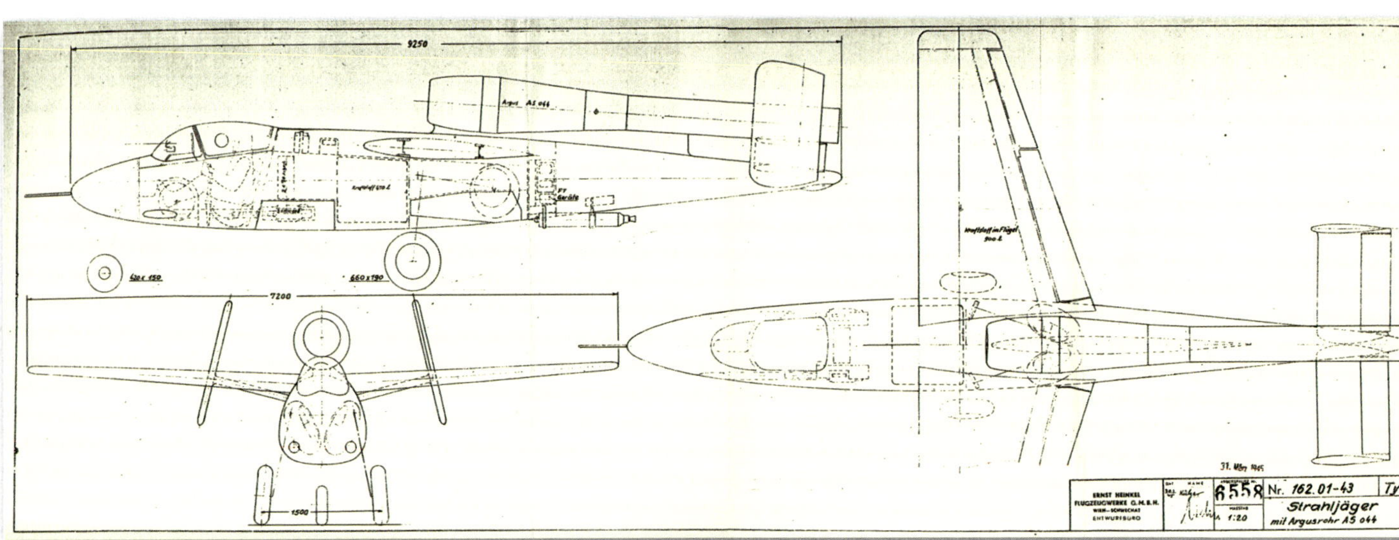

A Heinkel drawing dated 31 March 1945 in which a He 162 is fitted with one Argus As 044 pulsejet.

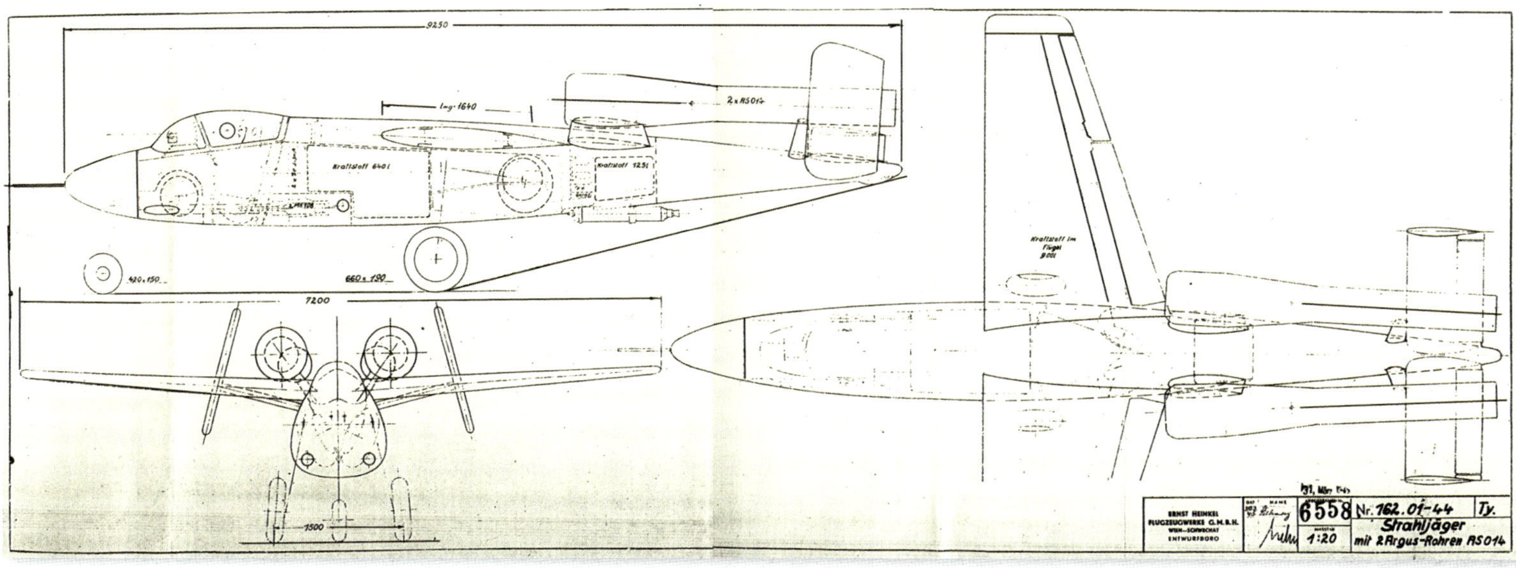

A Heinkel drawing dated 31 March 1945 in which a He 162 is fitted with two Argus As 014 pulsejets.

The Argus As 014 pulsejet.

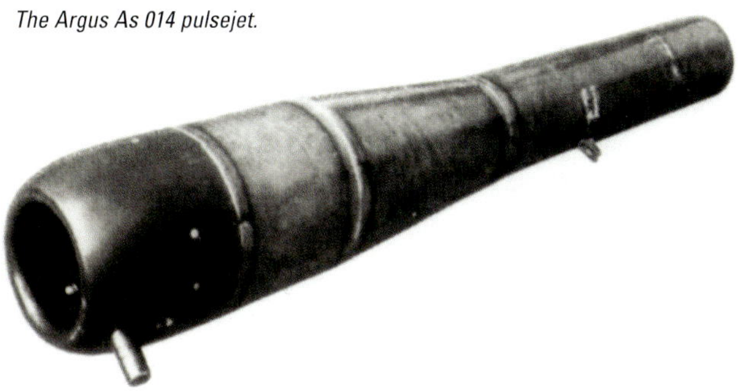

The Argus As 044 pulsejet.

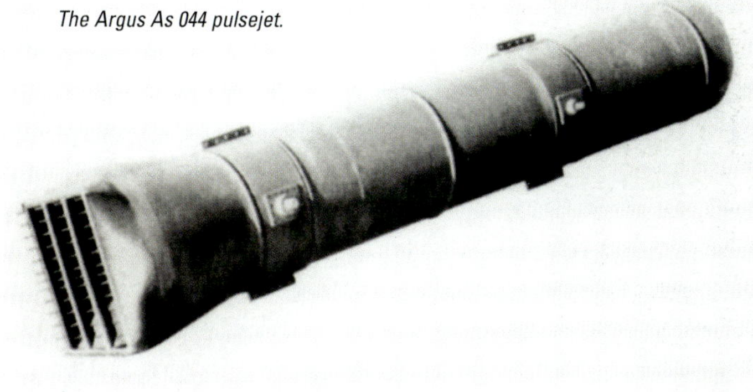

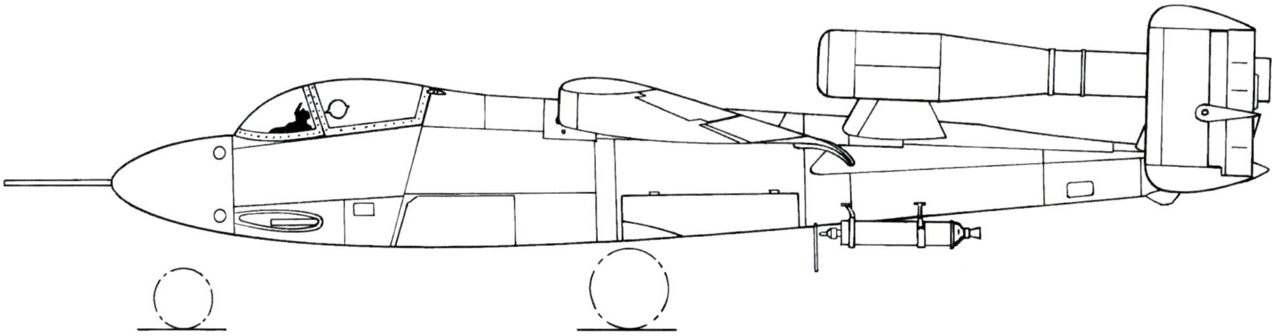

Side view of the Heinkel He 162 project dated 31 March 1945 fitted with two Argus As 014 pulsejets and RATO engines.

He 162 with SG 117

In 1945, ballistics specialists at the Automatic Weapons Munitions Department at WKW, the Weapons Research and Development Division of the Rheinmetall-Borsig Works and Proving Ground at Unterlüss, 50 km north-west of Celle, conducted feasibility studies to significantly increase the cannon armament of the He 162 for operations against Allied heavy bombers. In a report prepared for the Allies in July 1945, *Dr.-Ing.* Josef Schoetz, a ballistics technician at Rheinmetall-Borsig, explained that '... combat tactics deployed by fighters against bombers, consisted mainly of frontal or rear attacks. However, it became evident during 1943/44 that these tactics failed to guarantee successful destruction of the bomber.

'In the direct frontal and rear attack the bomber offered a small target which required accurate approach and accurate fire. This situation was made more challenging by the defensive fire from the bomber formation which was often intense enough to destroy the fighter...

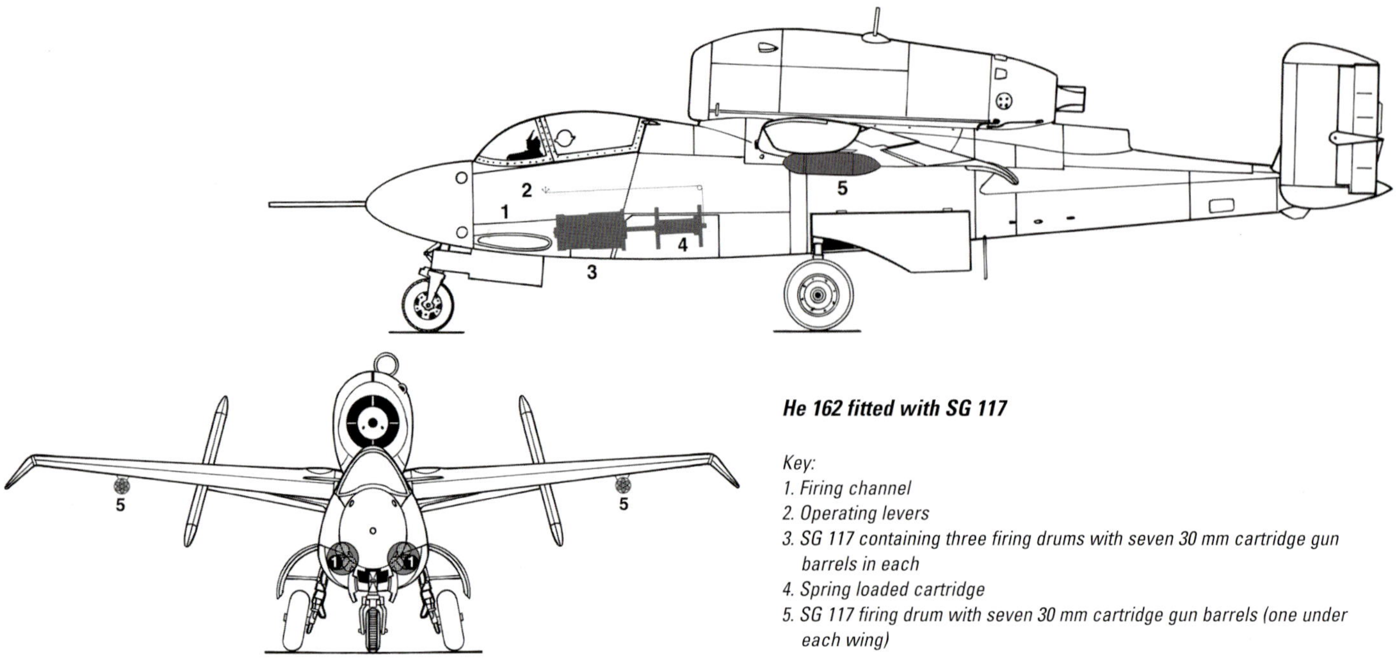

He 162 fitted with SG 117

Key:
1. Firing channel
2. Operating levers
3. SG 117 containing three firing drums with seven 30 mm cartridge gun barrels in each
4. Spring loaded cartridge
5. SG 117 firing drum with seven 30 mm cartridge gun barrels (one under each wing)

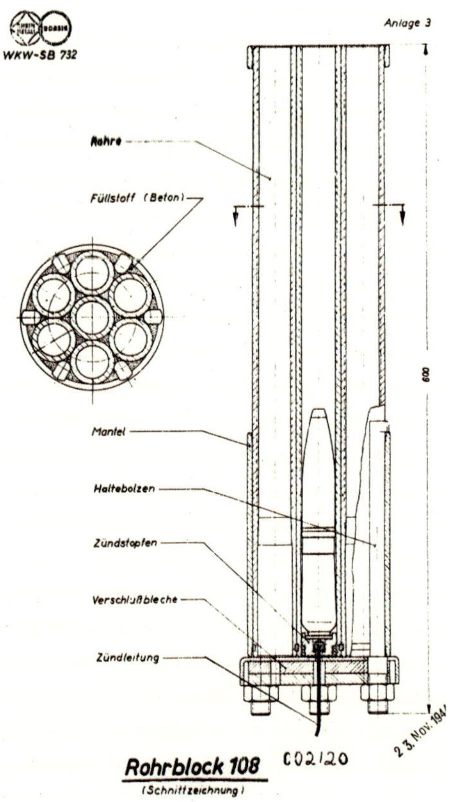

A Rheinmetall-Borsig drawing dated 23 November 1944 showing a cutaway of the Rohrblock 108.

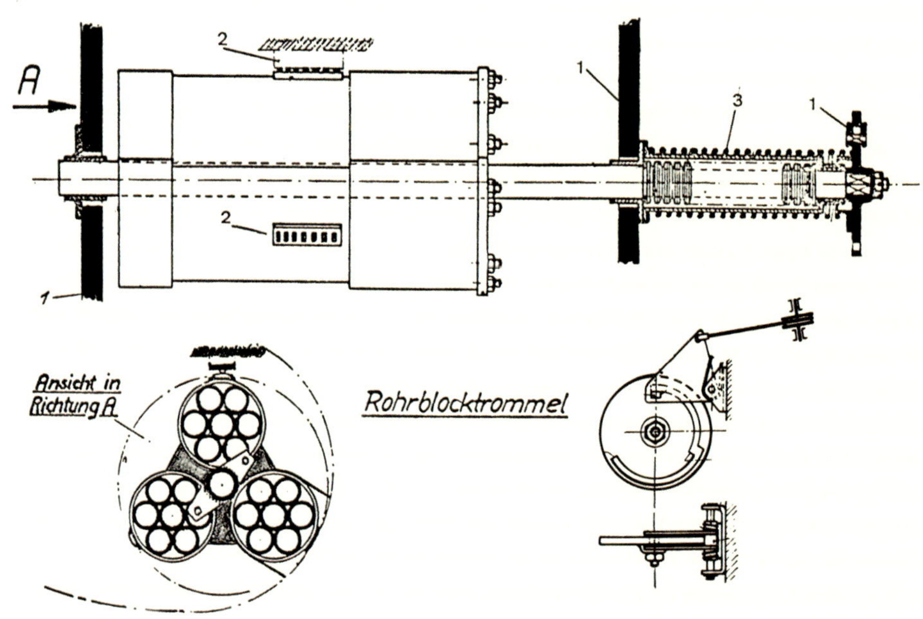

A Rheinmetall-Borsig drawing from 1945 showing the planned fuselage installation of two Rohrbatterie in the He 162.

The development of high-speed jet-propelled fighters of approximately 800 km/h, com-bined a high velocity with the minimum size of aircraft and a flight duration of only a few minutes – for example the He 162.'

Schoetz' point was that for the He 162 fighter – a fighter which was envisaged to be produced in great numbers, but dogged by limited combat endurance – to be tactically effective against '*Pulks*' of heavy bombers with massed defensive firepower it would need to be able to deliver the maximum weight of firepower in the quickest possible time. With rigidly fixed machine gun or cannon armament, such as the standard MG 151 or MK 108 installation in the He 162, a pilot was required to fly directly at the target and remain 'locked on' to it in his sights for several seconds in order to ensure a sufficient number of strikes with a comfortable degree of probability. In order to reduce this period, during which the pilot and fighter would be exposed to defensive fire, the Germans endeavoured to develop weapons offering a 'spray fire', 'fan fire' or '*Schrottschuss*' (shotgun fire) effect, resembling a wide 'blast' or arc of fire, rather than a single stream.

During the autumn of 1944, the engineers at Unterlüss had been developing a new weapons system known variously as the SG 117 ('SG' standing for *Sonder Gerät* – 'special device'), the 3 cm *Rohrbatterie* or the *Rohrblock* 108. The weapon comprised a battery of seven barrels each containing one 30 mm MK 108 cannon round. The barrels were clustered cylindrically, held together by a metal brace, running to a breech block and fired by means of an electric connection. The shells left the barrels sequentially.

It was proposed to group three such batteries into one revolving barrel drum made up of three *Rohrblocks* holding seven rounds per battery. The drums (a set of two) were to be installed in the fuselage where the usual MK 108s or MG 151s were housed, meaning that a pilot would be able to fire a salvo of 2 x 7 rounds at a bomber from the fuselage position. Additionally, a single SG 117 'barrel block' unit, (one that was made with a mounting rail) could be slung beneath each outer wing, offering a further 14 rounds in total.

The pilot of the He 162 would fire the weapons by means of a trigger-button on his control column, but a selector switch would allow him to fire salvos either from two batteries in the fuselage-mounted revolving drum or the two wing-mounted blocks, or to fire from the drums and wing blocks simultaneously.

The under-wing SG 117s were to be fitted with an aerodynamic, faired cover, which could be jettisoned by igniting combustible bands just before opening fire.

The three drum batteries were to be fitted around a tubular shaft and connected rigidly to it. The shaft was to be fitted to the aircraft by means of two flanged bearings, with the shaft being able to slide within the bearings. In order to absorb the projected recoil of some 2,000 kg, a buffer spring – composed of plate springs – was to be fitted on the shafts. A recoil of approximately 22 mm was anticipated. The recoil shock would be transmitted to the springs by means of a disc which was pushed along the shaft by means of a key. The other end of the springs would butt against a tubular cartridge by means of another disc. The tubular cartridge was to be connected by means of a flange with the rear flange bearing. At the end, the shaft would have carried a sliding sleeve, a locking disc and a castellated nut. This nut would have made it possible to modify the tension of the plate-shaped springs, but care would have had to be taken not to allow any axial play on the shaft. The recoil action of the drum pressed the rear disc rearward, through the sliding sleeve, the locking disc and castellated nut. The plate-shape springs would then be compressed forward and partly absorb the counter recoil energy.

A strong, pre-loaded torsion spring applied to the tubular sleeve connecting on one side to the flange of the tubular sleeve and on the other side to the locking disc, would have turned the drum in one direction. The free rotation would be controlled by a latch in the recess of the key way of the locking disc. The latch, fixed to the sheet metal segments and the hub would have taken part in the back-movement of the drum. The hub was to slide on the pin. The pin would be held by the bearing fastened to the aircraft. After the first barrel block had been fired, the pilot was to release the latch by means of a cable and the tension of the spring would make the drum revolve by one section, until the latch reached the recess. After firing the second barrel block, the pilot was to release the latch and the spring would turn the drum by one section until the latch reached the recess. In this position the third block could be fired.

Loading would have begun with the third block, turned one section backwards by hand, until the latch was brought in front of the surface. After the second block had been loaded, the drum would again be turned by hand, until the latch was in front of the surface, and then the first block was loaded.

The firing of each block was to have been effected by means of an electric cylindrical switch. The seven rounds of one barrel block followed each other at a distance of 6 m. The seven firing cables of the first barrel block led to a contact case on the second barrel block. The contact case was provided with sliding elements which pressed the contact springs of the contact case. The contact case was to be fixed to the aircraft. From this contact box, the firing cables were to be conducted to the cylinidrical switch. The firing cables of the second barrel block were to be linked to the contact case on the third barrel block, and then to the case on the first barrel block.

For loading, the cover of the third barrel block was to be removed and the cartridges with the contact cases were inserted into the barrels. The cover was screwed on the barrel block again after the firing cables were fed through the corresponding holes in the cover. The firing cables would then have had to be connected numerically to the contact case on the second barrel block. The loading of the second and first barrel blocks was carried out in a similar way.

The pulling cables of the left and right drums would have been united into one cable, which was brought through the different block pulleys near the pilot and ended there in a three-way lever.

There would have been a cover in the fuselage wall for the purpose of servicing the installation. The drum would have been sealed internally by a coating between the ribs.[2]

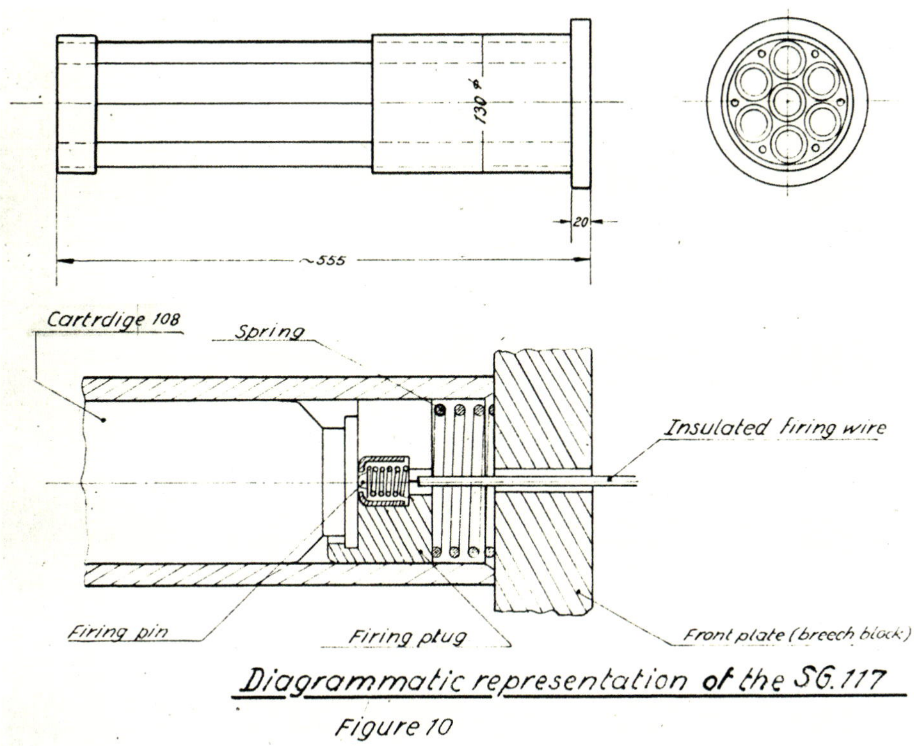

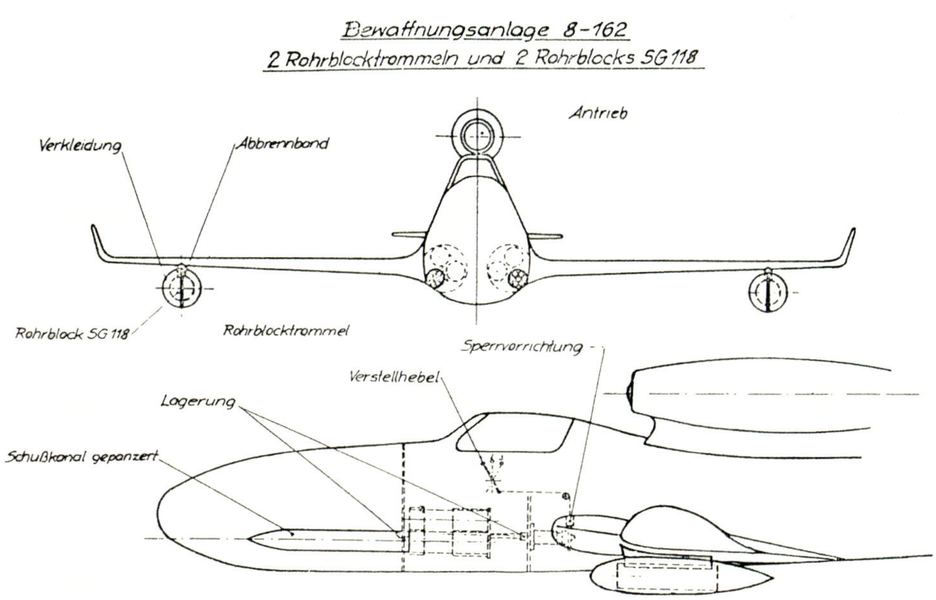

Two contemporary drawings from 1945 produced for the Allies by a former Rheinmetall-Borsig engineer showing (above) the design of a single SG 117 unit and (below) the installation of SG 117 batteries in both fuselage and on the outer wings of the He 162.

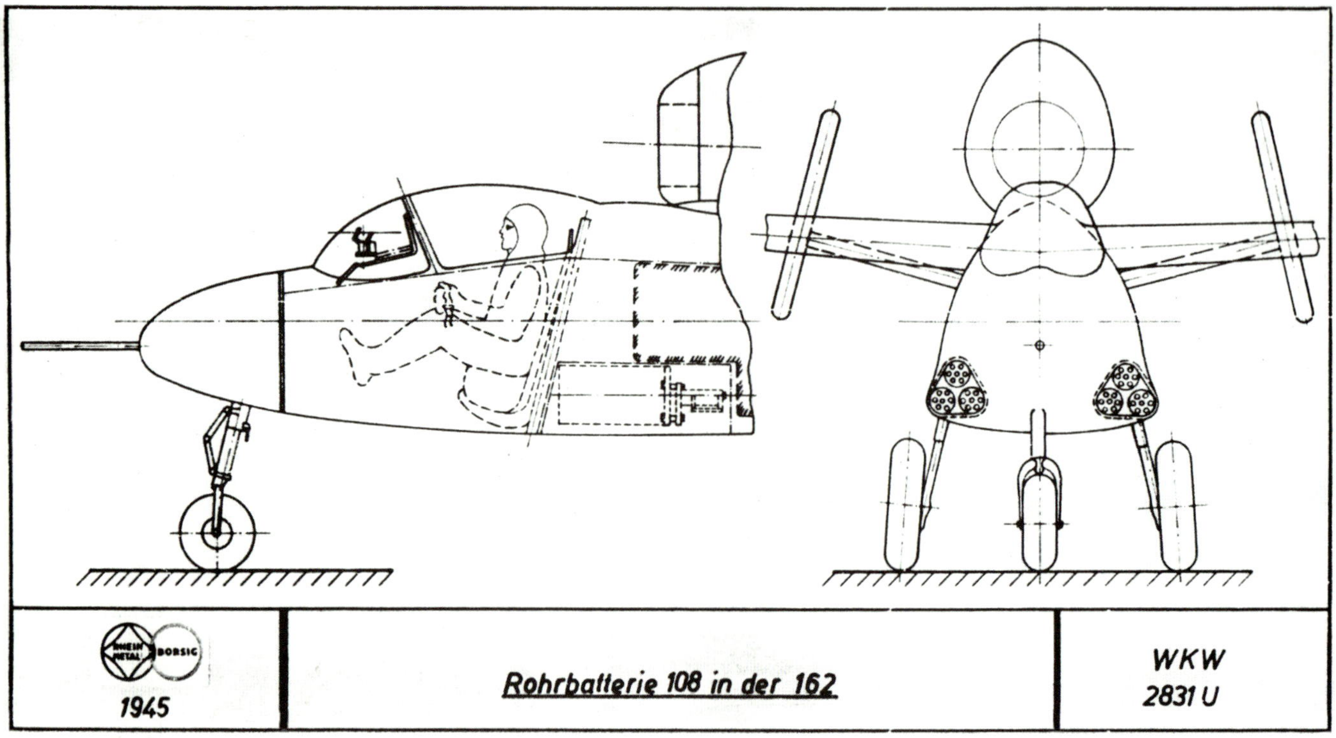

A contemporary drawing of a 'triple-barrelled' SG 117 configuration which was planned for installation in the He 162 and which was to be fitted in the bays where the MK 108 or MG 151 cannon would usually be located as per the drawing (left).

Front and rear views of the seven-barrel 30 mm Sondergeräte SG 117 Rohrbatterie intended for installation in the He 162. The weapon is rigged up to a test-firing stand at the Rheinmetal-Borsig firing range at Unterlüss.

He 162 with R4Ms

It will be recalled from Chapter Two that following his flight in the He 162 at Schwechat in February 1945, *Oberst* Gordon Gollob, the *General der Jagdflieger*, asked EHAG to study the possibility of fitting 55 mm R4M air-to-air rockets (as planned for the Me 262) and to report by 20 February. Long before that, as early as 14 October 1944, Dr. Francke's *Technische Direktion* at EHAG Wien-Schwechat had assigned their specialist, Töpfer, the task of examining as a project, in what form it would be possible to install two BR 50 BS projectiles or, alternatively, the R4M in the He 162.[3]

In early 1944 German ballistics engineers had recognised that the installation of rockets would become 'indispensable' as the possibility of introducing greater ranges of fixed armament into a single fighter aircraft became increasingly difficult, combined with the corresponding increase in defensive firepower of Allied bomber formations.

Throughout the latter half of 1943 and into 1944, following the mixed success of the W.Gr 21 cm mortar, German armaments experts recognised that the only plausible alternative was for a fighter formation to attack a bomber *Pulk* simultaneously firing batteries of rockets carried either in underwing racks or in nose-mounted 'honeycombs' with which a dense 'fire-chain' could be created and which would be impossible for the bombers to avoid. In June 1944, a requirement was put forward by the *Luftwaffe's* Technical Equipment Office for an electrically fired, fin-stabilised weapon whose warhead would contain sufficient explosive to destroy a four-engine bomber in one hit. Four weeks later, a powerful consortium of companies, each with individual responsibility for different components was formed and led by the Deutsche Waffen und Munitionswerke (DWM) Research Institute in Lübeck.

This consortium duly presented the Technical Equipment Office with a proposal for an 814 mm long, 55 mm calibre rocket with a warhead containing 520 g of HTA explosive and ignited by an AZR 2 detonator, all bearing a weight of 3,500 g. The rocket was intended to be launched against aerial targets from a range of 800 metres and be stabilised by eight fins which would open automatically by aerodynamic drag immediately after launching.

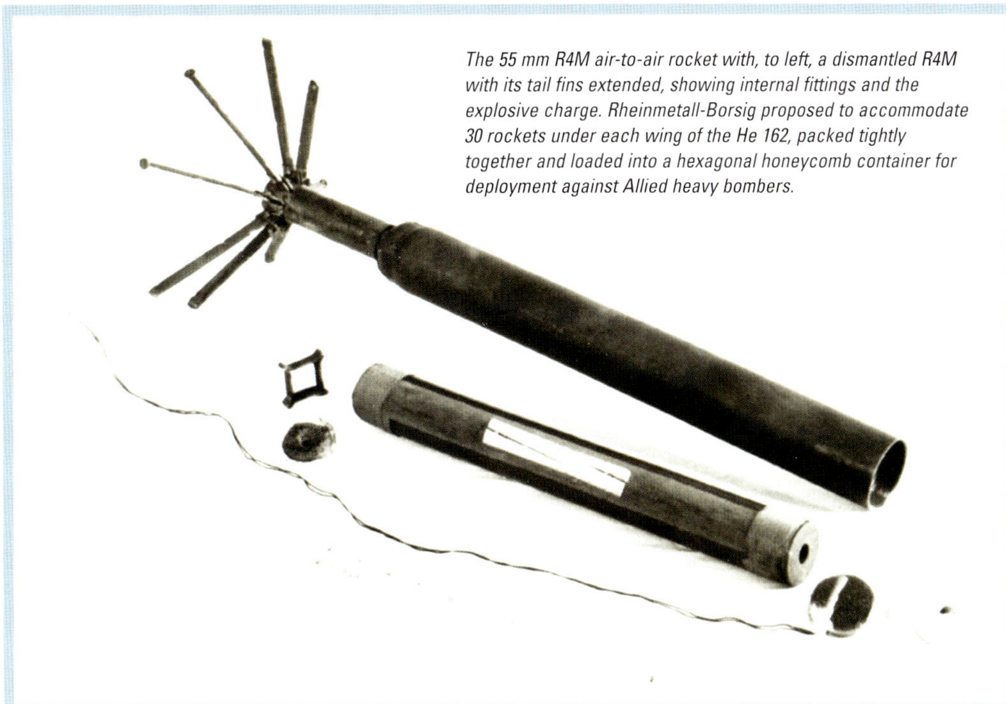

The 55 mm R4M air-to-air rocket with, to left, a dismantled R4M with its tail fins extended, showing internal fittings and the explosive charge. Rheinmetall-Borsig proposed to accommodate 30 rockets under each wing of the He 162, packed tightly together and loaded into a hexagonal honeycomb container for deployment against Allied heavy bombers.

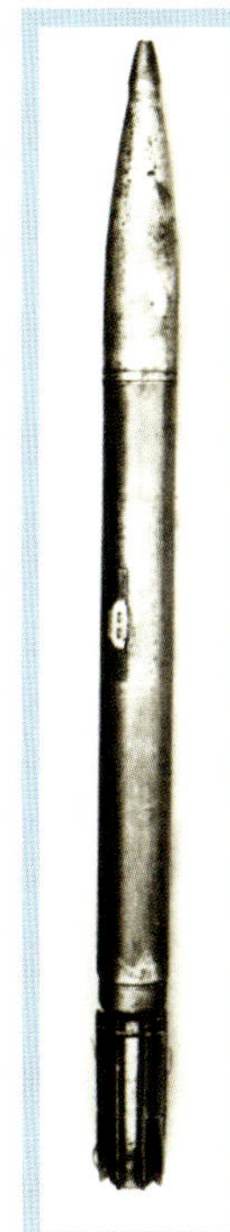

The proposal was received favourably and the designation 'R4M' (*Rakete 4 kg Minenkopf*) applied to the project. Firing trials took place at the end of October 1944 on the Strehla firing range at the Westin works of Brünn AG and at Kurt Heber at Osteroda. However, the *Erprobungsstellen* at Rechlin (which had conducted the first air launches in December 1944) and Tarnewitz both judged that the missile was still unsatisfactory as a result of the poor standard of manufacture of some individual parts. By the end of January 1945, once some initial burn-out problems had been solved, a general re-working of the rocket, incorporating various aerodynamic and warhead refinements, was conducted.

In its final form, the R4M appeared as an unrotated, rail or tube-launched, single venturi, solid-fuel propelled, multi-fin-stabilised missile, with the warhead contained in an exceptionally thin 1 mm sheet steel case enclosed in two pressed steel sections welded together and holding the Hexogen high-explosive charge. The missile bore a high charge weight to case weight ratio.

The weapon first saw action when fitted to the Me 262s of JG 7 and JV 44 in March and April 1945 when these units achieved some devastating success against B-17s and the ballistics specialists at Rheinmetall-Borsig wanted to emulate this success with the He 162. It was proposed to mount 'honeycomb' batteries of 30 R4Ms under each wing to be used in a similar manner to the SG 118 or *Rohrblock* 108 described previously.

A report prepared by Rheinmetall-Borsig on the feasibility of mounting R4M rockets into the He 162 stated: 'The R4M leaves behind a considerable stream of gas flows which means it cannot be installed in front of other cell components and consequently the only arrangement which can be considered is under the wings.

'It was planned to accommodate 30 rockets under each wing, packed tightly together and loaded into a hexagonal honeycomb container. With such an arrangement only 2 rounds can be fired at a time, one round from each honeycomb. There must be an interval of 70 m between rounds in order to prevent succeeding projectiles being obstructed by the preceding ones. A rate of fire of 1,700 rounds per minute is therefore achievable.

'By sub-dividing the 30-cell honeycomb into two combs with 15 rounds each and suspending them under the wing at a distance of approximately 500 mm apart, it is possible at any time to discharge 4 rounds simultaneously, thereby raising the cyclic rate to 3,400 rounds per minute. Since the R4M has a calibre of 5 cm, this is a considerable improvement in performance compared with other armament installations.

'The firing of a burst of 4 rounds is effected by means of an electrical cylinder switch, such as has been designed for the SG 119. It is possible in this way to fire continuous bursts, as well as release a pre-determined number of bursts.

'The honeycomb magazines are enclosed in an aerodynamic cover, which is discarded by the pilot before the attack by igniting a combustible tape.

'The weight of the complete weapon installation including the ammunition is approximately 250 kg. An advantage here is that after firing the rockets, the aircraft has only 40 kg to carry, and this can also be jettisoned if desired. In other weapon installations high dead weights or the armament remains with the aircraft.'[4]

Despite the development study by Rheinmetall-Borsig, the He 162 never carried R4M missiles.

Mistel 5

Planned in late November 1944, a concept was conceived to use the He 162 in a '*Mistel*' composite configuration in which the He 162 formed the upper component. Constructed from non-strategic materials in relatively few man-hours, the He 162 was considered by some to be the ideal delivery vehicle for a powered version of the Arado E 377 – known as the E 377a. In its original form the E 377 was to be an unpowered, expendable aircraft – in reality, an air-launched bomb – which would carry either a 2,000 kg hollow-charge warhead or a SC 1800 bomb mounted in its nose. The E 377a was to be fitted with a pair of BMW 003 A-1 engines.

In the final plan, no control surfaces or undercarriage were to be fitted to the E 377 because of the expense involved and the missile was intended simply to be aimed at its target and launched. Rheinmetall-Borsig had developed a 3.5-ton take-off trolley onto which the expendable aircraft could be hoisted. The He 162 would then be lifted on top and connected to it by struts fitted with explosive bolts. The five-wheeled trolley was to be jettisoned shortly after take-off.

In January 1945, development work for the proposed *Mistel* 5 was transferred by the RLM to Junkers who devised the Ju 268, their own version of an expendable aircraft, along the lines of the E 377a. A year later, in January 1946, a report on the proposed Ju 268/He 162

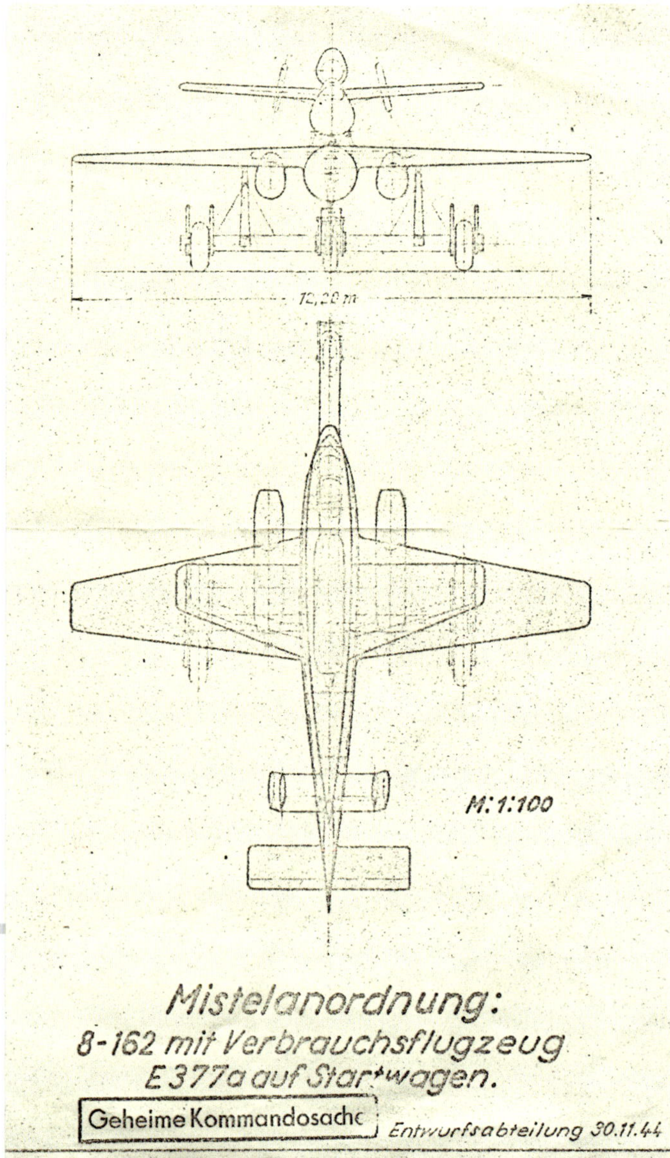

An original Arado drawing of the He 162 and Ar E377a proposed Mistel combination dated 30 November 1944.

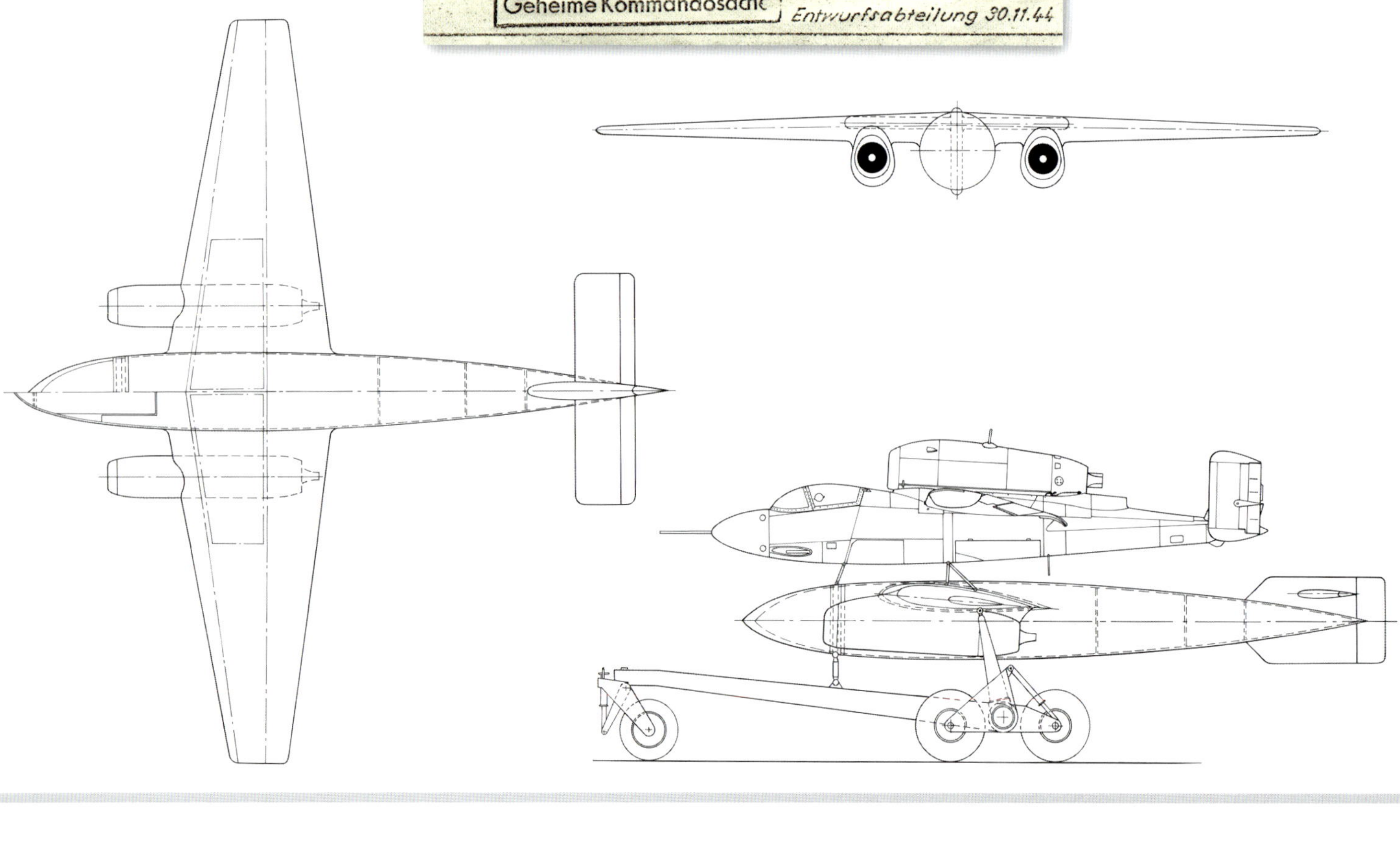

He 162 and three-view drawing of the Ar E377a, proposed as a Mistel combination from 30 November 1944.

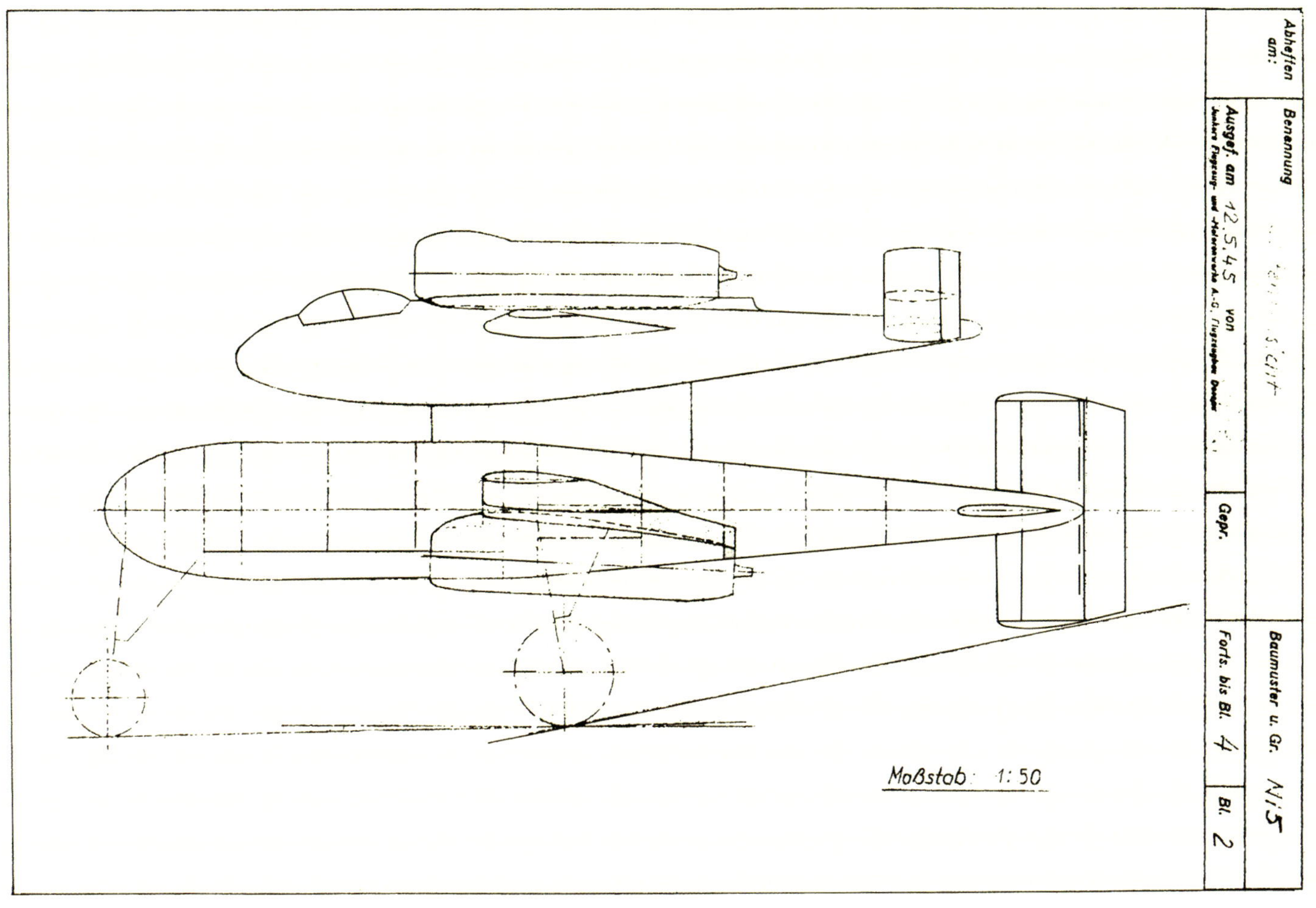

Two Junkers drawings of the He 162/Ju 268 Mistel combination proposals. These drawings were produced by Junkers personnel at the instigation of Russian forces occupying the Junkers factory after the war. The drawings are dated as 12 May 1945.

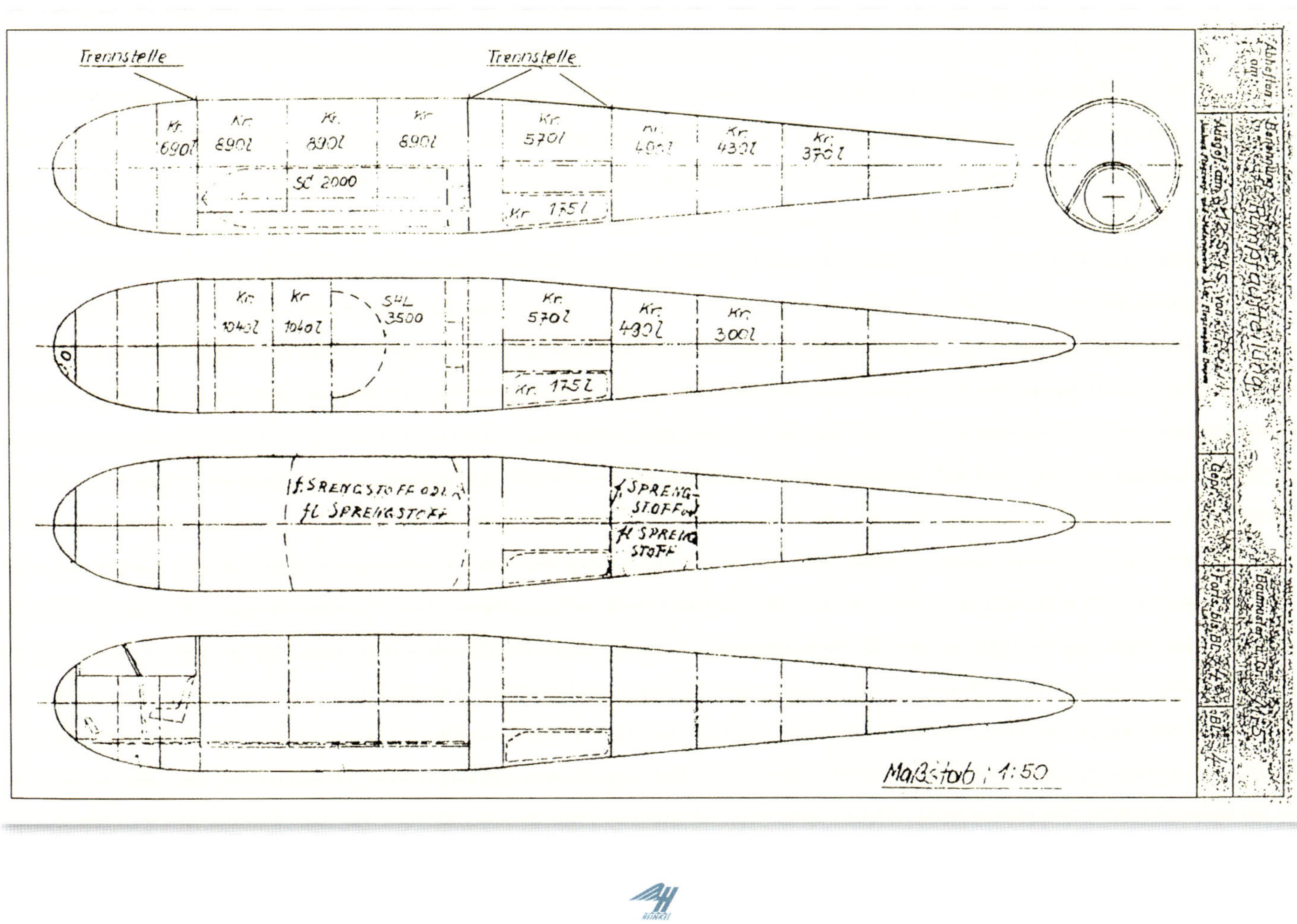

He 162/Ar E377a Mistel Composite	He 162A (upper)	Ar E 377a (lower)	Both together
Powerplant	1 x BMW 003E	2 x BMW 003A-1	3 x BMW 003
Thrust (kg), sea-level static	1 x 800	2 x 800	3 x 800
Wingspan (m)	7.20	12.20	
Length (m)	9.05	10.90	
Wing area (m²)	11.00	25.00	36.00
Fuel wt (kg)	870	4,500	5,360
Warhead wt (kg)	-	1,800-2,000	
Take-off wt (kg) w/o trolley	2,900	10,400	13,300
Wing ldg (kg/m²) w/o trolley	263.6	416.0	369.4
Take-off wt (kg) with trolley			17,300
Wing ldg (kg/m²) with trolley			480.6
Flight wt (kg) over target at maximum penetration depth	2,900	5,900	8,800
Wing loading (kg/m²) at target	263.6	236.0	244.4

The specifications for this Mistel variant were given as follows:

He 162/Ju 268 Mistel Composite	He 162A (upper)	Ju 268 (lower)	Both together
Powerplant	1 x BMW 003E	2 x BMW 003A	3 x BMW 003
Wingspan (m)	7.20	11.50	
Length (m)	9.05	10.90*	
Wing area (m²)	11.00	22.00	33.00
Fuel capacity (ltrs)	1,540	5,080	6,620
Explosive load (kg)	-	2,000**	2,000
Equipped wt (kg)	1,725	4,300	6,025
Take-off wt (kg) (w/o RATO and jettisonable undercarriage)	3,100	10,500	13,600
Max. speed (km/h) at sea-level	790		780
Max. speed (km/h) at 6 km	840		820
Cruising speed (km/h) at 11 km			800
Rate of climb (m/sec) at 0 km			16.0
Rate of climb (m/sec) at 6 km			8.5
Take-off run (m) (with 6 x RATO units)			1,400

* With 2,000 kg warhead.

** Alternative warheads were a 3,500 kg hollow-charge warhead, and a steel-cased warhead also of 3,500 kg weight.

combination prepared by AI2(g) of British Air Ministry Intelligence stated: 'The upper component of this composite aircraft is the He 162 single-jet fighter. The lower component, a Junkers aircraft designated 8-268, carries the warhead and is a twin-jet mid-wing monoplane of wood construction with twin fins and rudders, powered by two BMW 003 jet units. A jettisonable tricycle undercarriage is fitted.

'Three alternative warheads were projected for the 8-268, (a) the first consisting of one SC 2000-kg bomb cradled in the lower forward part of the fuselage, (b) the second, a steel-cased hollow-charge warhead of 3,500 kg mounted near the centre of gravity, and (c) the third, a steel-cased solid head of the same weight mounted in a similar position.

'It was also foreseen that the lower component should be used as a separate aircraft with conventional controls.'[5]

The specifications for this Mistel variant are shown in the above table.

In mid-January 1945, Junkers had calculated that a range of 1,600 km with a maximum speed of 820 km/h at 6,000 m altitude was attainable. Although the project was reported to have been '... in preparation in its final form' in March 1945 and a low-speed wind tunnel test on a '*Mistel* 5 twin jet aircraft' was carried out at Junkers Dessau on 19 April, no such *Mistel* were ever produced.[6]

A drawing showing the Ju 268 configuration survives which was dated 12 May 1945, by which time the Junkers factory had fallen into Russian hands.

Investigations had also been made to fit the WVR-1 and FS-Revi target-aiming devices in the Ju 268/He 162 and Me 262/He 162 composites, but remained only a project.[7]

CHAPTER FIVE

'Falling Leaf'

Allied Testing, Assessment and Further Development

'We removed the propellers and rudders from the aircraft and ensured the magazines were empty. As airmen, this vision alone was enough to plunge us into a deep sadness. Our pride, our weapons, our world – all this is is now nothing. Between 30 and 40 He 162 jet fighters – the fastest aircraft in the world – weapons that could have given us victory and swept the bomber Pulks from the skies – are lined up forlornly in front of the hangars ready to be surrendered to the enemy. The same fate awaits our machine guns, our Panzerfauste… even the rifles carried by our guards.'

WAR DIARY OF *JAGDGESCHWADER* 4

'I cannot help but feel that the Allies were fortunate for, had another month or two and the necessary fuel been available, the He 162 might well have got in among our bombers in numbers at a time when desperate measures might just have achieved sensational results.'

TEST PILOT CAPTAIN ERIC BROWN, CBE, DSC, AFC, RN

BY 6 May 1945, armour and infantry units from 8 Corps of Field Marshal Montgomery's 21st Army Group had pushed into Schleswig-Holstein in northern Germany and had reached Leck. Here they discovered the large assembly of *Luftwaffe* aircraft gathered there, including the He 162 jet fighters of *Jagdgeschwader* 1 which were dispersed around the airfield. They raised considerable interest amongst the British troops and *Obstlt*. Nordmann, the local overseeing commander of air units, and *Obstlt*. Ihlefeld, the *Geschwaderkommodore*, were duly requested to rearrange the aircraft so that they could be more easily and closely inspected when further British forces, including technical intelligence personnel, arrived at the airfield over the next few days. The German officers were informed, meanwhile, that as long as they co-operated, they would be allowed to retain their sidearms. An agreement was reached between the British and the Germans and Ihlefeld instructed his staff accordingly. The bulk of the British units rumbled off.

The RAF moved reasonably quickly to examine its war booty. In the evening of 29 May 1945, Group Captain G. Mungo Buxton, the Chief Technical Officer of the Central Fighter Establishment (CFE) at Tangmere in Sussex, together with Squadron Leader R.M. Cracknell, Engineering Officer at the Royal Aircraft Establishment (RAE) at Farnborough, landed at Schleswig airfield following a flight from Tangmere. This was to be their base in Germany from where they would arrange to examine, assess and exploit captured German aircraft and aeronautical equipment: according to Mungo Buxton, the first stage of the mission was to '…select the total number of German aircraft to be flown so that the servicing could be organised in a systematic way.'[1] One of the first jobs was to inspect two Me 262s on the airfield which were in the hands of a team from the RAE under Lieutenant Commander Eric Brown, an extremely experienced Royal Navy test pilot who was fluent in German. Mungo Buxton directed that these aircraft should be flown

A rare view of up to five He 162s of JG 1 photographed outside a hangar at Leck very shortly after the German surrender.

The derelict and engineless airframe of a He 162 photographed at an unknown location in mid-1945. The wings of the aircraft lie inverted on a pallet in front of the nose, while the nose cone is on the ground in front of the fuselage. This would have been a common site at certain locations around Germany and Austria at this time.

With the cessation of hostilities and their aircraft under British control, from left, Leutnant Hans Berger, Oberleutnant Emil Demuth, Staffelkapitän of 3./JG 1, Leutnant Gerhard Hanf and Oberleutnant Wilhelm Krebs, play a game of 'Doppelkopf' in the May sunshine. Behind them, fixed to the tent pole are three emblems of JG 1: top – the red '1' of JG 1; centre – the demon emblem of I./JG 1; and bottom, the Lion of Danzig of 3./JG 1.

Volksjäger in the scrap dump: the remains of a He 162 lie abandoned next to a He 111 bomber. This photograph could well have been taken in the north of Germany, possibly at Leck, since a number of similarly camouflaged He 111s belonging to KG 3 and KG 53 were found on airfields in the Leck area.

to England via refuelling stops at Twente and Gilze-Rijen. Brown had already encountered the He 162 by this point and had noted down his first impressions: 'An exciting-looking aeroplane, though not exactly beautiful. There is so much wood around that it looks as though it has been built by a modelling enthusiast. Its narrow-track undercarriage is likely to make it a handful in a crosswind. An oversize V-1 on wheels!'[2]

At Schleswig Mungo Buxton and Cracknell also met Wing Commander Wheeler of 2nd TAF's Air Technical Intelligence. Shortly after, Mungo Buxton flew one of the Me 262s personally to Gilze-Rijen. Over the course of the next few days, and accompanied by Flight Lieutenant Calvert of Signals Intelligence, the team journeyed back into Germany stopping at Schleswig, Flensburg, Leck, Eggebeck, as well as at Grove and Kastrup in Denmark. In all, as an initial selection, a total of 42 German aircraft were assigned for ferrying to the United Kingdom for 'research and trials', including Bf 109s, Fw 190s, Bf 110s, Ju 88s, Si 204s, Ju 352s, Ar 234s, a Ju 290, an Ar 232, He 219s, a Ta 152, an Fw 189, and an Me 410. Conspicuously absent from this list were the He 162s of JG 1 which, by now, had been neatly lined up at Leck by German crews to await their fate at the hands of Mungo Buxton's group. This was because the range of the He 162 was '... unknown but believed to be too small.'

By 29 May, the Enemy Aircraft Flight of the CFE had established working parties at Schleswig, Leck and Husum to attend to any mechanical or technical problems on both 'orthodox and jet aircraft' and their recovery for British inspection, assessment and trials. In a report prepared by Flight Lieutenant R.T.H.Collis, DFC, commanding the Enemy Aircraft Flight, it was stated that: '10 He 162s had been made serviceable at Leck and were ready to fly, when a last minute inspection showed the wooden control surfaces to have been affected by weather, and the machines were grounded pending further examination by a British Engineer (S/Ldr. Cracknell). Two spare

A bemused Leutnant Gerhard Stiemer peers at a sign erected by the 'new owners' at Leck in May 1945.

Left and above left: Oberleutnant Wolfgang Wollenweber (in the leather overcoat standing on the tarmac), former leader of 2./JG 1, supervises work on He 162 A-2 'White 3' outside one of the hangars on a rainy day at Leck in mid-May 1945. Wollenweber was assigned by the British to brief their test pilots on the characteristics of the Volksjäger. Note the barrel of the MG 151/20 20 mm cannon visible in its port, the red ring surrounding the BMW 003 engine intake and the starter cart nearby. Wollenweber is evidently unconcerned about his proximity to volatile jet fuel, for he seems to be enjoying a cigarette!

The cockpit of W.Nr. 120 086 as seen opposite.

The British carefully examined He 162 W.Nr. 120 086 at Leck, the aircraft of Leutnant Alfred Dürr of II./JG 1. This aircraft was noteworthy from the point of view that Dürr had been forced to land on the Autobahn north of Dänischburg near Lübeck due to a lack of fuel on 30 April 1945 (see Chapter Three). The aircraft is not believed to have carried a tactical number or unit markings. These two photographs offer good views of the canopy structure and frame, with the communication panel and, inside the cockpit, the headrest for the pilot and the Revi 16 b gunsight above the instrument panel. Also seen in these photographs is the barrel for the MG 151/20 cannon. Note the crude join between the fuselage and the nose cone. The photograph to above right provides a detailed view of the nosewheel construction. The stencilling on the nose reads: 'Aussenbordsteckdose im Bugradraum' = 'External socket box in nosewheel bay' and 'Hier unterbocken' = 'Prop here'

The hand pump in He 162 W.Nr. 120 086 to extend the flaps and the toggle release to lower the undercarriage.

A view of W.Nr. 120 086's throttle in the ground-idling position, with the fuel cock shut and undercarriage retraction lever in neutral.

Detailed view of lower instrument panel and nosewheel observation window.

The parachute as provided for the He 162, showing spring hook, transfer cock and installed oxygen.

Safety buckle for harness release on the He 162 pilot parachute.

The catapult seat removed from W.Nr. 120 086 to demonstrate the safety arm and trigger for ejection.

The nozzle (or 'tulip valve') position indicator markings for ground crew to check before take-off.

Below: View of port-side 'Lippisch ear' on W.Nr. 120 086 looking forward towards cockpit, Leck, May 1945.

Tail assembly of W.Nr. 120 086. Just visible in the background is the tail assembly of W.Nr. 120 076, 'Yellow 4', further along the right-hand row in the line-up at Leck.

The BMW 003 engine of this He 162 appears to have been removed and may be the engine unit in the foreground with the cowling removed. Note the unusually marked figure '8' as a tactical number on the aircraft. The British would need spare engines for the aircraft they were planning to ship to England.

Below: A He 162 of JG 1 as found by the British on Leck airfield.

Above and right: Front and rear views of a BMW 003 turbojet from JG 1's inventory at Leck in May 1945. The BMW emitted a violent streak of flame and efflux on starting, but if the start failed, the engine would have to be allowed to cool right down (taking some minutes) before re-start. Furthermore, the inside rims of the cowling around the rear nozzle would have to be thoroughly washed out to prevent a fire hazard when re-starting. One pilot from JG 1 recalls how, at Warnemünde, pilots would attempt to push the rear end of the diminutive jet fighter to the ground in order to drain any excess fuel out of the engine.

Two Luftwaffe personnel involved in briefing British test pilots and technical intelligence personnel on the characteristics of the He 162 at Leck. The officer on the left is believed to be Oberleutnant Wolfgang Wollenweber, former Kapitän of 2./JG 1. This photograph is taken from Squadron Leader R.M. Cracknell's report.

turbines and a collection of He 162 spares and tools were assembled at Leck... Ten special parachutes for the ejector seat of the He 162 had been repacked under supervision and assembled for the use of pilots flying the He 162s.'[3]

It would not be until 2 June that S/Ldr. Cracknell would make two assessment flights in a He 162 at Leck with the aim of taking readings for the RAE from which a rough estimate of the aircraft's ferrying range could be made. According to Cracknell: 'A German pilot and engineer was used to give information about the He 162. The pilot stated before take-off that he would like to demonstrate it to prove that it was satisfactory, which was reassuring about his good faith.'

Against a summer sky, an unidentified He 162 makes its landing approach at Leck. This is possibly a photograph of the He 162 being flown by the British test pilot, Squadron Leader R.M. Cracknell, who made two flights in a Volksjäger there on 2 June 1945. The photograph is taken from Cracknell's subsequent report.

The recollections of *Oblt.* Wolfgang Wollenweber, formerly of 3./JG 1, are of interest: 'When the Allied pilots came to Leck to take over our He 162s, *Oberst* Ihlefeld ordered me to explain to them the way to pilot these aircraft. To do this, I ordered the technicians to put my 'White 3' into flight readiness. Nevertheless, my 'show flight' was cancelled, the British test pilot considering that my help would not be necessary. Indeed, he made a perfect flight. After its landing, he said to us how much he was enthusiastic about the aircraft. My He 162 was refuelled for me but I would never receive authorisation to fly it. Surely, were they still suspicious of German pilots?'[4] Shortly after Cracknell's flights, there was a change in policy whereby the RAE assumed full responsibility for the recovery of all German aircraft from the CFE and the latter's ground crews and pilots were to work under RAE orders. By this stage F/Lt. Collis reported that: 'He 162s serviceable at Leck and waiting for disposal. Spares and tools and 400 gallons of J2 fuel assembled and ready for collection.'[6]

Altogether, eleven He 162s formerly belonging to JG 1 were eventually assigned 'AM' (Air Ministry) numbers by the British at Leck. These numbers were intended to identify an aircraft as being of interest to technical intelligence personnel at their place of surrender and as a means of differentiating such machines from the bulk which would, eventually, be scrapped. The teams headed by Mungo Buxton, and others, were to report on their selections directly to the Air Ministry's Under Secretary of State and 'AI2(g)' (Air Intelligence 2(g)) and to the Ministry of Aircraft Production.[7] Ordinarily, the aircraft were '...numbered in white paint on the port side of the fuselage, in

(Continued on page 158)

APPENDIX "B"

H.E. 162 FERRY TESTS

PRELIMINARY ACCOUNT

Information from Germans.

1. A German pilot and engineer was used to give information about the H.E. 162. The pilot stated before take-off that he would like to demonstrate it to prove that it was satisfactory, which was reassuring about his good faith.

2. He stated that the 1,200 metre runwa at Leck is only just sufficient, as the take-off and landing run is long. The Tulip valve should be switched to "A" at touch-down to reduce the thrust. Alternatively, the turbine can be closed down at touch-down to eliminate thrust during the landing run. He said the undercarriage is strong and that there is no disadvantage in the narrow track (presumably because of the good tricycle characteristics). He stated that there is a variation of up to 100 km. in top speed of different aeroplanes.

3. He said also that the undercarriage release might be stiff and that two hands should be used if necessary.

4. He lay great emphasis on the need for flying with the bubble central and using a minimum of rudder. He said that crashes had occurred through a yaw-roll oscillation which can build up until the aircraft goes out of control, if rudder is used. This is more likely to occur when flaps and undercarriage are down and he recommended a long, straight approach. He said that this aircraft will not spin.

PECULIARITIES FOUND

5. The first take-off in a cross wind was prolonged (the throttle may have slipped back slightly) and the aircraft had to be pulled off and it began to do this yaw-roll "falling leaf" oscillation. The undercarriage was retracted, which is a quick action; and at a safe height the flaps were retracted with marked loss of height. The second take off and landing on 1,200 metre runway were satisfactory, the wind being about 20 m.p.h. and dead in line.

6. The perspex is not optically good, which is rather a disadvantage for landing.

7. Oxygen endurance is small, being exhausted about half-way through the first flight which lasted 50 minutes. It had been turned on perhaps 5 minutes before take-off. On the second flight which lasted 45 minutes, oxygen was not turned on until about 7,000 feet had been reached and lasted until the descent.

Cockpit Controls

8. Cockpit Controls are ropey. The flap extending pump must be worked vigorously to start it and the flap can only be extended with comfortable pressure when at low speeds. On the second flight, I made a long straight approach and slowed to 240 kilometres per hour to do this. The undercarriage hydraulic kick-out occurred once before retraction was complete. The undercarriage spring release for extension worked with a strong one hand pull and the nose wheel can be seen extending, through the observation window between the pilots knees.

9. Tulip valve control is a new vital action. It has four positions:-

(A) For starting and for landing run.
(H) For high altitude use.
(S) For take-off, climb, normal flying, and full speed at moderate altitudes.
(F) For full speed at low altitudes.

/Before

-2-

Before take-off the ground crew should check that the tulip valve has moved to the correct position(s), marked on the fuselage(Photo:) to ensure there is thrust for take-off.

Cockpit Drill

10. The vital actions which are unfamiliar to English pilots and need attention in cockpit drill are:-

Flap Control.	Flaps are extended and retained by pumping and engaging pump handle in bayonet catch by pushing and turning to the RIGHT. Flaps are freed to fly up when the pump handle is pushed in and turned to the LEFT and a loss of height then occurs.
Tulip Valve Control.	This control must be operated before take-off and on touch down. Also, as may be expected in a cheap construction, throttle friction nut should be tight.

A.I.2(g) REPORTS

11. The following corrections are needed to A.D.I.(K) Report No. 309(b)1945 dated 16th May, 1945 and No. 234(D):-

The igniter-primer button is on the throttle, not on the stick.
Difficult to taxi, tow out if possible.
Elevator trim must be full TAIL HEAVY by the marking "START" on scale not central.
Rudder trim central.
Tulip valve must be at "S" not "H".

SUMMARY

12. The controls and aiming stability are good and will probably be of great interest to a fighter pilot. Undercarriage and brakes are satisfactory. Endurance is small and the oxygen endurance smaller still.

13. The "falling leaf" oscillation is peculiar, but may be explained by several unusual features in the aircraft:-

First, there are the anhedral wing tips which must give a high destabilizing moment in a skid, reinforced by the inertia moment of the heavy turbine on top. The pilot may instinctively use the rudder which is light, and this may aggravate the condition.

On take off, it is easy to try to guide the aircraft by using rudder, which is clearly undesirable because too much rudder may be on at the moment of leaving the ground. On the other hand, brakes cannot be used too much for steering on a short runway so that particular care must be given to lining up and keeping straight at the beginning of the run.

-3-

READINGS TAKEN DURING SECOND FLIGHT

TIME	R.P.M.	HEIGHT K.M.	SPEED AS SHEWN ON A.S.I.	TEMP: C.	INJECTION PRESSURE	REMARKS
1545	9700					Take-off
1546	9400	.4		585	35	Climb. Speed reduced 10 km/hr at each km. of height.
1547	9400	1	+350/340			
1548.45	9400	2	+340/330	580	30	
1550.30	9400	3	+330/320	580	25	
1552.45	9400	4	+320	590	21	
	9500	4	+495	540	+15	Full speed level.
1600	8900	4	+405	480	17	Level cruising speed for ferrying R.P.M. suggested by German pilot.
1608	8900	4.4	+340	500	17	
1611	8900/7000	(Contents gauge 410 litres).				Began descent
1615	7000/6000	3				Vibration note from engine at 7,000 r.p.m.
1617.40	6200	2	(330 approx. 340 litres)			
1628	landed, engine off during landing run. 180 litres on gauge.					

+ NOTE: Cockpit notice that A.S.I. reads 10% low.

ENGINE STARTING INSTRUCTIONS

1. Cockpit cover shut.

2. Switch on following switches, numbered from front:-

2. Immersed fuel pump.
5. Instruments.
6. Tulip valve. (Note selector is separate)
9. Two-stroke.

3. Tulip valve selector at "A".

4. Throttle against flap(not right back).

5. Two-stroke switch twice forward, then back, when it should start (this switch also selects inner scale on tachometer).

6. At a 1,000 r.p.m., open fuel cock and immediately press ignition - petrol injection button on throttle and open the throttle a little, quickly, if necessary.

7. At 1,100 r.p.m., release two-stroke switch and watch that the throttle is reduced enough to avoid exceeding 700° momentary maximum temperature.

8. Turbine idles at 3,000 r.p.m. against the flap while battery plug is taken out, No. 1 switch is to be on (aircraft battery).

General instructions were that No. 2 switch (immersed fuel pump) could be off for all flight, but it might be desirable to use it for take-off. The engine should be idle for one minute before take-off.

NOTE: There is no parking brake and brakes must be held on if chocks are not used.

/AIRFRAME AND ENGINE LIMITS

- 4 -

AIRFRAME AND ENGINE LIMITS

Engine Limits

r.p.m. maximum, 9,500
Temperature maximum, 600° .(700° momentary during starting)
Oil, 6 - 7.
Fuel, 45(?) about, decreasing to 10 at height or low power.

NOTE: Throttle must not be closed past the gate which gives 6,000 r.p.m. when in flight. It must be closed past the gate and back to the flap to reduce thrust on landing.

Airframe Limits

Acceleration, 4(g) maximum. (Cockpit placard)
Negative(g) not to be used. (Cockpit placard)
Maximum speed flaps in take-off position 500 Km/hr.
" " " in landing position, 300 Km/hr.
" " undercarriage out, 350 Km/hr.

NOTE: It is suspected that these speeds are high. The flaps cannot easily be extended by hand pump above about 240 kilometres per hour.

TO STOP THE ENGINE

Lift flap and close throttle completely, and immediately close fuel cock.

NOTE: On a short runway, this can be done on touching down and will eliminate the thrust during the landing run.

Squadron Leader R.M. Cracknell's report of June 1945 following his test flights in the He 162 at Leck.[5]

Heinkel He 162 A-2 W.Nr. 120230, 'White 23', Stab JG 1, Leck, May 1945

Although *Oberst* Herbert Ihlefeld, *Geschwaderkommodore* of JG 1, never flew an operational mission with the He 162, this aircraft is believed to have been his personal machine. It was the last He 162 built by the Heinkel-Rostock plant that was painted as per the paint specification '*Oberflächenschutzliste 8-162*' dated 9 January 1945. The fuselage was RLM 82/76, the upper wing surfaces RLM 81/82 and the tail fin and rudder were in RLM 76. The high tactical number and the black-white-red nose indicate that this was a *Stab* aircraft. The red arrow painted on the nose was typical of He 162s flown by JG 1 although the significance is not known. The aircraft was captured at Leck in May 1945.

This page and opposite: He 162 A-2 W.Nr. 120230 'White 23' at Leck, May 1945. The aircraft wears a scheme typical of I./JG 1's Heinkels, with a black/white/red nose tip, red arrows on either side of the nose section, the aircraft's tactical number in white applied just behind the cockpit and the engine intake ring in red. The other He 162 seen collapsed on one wheel in this sequence, above, is W.Nr. 120233.

In the summer of 1945, partially finished He 162 fuselages were hauled out of the 'Languste' facility in the Hinterbrühl in Austria and were lined along the quiet country roads ready for scrapping.

Some thirty or so He 162 fuselages line one of the main 'assembly halls' at the Junkers facility housed in a former salt mine at Tarthun, near Egeln in mid-1945. The Tarthun facility served as a production outstation of the Bernburg plant 30 kilometres to the east. All the fuselages have had their canopies fitted, but await delivery of tail sections from a sub-contractor. The three units to the left, in jigs, are at a slightly more advanced state of build.

American and British servicemen are shown the Tarthun facility by Junkers personnel and use the opportunity to examine the He 162 at close quarters.

When American troops reached the Junkers factory at Bernburg, amongst the plant's stock of aircraft they discovered a number of complete and partially complete He 162 airframes, including W.Nr. 310 020 seen here. The aircraft had not received its application of paint and was found in its bare metal and primer paste finish, except for the nose cone which was probably a sub-contractor-supplied component. The last two digits of the Werk Nummer were applied to the forward fuselage below the cockpit. The aircraft would appear to be fitted with MK 108 cannon rather than MG 151s and the BMW engine appears to have been removed, semi-forcibly rather than not having been installed at all. The canopy has been damaged, probably by Allied troops, who have also taken pot-shots at the vertical stabilizers.

A view of the cockpit of W.Nr. 310 020, which was either incomplete, or from which certain items have been 'liberated'.

Heinkel He 162 A-1 W.Nr. 310027 built by Junkers Zweigwerk, Bernburg, April 1945

W.Nr. 310027 was almost complete when it was found by US troops at Bernburg in April 1945. Because of the unpainted finish the construction lines of the He 162 are still clearly visible. The fuselage was constructed of Dural aluminium with the rivets and panel lines having been partially filled with smoothing/filler paste. The nose cone and weapons bay doors and their coverings were manufactured from timber. These parts were manufactured by different sub-contractors, which is why their colour shades differ slightly. The undercarriage doors were left in natural metal finish, while the tail fins were painted with primer paint, Flieglack 7139.99.

This page and opposite: Alongside W.Nr. 310 020 at Junkers Bernburg, US troops also discovered W.Nr. 310027, which was in a similar bare metal and primer paste finish, but which had its BMW 003 engine in place and which was finished in a darker paint, possibly RLM 81. As with its sister machine, the last two digits of the Werk Nummer were applied to the forward fuselage below the cockpit.

27

27

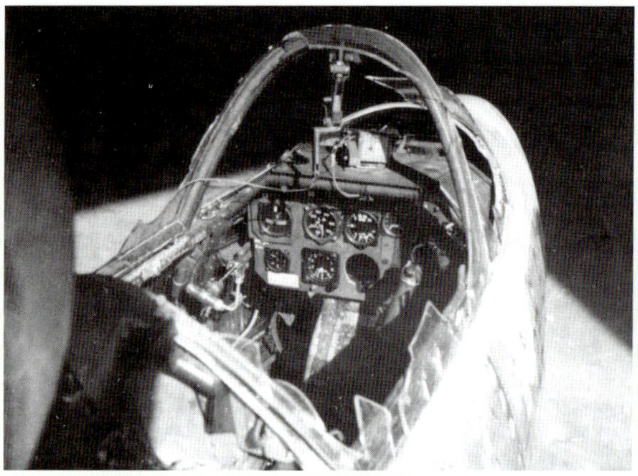

A view looking into the cockpit of W.Nr. 310 027 (seen on previous page), made possible because of its missing hood.

A close-up view of the engine intake of the BMW 003 of W.Nr. 310 020 seen on previous page.

front of the tailplane, with the words 'Air Ministry' so that they could be recognised', although whether this practice was applied to all the selected He 162s at Leck is not known.[8]

Of the selected He 162s, the known *Werk Nummern* are:

W.Nr. 120 221
W.Nr. 120 076
W.Nr. 120 074
W.Nr. 120 072
W.Nr. 120 086
W.Nr. 120 095
W.Nr. 120 097
W.Nr. 120 227
W.Nr. 120 091
W.Nr. 120 098

Meanwhile on 15 May 1945, 1280 km to the south, in Wien, all the EHAG drawings and documents which had been hidden in a cellar near the Achensee at Jenbach were handed over to the Allied Commission and placed into the hands of eager RAF officers, F/Lt. Bingham and F/Lt Lee.

As *Prof.* Ernst Heinkel and Karl Frydag told their Allied interrogators in July 1945: 'At the time we had to leave Wien, about twelve complete machines were ready there; they were to be flown to Hörsching, near Linz, and on to Lechfeld, but as we heard it, not all of them arrived. Additionally, a larger number of fuselages and stabilizers were ready to be mounted up in Wien. We tried to transfer them, but without success. Up to ten or twelve aeroplanes, the fittings of which were ready for final mounting in the workshop of our sub-contractors, Amme-Luther in Wien, were transported firstly to Ainring, and then directed to a small factory at Lent near Schwarzach (Salzburg).

'Because of the lack in communications, we didn't receive any information about what became of the machines at Rostock. There must have been about 20-30 complete aeroplanes there and some 60-80 others without powerplants.

'In order to prevent too great a storage of aircraft in one place, we established an additional airfield for trial purposes at Oranienburg with the aid of *Lufthansa*. There may have been up to 25 machines left there in a more-or-less complete state. Junkers had delivered 20 complete aeroplanes at the end of March, and a further 60-80 machines may have been ready for mounting, excepting powerplants.'[9]

On 4 July, Heinkel and Frydag boarded an Allied aircraft in Frankfurt and were flown to London. In his memoirs, Heinkel recorded: 'At first we were lodged in a boarding house which had been taken over

The personnel of the Experimental Flying Detachment of the RAE at Farnborough, England, photographed in 1944. At least four of the pilots seen here are known to have test-flown the He 162 in England: Squadron Leader R.M. Cracknell (front row, third from left), Wing Commander R.J. 'Roly' Falk (front row, sixth from left), Squadron Leader Tony Martindale (front row, fifth from right) and Captain Eric Brown, RN (front row, fourth from right). Cracknell would fly the Heinkel at Leck, the only British pilot believed to have flown the aircraft in Germany.

by the Royal Air Force. The first person we met on the doorstep was Schelp, the jet propulsion inspector of the German Air Ministry.[10] We spent a short time there... On July 7th we were transferred to a former children's home in Wimbledon, with a garden surrounded by barbed wire. About a week later the interrogations began.[11] The emphasis lay on my jet units and planes.

'The chief interrogator admitted frankly that I and my workers had been first in the field, that we were in advance of England and that Whittle, though later knighted, had come up against difficulties and opposition which were not very far removed from my own experience.

'On July 17th we drove out to Farnborough so that I could explain the German machines which had been captured. My heart beat faster when I saw eight airworthy He 162s which had been flown to England undamaged. I read the report of an English test pilot, who had achieved 740 km/h with one, and had described the machine from take-off to landing as the best in the world.'[12]

If *Prof.* Heinkel recollected that he saw eight airworthy He 162s at Farnborough on 17 July, he was mistaken. According to the exhaustive research carried out by Phil Butler into the fate of captured Axis aircraft, the first He 162 to arrive at Farnborough was W.Nr. 120 098 (AM 67) on 11 June.[13] This was followed by W.Nr. 120 076 (AM 59) on 15 June, W.Nr. 120 221 (AM 58) on 16 June, W.Nr. 120 072 (AM 61), W.Nr. 120 097 (AM 64), W.Nr. 120 227 (AM 65) and W.Nr. 120 091 (AM 66) on 31 July, W.Nr. 120 074 (AM 60), W.Nr. 120 095 (AM 63) and a machine with no *Nummer* recorded on 10 August (AM 68), and W.Nr. 120 086 (AM 62) on 22 August. All the aircraft were transported to England via ship.

From 29 June 1945, a quite rigorous flight-testing programme of the He 162s was commenced at the RAE. That day W/Cdr R.J. 'Roly' Falk took to the air at Farnborough in W.Nr. 120 076 (AM 59), the serial number, VH532, having been applied ten days previously. Falk had flown as a press pilot during the Abyssinian War of 1935-1936 and during the Spanish Civil War. After a spell on the London-Paris newspaper service in 1937, he had joined the Air Registration Board as a test pilot, remaining there until the outbreak of war. From 1939-1946 he served with the RAF, becoming Chief Test Pilot with the rank of Wing Commander at the RAE at Farnborough in 1943.

Falk flew W.Nr. 120 076 again on 5 July, before S/Ldr. A.F. Martindale possibly took over the controls on the 6th. The aircraft was flown again on 23 July, possibly by F/Lt Cleaver. None of the aircraft's flights had lasted more than 20 minutes and its total flying time was 1 hour 30 minutes.

On 2 August, Jack Woolams, the renowned Chief Test Pilot at the American Bell Aircraft Corporation, who had been the first to fly a fighter aircraft in September 1942 coast-to-coast non-stop over the United States without stopping and who had set a new altitude record of 47,600 feet in the summer of 1943, flew the He 162 for 15 minutes

Jack Woolams, Chief Test Pilot of the American Bell Aircraft Corporation, seen here right, providing classroom instruction to trainee test pilots, made a brief flight in the He 162 over England. Woolams was working on Bell's rocket interceptor, the XS-1, at the time.

He 162 A-2 W.Nr. 120 098, formerly of JG 1 and captured at Leck, is seen here in England in the late summer of 1945. It was the first Volksjäger to arrive in the country in June 1945 and was assigned the Air Ministry number AM 67 and the RAF serial VH513 on 14 June. The aircraft carries JG 1's red nose arrows and a coloured band at the nose/fuselage join. The mark just below the cockpit may have been a patch left by repair or crude modification to the flare pistol port. W.Nr. 120 098 was known to have been flown by at least four Allied test pilots. It is possible the officer seen here is either F/Lt. Foster or F/Lt/ R.A. Marks.

He 162 A-2 W.Nr. 120 098, AM 67, coded VH513 by the British, in flight over Farnborough in the summer of 1945. The aircraft has been erroneously identified as W.Nr. 120 227.

W.Nr. 120 098 touches down at the RAE Farnborough following a test flight during the summer of 1945.

He 162 W.Nr. 120 086 was included in a public exhibition of captured German aircraft held in Hyde Park, central London. If this photograph shows that aircraft, then it would appear that it was repainted with a fresh Balkenkreuz and new red JG 1 Geschwader arrows added, since photographs taken of the aircraft at Leck in May 1945 do not show such arrows in place.

on a transfer flight from Farnborough to RAF Brize Norton, in Oxfordshire, a major training base some 50 miles north-west of London. Woolams was in Europe mainly because of Bell's interest in the Me 163, the company working on its own rocket interceptor, the XS-1.[14]

When Woolams delivered the He 162 to Brize Norton, it was placed into storage with No. 6 Maintenance Unit (No. 6 MU). The prime role of No. 6 MU had been as a glider assembly unit, working on Horsa gliders, the General Aircraft Hotspur and various types of tug aircraft. However the unit also assumed the responsibility for the storage of captured German aircraft after their evaluation at Farnborough, or following use as 'hacks' by the occupying forces. In addition to storage, German aircraft were also sent out from No. 6 MU to various exhibitions, including that held in Hyde Park, London in September 1945 when an Me 163, He 162, Bf 108, Bf 110, Fw 190, Ju 88 and Fi 156 were exhibited, as well as Brize Norton's own 'At Home' day on 15 September 1945 when various machines were displayed including a He 162 alongside a Ju 52, Ar 234B, Fw 190, Fw 189, Ju 188, Ju 88, Me 262, He 219, and Si 204. In addition, another He 162 as well as an Me 163, were despatched to Little Rissington on loan for an open day there.[15]

On 3 August, He 162 W.Nr. 120 098 (AM 67) was test-flown for the first time and on 10 August, having just arrived at Farnborough, W.Nr. 120 074 (AM 60), was moved by road to Brize Norton the same day, while W.Nr. 120 098 (AM 67) was test-flown for a second time. On 11 August, W.Nr. 120 074 (AM 60) also arrived at the RAE, but was moved by road to Brize Norton the same day. W.Nr. 120 098 (AM 67) was test-flown for the third time this day. Similarly, on the 22nd, when W.Nr. 120 086 (AM 62) arrived at Farnborough, it too was moved immediately by road to Brize Norton.

Testing resumed on 7 September, when Captain Eric Brown, a test pilot attached to the Aerodynamics Flight (the 'Aero Flight') of the Experimental Flying Detachment at the RAE, flew the Rostock-built He 162 W.Nr. 120 098 (AM 67). Brown had endeavoured to obtain aeronautical information on the He 162 from a former German test pilot who had been assigned to EHAG from the *Luftwaffe*, but he was concerned about the reliability of his information and his experience. There was only one thing to do and that was to fly the He 162 himself. 'Therefore, at 10.25 hours on the morning of 7 September 1945, armed with the notes I had made during the interrogation, I clambered into the cockpit of He 162 A-2 W.Nr. 120 098.

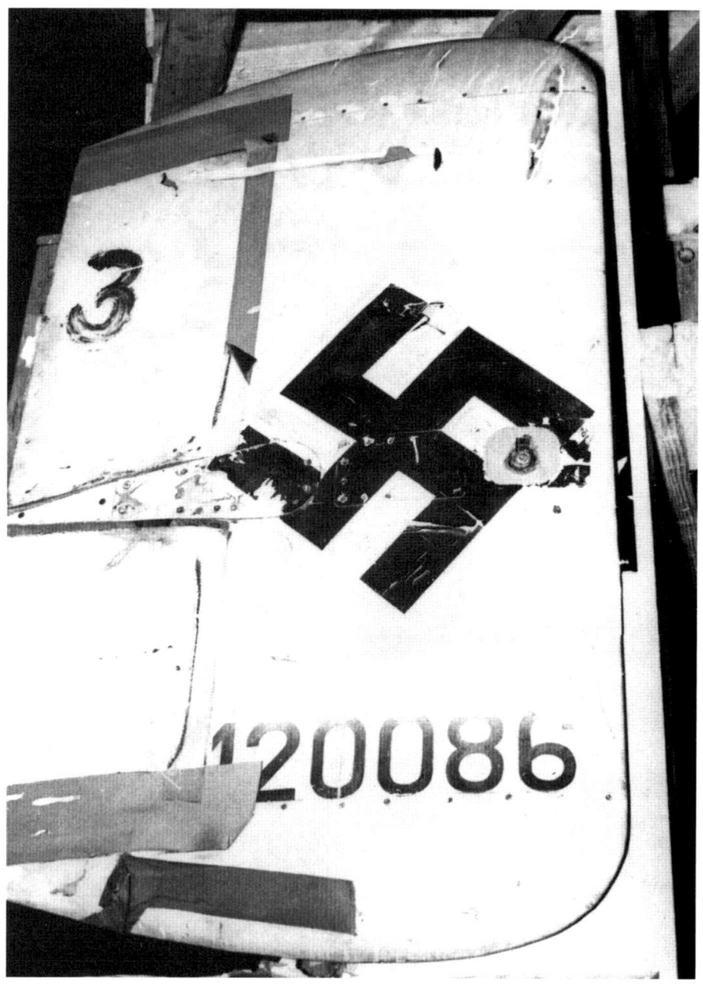

The starboard tail fin of He 162 W.Nr. 120 086, which had been flown by Leutnant Alfred Dürr of II./JG 1 and which was examined in considerable detail by British technical intelligence teams at Leck in May 1945 before being shipped to England. The fin is seen here in England, possibly in late 1945, following considerable handling by the British. It is worth comparing this photograph with that on page 146 which shows the port side fin while the aircraft was still at Leck.

A few He 162s found their way to Kassel and into American custody, though how each got their and under what circumstances is not known entirely. Here, W.Nr. 310 012, 'Yellow 6' and W.Nr. 120 028 'White 3' lie derelict outside a hangar at Kassel. A third Heinkel is just visible behind and some researchers believe that this airframe could be W.Nr. 310 078 'White 5'. All these aircraft would have flown south, from Leck.

'I had to pick what I believed were the best…' – the hunt for German technology. Colonel Harold E. Watson, the leader of 'Watson's Whizzers', was briefed to organise a unit to locate the newest forms of German aeronautical technology, including the He 162 which was viewed as a priority, and ship them to England, and eventually to the United States, as fast as possible. Watson is seen here, with some of his pilots, pointing across Schleswig airfield. Also seen, in civilian clothes leaning over the Jeep, is German test pilot Ludwig Hofmann, while behind the group is an Me 262 B-1a being inspected by one of Watson's team.

The diving eagle emblem of 1./JG 1.

Heinkel He 162 A-2 W.Nr. 120067, 'White 4', 1./JG 1, Leck, May 1945

A starboard view of He 162 A-2, W.Nr. 120 067, 'White 4' of 1./JG 1 which was brought to Kassel and which proved of great interest to curious American servicemen (see also following pages).

Heinkel He 162 A-2 W.Nr. 120067, 'White 4', 1./JG 1, Kassel, summer 1945

This mid-series production aircraft was produced by the Heinkel-Rostock factory. It was later captured at Leck and was then brought to Kassel where it was eventually scrapped. The fuselage, tail and wings were painted in RLM 82/76. The 'Diving Eagle' emblem was only painted on the port side of the fuselage. Also of note are the cannon firing ports and channels which have been painted black. Note that by the time the aircraft was at Kassel, the wings and tail assembly had been replaced.

An aircraft that attracted much interest at the American-occupied airfield at Kassel throughout the summer and autumn of 1945, was He 162 A-2, W.Nr. 120 067, 'White 4' of 1./JG 1 which had come in from Leck. As a result, it was frequently photographed by camera-wielding US servicemen. This sequence of photographs, including the one on the previous page, illustrate the starboard side of the aircraft, which, when compared to the photograph at top of page 123 shows how worn and changed the airframe became during its time at Kassel. The red nose arrows of JG 1 gradually faded, the filler paste on the panel join lines became much more visible through the weathered late-war quality paint, and as far as structure was concerned, both the aircraft's original wing and tail assembly (as seen in the photographs of the line-up at Leck) had been replaced.

In this view of the port side of He 162 A-2, W.Nr. 120 067, 'White 4' of 1./JG 1 at Kassel, the general appearance of the nose markings, unit emblem and tactical number seem in much better condition, suggesting the photograph was taken fairly soon after the aircraft's arrival there.

The diving eagle emblem of 1./JG 1 as seen just below the cockpit of He 162 A-2, W.Nr. 120 067.

'Caution had to be exercised in handling the throttle in order to avoid overheating, although the BMW 003 was better in this respect than the Jumo 004. View from the cockpit was perfect, although the non-adjustable seat was too low if a British-type seat parachute was used. At the runway threshold I applied about 20 deg of flap by pumping them down until they could just be seen from the cockpit, no flap position indicator being provided. I set the elevator trim and moved the jet nozzle control to the S (start) position. The fuel indicator showed 450 litres. Moving on to the runway, I lined the aircraft up and opened the throttle slowly to 9,500 revs, meanwhile holding the aircraft on the brakes and checking that the temperature gauge did not exceed the maximum 600 deg C, although a momentary 700 deg C was permissible on moving the throttle or on start-up. The throttle movement from closed to full revs occupied 15 seconds if the temperature limit was observed.

'The take-off was much longer than I had expected, and any attempt to pull the aircraft off prematurely under 118 mph (190 km/h) resulted in a tendency to wing dropping. Ideally the nosewheel was lifted off at about 105 mph (170 km/h) and the aircraft allowed itself to fly off. So much for the take-off distance specified by the original requirement!'

'I then began a climb to 30,000 ft (9144 m) and this necessitated a change of nozzle control to H as I passed to 26,000 ft (7925 m). On the climb, the fuel gauge began to drop, indicating that the two ungauged wing tanks had completely drained their contents into the main tank. Handling at 30,000 ft (9144 m) still displayed very good stability and control characteristics, apart from that very touchy rudder which had to

This page and page 168: A selection of views of the port side of He 162 A-2, W.Nr. 120 067, 'White 4' of 1./JG 1 at Kassel. The photographs illustrates well the replacement tail assembly fitted to the aircraft which, it has been suggested, had been taken from W.Nr. 120 097, another aircraft from Leck.

be used sparingly. I put the nose down to commence a powered dive, at the same time moving the nozzle control to position S. There was no buffeting or vibration, and a check on the rate of roll at 400 mph (644 km/h) revealed the highest that I ever experienced outside the realm of hydraulically-powered ailerons, and the stick force demanded to produce those exhilarating gyrations was delightfully light.

'Levelling off at 12,000 ft (3658 m), once again changing the nozzle position (this time to F) for high-speed flight below 13,123 ft (4000 m), I settled down to another spell of the pleasures of the phenomenal roll rate of this delightful little aeroplane, but I was careful not to impose negative *g* for more than three seconds. The thought of extinguishing the jet burner and trying the He 162 as a glider was not really to my fancy. When level speed had built up to 350 mph (563 km/h) I pulled the He 162 into a loop. It skimmed round but I had the inescapable feeling that I was playing pretty close to the minimum speed for this manoeuvre. Finally, I tried a few stalls to get the feel of things before landing. As the stall was approached a gentle lateral lurching and some mild elevator buffet set in, being followed by a mild porpoising motion before the nose pitched down indicating stall had been reached. And so back to base.

'The landing proved difficult for technical rather than aerodynamic reasons. In the first place it took a full minute to pump down the flaps, although the undercarriage came down quickly under the action of the springs when a red toggle was pulled to release the up locks. In the second place, the throttle had to be shut beyond the cruising gate into the idling gate (3,000 rpm) as soon as it was certain that the runway would not be undershot, thus cutting the thrust. The approach speed had to be held at 125 mph (200 km/h) almost up to the runway threshold as there was no question of going round once again once the throttle had been moved to idling, and there was therefore an inevitable tendency to arrive with excessive speed. This called for good braking, and no German aircraft that I had ever flown had brakes that came up to British standards. By *German* standards, however, the He 162's brakes were good, and I had already been favourably impressed by them during taxying, but now they proved too weak for the speed involved, and I burned up a lot of runway.

'Touchdown speed was 105 mph (170 km/h), and after two or three more flights in the He 162 I got used to judging the correct spot for closing the throttle to idling, and this expertise, coupled with the powerful elevator keeping the nosewheel off the ground down to a very low speed, greatly reduced the landing run. Stopping the engine was merely a matter of closing the throttle completely, closing the fuel cock, and switching off the fuel pump. All very simple, but there *was* a

British test pilots, Squadron Leader Tony Martindale (far left) and Captain Eric Brown, RN (second from right) both flew the He 162 at the RAE Farnborough throughout the summer and autumn of 1945. They are seen here with fellow test pilots, Squadron Leader Jimmy Nelson (second from left) and Squadron Leader Doug Weightman.

The end of the road for He 162 A-2, W.Nr. 120 067, 'White 4'. The next destination was probably the scrap-heap.

He 162 A-2 W.Nr. 120 097, formerly 'White 3' of JG 1 which was captured at Leck in May 1945. The aircraft is photographed in 'A' Shed at the RAE Farnborough during the 'German Aircraft Exhibition' held in October 1945. It was assigned the RAF serial VN153 the following month. The outline of the aircraft's tactical number is still just visible on the paintwork aft of the cockpit. To the right of the photograph is the (removed) BMW engine of He 162 A-2 W.Nr. 120 091.

After the 'German Aircraft Exhibition', He 162 A-2 W.Nr. 120 097 was removed from the hangar and the following month after its evaluation had been completed, it was parked on a grass area where the machine gradually deteriorated as a result of weather and looting, before eventually being scrapped.

W.Nr. 120 097's 'neighbour' at the RAE's 'German Aircraft Exhibition' was He 162 A-2 W.Nr. 120 091, possibly assigned the tactical number 'Red 5' by JG 1. It is seen here in a partly dismantled condition with the cowlings to its BMW 003 engine open, and which has been suspended from the roof girders of 'A' Shed. The wings have also been removed to show the wing fuel tank. W.Nr. 120 091 was assigned the Air Ministry number AM66 and was later moved to the Science Museum in London.

catch for the unwary. The fuel cock and the undercarriage retraction lever nestled side by side, and requiring a downward motion to close the fuel cock *and* to retract the undercarriage was just asking for trouble!'[16]

In mid-September, a public exhibition of captured German aircraft was held in Hyde Park, central London to coincide with a 'Thanksgiving Week'. Curious Londoners were able to inspect W.Nr. 120 086 (AM 62). This was the aircraft that *Leutnant* Alfred Dürr of II./JG 1 had collected from Rostock-Marienehe to ferry to Leck on 30 April, and in which he had to make a forced-landing on the Autobahn near Lübeck (see Chapter Three). Meanwhile, for several months W.Nr. 120 095 (AM 63) toured cities in the Midlands of England, such as Birmingham, also as an exhibition item.

During the late summer of 1945, at least three He 162s were shipped across the Atlantic from Europe to the United States on merchant vessels. The Heinkels formed part of a batch of some 50 captured German aircraft gathered by US forces in the immediate post-war period. Following the invasion of North-West Europe in June 1944, it became increasingly apparent to the Americans that the main goal for their intelligence teams was to exploit the advances made by German aviation engineers. Consequently, on 22 April 1945 an exploitation division was established under the code name of 'Operation Lusty', an acronym for **LU**ftwaffe **S**ecret **T**echnolog**Y**. The main purpose of the operation was to collect examples of the latest German aircraft and equipment for examination and eventual transport to the USA. High on the list of priorities were the three major *Luftwaffe* jet types, the Me 262, He 162 and Ar 234.

In this regard, a dedicated squadron was set up to transport such aircraft back to the US. To lead this unit, the US Director of Intelligence, General George C. McDonald, appointed the experienced young test pilot with the Air Technical Intelligence division, Colonel Harold E. Watson. Watson, a man with rare charm and organisational ability, had arrived at Merseburg during the spring of 1945, bringing with him Capt. Fred McIntosh who was to look after the acquisition of German piston-engined aircraft. During May, Watson added nine American pilots to his team, all of them from the Ninth Air Force, and many with engineering backgrounds or rated as instructors. Watson remembered: 'There was the greatest competition in the world between the RAE team and ourselves as to who was going to get there first. Eric Brown and I knew each other quite well. Brown had a team and I had a team, and we were driving them as fast as we could. He had to get his airplanes over to England, whereas I had to get them to Cherbourg. I had to pick what I believed were the best of the new developments such as the Ar 234, He 162, Me 163 and 262 and the Ju 388. These were the aircraft we went for, and were the ones we got.'[17]

Forty-one aircraft were shipped to the US aboard the Royal Navy aircraft carrier, HMS *Reaper,* which left Cherbourg for New York on 19 July, arriving there on 31 July, but the Heinkels were not in this consignment and followed shortly after on other vessels. At least one Heinkel, an A-2, W.Nr. 120 077, Gerhard Hanf's 'Red 1', was taken over at Leck, while there is some uncertainty over the provenance of the remainder, but some sources state that they were found in the Halle area, possibly in an incomplete condition.[18] Whatever the case, a number of He 162s found their way to the USA during 1945 following Watson's work, but little would be heard of them until the following year.

Testing continued at Farnborough using W.Nr. 120 098 (AM 67) throughout September, during which it was flown four times, and October, during it which it was flown on a further 11 days, and on some days, more than once. The aircraft had increased fuel capacity which gave an increased flight duration of up to 40 minutes. A number of pilots flew the aircraft including Eric Brown, Squadron Leader Tony 'Marty' Martindale, ('a big, powerful six footer' according to Brown) who holds the highest fully documented flight speed in a piston-engined aircraft, Flight Lieutenant Foster, and Flight Lieutenant R.A. Marks. 'Bob' Marks

He 162 A-2 W.Nr. 120 072 at the RAE Farnborough on 11 September 1945. The aircraft was originally flown by Günther Kirchner and Gerhard Stiemer of JG 1 with the tactical number 'Yellow 3'. The outline of the '3' is just visible here on the paintwork aft of the cockpit. The aircraft was assigned the British Air Ministry number AM61, but it crashed on 9 November 1945 during a demonstration flight at Farnborough, killing its pilot, F/Lt. R.A. Marks. Comparison should be made with the photograph on page 121.

Heinkel He 162 A-2 W.Nr. 120072, AIR MIN 61, formerly 'Yellow 3', 3./JG 1, RAE Farnborough, August 1945

JG 1's 'Yellow 3' was shipped to the United Kingdom from Leck where it arrived on 10 August 1945. The aircraft was lost on its fourth test flight killing Flight Lieutenant R.A. Marks. Although the original German camouflage was retained, only the national and tactical markings were overpainted with RAF markings. The red arrows painted on the nose were added after being captured as well as the small 'Yellow 3' on the BMW 003 engine.

had only recently returned from Germany where he had been a POW and as Eric Brown remembers '… was new to the game.'[19]

Another Allied test pilot to fly the He 162 at the RAE was Commander William Benson. He recalled his first flight: 'My ground crew chief, as I strapped in 30 minutes earlier, with typical RAF humour, had saluted with seemingly special reverence, obviously not expecting to see me in one piece again, and, formalities over, had confided to me earnestly, "If you are really barmy enough to want to fly this carpenter's nightmare, Sir, I feel I should point out that this 'ere glorified bloody blow torch you are 'anging under is only 'anging by two ****** bolts." Of course, to stay ahead, I had to come back quickly and coolly with, "Well, Sarge, if the bloody blow torch comes off, I'll just have to glide the jolly thing back, won't I?"

'My westerly cruise from Farnborough had taken me out over Laffens Plain, Basingstoke, and towards the desolate Salisbury Plain, the plan being that I could reach either Boscombe Down or Base quickly, but conduct the tests over a deserted area. The positive ailerons gave me a good rate of roll, but after about three I sensed that the top-heavy turbojet was causing a sort of "swinging effect" so that the shape around the selected reference point became more elliptical than round. Next, a gentle loop, no tight *gs*; about 3,000 feet was used. Continuing, I half-rolled off the top. Back at 28,000 again. I began to enjoy flying the thing.

Perhaps it was possible, after all, for 16-year old, glider-trained, Hitler Youth pilots to have gone straight to this. Watching my fuel, it was time to head back (a safe 30-minute maximum away from the circuit was strictly recommended). Descending to home base, I slowed down... Here was the catch. Lateral control became poor and she wanted to roll that turbojet from above to below. Checking with flaps and gear down, I decided to add 15 mph to the 110 advised. Making a long, steady approach, I kept plenty of excess speed until close to home. At 1,000 feet, I dropped 30 degrees of flaps at 130 indicated, the gear down. This was a rather startling experience until you realised what was happening with a *twang-bang-clank* from the springs etc. The first time I was ready to squeeze the trigger, but a glance through the floor panel reminded me of what happened. Easing her down now, I was skimming the ever-patient inhabitants of Farnborough village.'

'During the next two weeks, I explored the performance range of the 162; the results were as follows: low speed, very tricky; lateral and longitudinal stability were poor mainly because of the high-mounted turbojet. Control movements were *always* smooth and careful, *no* sudden movement. Maximum altitude reached was 41,200 feet, maximum speed level 562 mph at 18,400 feet. In a dive, at around 585 mph at 25,000 feet (having commenced the dives at 25,000), aileron snatch and buffet on the rudders started to get severe and I would throttle back and ease *very* carefully level. High angles of attack resulted in a near fatal spin (I still don't quite know how I got out of that one) so the message was 'don't stall' (at least not below 35,000 feet!) Treated properly and smoothly, the 162 was very good, and speed was its weapon rather than a dog fight. There was no way that you could haul that plane around like a Spitfire or Fw 190. It needed the touch of a well-trained pilot, say at least 2,500 hours to be really safe. I am afraid the dream of training 16-year old boys from the Hitler Youth on gliders and then putting them straight into the planned 4,000 per month production He 162s was just that – a dream. The poor kids would never have stood a chance.'

'Visibility, while excellent ahead and to the side, was poor to nil behind you, never a popular arrangement with a fighter jock. I suppose the plan was, "It is too fast to bother about behind you." I wouldn't buy that one, I'm afraid. The Me 262 and Gloster Meteor were far superior from this point of view, but the 'Salamander' was quite a plane all the same, and, flown correctly, could have been a very serious problem for the Allies.'[20]

On 27 October 1945, it was the turn of He 162 W.Nr. 120 072 (AM 61) – which *Fhj.Fw.* Günther Kirchner of I./JG 1 had ferried from Marienehe to Ludwigslust on 10 April (see Chapter Three), when it was flown from Farnborough by F/Lt Foster.[21] Foster was airborne in the aircraft again on the 29th, the opening day of the 'German Aircraft Exhibition' held at the RAE Farnborough which formed part of a larger exhibition of both British and German wartime aircraft, equipment and weapons. The event drew thousands of visitors from the aviation industry, the armed forces, civil service and, during its closing days in early November, even the general public. Air Marshals and schoolboys got a chance to see He 162s W.Nr. 120 097 (AM 64) and W.Nr. 120 091 (AM 66) – given the RAF serial number VN153 – on static display in the facility's 'A' Shed.[22]

In addition to a large static demonstration of the captured machines held in the various hangars and sheds, there were also flying demonstrations by British Meteor and Vampire jets, but Foster's flight on the 29th in a He 162, as well as a flight by an Me 262, were apparently high points of the event. The euphoria and sense of victory were dashed however, when tragedy struck on 9 November, the day that F/Lt R.A. Marks chose to fly a demonstration in W.Nr. 120 072 (AM 61) for members of the Army Staff College. It was Marks' fourth flight in the He 162 (he had also flown the aircraft on the 4th). While airborne, and after a flight time of just 50 minutes while at the RAE, the Heinkel suddenly yawed violently, stalled and plummeted towards the earth.[23] As Capt. Eric Brown recorded in his memoirs: 'I warned him that she had a very sensitive rudder and a very high rate of roll, and that he should be careful using the rudder to assist rolling action.'

Brown recalled: 'I had flown the aircraft in the first three days of the display, but Bob had wanted to have a go on the last day. In his enthusiasm he must have forgotten the advice, used too much rudder, and made the whole fin and rudder collapse. The machine literally tumbled, head over heels, out of the sky, the only time I have seen such a thing happen. It crashed straight into Aldershot Barracks, where it killed a soldier as well as its pilot.'[24]

The subsequent investigation attributed the crash to a loss of control following an upward roll. During the roll, excessive rudder yawed the aircraft sufficiently to initiate a stall at too low a level to permit recovery.[25] The wing broke up.

W.Nr. 120 098 (AM 67) was back in the air on 18 September, and later, on 29 and 30 November. The aircraft's total flight time for all flights in England would amount to 11 hrs 40 mins.

On 21 December 1945, a high-level meeting had taken place at Bad Eilsen in Germany to discuss French requirements for former German war material. It was decided at this meeting that, as far as servicing parties and administration were concerned '... only one French Servicing Party would be necessary – at Leck, this Party to be attached to No. 8302 Wing for administrative purposes.' In early January 1946, an officer from the French Air Ministry was attached to the British Air Forces of Occupation – BAFO (Disarm) – with members of his staff with the objective of drafting a so-called 'French Supplement' – essentially, a quantity of aircraft and equipment that the French would *like* to have, provided the British deemed them surplus. The French response, in terms of aircraft, was forthcoming at the end of February: they were interested only in '...Ju 52, Ju 88, Me 108, Ar 96, plus a few jet propelled aircraft.'[26]

Eventually, after what amounted to some low-level military and diplomatic 'horse-trading' between the British, the French and the Americans, an initial – and 'official' offer of seven He 162s for the French was whittled down to five examples: Bernburg-built He 162 A-1s W.Nr. 310 003 and W.Nr. 310 005, and Rostock-built He 162 A-2s W.Nr. 120 015, 'White 21' of 1./JG 1, W.Nr. 120 093, and W.Nr. 120 223 'Yellow 1' which *Oblt.* Wollenweber of 3./JG 1 had flown on 22 April.

These were assigned to a French unit at Leck whose officers comprised *Cmdt.* Bouvarre and *Cmdt.* Hirschauer, with *Capt.* Petit, *Capt.* Boitelet and a mechanical specialist, *Sous-Lt.* Schall.[27] It was decided that the aircraft would need to be transported by rail to France from Leck, under British guard as a deterrent to the 'pilfering of attractive stores and/or armament', a challenging exercise in itself, given that by February 1946 it was still impossible to cross the Rhine into France because of the earlier destruction of the bridges. It was thus decided, initially, to move the airframes as far as the *Armée de l'Air* depot at the *Gare de Neuwied* near Koblenz. Unfortunately, the rail facilities there were judged to be poor and the train carrying the He 162s was eventually and successfully moved across the Rhine to Andernach station on the French side of the river, where it arrived some time in March 1946.

The Heinkels were then moved to the *Societé Nationale de Construction Aéronautique du Centre* (SNCAC) at Boulogne-Billancourt for further evaluation. It was decided to retain the three aforementioned A-2 machines for restoration to flying condition, while the two others – A-1s each equipped with MK 108s – would have their wings removed for further analysis and the cannon sent to the *Direction des Études et Fabrications d'Armement*. The three A-2s were then moved again by road to the airfield at Toussus-le-Noble, where over a period of one year they were carefully returned to flying condition, a remarkable achievement when it is considered that no manuals were available to the technicians. The BMW 003 engines, which had been removed from the fuselages for the rail journey from Germany, were sent to the Compagnie Electro Mécanique in Paris for overhaul. [28]

1946

In England in mid-February 1946, He 162 W.Nr. 120 091 (AM 66) was placed on display at the Science Museum in South Kensington, London. It remained there until mid-May of that year after which its fate is not known.

On 21 March, W.Nr. 120 086 (AM 62) is known to have been in store at No. 6 MU, Brize Norton, while on 29 June the maintenance unit handed W.Nr. 120 076 (AM 59) over to No. 47 MU at Sealand for shipping to Canada.[29]

Although some aircraft would eventually be passed to No. 47 MU at Sealand, No. 76 MU at Wroughton and various other RAF stations, the vast majority lingered on at Brize Norton, with the larger aircraft open to the elements until the bad winter of 1946/47 took its toll. Many of the aircraft were overturned in gales, and others suffered from falling trees. Shortly after this, wholesale scrapping began. The aircraft were taken to the south side of the airfield where No. 6 MU was already scrapping Spitfires, Spitefuls and Liberators. After all useful pieces and large metal areas had been removed, the mortal remains were buried in holes 20 ft deep where, apparently, they remain to this day.[30]

Far away to the east, in Soviet Russia, a captured He 162, number '02', was flown by LII NKAP (*Letno-Islyedovatel'skiy Institut Narodny Kommisariat Aviatsionoy Promishlinosti* – Flight Research Institute of the People's Commissariat for the Aircraft Industry) pilot, Georgi M. Shiyanov, for the first time on 8 May 1946. Russian aerodynamicists treated the Heinkel with caution and, before the first flight, a technical commission had established several speed, overload, and flight weight restrictions.[31] Shiyanov, nevertheless, made two further flights five days later as well as a demonstration flight before the Minister of Aircraft Production, Mikhail V. Khrunishev, his deputy, Pyotr V. Dementyev, as well as the aircraft designers, Aleksandr S. Yakovlev and Artyom I. Mikoyan, on 11 July 1946. Another test pilot, A.G. Kochetkov, also made flights.[32]

Both the LII and the NII VVS (*Nauchno-Ispitatel'niy Institut Voyenno-Vozdushikhv Sil* – Scientific Test Institute of the Army Air Forces) test-flew He 162s, and although a number of such aircraft had been found at the EHAG works in Wien by members of the 212 Guards IAP (Fighter Aviation Regiment) during the advance into Austria in the

Heinkel He 162 A-1 W.Nr. 310003, 'Yellow 5', 3./JG 1, Leck, May 1945

This aircraft from the Junkers Bernburg production plant was captured at Leck before being transferred to France where it was stripped down in order to study the construction of the airframe. The aircraft was camouflaged in the typical Bernburg style. Of particular interest is the emblem, which contains three different JG 1 Staffel badges, painted under the cockpit.

Bound for France: two dismantled He 162 airframes lashed to a railway flat car at Leck while awaiting transport to France. The fuselage to the left is Bernburg-built He 162 A-1 W.Nr. 310003, 'Yellow 5', possibly the same aircraft flown by Hans Berger of 3./JG 1 to Leck on 15 April 1945. The aircraft carries a colourful trio of JG 1's unit emblems representing from left, the demon of I./JG 1, the Lion of Danzig of 3. Staffel, and the winged '1' of JG 1 as a Geschwader. The airframe to the right is W.Nr. 310005 'Red 7', the stem of the number just visible in the usual position aft of the cockpit. Note the rail wagon is marked 'France': it would not arrive on French soil until March 1946.

'A comic-looking job': at least one He 162 made it as a cartoon – A-2 W.Nr. 120 091, once possibly JG 1' s 'Red 5'. Here the aircraft has been caricatured during its tenancy at the Science Museum in Kensington, London, by the illustrator, Chris Wren, in February 1946 for his popular 'Oddentification' series of cartoons in the British 'Aeroplane' magazine.

spring of 1945 and before the area was reassigned as part of the American zone of occupation, the Soviets never, apparently, obtained any operationally ready examples.[33] In all, the Soviets are believed to have acquired seven He 162s in varied conditions; and at least two A-2s, coded '01' and '02', one of them believed to have been W.Nr. 120 020,[34] were assembled at EHAG Rostock under Russian supervision. These were later moved to the Soviet Union where the aforementioned flight tests were conducted as well as wind tunnel tests in the T-101 wind tunnel at TsAGI (*Tsentral'niy Aero-Gidrodinamicheskiy Institut* – Central Aero-Hydrodynamics Institute) in Zhukovskiy, the 'Aero-city of the Soviet Union' on the outskirts of Moscow. The subsequent LII report on the trials with the He 162 commented: 'According to the pilot, the aircraft has a low longitudinal stability margin; lateral stability is close to neutral. The aircraft is unpleasant to fly thanks to negative stability and the extra efficiency of the rudders. The long take-off roll of 1350 metres (with a flight weight 9.6 per cent below normal) indicates a very low take-off lift coefficient… Further tests have ceased, because the take-off roll is too long.'[35]

This take-off distance was considered unacceptable in view of the size of most Soviet airfields. Despite captured German manuals stating that maximum take-off speed was 190 km/h, the Russian test pilots found that they could not lift off at less than 230 km/h. Maximum speed at 4000 m was not to exceed 700 km/h and the load factor was not to exceed 2.5 g, with a maximum angle of roll at maximum speed of 5 degrees. They drew performance comparisons with the Lavochkin La-7.

The Russians did not view the upward-opening canopy hood favourably, nor the fact that the engine could not be started and run up with the hood open, although the aircraft's simple production methods which, however, embraced ejection seat technology, did hold appeal. It was the recommendation of the LII that such features be incorporated wherever possible into existing and future Soviet designs.[36]

Subsequently, at least one He 162 was placed in a static exhibition in a partly disassembled state in the TsAGI New Equipment Bureau and the *Institut's* technicians produced detailed drawings of the type based on the examples in their hands. There, it seems, things stopped.[37]

Gerhard Hanf's He 162 A-2, W.Nr. 120 077, 'Red 1' had been handed over to Colonel Watson of the USAAF at Leck. In 1946 the aircraft had been shipped to the United States where it was overhauled at the USAAF experimental facility and test centre at Freeman Field, Indiana. It may also have spent a brief spell at Headquarters, Air Materiel Command, Wright Field at Dayton, Ohio. On 14 May 1946, 1st Lt. John R. Byers of the Technical Section of the Analysis Division, Intelligence (T-2) at Wright Field drafted an interim report on the He 162: 'The Heinkel 162 employs as little critical material as possible. The most remarkable features of the design are the low span/length ratio, the mounting of the jet unit above the fuselage, the tricycle undercarriage which retracts into the fuselage, and the sharp dihedral of the tailplane.'

The report went on to portray, in depth, the features of the fuselage, wings, flight controls, undercarriage, hydraulics, brakes, electrical systems, fuel system and throttle control and concluded: 'It is felt that many novel features in design and construction of this German jet

The clean, almost pristine, forward section of what is probably He 162 '01' at a Soviet testing site in 1946.

The second of two He 162 A-2s that were assembled at EHAG Rostock in 1945 under Russian supervision and later moved to the Soviet Union. This is aircraft '02', finished, as with aircraft '01', in an overall light grey paint with the same Soviet markings.

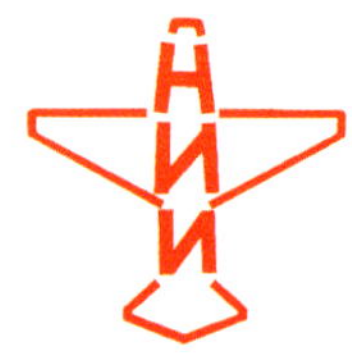

The emblem of the Soviet LII.

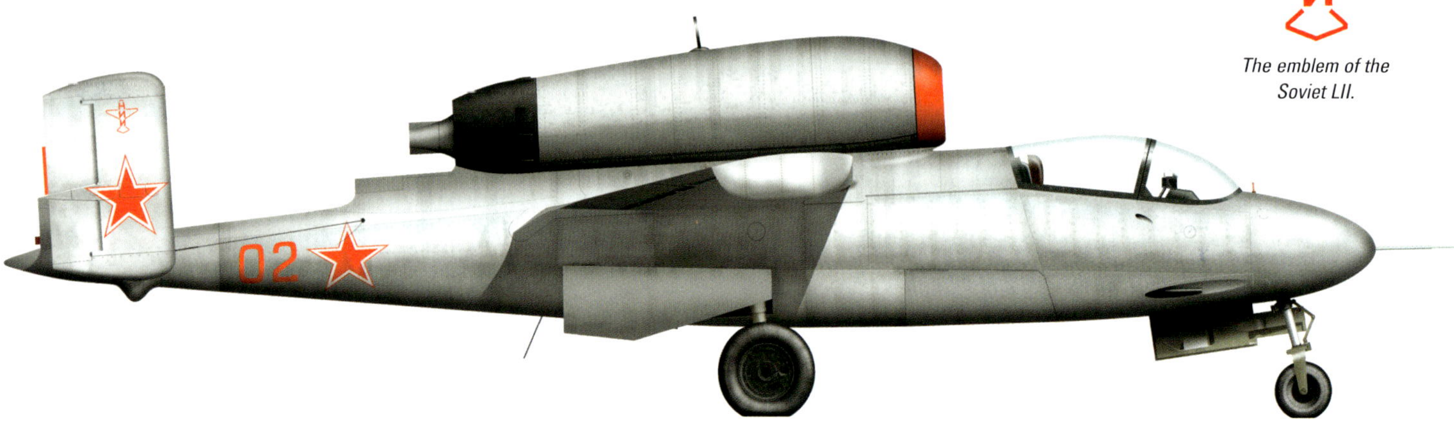

Heinkel He 162 A-2 'Red 02', Letno-Islyedovatel'skiy Institut, Ramensky, near Moscow, spring 1946

This was the second Heinkel He 162 A-2 that was tested in the Russian L II facility in the spring of 1946. The aircraft was completely overpainted in silver-grey with the engine air intake, national star insignia and the emblem on the tail fin all painted in red.

Left and opposite page: A selection of views offering a 'walk-around' sequence of the first of two He 162 A-2s that were assembled at EHAG Rostock in 1945 under Russian supervision and later moved to the Soviet Union. This is aircraft '01', finished in an overall light grey paint with Soviet markings and photographed at the LII (Letno-Islyedovatel'skiy Institut – Flight Research Institute) airfield at Ramensky, near Moscow in 1946. The aircraft carries the emblem of the LII on its tail fin and was used for ground tests.

01

The BMW 003 engine of one of the two Heinkels to be tested in Russia after the war. The Russians planned to manufacture the engine as the RD-20, and the Jumo 004 as the RD-10.

fighter should be studied further relative to the possibility of incorporating the best features in future American types.'[38]

Subsequently, by 24 July, the aircraft was transferred to Muroc Army Airfield in California where it was flown on just one occasion by Air Force test pilot Bob Hoover. The single flight may have been attributable to incorrect rigging during reassembly in the USA which greatly increased the aircraft's landing speed.

Still at Freeman Field by 1 August were W.Nr. 120 017 (in storage) and W.Nr. 120 230 'White 23' (assigned to the Display Branch but with the tail section of W.Nr. 120 222), while a third machine, possibly W.Nr. 120 067 was transferred from Freeman Field to No. 803 Special Depot at Park Ridge.

On 26 August, the British freighter, SS *Manchester Commerce*, steamed out of Salford Docks in Manchester, bound for Montreal. On board were two He 162 jet fighters and three Me 163 rocket-powered interceptors destined for the Canadian government. The He 162s were W.Nr. 120 076 (AM 59) and W.Nr. 120 086 (AM 62). The SS *Manchester Commerce* berthed in Montreal on 9 September 1946 and the Heinkels would, ultimately, be deposited with the Canadian National Aeronautical Collection (CNAC) at Rockliffe, near Ottawa.

A partially disassembled He 162 airframe was displayed at an exhibition of captured German aircraft held at TsAGI (Tsentral'niy Aero-Gidrodinamicheskiy Institut – Central Aero-Hydrodynamics Institute) in Zhukovskiy. Behind the He 162 is an Me 262.

RLM 82

RLM 81

RLM colours used on the He 162 (Translated from an original German document - See this document on page 191 bottom right).

Part	upper: Left	upper	upper: Right	lower	
Fuselage		82		76	Upper third in 82 with lower edges soft spray.
Removable engine panels		81			
Wings	82		81	76	Leading edge in 100mm 76 with up to 150mm soft spray.
Landing flaps	81		82	76	From leading edge soft spray up to 25mm underneath
Ailerons	all sides 82				fully interchangeable
Tail plane	82 upwards 50mm		81	76	leading edge 17mm in 76 and feather sprayed
Elevators	81		82	76	"
Fin and Rudders	all sides 76				

Cockpit interior and instrument panels 66

RLM 76

RLM 66

Leutnant Gerhard Hanf's W.Nr. 120 077 'Red 1' 'Nervenklau' seen shortly after arriving in the USA. After an initial period at the USAAF experimental facility and test centre at Freeman Field, Seymour, Indiana where it became the subject of a detailed technical intelligence report and was assigned the serial T2-489, the aircraft was moved to Muroc Flight Test Base at Muroc Dry Lake, California.

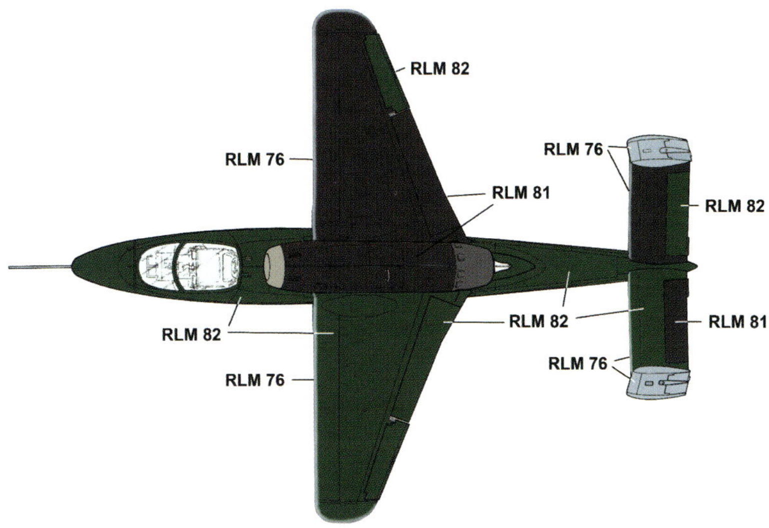

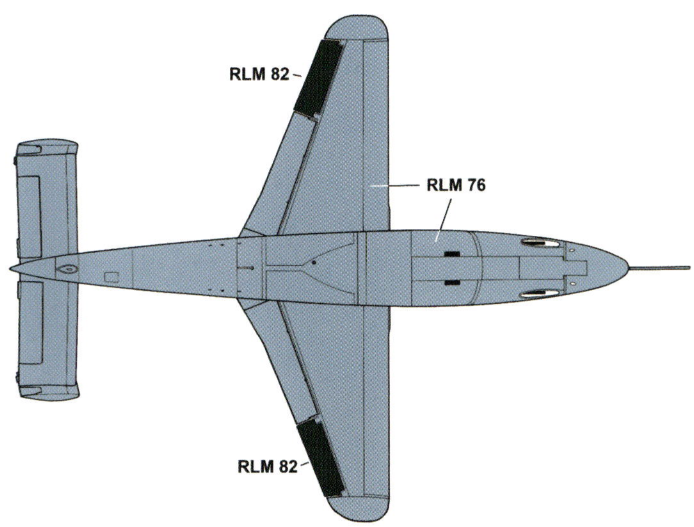

He 162 W.Nr. 120 077, formerly 'Red 1', 'Nervenklau', flown by Leutnant Gerhard Hanf of JG 1, lands at Muroc Flight Test Base in California with test pilot Bob Hoover at the controls. The aircraft still carries its unit emblem but has received a 'new' and inaccurate fuselage Balkenkreuz and tail fin Hakenkreuz. It was eventually relocated to the University of Kansas at Lawrence, Kansas before becoming a long-term resident at the Planes of Fame Museum at Chino, California.

Among those airframes left in England were W.Nr. 120 221 (AM 58), W.Nr. 120 097 (AM 64) and W.Nr. 120 098 (AM 67 – noted as being in a 'wrecked condition'), all of which were reported as being in a scrap area at the RAE Farnborough by 15 December 1946. W.Nr. 120 227 (AM 65) which had been assigned the RAF serial number VN679, was also reported on a scrap area at the RAE, but was rescued for use as a display exhibit and appeared at the Blackpool Air Pageant in July 1947.[39]

Meanwhile, in France in September 1946, a pilot from the *Centre d'Expériences Aériennes Militaires* (CEAM) at Mont-de-Marsan, accompanied by four mechanics, was sent to the Compagnie Electro Mécanique in Paris for a short training course on the BMW 003 engine. *Col.* Kostia Rozanoff, the commander of the CEAM, was anxious that France should learn all it could about captured German jet technology in readiness for when the country took delivery of its own jets.[40]

He 162, W.Nr. 120 077, bearing the serial T2-489, photographed just before its only known flight in the USA at Muroc Dry Lake, California.

1947

The French first test-flew their He 162s, as part of ongoing trials by SNCAC, in May 1947 from the 2,150-metre runway at Orléans-Bricy airfield. The aircraft had been reassigned French identification numbers with W.Nr. 120 223 becoming 'No.1', W.Nr. 120 015 becoming 'No.2' and W.Nr. 120 093 becoming 'No. 3', with all three machines carrying the French tricolour and the SNCAC emblem on their fins. The testing took place with factory pilots Abel Nicolle and Louis Bertrand at the controls.

Following his first flights in W.Nr. 120 223/'No.1', Nicolle wrote an appraisal for the CEAM in which he stated: '... The take-off run is rather long, about 2000 m for an indicated airspeed of 190-200 km/h; the aircraft has no tendency to swing. Retract the undercarriage as soon as possible, keeping the lever in the low position until the three wheels are locked (apply brakes to avoid vibration)...

'For landing... As soon as the pilot judges he is in the best situation for landing he should reduce the power below 6,000 rpm, slow the aircraft down to about 250 km/h, and set the flaps to their maximum 'down' setting (again this must be done at a safe altitude, as the aircraft sinks rapidly in these conditions). If necessary add some power carefully to avoid any rough running. If the aircraft is kept straight and level the approach is made between 200-210 km/h. Landing is easy; keep the aircraft as long as possible on its mainwheels and brake gently. If the landing run is too long, shut the fuel feed and set the throttle to 'idle'.

'Do not fly longer than 30 min (including take-off and landing). In case of engine failure, the pilot should land with the undercarriage up if he is not absolutely sure he can reach the runway. If the engine stops it is impossible to retract undercarriage. Therefore the pilot should not lower the undercarriage unless he is absolutely certain to touch down on the runway.'

He 162 A-2 W.Nr. 120 230 'White 23' of I./JG 1, captured by the British at Leck, finally ended its days in the USA. It was at Freeman Field, Seymour, Indiana by August 1946, but had received the tail unit of another Heinkel, W.Nr. 120 222, also a Leck aircraft. In these three photographs, the aircraft is seen having been transferred from Freeman Field to Wright Field where it underwent further evaluation. It was assigned the 'Foreign Equipment (FE)' number, 'FE-504' (later T-2 504). The aircraft subsequently appeared at air shows across the USA before being consigned to the Paul E. Garber Facility for restoration at the National Air and Space Museum in Washington, DC.

Heinkel He 162 A-1 W.Nr. 310005, 'Red 7' 2./JG 1, Leck, May 1945 and SNAC, Boulogne-Billancourt, March 1946

This Bernburg-produced machine was first flown by H.J. Pancherz on 26 February 1945. It later joined the 2. Staffel of JG 1 and was captured at Leck in May 1945. 'Red 7' was the second He 162 A-1 that was transferred to France after the war. The machine was painted according to 'Oberflächenschutzliste 8-162' with the special colour demarcation line. The 'Wolf's head' emblem, taken from III./JG 77, was applied on both sides of the fuselage.

The fuselage and wings of He 162 A-1 W.Nr. 310 005, 'Red 7', rest on trestles at SNAC, Boulogne-Billancourt, March 1946. The aircraft would appear to have had a fresh coat of green paint applied to its upper fuselage which has masked both the tactical number and the upper Balkenkreuz, but not the unit emblem. Note the tail assembly has been removed. The MK 108 cannon were also removed for inspection by French armaments experts.

A view of the nose bulkhead of He 162 A-1 W.Nr. 310 005, 'Red 7', with its exposed nosewheel assembly, hydraulics and springs, photographed at the Societé Nationale de Construction Aéronautique du Centre (SNCAC) in the former Farman factory at Boulogne-Billancourt in March 1946, shortly after the aircraft's arrival in France. The Heinkel, which bears the wolf's head emblem of III./JG 77 adopted by 2./JG 1, was in the process of being stripped down for analysis and technical appreciation.

The emblem of 2./JG 1.

A view of He 162 A-2 W.Nr. 120 093 'White 2' at SNCAC in Boulogne in March 1946. Note the tail cone has been removed, but the landing gear is still in place.

A further engineering report of 8 May concluded: '... the performance charts attached to the German manual seem to be very optimistic, especially for the take-off run... The aircraft does not seem very steady on its course. Especially when landing with undercarriage and flaps down, the aircraft is difficult because of its lack of stability in the yaw and pitch axes.'

Following these initial findings, a team from the *Direction Technique et Industrielle* (DTI) including a former fighter pilot from 329 (French) Squadron (*Groupe de Chasse* I/2 *'Cicognes'*), *Lt* Raphaël Lombaert, tested the He 162 on behalf of the *État-Major Général Air* (EMGA). Lombaert noted: '... I stress the sluggish acceleration, which requires a run of 900-1000 m before the aircraft leaves the ground at a speed of 190 km/h... Climb at 350 km/h was very pleasant, with no vibration and a very soft noise; levelling off the aircraft at the cruise setting of 9,000 km/h IAS did not alter the pleasure of the climb. Unfortunately, this apparent docility vanished as soon as one started to feel for the control reactions, especially its incredible sensitivity to the slightest amount of slip, which made one think, because of the sinking in pitch or roll, that a spin was imminent.

'The pilot can't see in the crucial area, i.e. to the rear and to the top. Moreover the very short range and the scanty equipment makes flights in bad weather or flying through clouds somewhat problematic.'

Further testing was plagued by worrying incidents, such as an almost fatal take-off when runway length proved insufficient and another when, after repeated attempts to land one of the Heinkels, it was found that an undercarriage door had been torn away.

During the summer of 1947, the three He 162s were moved by rail from Orléans-Bricy to the CEAM facility at Mont-de-Marsan, where they were thoroughly overhauled and repaired by CEAM mechanics with specialisation in jet technology, civilian technicians from SNAC and a former engineer from BMW. By September the aircraft were ready for further flight trials and on 25 October, no fewer than eleven

A rare photograph of He 162 A-2 W.Nr. 120 223, 'Yellow 1', in its new incarnation with the French identification number, 'He 162 No. 1', photographed at the Centre d'Expériences Aériennes Militaires (CEAM) at Mont-de-Marsan, France, in 1947. The aircraft still has its MG 151/20s fitted and is finished in overall grey/beige paint with a band of protective paint around the fuselage/nose join, an area susceptible to forces of air when in flight. A French tricolour has been applied to the rudders.

A good view of He 162 A-2 'No. 2' (W.Nr. 120 015), formerly 'White 21' of 1./JG 1, in its new French colours of overall grey/beige with French fuselage roundels and tricolours on the rudders outside a hangar at Orléans-Bricy in 1947.

A mechanic poses for a snapshot by the cockpit of He 162 A-2 'No. 2' at Orléans-Bricy, France, in the summer of 1947. The aircraft appears to be in a good overall condition.

A mechanic crouches under the wing of He 162 A-2 'No. 2' at Orléans-Bricy, France, in the summer of 1947 while the aircraft undergoes engine maintenance.

pilots flew the Heinkels on 20-minute high-speed familiarisation flights. Despite starting problems involving the Riedel starter motor, 13 flights had been logged by the end of the month, totalling 4 hours 35 minutes. The following month saw a further six flights of 2 hours 7 minutes, with seven flights in December totalling 2 hours 15 minutes. During one of these latter flights, on 12 December, it was the turn of the experienced CEAM pilot, *Lt* Lucien Inguimbert, formerly of GC 1/G *Champagne*, who had also flown 150 hours flight-testing captured Ju 88s. It was his first jet-powered flight and he remembered: 'As soon as the Heinkels arrived, the mechanics took over the machines to learn how they worked. This took several days, proceeding by trial and error, because we did not have any technical manuals… I clearly remember the cramped cockpit, which contained the bare minimum, just the basic instruments. The throttle levers were simple iron rods, and strings with pieces of wood tied on their ends were the handles for the flaps and the undercarriage.'

Other very qualified French pilots to fly the *Volksjäger* included Pierre 'Tito' Maulandi, who found acceleration and take-off very slow but visibility to front and sides and taxying, good, and *Lt.* Jean Bourguignat, formerly a Spitfire pilot with 341 (French) Squadron (*Group de Chasse* III/2 *'Alsace'*), who, despite flying in a machine which had starting problems and in which the ejector seat did not function, found that his overall impressions of taxying, take-off and landing were good.[41]

Meanwhile, back in England, on or by 14 August 1947, He 162 W.Nr. 120 074 (AM 60) and W.Nr. 120 095 (AM 63) are believed to have been Struck off Charge by No. 6 MU, meaning effectively that they no longer remained on RAF strength.[42]

In the USA, W.Nr. 120 077, 'Red 1' had been relocated to the University of Kansas at Lawrence, Kansas.

1948

The French continued with the testing of their three He 162s three years after the end of the War. In April 1948, *Lt. Col.* Hervé Longuet attempted to take off in He 162 'No. 2' from Mont-de-Marsan but an undercarriage leg collapsed during taxying.

The following month, *Capt.* Pierre Douard, an experienced former *Normandie-Niemen* pilot, flew the He 162 at Mont-de-Marsan for some 15 minutes prior to being posted as air attaché to Poland, where it was believed he would be able to obtain intelligence on what were assumed to be Soviet attempts at building their own version of the He 162. Once again, on landing and without functioning brakes, Douard was another pilot who found himself stopping just a few metres from the end of the runway.

On 14 July, *Lt. Col.* Longuet madeanother attempt to fly the *Volksjäger*, this time in 'No. 1' for a flypast. At 200 metres, Longuet entered into a dive across the runway, but managed to pull up at the last moment, while the Heinkel continued to lose height even as he pulled out.

The last recorded flight of the He 162 would take place nine days later on 23 July 1948, when French pilot, *Capt.* Schlienger, took off in clear weather with a very light south-easterly wind in Rostock-built W.Nr. 120 223, 'No. 1' from Mont-de-Marsan to conduct a demonstration flight for student officers. It was observed by the control tower that Schlienger's take-off appeared somewhat slow, lifting only a few metres off the ground with the undercarriage not retracting. The tower immediately ordered the road at the end of the 2450-metre runway to be kept closed to passing traffic, but after just one minute in the air above the surrounding pine trees, the Heinkel turned to port, with its wheels still down, stalled and crashed into the ground, exploding into flames with its BMW engine flung more than 60 metres from the scene of impact.

The aircraft had flown for 7 hrs 45 mins since being overhauled and its engine had run for 7 hrs 55 mins. The report of the investigation into the crash pointed to *Capt.* Schlienger possibly encountering difficulties with the electrics systems during take-off. The report further concluded that the He 162s were of 'no military value and of no practical interest'. The two remaining machines were to be written off.[43]

Mechanics conduct pre-flight checks on He 162 'No. 2' while pilot, Pierre Maulandi, checks the instruments in the cockpit ahead of a flight at the Centre d'Expériences Aériennes Militaires (CEAM) at Mont-de-Marsan, France, in December 1947.

A team of SNAC mechanics take a break from working on the BMW 003 engine of He 162 'No. 2' at Orléans-Bricy in the summer of 1947. The stencilled French maintenance markings were applied in red paint. Note the barrel of the MG 151/20 cannon in the gun trough.

Known French test flights, 1949-1952

Date	Number of aircraft	Not available	Available	Number of flights	Flying time	Pilots
04/05-47	3 aircraft	N°3	N°01& 2	4/7 flights	3h00	SNCAC (Bertrand & Nicolle)
27-05-47	3 aircraft	N°01 + N°3	N°2	5 flights	1h45	CATRE (du Merle, Descaves, Le Martelot, Lombaert)
10-47	3 aircraft	N°01 + N°3	N°2	13 flights	More than 4h35	CEAM (including de Pins, Vinçotte, Maurin and Thierry on 16th in N°2)
11-47	3 aircraft	1 not available	2 available	6 flights	2h00	CEAM
12-47	3 aircraft	N°01 + N°3	N°2	7 flights	2h15	CEAM (including Inguimbert and Maulandi)
01-48	3 aircraft	2 not available	1 available	3 flights	1h15	CEAM
02-48	3 aircraft	?	?	?	?	?
03-48	3 aircraft	1 not available	2 available with N°2	2 flights	1h10	CEAM (including Thierry, the 1st in N°2)
04-48	3 aircraft	N°2 + N°3	N°01	1 flight	0h20	CEAM (Longuet)
05-48	3 aircraft	N°01under repair.	N°2 + N°3	5 to 6 flights	2h00	CEAM (including Douarre)
06-48	3 aircraft	N°01 + N°3	N°2 available	?	?	?
07-48	3 aircraft	N°2 + N°3	N°01	1 flight + 1 accident	0h15	CEAM (Longuet and Schlienger)
08-48	2 aircraft	N°3	N°2	0	0	grounded
09-48	2 aircraft	N°3	N°2	0	0	grounded
10-48	2 aircraft	N°3	N°2	0	0	grounded
11-48	2 aircraft	N°3 written-off ?)	?	0	0	grounded
12-48	2 aircraft	?	?	0	0	grounded
01-49	0 aircraft	-	-	-	-	CTAR on DH Vampire F1

(via Philippe Couderchon)

1949-1952

By 1949 in England, W.Nr. 120 227 (AM 65), the former 'Red 2' of 2./JG 1 captured at Leck was to be found at the Central Gunnery School at Leconfield in Yorkshire.[44]

In France, the He 162 having been flown on some forty test-flights for a total of around 23 hours, aircraft '02' and '03' were slowly mothballed. However, as researcher and restorer Philippe Couderchon points out, they had actually performed a service of value in preparing some 30 CEAM pilots for their transition to the Vampire. The table above lists the known French test flights.

In January 1949, 'No. 02' was assigned as an instructional airframe to a mechanics' school in Rochefort-sur-Mer where it remained until July 1952, on one occasion painted bright red while paraded through a nearby village for a local fête.

'No. 3' which had been flown on only a few occasions, was moved to Salon-de-Provence for similar instructional purposes on behalf of officer mechanics of the *École de l'Air*. Here the aircraft was painted in overall blue and its BMW fired up on a number of occasions. Eventually, the engine broke down completely and the aircraft was relegated as a training airframe for the base fire brigade at Salon-de-Provence where it languished, with its wing removed, until disappearing during the mid-1950s.

A number of He 162s would survive, however, into the 21st century as exhibits in Great Britain, France, Canada and the USA.

In the same way that this chapter started, so it is perhaps fitting to end it with a view from Capt. Eric Brown, the British test pilot: 'The *Volksjäger*, with its pygmy size and very limited range, was an impracticable proposition. A more powerful jet and a swept-back wing might have made it a phenomenal machine, provided there had been more time to develop it properly…'[45]

An unidentified pilot or engineer in the cockpit of He 162 A-2 'No. 3' prepares to perform an engine test at the École de l'Air at Salon-de-Provence in 1949. Even by this late stage, the aircraft was still equipped with its MG 151/20 cannon and its FuG 24 and FuG 25 radio equipment and antennae.

A streak of flame blasts from the BMW 003 jet engine of He 162 A-2 'No. 3' as it undergoes an engine test at Salon-de-Provence in February 1949.

Heinkel He 162 A-2 W.Nr. 120093, 'No. 3', formerly 'White 2' of 1./JG 1, École de l'Air, Salon de Provence, 1949

This He 162 was one of five machines that were transported to France after the war and where it was assigned the individual number, '3'. During the French testing period the aircraft was initially painted in brown/green. In January 1949 the aircraft was still on the CEAM inventory and was transferred to the École de l'Air in Salon de Provence where it was used for airframe instruction purposes. The aircraft was then repainted in 'French cockade blue'. It had been captured at Leck in May 1945.

Following an engine test, He 162 A-2 'No. 3' is left parked on the taxiway outside the hangars at the École de l'Air at Salon-de-Provence. By 1949, the aircraft had had a resplendent new paint scheme of overall French 'cockade blue' applied, with national fuselage roundels and rudder tricolours. The nose cone was in a darker finish and the rear engine section was in black. Note the Siebel Si 204 visible just beyond 'No. 3'.

By 1949 He 162 A-2 'No. 3' had been returned to the hangar.

Left and above: He 162 W.Nr. 120 077, formerly 'Red 1', 'Nervenklau' / T2-489 photographed while on exhibition in the USA during the 1950s, possibly while owned by the first of two private museums in California.

Above, right and following page: These photographs of He 162 W.Nr. 120 227, 'Red 2', were taken at RAF St. Athan, South Wales in 1985. The aircraft had been refurbished with the exception of the ejector seat, which had been removed and forwarded to Martin Baker for research purposes. Since these photographs were taken, the aircraft has been moved to the RAF Museum Hendon in north London and has been on display since 22 November 1989 in the Bomber Command Hall.

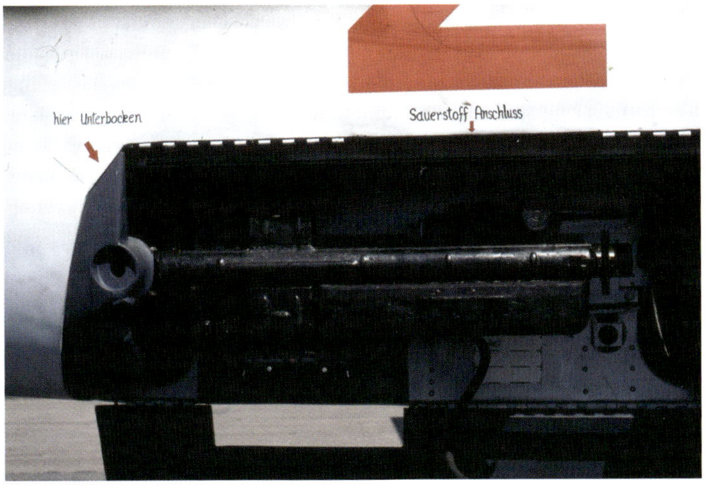

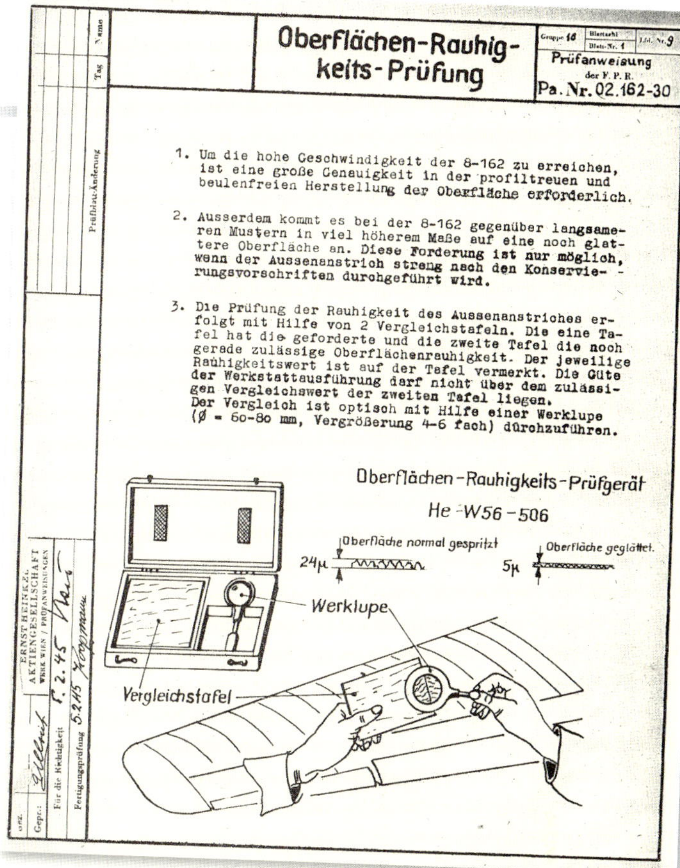

Oberflächen-Rauhigkeits-Prüfung

Gruppe 16 | Blatt-Nr. 1 | Lfd. Nr. 9
Prüfanweisung der F. P. R.
Pa. Nr. 02.162-30

1. Um die hohe Geschwindigkeit der 8-162 zu erreichen, ist eine große Genauigkeit in der profiltreuen und beulenfreien Herstellung der Oberfläche erforderlich.

2. Ausserdem kommt es bei der 8-162 gegenüber langsameren Mustern in viel höherem Maße auf eine noch glattere Oberfläche an. Diese Forderung ist nur möglich, wenn der Aussenanstrich streng nach den Konservierungsvorschriften durchgeführt wird.

3. Die Prüfung der Rauhigkeit des Aussenanstriches erfolgt mit Hilfe von 2 Vergleichstafeln. Die eine Tafel hat die geforderte und die zweite Tafel die noch gerade zulässige Oberflächenrauhigkeit. Der jeweilige Rauhigkeitswert ist auf der Tafel vermerkt. Die Güte der Werkstattausführung darf nicht über dem zulässigen Vergleichswert der zweiten Tafel liegen. Der Vergleich ist optisch mit Hilfe einer Werklupe (Ø = 60-80 mm, Vergrößerung 4-6 fach) durchzuführen.

Oberflächen-Rauhigkeits-Prüfgerät
He-W56-506

Oberfläche normal gespritzt 24μ
Oberfläche geglättet. 5μ
Werklupe
Vergleichstafel

ERNST HEINKEL AKTIENGESELLSCHAFT WERK WIEN / PRÜFANWEISUNGEN

Translation of an EHAG document stipulating the smoothness required for the upper wing surface of a He 162.

1. In order to achieve the highest performance in the He 162 it is necessary to have the smoothest finish over the wing profile surface by elimination of all roughness and bumps especially on the upper surface.
2. In addition, as the production of the 8-162 slowly increases, it is paramount that the smoothness of the upper wing surface is maintained. However, this is only possible if the final external finish complies with the highest manufacturer's specifications.
3. The testing for roughness of the external paint finish can be carried out by comparing the 2 sample tablets. The first sample tablet shows the normal factory finish and the second shows the preferred acceptable upper surface finish after smoothing.
   This comparison can be carried out optically by using the second tablet and a magnifying glass [Diam between 60-80 mm with an enlargement capacity of between 4 to 6 times].

Key to annotation:
Upper surface- roughness-test equipment
He-W56-506
Upper surface normal finish	Upper surface after smoothing
Comparison sample	magnifying glass

Pages 190: Two documents produced by EHAG in Wien giving the painting specifications for the He 162. The documents include information regarding the RLM paint colours as well as preservation lacquers and primer coatings for both metal and timber parts of the aircraft. Included with each of these specified items are the names and addresses of the various manufacturers. The two documents are dated and appear in that sequence.

The first document, consisting of seven pages, is dated 9 January 1945 and is headed 'Preliminary preservatives list for the series production He 162.

The second, single page, document (page 190-bottom right), dated 27 January 1945, is headed 'Camouflage scheme and stencilling for 8-162'. A note at the bottom of the page states that the drawings to accompany the camouflage scheme and stencilling had not been completed. It should be noted that all the documents were typed and not printed on a printing press.

Please refer to caption at bottom right of previous page.

Ernst Heinkel
Akt.-Ges.
Werk Wien.

Vorläufige Konservierung für He 162 Serie — OS-Liste vom 9. 1. 1945

Bauteil bezw. Werkstoff	Konservierung
1. Teile aus Aluminium-Legierungen nach Fliegwerkstoff-Leistungsblättern. Z.B. Fl.W. 3000, 3115, 3116, 3125, 3355	Kein Anstrich
Ausnahmen:	
Blendschutz im Führerraum	Fl.L. 7101.66
Tarnanstrich für Rumpf und Höhenleitwerk	Fl.L. 7121.76 oder 81 oder 82 nach Tarnvorschrift. Anstrich mit feinster Stahlwolle abreiben. Strich in Strömungsrichtung.
Außen sind Blechstöße und Nietreihen sorgfältig zu entfetten und darauf auf blankem Blech zu spachteln. Am Rumpf werden dabei nur im Bereich des vorderen Drittels die von oben nach unten verlaufenden Stöße und Nietreihen gespachtelt. An der Höhenflosse sind Stöße und Nietreihen nur im Bereich der vorderen Hälfte zu spachteln.	Ikarol-Spachtel 119D
In offenen Schächten (z.B. Fahrgestell) sind Teile aus Fl.W. 3115 sowie hydraulische Leitungen und Fl.W. 3125 1 x zu spritzen.	Fl.L. 7101.66
Rohrleitungen	Nur Kennzeichnung durch Tupfen mit Fl. L. 7160, Farbtöne 21 bis 27 oder mit Kennbändern der Fa. Beiersdorf, Hamburg.
Gewindeteile sind nach OKL-Vorschrift Az 70 k 10 Nr. 4135/44 v. 30.V. 44 zu konservieren, die lautet:	Eloxieren nach OKL-Vorschrift
a) Bei Normteilen werden die Innengewinde gemäß Vorschrift GL/C-E 10 4399/42 v. 19.9.42 weiterhin eloxiert, falls nicht diese Teile im eigenen Werk hergestellt werden oder bisher im eigenen Werk oberflächengeschützt wurden (Teile sind vor dem Zusammenbau gut zu fetten).	
b) Gewinde, die im Fluge verstellt werden (z.B. Verstellspindeln für Trimmgetriebe).	

- 2 -

Bauteil bezw. Werkstoff	Konservierung
2. Teile aus Magnesiumlagierungen nach Fliegwerkstoff-Leistungsblättern. z.B. Fl.W. 35o1, 351o u.s.w.	1xFl.L.71o1.66 od. 99 und 1xFl.L. 71o9.66 oder 2xFl.L. 71o1.66
Gewinde und Passungsteile sind nach OKL-Vorschrift Az 7o k 1o Nr.4135/44 v.3o.5.44 zu konservieren, die lautet: Für Gewinde und Passungsteile aus Fl.W. 351o wird anstelle des bisherigen Kochverfahrens mit 5%igem Kaliumbichromat das Kochverfahren ABL 35 (Fa.Dr.W. Proben, Chem.Fabrik, Kitzingen a.M. Postfach 44) eingeführt.	Bichromatisieren
3. Teile aus Stahllegierungen nach Fliegwerkstoff-Leistungsblättern	
Knotenstücke, Rohre, Schweißteile, Stahlguß- und Schmiedestücke	Fl.L. 71o1.66 1x
Ausnahmen:	
Im freien Luftstrom oder in offenen Schächten	2xFl.L.71o1.66 oder 1xFl.L.71o1.66 oder 99 und 1xFl.L.71o9.66 od.76 od,81 od.82
Kleinteile: Unterlegscheiben, Sicherungsscheiben, Federn, bei denen Anstrich unzweckmäßig.	verzinken oder phosphatieren
Nietköpfe (ungeschützt geschlagen):	1xFl.L.71o1.66 od. 99
Verzinkte Nieten:	ohne Anstrich
Dichtgeschweißte Hohlräume: Innenseite	ohne Oberflächenschutz
Rohrleitungen:	innen ungeschützt außen: 1xFl.L.71o1.66, dann durch Tupfen mit Fl.L.716o Farbtöne 21 bis 27 oder durch Kennbänder der Fa. Beiersdorf, Hamburg, kennzeichnen.
Gewinde- und Paßteile sind nach OKL-Vorschrift Az.7o k 1o Nr.4135/44 vom 3o.5.44 zu konservieren, die lautet:	
a) Teile nur mit Gewinde sind grundsätzlich zu schützen. Bestimmte, von den Stammwerken besonders festzulegende Teile sind nur verzinkt einzubauen, z.B. Überwurfmuttern an Trennstellen der Großbauteile, sämtliche Kugelpfannen, bei denen Gegengewinde unverzinkt ist, Fahrwerks- und Spornradachsen, Gabelköpfe, Spannschrauben für Zurrungen an Behältern u.sonstige	verzinken oder phosphatieren

- 3 -

Bauteil bezw. Werkstoff	Konservierung
wichtige Teile mit einstellbarem Gewinde, Spreizbuchsenverschraubungen an Klappen und Schrauben für Klappen, die im Einsatz geöffnet werden müssen.	
Im übrigen ist das Verzinken von Schrauben und Muttern überall dort beizubehalten, wo Verzinkungsanlagen vorhanden sind. Phosphatiert und brüniert angelieferte Schrauben keinesfalls abbeizen und nachverzinken. Ungeschützt angelieferte Schrauben und solche aus eigener Fertigung in den Flugzeugwerken verzinken oder phosphtieren. Bei Innenteilen von Geräten, die nicht ständig von Oel berührt sind, muß von Fall zu Fall entschieden werden, ob Verzinken beibehalten werden muß. Bei Anwendung von Phosphatierungsverfahren und Brünieren ist Voraussetzung, daß derartige Gewindeteile mit Fett eingesetzt werden. Bei solchen Schrauben ist im freien Luftstrom oder in offenen Schächten das freistehende Gewindeende nach Zusammenbau mit Flieglack 7101.66 oder 99 zu streichen.	
Abbrennen in Oel ist verboten.	
b) Teile nur mit Passungen	gefettet
Grundsätzlich nur gefettet anliefern, beim Einbau, falls erforderlich, nachfetten. Freie Bolzenenden, wie bisher, nach Einbau streichen mit Flieglack 7101.66.	
4. Teile aus Holz. Z.B. aus Kiefer, Buchensperrholz, TBu 7 und TBu 20.	
Holzteile sind immer so schnell wie möglich zu konservieren, da bei Verzögerungen sehr leicht Rißgefahr durch Feuchtigkeitsaufnahme besteht. (Ausnahme: Teile, die im Tankraum liegen!)	
A. Außenseite.	
1. Arbeitsgang: 1 x streichen oder tauchen.	Fl.L. 7141.99
2. " Spitzen brechen.	
3. " 1 x streichen oder tauchen.	Fl.L. 7140.99
4. " Spitzen brechen	
5. " 1 x streichen oder tauchen	Fl.L. 7140.99
6. " 1 x spritzen mit Fl.L.7116, der im Verhältnis 3:1 mit Fl.L.7139 gemischt ist. Diese Mischung kommt in Wegfall, wenn der Fl.L. 7116 von von der Fa.Herbig-Haarhaus spritzfähig geliefert wird.	
7. " 1 x spritzen mit Gemisch von Fl.L. 7116 und 7139 im Verhältnis 3:1, wie unter Arbeitsgang 6.	
8. " 1 x naß schleifen.	
9. " 1 x spritzen.	Fl.L. 7139.99
10. " Spitzen brechen.	

- 4 -

Bauteil bezw. Werkstoff	Konservierung
11. Arbeitsgang: 1 x spritzen	Fl.L.7115.76 od. 81 oder 82 nach Tarnungsvorschrift
12. " Die Übergangsstellen im Bereich der Flügelnase (50 % der Flügeltiefe) mit einem Lappen, der mit Fl.L. Verdünner 7215.00 getränkt ist, verteilen.	
Anmerkung: Unter Spitzenbrechen ist das Wegnehmen der Spitzen durch leichtes Überfahren mit feinem abgestumpftem Schleifpapier zu verstehen. Für Stöße ist der reine Ziehspachtel 7216.99 zu verwenden, der vor dem Spritzspachteln aufzubringen ist.	
B. Innenseite (ohne Tankraum!).	
1. Arbeitsgang: 1 x streichen, tauchen oder ausgießen.	Fl.L.7141.99
2. " 1 x streichen, tauchen oder ausgießen	Fl.L. 7140.99
3. " 1 x streichen, tauchen oder ausgießen.	Fl.L. 7141.99
C. Tankraum im Flügel. Die Tankraumteile des Flügels, die innen liegen, also die Teile, die mit dem Kraftstoff in Berührung kommen, dürfen auf keinen Fall mit den vorgenannten Holzkonservierungsmitteln geschützt werden, sondern diese Teile müssen unbedingt roh bleiben. Für die Konservierung des Tankraumes selbst ist eine zweimalige Behandlung mit Luphen L vorgesehen, das von der Fa. Duco, Berlin-Spindlersfeld, vertrieben wird. Diese Firma übernimmt auch vorläufig durch besondere Arbeitsanweiser die fabrikatorische Konservierung. Von Herrn Pelizaeus vom OKL/Fl E-10 IV wird eine entsprechende Konservierungsanweisung aufgestellt und verteilt.	Luphen L
D. Kanten. Auf eine besonders gute, wasserdichte Kantendichtung bei allen Holzteilen, insbesondere bei den Waffenklappen, Fahrwerksklappen u.s.w., ist besonderer Wert zu legen. Von der Fa. Herbig-Haarhaus in Erkner wird zu diesem Zweck eine Paste entwickelt, die der Flieglackkette 33 angeglichen ist.	
5. Akku-Lagerung	1x Fl.L.7101.66 od.99 und 1x Fl.L.7119.66
6. Beschriftung und Balkenkreuz.	1x spritzen mit Fl.L. 7160.21/22 /23/24 oder 1x streichen mit Fl.L.7164/21 /22/23/24

5

Bauteil bezw. Werkstoff	Konservierung
7. Heißwerdende Teile. Das sind solche, die höheren Temperaturen als 150°C ausgesetzt sind.	Aluminium-Glasurit W 9544
8. Punktschweißungen. Nur für Konservierung zwischen der Überlaschung.	
a) Stahl- und Magnesiumlegierungen	Fl.L. 7191.99
b) Aluminiumlegierungen	ohne Schutz.

9. Lieferanten der Konservierungsmittel.

Konservierungsmittel	Lieferant
Flieglack 7101, " 7109, " 7119, " 7121; Flieglackverdünner 7200.00, 7201.00; Ikarol-Spachtel 119 D	Warnecke & Böhm, Berlin-Weißensee, Goethestraße
Flieglack 7160, 7164; Flieglackverdünner 7232, " 7234	Beck, Koller & Co., Berlin-Weißensee.
Aluminium-Glasurit W 9544	Glasurit-Werke M. Winkelmann, A.-G., Hiltrup /Weißensee.
Flieglack 7115, " 7139, " 7140, " 7141; Flieglack 7116 (Spachtel); Flieglackverdünner 7213.00, " 7233.00; Flieglackverteiler 7215.00; Abdichtpaste	Herbig-Haarhaus, Erkner b.Berlin
Luphen L	Duco A.G., Berlin-Spindlersfeld
Flieglack 7191	Dr.Kurt Herberts, Wuppertal-Barmen.

- 6 -

10. Arbeitsanweisung.

A. Metallanstriche.

Beim Aufbringen der Anstriche ist zu beachten:
I. Die Oberfläche der Flugzeugteile ist sorgfältig zu entfetten.
II. Die Verarbeitung muß in temperaturbeständigen, sauberen und staubfreien Räumen erfolgen.

1. Flieglack 7101	TZ 6 h	
	Spritzkonsistenz	19 bis 23 sec
	Verbrauch pro m²	0,250 kg ca. +)
	Fliegl.Verdünner	7200.00 od. 7201.00
	Verbrauch pro m²	0,070 kg ca. +)
2. Flieglack 7109	TZ 3 h	
	Spritzkonsistenz	27 bis 32 sec.
	Verbrauch pro m²	0,10 kg ca +)
	Fliegl.Verdünner	7200.00
	Verbrauch pro m²	0,030 kg ca +)
3. Flieglack 7119.99	TZ 3 h	
	Verdünnungsverh.	3:5
	Verbrauch pro m²	0,060 kg ca.+)
	Fliegl.Verdünner	7200.00
	Verbrauch pro m²	0,100 kg ca.+)
4. Flieglack 7121	TZ 3 h	
	Spritzkonsistenz	21 sec.
	Verbrauch pro m²	0,250 kg ca +)
	Fliegl.Verdünner	7200.00
	Verbrauch pro m²	0,070 kg ca +)
5. Flieglack 7160	TZ 3 h	
	Spritzkonsistenz	45 sec.
	Streichkonsistenz	250 sec.
	Verbrauch pro m²	0,150 kg ca +)
	Fliegl.Verdünner	7232.00
	Verbrauch pro m²	0,100 kg (b.spr.)ca +) 0,050 kg (b.str.)ca +)
6. Flieglack 7164	TZ 3 h	
	Streichkonsistenz	80 sec.
	Verbrauch pro m²	0,150 kg ca +)
7. Ikarol-Spachtel	119 D TZ 3 h	
	Fliegl.Versünner	7200.00

+) Die Verbrauchszahlen sind größeren betriebstechnisch bedingten Schwankungen unterworfen und daher nur für für Zwecke der Vorkalkulation mit Vorbehalt anzusetzen. Die Werte sind unterschiedlich, je nachdem ob gespritzt, gestrichen, getaucht wird bezw. ob große Flächen oder Kleinteile behandelt werden.

B. Holzanstriche

Die Holzflächen müssen trocken sein und vor Aufbringen der Anstriche staubfrei gemacht werden.

a) Verdünnungsverhältnisse, Verarbeitungsviskositäten und Trockenzeiten, die bei den Lacken der Flieglackkette 33 anzuwenden sind, sind den Vorschriften der Firma Junkers anzupassen, [illegible]e für ihre Ju 352 ebenfalls die Flieglackkette 33 v[illegible]ndet.

- 8 -

- 7 -

b) Das für den Tankraum vorgesehene Lacksystem Luphen L wird von der Firma Duco durch besondere Arbeitsanweiser eingeführt. Die Arbeitsanweisung selbst wird von Herrn Pelizaeus, OKL,TLR/FL-E 10 IV, aufgestellt und verteilt.

C. Für die Ausführung des Balkenkreuzes und des Lichtsschutzanstriches sind besondere Anweisungen ergangen.

Die vorstehende Liste war bereits mehrfach Gegenstand von Besprechungen mit den amtlichen Stellen (OKL, TLR/FL-E 10 IV in Berlin und E-Stelle Travemünde). Es sind deshalb wesentliche Änderungen nicht zu erwarten, wenn nicht aus besonders dringenden Gründen (z.B. Rohstoffknappheit) anders disponiert werden muß.

Der Antrag auf offizielle Genehmigung dieser OS-Liste von der zuständigen Stelle (Fl.Stabsing. Hoppe bei der E-Stelle Travemünde) läuft.

Wien, den 9.1.45

Baumusterleitung
gez.Hart

gez. Althof gez. Bünger

Tarnschema und Beschriftung 8-162:

Bauteil	oben links	oben rechts	unten	Bemerkungen	Beschriftung nach Zeichng 8-162
Rumpf	82		76	Rumpfseiten im oberen Drittel 82 wolkig nach unten verlaufend	100 Blatt 3
Abnehmbare Triebwerk-Verkleidung	81		-	-	-
Tragfläche	82	81	76	Nase: 100 mm in 76, anschließend 150 mm nach oben wolkig verlaufd.	500-075
Landeklappe	81	82	76	von Nasenvorderkante nach oben und unten je 25 mm wolkig verlaufend.	320-026 321-026
Querruder	allseitig 82			so dass völlig austauschbar	305-016
Höhenflosse	82	81	76	Nase: 17 mm in 76, anschließend 50 mm nach oben wolkig verlaufd.	350-016 (keinerlei Schrift)
Höhenruder	81	82	76	" "	360-015 361-015
Seitenflosse	allseitig 76			-	370-014
Seitenruder	allseitig 76			-	380-016

Ferner wird benötigt:

Abschiebebild "Kraftstoff" nach Zeichnung 500-075.001
" "Anlasskraftstoff" " 500-075.002

T a r n s c h e m a Z e i c h n u n g f ü r d i e g e s a m t e M a s c h i n e w i r d v o r l ä u f i g n i c h t a n g e f e r t i g t , d a obige A n g a b e n g e n ü g e n .

Sämtliche Angaben über anzuwendende Lacke für Metall- und Holzteile vergleiche OS-Liste.

gez. 27.1.45
gepr. 28. Feb. 1945

1 Pitot tube
2 Moulded plywood nose cap
3 Nosewheel retraction mechanism
4 Spring-loaded nosewheel extension assembly
5 Shock absorber scissor
6 Nosewheel
7 Nosewheel fork
8 Nosewheel leg
9 Nosewheel door
10 Gun trough
11 Nosewheel well
12 Rudder pedal
13 Window panel (visual nosewheel retraction check)
14 Wooden instrument panel
15 One-piece moulded windscreen
16 Revi 16G gunsight (interchangeable with the Revi 16B)
17 Jettisonable hinged clear-vision canopy
18 Ventilation disc
19 Heinkel cartridge-operated ejection seat
20 Ejection seat handle grip
21 Throttle control quadrant
22 Retractable entry step
23 Gun barrel shroud in cockpit wall
24 Port 20-mm MG 151 cannon
25 Ammunition chute
26 Main oxygen supply bottle (2 litre/3.5 pint capacity)
27 Explosive charge ejector rail
28 Pilot's headrest
29 Canopy hinge
30 Ammunition box behind cockpit (120 rounds per gun)
31 Flexible main tank (695 litre/153 Imp gal capacity)
32 Fuel lines
33 FuG 25a IFF radio compartment
34 Beech plywood wing skinning
35 Jet intake
36 Riedel two-stroke starter motor bullet
37 Oil tank
38 BMW 003E-1 Sturm axial-flow turbojet
39 Riedel starter fuel tank
40 Seven-stage axial compressor casing
41 FuG 24 R/T homing loop
42 Annular combustion chamber
43 Exhaust centre body
44 Exhaust outlet
45 Jet efflux fairing
46 Heat-resistant aft dorsal decking
47 Light metal tailplane
48 Starboard fin housing R/T receiver aerial
49 Starboard rudder
50 Rudder tab
51 Elevator
52 Elevator tab
53 Tailcone (movable through +3° to -2°)
54 Port tailfin structure
55 Rudder structure
56 Tailplane/tailfin attachment
57 Port tailfin upper and lower plates (housing R/T transmitter and IFF aerials)
58 Tailskid
59 Dural fuselage skinning
60 Monocoque fuselage construction
61 Control cables
62 Downswept wing root fillet
63 Hydraulically-operated flaps
64 Port aileron
65 Detachable downswept aluminium wingtip
66 Wooden T-section rear spar
67 Wooden wing structure
68 Wooden T-section forward mainspar
69 Impregnated integral wing tank (180 litre/39.6 Imp gal capacity)
70 Vertical wing/fuselage attachment bolts (four stations)
71 Single rear horizontal engine mounting/attachment bolt
72 Two forward vertical engine mounting/attachment bolts
73 Pressure-fed oil tank
74 Mainwheel hydraulic retraction jack
75 Mainwheel extension spring
76 Wooden mainwheel door
77 Mainwheel leg
78 Mainwheel tyre (660 mm 3 190mm)
79 Shock absorber scissor
80 Narrow-track main undercarriage assembly
81 Assisted take-off rocker unit (attached to fuselage immediately aft of mainwheel well)

Heinkel He 162 A-2

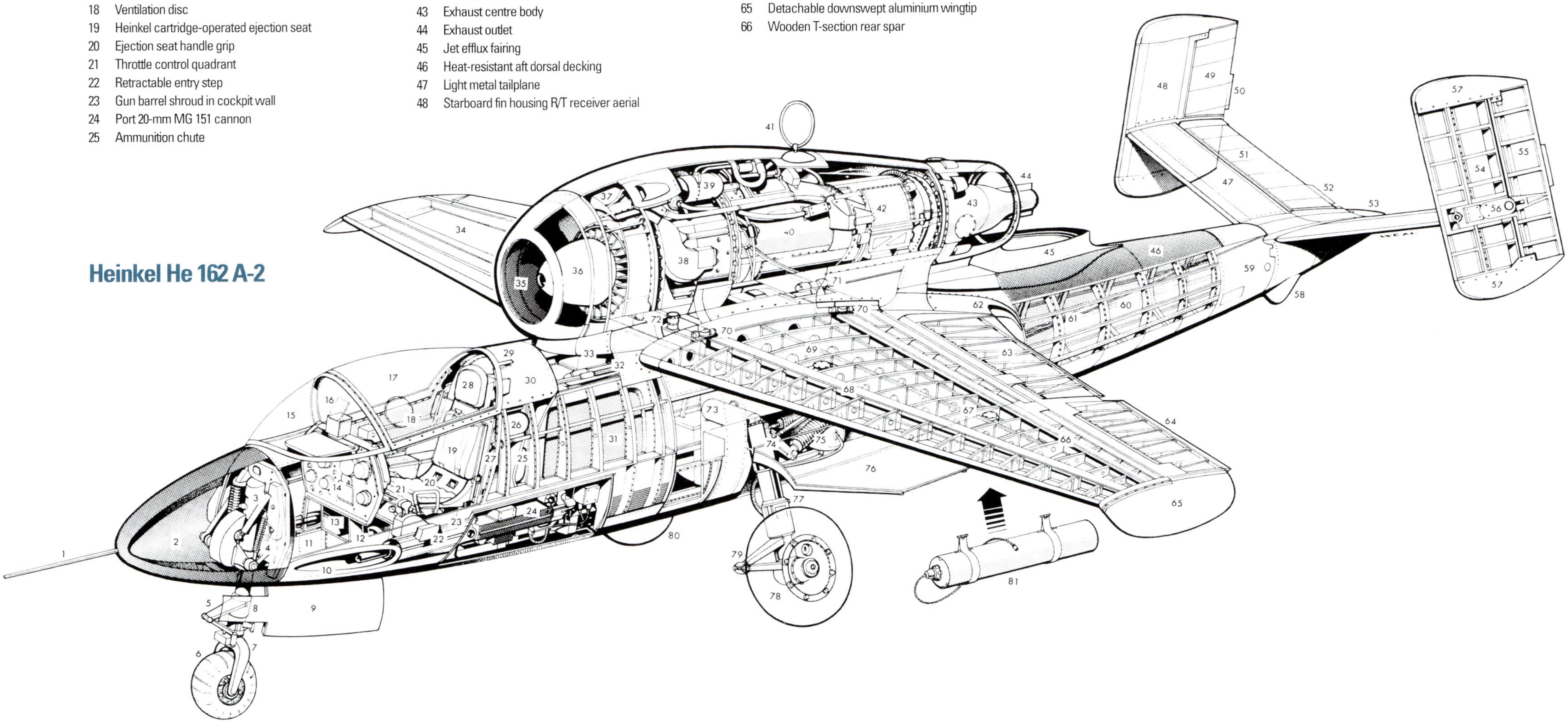

CHAPTER NOTES

Chapter One

1 Gilbert, *The Second World War*, pg. 553
2 UKNA/AIR20/7709
3 Speer, *The Slave State*, pg. 127
4 UKNA/AIR20/7709
5 Galland, *The First and the Last*, pg. 303
6 Caldwell & Muller, *The Luftwaffe over Germany – Defense of the Reich*, pg. 269
7 Ries, *Luftwaffen Story 1935-1939*, pgs. 27 & 40
8 Smith & Creek, *Jet Planes of the Third Reich*, pg. 239
9 UKNA/WO208/4170
10 Lloyd, *Heinkel He 162*, Aero Modeller article
11 Forsyth, *Jagdwaffe – Defending the Reich 1944-1945*, pg. 225
12 Air P/W Interrogation Unit, Main Headquarters Second TAF *Trends of Development in the GAF – Part IV – The Story of the 8-162*, AP/WIU (2nd TAF) 87/1945, 12.7.1945
13 Redemann, Hans, *Henschel Hs 132, Flug Revue*, 3/1970 and Smith & Creek, *Jet Planes*, pg. 229
14 Griehl, *Heinkel He 162*, pg. 3
15 Müller, *He 162 'Volksjäger' – Last Ditch Effort by the Luftwaffe*, pgs. 22 & 419
16 ADI(K) Report No. 340/1945, *Arguments for and against the Volksjäger*, 26 June 1945 and Smith & Norton *Heinkel He 162 – A Bird of a Different Feather*, unpub. draft
17 Heinkel, *He 1000*, pg. 269
18 UKNA/AIR40/2421
19 Heinkel, *He 1000*, pgs. 129-31
20 Ernst Heinkel Flugzeugwerke GmbH: *P.1073 – Schneller Strahljäger*, 10. Juli 1944 and Smith & Norton, unpub. draft
21 Schick & Meyer, *Luftwaffe Secret Projects – Fighters 1939-1945*, pg. 93
22 Hiller, *Heinkel He 162 'Volksjäger' – Entwicklung – Produktion – Einsatz*, pg. 27
23 Smith & Norton, unpub. draft
24 Griehl, pg. 3
25 Kay, Antony L., *German Jet Engine and Gas Turbine Development 1930-1945*, pg. 99 et passim, and Smith & Creek, *Jet Planes*, pgs. 53-54, 169
26 Smith & Norton, unpub. draft
27 Teleprint message RLM Berlin to Blohm u.Voss, Nr. 2267, 10.9.1944
28 *Projekt Volksjäger – Stellungnahme zum Projekt Volksjäger von Dr. Vogt (Blohm & Voss) unter Berücksichtigung des Entwurfs Heinkel He 162* (undated)
29 ADI(K) Report No. 340/1945, 26 June 1945
30 Ernst Heinkel Aktiengesellschaft, Wien: *Kleinst-Jäger P.1073 mit BMW 003*, 11.9.1944
31 Müller, pg. 43
32 Prof. Messerschmitt, *Stellungnahme zum Projekt 'Volksjäger'*, Oberammergau, October 1944 (and English translation as Appendix to ADI(K) Report No. 340/1945, 26 June 1945)
33 Müller, pg. 49
34 Schick & Meyer, pg. 98
35 *Dr.-Ing.* Richard Vogt, *Projekt Volksjäger – Stellungnahme zum Projekt Volksjäger von Dr. Vogt (Blohm & Voss) unter Berücksichtigung des Entwurfs Heinkel He 162*, undated
36 UKNA/AIR40/164 Günter, S and Hohbach *History and Experiences of He 162 and He 162 Report No. 2 Performances with Jumo-004* (Heinkel Report), Translation No. F-TS-672-RE, Headquarters Air Materiel Command, Wright Field, Dayton, Oh., October 1946
37 APWIU (2nd Air Disarmament Wing) 63/1945, *A View on the Volksjäger He 162*, 14 June 1945
38 Schick & Meyer, pg. 97
39 Müller, pg. 50
40 Smith & Norton, unpub. draft
41 Galland, pgs. 347-48
42 ADI(K) Report No. 340/1945, *Arguments for and against the Volksjäger*, 26 June 1945
43 Smith, J. Richard & Creek, Eddie J., *Volksjäger*, Monogram *Close-Up* 11, Monogram Aviation Publications, Boylston, 1986, pg. 5
44 Müller, pg. 50
45 EHAG Wien, *Bericht 105a/44 P.1073 Strahljäger*, 23.9.1944, Smith & Norton, unpub. draft and Müller, pg. 51
46 Müller, 51 & 421, Albert Speer, *Inside the Third Reich*, Weidenfeld & Nicolson, London 1970, pg. 286 and Dan van der Vat, *The Good Nazi – The Life and Lies of Albert Speer*, Weidenfeld & Nicolson, London, 1997, pg.141
47 Baumbach, Werner, *Broken Swastika – The defeat of the Luftwaffe*, Hale, London, 1986, pg. 172
48 Der Reichsminister für Rüstung und Kriegsproduktion: Entwicklungshauptkommission Flugzeuge, B.Nr. 181/44, Bericht über die Besprechung am 24.10.44 betr. Schulflugzeuge, 27.10.1944
49 Galland, pg. 348
50 Baumbach, pg. 172
51 Smith & Norton, unpub. draft
52 Hiller, pg. 35
53 *Dr.-Ing.* Richard Vogt, *Projekt Volksjäger – Stellungnahme zum Projekt Volksjäger von Dr. Vogt (Blohm & Voss) unter Berücksichtigung des Entwurfs Heinkel He 162*, undated
54 Smith & Norton, unpub. draft and Griehl, pg. 4
55 Farren Mission to Germany: *He. 162 – An Achievement in Rapid Aircraft Development and Manufacture* (undated report)
56 Griehl, pg. 4
57 IWM/GDC/18/205 EHAG Aktenvermerk Nr. 5/44, 162 Konstruktionbespechung, 7.10.44
58 Farren Mission to Germany: *He. 162 – An Achievement in Rapid Aircraft Development and Manufacture* (undated report)
59 Griehl, pg. 4
60 Prof. Messerschmitt, *Stellungnahme zum Projekt 'Volksjäger'*, Oberammergau, October 1944
61 Smith & Norton, unpub. draft
62 Prof. Messerschmitt, *Stellungnahme zum Projekt 'Volksjäger'*, Oberammergau, October 1944
63 Air P/W Interrogation Unit, Main Headquarters Second TAF *Trends of Development in the GAF – Part IV – The Story of the 8-162*, AP/WIU (2nd TAF) 87/1945, 12.7.1945

Chapter Two

1 Farren Mission to Germany: *He. 162 – An Achievement in Rapid Aircraft Development and Manufacture* (undated report)
2 Müller, pg 70
3 UKNA/AIR40/2421: ADI(K) Report No. 185/1945, *Heinkel – Wien/Schwechat and Ludwigslust*, July 1945
4 IWM/CIOS Evaluation Report 40, 29.5.1945
5 Müller, pg. 425
6 Müller, pg. 180
7 Müller, pg 193
8 Müller, pg 194
9 Farren Mission to Germany: *He. 162 – An Achievement in Rapid Aircraft Development and Manufacture* (undated report)
10 Müller, pg. 126 and EHW 159/44, 1.11.44
11 Chef TLR Fl.Nr.8582/44 (E-2), *Flugzeug-Baureihen-Blatt 8-162*, 1.11.44
12 Erprobungstelle der Luftwaffe, Tarnewitz, B. Nr. E6 4684/44, *Schwerpunkterprobungsbericht Nr. 44/44*, 4.11.44
13 According to the author Heinz Höhne in *The Order of the Death's Head* (Secker & Warburg, 1980, pg. 406), Kurt May was a furniture manufacturer from Stuttgart who held SS rank.
14 Letter Der Chef des SS-Hauptamtes, 9. November 1944 and Bra/H. 2091/44 betr: Baumuster Me 162, 25. November 1944 (via Rose)
15 Erprobungsstelle der Luftwaffe Tarnewitz, B.Nr. E6 4806/44: *Schwerpunkterprobungsbericht Nr. 45/44 für die Zeit vom 5.11-11.11.44.*
16 EHAG TD 188 Dir.Fr./nie. 16.11.1944 '162'
17 EHAG TD Francke/*Me. 162 Wochenbericht*, 17.11.44
18 EHAG *Punkte für Wochenbericht 162*, 16.11 / TD Schrö/Nie
19 EHAG file note 20.11.44
20 Beauvais, Heinrich; Kössler, Karl; Mayer, Max & Regel, Christoph, *German Secret Flight Test Centres to 1945*, Midland Publishing, Hinckley, 2002, pgs. 70, 74, 80 & 140 and Brütting, Georg, *Das Buch der deutschen Fluggeschichte: Band 3*, Drei Brunnen Verlag, Stuttgart, 1979, pgs. 26 & 138
21 EHAG TD Francke/*Me. 162 Wochenbericht*, 17.11.44
22 OKL, Gen.d.Fl.Ausb/V.u.L.Abt. IC Br.B.Nr. 3608/44 *Besprechungsbericht Nr 379*, 19.11.44
23 Ransom, Stephen and Cammann, Hans-Hermann, *Me 163 Rocket Interceptor, Volume One*, Classic Publications, Crowborough, 2002, pg 200
24 EHAG TD 548, 18.11.44
25 EHAG 191/44 Dir.Fr./Me.36 21.11.44
26 EHAG file note 21.11.44
27 EHAG Francke via Bentow, 21.11.44
28 Francke note, 21.11.44
29 EHAG TD Dir.Fr./Nie, 22.11.44
30 EHAG TD/Dir.Francke/*Me., 162 Holzfertigung*, 22.11.44
31 EHAG TD/ 51/44, *162 Wochenbericht*, 24.11.44
32 Francke to May, *162 – Fläche*, 25.11.44
33 Francke to Frydag, *162 – Fertigung*, 25.11.44
34 Müller, pg 194
35 EHAG TD/ 51/44, *162 Wochenbericht*, 24.11.44
36 Erprobungsstelle der Luftwaffe Tarnewitz, B.Nr. E6 5045/44: *Schwerpunkterprobungsbericht Nr. 47/44 für die Zeit vom 19.11-25.11.44.*
37 EHAG TD 199 Dir.Fr./Nie, 26.11.1944
38 EHAG TD/Francke to Frydag, *162 – Leitwerk*, 27.11.4
39 EHAG TD/Francke/Nie, *162 Anderungen*, 27.11.44
40 Müller, pg 126
41 EHAG TD 201 Dir.Fr./Nie. 28.11.44 – *162 Motors*
42 EHAG A 37 089 Dir.Fr./Nie. 1.12.44
43 EHAG TD/Fr./Nie., 28.11.44
44 EHAG 200/44 DIR.FR./NIE. 36, 28.11.44
45 Only one other aircraft, the British-designed Miles M.20 fighter, has been designed and built in a shorter period than the He 162. The M.20 was conceived in June 1940 as a high-performance utility fighter, to supplement Spitfire and Hurricane production, and, wherever possible, utilised components from the Miles Master advanced trainer. The M.20 prototype flew only 65 days after a contract was placed for its construction, but the anticipated shortage of Spitfires and Hurricanes never arose, and further development was cancelled. The He 162 remains unique in that its development, prototype construction, and preparations for quantity production all proceeded in parallel.
46 Smith, Richard J and Norton, Mike, unpublished draft & Müller, pg 126
47 EHAG A 37 098 TD/Nie, *Einberufungsbefehl Erwin Mikysa*, 30.11.1944
48 Smith, J. Richard & Creek, Eddie J. with Rolotschek, Gerhard, *Dornier Do 335 Pfeil*, pg. 65
49 Erprobungstelle der Luftwaffe, Tarnewitz, B. Nr. E6 5321/44, *Schwerpunkterprobungsbericht Nr. 48/44*, 2.12.44
50 EHAG file note 1.12.44
51 EHAG TD 54, Dir. Francke/Nie. *162 Wochenbericht*, 7.12.1944
52 UKNA/AIR34/274
53 EHAG Wien 8-162 Muster-Übersicht 6/10.2.45
54 The authors have found no evidence to suggest that the name '*Salamander*' was anything other than a coded reference to the wings of the He 162. See reference by *Dipl.-Ing.* Fritz Stenzel of Gotha in USSAFE Tech. Intelligence Report No.I-66, 10 June 1945: '*Interrogation of Dipl.-Ing. Fritz Stenzel, Gothe (sic), Germany M51-J06, on a new method of aircraft construction as developed by the subject engineer.*' See also reference in EHAG Francke to Hansen & Schwarz at Marienehe, 7.12.1944: '*Salamander ist der Tarnname für die Flächen, sonst für nichts!*'
55 EHAG file note *Anruf Frau Bantow*, 7.12.44
56 EHAG Francke/Nie, *162 Wochenbericht*, 7.12.44
57 EHAG file note, 6.12.1944 '*Besuche zum 10.12.44*'
58 EHAG *Flugbericht* Nr. 2, 13.12.44
59 EHAG Werk Wien to OKW *Filmstab*, 13.12.1944
60 Schwärzler in EHAG *Besprechung über den Unfall 162*, 14.12.1944
61 EHAG *Aktenvermerk, 20 Dez 44 'Über den Unfall des Flugzeuges 8-162 V1 am 10.12.44. Stand der Untersuchung am 20.12.44'* Smith, Richard J and Norton, Mike, *Heinkel He 162 – A Bird of a Different Feather*, unpublished draft, via authors
62 Hiller, p. 49
63 Smith, J. Richard & Creek, Eddie J. Close-Up, pg 8
64 CIOS: '*Jet-Fighter Heinkel 162 (Volksjäger)*'. Evaluation Report 166a, 7 July 1945

65 CIOS:'*Jet-Fighter Heinkel 162 (Volksjäger)*'. Evaluation Report 166a, 7 July 1945
66 Erprobungsstelle der Luftwaffe Tarnewitz, B.Nr. E6 5045/44: *Schwerpunkterprobungsbericht Nr. 47/44 für die Zeit vom 19.11-25.11.44.*
67 CIOS:'*Jet-Fighter Heinkel 162 (Volksjäger)*'. Evaluation Report 166a, 7 July 1945
68 CIOS:'*Jet-Fighter Heinkel 162 (Volksjäger)*'. Evaluation Report 166a, 7 July 1945
69 Müller, pg. 135
70 EHAG Francke to Schüngel, TD 217, 7.12.1944
71 Smith, Richard J and Norton, Mike unpublished draft
72 EHAG Telegram Francke-CAG Hermann Wächter, Neustadt a.d.Orla, *162 – Holz Anderungsbesprechung*, 1.12.1944
73 EHAG, *Program für die Holz-Anderungsbesprechung 162 am 12.12.44 in der Fichtegasse*, 8.12.44
74 OKL/TLR Fl.E3 VII A, Nr. 16 734/44, *Aktenvermerk über die Besprechung am 14.12.44 bei der Firma Muldwerke*
75 EHAG file note – *Anruf Brünn*, TD/Su, 6.12.44
76 EHAG 227/44 Fr./Nie. 19.12.44.
77 Musterprüfkommission 8-162 (Festigkeit u. Konstruktion): Betr. *Tatigkeit der von TLR Chef Ing. Beauftragten Musterprüfkommission 8-162 vom 16-20.12.1944* (20.12.1944)
78 EHAG Wien, *8-162 Muster-Übersicht* 6/10.2.45
79 EHAG Wien, 8-*162 Muster-Übersicht* 6/10.2.45
80 Farren Mission to Germany: *He. 162 – An Achievement in Rapid Aircraft Development and Manufacture* (undated report)
81 EHAG Flugbericht Nr. 25.12.44 & Dir.Francke/Nie, *162 Wochenbericht, vom 7.12. bis 22.12.44*
82 *Flugbericht 162 M-2 am 22.12.1944 vom Fl.Stabsing. Bader*
83 Smith, J. Richard & Creek, Eddie J. *Close-Up* pg. 5
84 EHAG TD 228 Dir.Fr./Nie., 27.12.1944.
85 Smith, J. Richard & Creek, Eddie J. *Close-Up* pg. 9
86 USSAFE Tech. Intelligence Report No.I-66, 10 June 1945:'*Interrogation of Dipl.-Ing. Fritz Stenzel, Gothe (sic), Germany M51-J06, on a new method of aircraft construction as developed by the subject engineer.*'
87 UKNA Ultra Decrypt CX/MSS/T420/37 (via Beale)
88 *BAL 162 – Flugerprobung*, Hart, 3.1.45 and Müller, pg. 146
89 EHAG Wien, *8-162 Muster-Übersicht* 6/10.2.45
90 Smith, J. Richard & Creek, Eddie J. *Close-Up* pg. 5 & Müller, pg. 148
91 Griehl, *Heinkels Verschleißjäger – Die Entwicklung der He 162 (Teil 1)*, Flugzeug 5/95
92 *4. Bericht über den Fertigungsstand des Baumusters 162 (100 in Rostock)*, HF 85/45, 5.2.45
93 EHAG, *8-162 Muster*, 31.1.45
94 EHAG, *Wien, 8-162 Muster*, 31.1.45, *8-162 Muster-Übersicht* 6/10.2.45 and Griehl, *Heinkels Verschleißjäger*
95 EHAG Wien, 8-*162 Muster-Übersicht* 6/10.2.45 and Müller, pg. 146 & 148
96 *4. Bericht über den Fertigungsstand des Baumusters 162 (100 in Rostock)*, HF 85/45, 5.2.45
97 EHAG Wien, *8-162 Muster-Übersicht* 6/10.2.45
98 EHAG Trbw/Ja/Ba. Betr. 19, *162 Führeraum 17.1.45*
99 Müller, pg. 149
100 Smith, J. Richard & Creek, Eddie J. *Close-Up* pg. 9
101 EHAG Wien, *8-162 Muster-Übersicht* 6/10.2.45
102 EHAG, *8-162 Muster*, 31.1.45
103 EHAG Wien, *8-162 Muster*, 31.1.45 and 8-162 Muster-Übersicht 6/10.2.45
104 See EHAG Wien, *8-162 Muster-Übersicht* 6/10.2.45 and Smith, J. Richard & Creek, Eddie J. *Volksjäger* & Müller – various
105 4. *Bericht über den Fertigungsstand des Baumusters 162 (100 in Rostock)*, HF 85/45, 5.2.45
106 EHAG Wien, *8-162 Muster-Übersicht* 6/10.2.45
107 EHAG TD 35 Dr.Fr./Nie., 26.1.1945
108 BF 92/45 and *Lagebericht für Fertigung Heinkel Rostock*, 27.1.45 and *Lagebericht für Fertigung Heinkel Rostock*, Meyer, 27.1.45
109 EHAG Wien, *8-162 Muster*, 31.1.45 and 8-162 Muster-Übersicht 6/10.2.45
110 EHAG 31/45, Hart/Pi.14, *8-162 – Flugbetrieb am 27. und 28.1.45* (29.1.45)
111 EHAG Wien, *8-162 Muster-Übersicht* 6/10.2.45 and Müller, pg. 149
112 OKL, Lw.Organisationsstab, Genst.Gen.Qu. 2.Abt. (IIB), 30.1.1945
113 EHAG 35/45, Hart/Pi.14, *Flugbetrieb am 30.1.45* (30.1.45)
114 IWM GDC/18 64, EHAG Wien, *Prüfmappe Flugzeug 162*, 1.2.45
115 EHAG Aktenvermerk 8/45 *162 Wochenbericht vom 29.1-4.2.45* & Müller, pg 206
116 EHAG 38/45 *Flugbetrieb am 2.2.45* (3.2.45)
117 EHAG Wien, *8-162 Muster-Übersicht* 6/10.2.45
118 EHAG file note
119 EHAG Aktenvermerk Nr. 8/45, *Wochenbericht vom 29.1-4.2.45* (5.2.45)
120 EHAG Besprechung am 12.2.45 in der Angermayergasse
121 EHAG *Flugbetrieb am 4.2.45* (5.2.45)
122 EHAG *162 Wochenbericht vom 29.1.-4.2.45* (5.2.45)
123 BF 92/45 *5. und 6. Berichte über den Fertigungsstand des Baumusters 100 in Rostock.*
124 *4. Bericht über den Fertigungsstand des Baumusters 162 (100 in Rostock)*, HF 85/45, 5.2.45
125 EHAG TD Francke/Nie., 6.2.45
126 EHAG 26/45 KOL/Bt./He den Betrieb 162 6.2.45
127 EHAG Wien, *8-162 Muster-Übersicht* 6/10.2.45 and Müller, pg. 150
128 EHAG Wien, 8-*162 Muster-Übersicht* 6/10.2.45 and Griehl, Heinkels Verschleißjäger
129 EHAG 55/45 Dir.Fr./Nie. 36, 9.2.45
130 EHAG 55/45 Dir.Fr./Nie. 36, 9.2.45
131 Müller, pg. 149
132 EHAG Wien, *8-162 Muster-Übersicht* 6/10.2.45
133 EHAG Wien, *8-162 Muster-Übersicht* 6/10.2.45
134 Dahl had 93 known victories at the time of his visit to Schwechat, but his final score was 128.
135 In his memoirs, *Rammjäger*, published in Germany in 1961, Dahl states that the visit to Schwechat took place on 26 March 1945, but this conflicts with original Heinkel and RLM documents drafted following the meeting, all of which refer to the visit as taking place on 11 February.
136 EHAG Aktenvermerk Nr. 11/45 *Besuch GdJ und KdE am 10-11.2.45* (12.2.45)

137 Dahl, Walter, *Rammjäger*, Orion Verlag, Heusenstamm, 1961, pg.187-89
138 EHAG Aktenvermerk Nr. 11/45 *Besuch GdJ und KdE am 10-11.2.45* (12.2.45)
139 EHAG *Aktennoitz über Telefongespräch mit Gen.Dir. Frydag am 19.2.45*
140 Kommando der Erprobungsstellen Rechlin, 430/45 8-161 – *Besprechung am 11.2.1945 in Wien-Schwechat*, (13.2.1945)
141 EHAG Besprechung am 12.2.45 in der Angermayergasse
142 EHAG Besprechung am 12.2.45 in der Angermayergasse and Müller, pg 197
143 EHAG Wien, *8-162 Muster-Übersicht* 6/10.2.45
144 Steckhan *Flugbuch*
145 EHAG A 51078 *Zufahrtswege zur Startbahn in Heidfeld*, 15.2.45
146 EHAG Wien, Protokoll Nr. HG-1, *Umrüsting 162 – Wien (Anderungsanweisung 1, 2 und 3)*, Dir.Huf/Mg, 18.2.1945
147 Hammel, Eric, *Air War Europa*, Pacifica Press, Pacifica, 1994, pg. 446
148 EHAG *Wochenbericht vom 13.2-18.2.45*, TD/Dir.Francke/Ne., 19.2.45
149 EHAG *Wochenbericht vom 13.2-18.2.45*, TD/Dir.Francke/Ne., 19.2.45
150 EHAG 373/45 *Umrüstung 162*, 15.2.1945
151 UKNA/AIR34/274 Interpretation Report No. L.294, 5.4.45
152 EHAG *Wochenbericht vom 13.2-18.2.45*, TD/Dir.Francke/Ne., 19.2.45
153 EHAG *Aktennoitz über Telefongespräch mit Gen.Dir. Frydag am 19.2.45*
154 E-Stelle Tarnewitz, *Schwerpunkterprobungsbericht Nr. 3/45*, 19.2.1945
155 EHAG 66/45 Hart/Pi 162 – *Flügelauskleidung und Flügelanstellung, 21.2.45* and Steckhan *Flugbuch*
156 Interview Creek & Götz/Steckhan, Germany, September 1980
157 EHAG 66/45 Hart/Pi 162 – *Flügelauskleidung und Flügelanstellung*, 21.2.45 and Steckhan *Flugbuch*
158 Smith, J. Richard & Creek, Eddie J., *Close-Up*, pg 5
159 Steckhan *Flugbuch*
160 UKNA/DEFE/CX/MSS/T442/52 15.2.45 (via Nick Beale)
161 EHAG Francke to Kessler 162-EZ 42, 24.2.45
162 EHAG TD/Francke to Schüngel, *Startbahn*, 24.2.45
163 UKNA/DEFE/CX/MSS/T474/41 BT 5956 (via Nick Beale) and Smith, J. Richard & Creek, Eddie J., *Volksjäger*, pg 10
164 Gilbert, pg. 644
165 Mombeek, Eric, *Defending the Reich*, pg. 297
166 EHAG 69/45 Dir.Fr./Me. 36, 2.3.1945
167 Smith, J. Richard & Creek, Eddie J., *Close-Up*, pg. 11
168 EHAG Wien, *8-162 Muster-Übersicht* 6/10.2.45
169 EHAG 69/45 Dir.Fr./Me. 36, 2.3.1945
170 EHAG 89/45 Dir.Fr./Me.-36, 2.3.1945 Betr. 162
171 EHAG Wien, 8-*162 Muster-Übersicht* 6/10.2.45
172 EHAG 69/45 Dir.Fr./Me. 36, 2.3.1945
173 Smith, J. Richard & Creek, Eddie J., *Jet Planes* pg. 312
174 Steckhan *Flugbuch*
175 Compiled from '*Flying the 162*': from ADI(K) Report No. 309B/1945, 16 May 1945
176 EHAG TD Francke/*Me. Unfall 162 - M8 am 12.3.45*
177 EHAG TD Francke/*Me. Unfall 162 – M19 am 14.3.45* (16.3.45)
178 Betr: *Leistungsvermessung der 162: Besprechung am 17.3.45.*
179 Smith, J. Richard & Creek, Eddie J., *Me 262 Volume One*, pg. 300-301 and *Me 262 Volume Two*, pg 136-137
180 Francke to Bruckmann, 19.3.45 and Huber/Reiniger report '003 R in 162', Nr. 506, EZS Hu/C 27.3.45
181 *Salamander – Zusatzmessung in A 3*, Braunschweig, 19.3.45
182 Hiller, pg. 68
183 IWM/GDC 18/106: OKL-Chef-TLR-Fl-E-10/IV, *Vorläufige Dichtungsvorschrift für Flächentankraum Baumuster 8-162*, 12.3.1945
184 UKNA/AIR34/274 Interpretation Report No. L.294, 5.4.45
185 Osterwald *Flugbuch*
186 Wollenweber, *Thunder*, pg. 110-112
187 Steckhan crash report, 27.3.1945
188 Wollenweber, *Thunder*, pg. 110-112
189 Steckhan *Flugbuch*
190 Letter Heinz G. Gülzow to R. Forsyth, 17.1.2002
191 Kröger *Flugbuch*
192 Osterwald *Flugbuch*
193 Kröger *Flugbuch*
194 Smith, J. Richard & Creek, Eddie J. *Jet Planes*, pg. 313
195 Müller, pg 176
196 CIOS Evaluation Report 166a, *Jet-Fighter Heinkel 162 (Volksjäger)* by Dr Ernst Heinkel and Karl Frydag, 7 July 1945
197 Information via Simon Schatz, 1.12.2008
198 UKNA Ultra Decrypt KO 326 (via Nick Beale)
199 APWIU (2nd Air Disarmament Wing) 63/1945, *A View on the Volksjäger He 162*, 14 June 1945
200 Osterwald *Flugbuch*
201 Betr.: *8-162 Besprechung am 5.4.45 in Lager-Lechfeld*, Hilber, 10.4.45
202 Smith, J. Richard & Creek, Eddie J., *Me 262 Volume Two*, pg. 310
203 Kröger *Flugbuch*
204 *Vorhandene Flugzeuge*, Abschrift v. E2, 10.4.45
205 Osterwald and Kröger *Flugbuch*
206 UKNA/HW13/47 War Department, Military Intelligence Service, *German Technical Aid to Japan*, 31 August 1945
207 Borsdorff *Flugbuch*
208 Beauvais, et al, *German Secret Flight Test Centres*, pg. 102
209 UKNA Ultra/CX/MSS/R.540 (A) (via Nick Beale)
210 Kröger *Flugbuch*

211 UKNA/AIR40/2423: ADI(K) Report No. 379/1945 – *Some Notes on the German Aircraft Industry and German Aircraft Production during the War*

212 UKNA/AIR40/164 Günter, S and Hohbach, *History and Experiences of He 162 and He 162 Report No. 2 Performances with Jumo-004 (Heinkel Report)*, Translation No. F-TS-672-RE, Headquarters Air Materiel Command, Wright Field, Dayton, Oh., October 1946

213 OKL, Lw. Organisationsstab, Genst.Gen.Qu.2.Abt. (IIB), Betr. *Besprechung bei 6. Abt am 29. 1. 1945*, (30.1.1945)

214 Farren Mission to Germany: *He. 162 – An Achievement in Rapid Aircraft Development and Manufacture* (undated report)

Chapter Three

1 Müller, pg 262-63 and Beauvais et al, *German Secret Flight Test Centres to 1945*, pg. 236

2 Müller, pg 262 and Interview Forsyth-Geyer, Germany, 1989

3 Müller, pg 263

4 OKL, Lw.Organisationsstab, Genst.Gen.Qu. 2.Abt. (IIB), 30.1.1945

5 Gollob, Brb.Nr. 466/45 (date not known)

6 Eric Mombeek, *Defenders of the Reich – Jagdgeschwader 1: Volume Three 1944-1945*, Classic Publications, Hersham, 2003. The authors are grateful to Eric Mombeek for his kind permission to quote extensively from his detailed account of JG 1's operations.

7 Obermaier, Ernst, *Die Ritterkreuzträger der Luftwaffe 1939-1945 – Band I Jagdflieger*, Verlag Dieter Hoffmann, Mainz, 1966, pg. 40

8 Manrho, John and Pütz, Ron, *Bodenplatte – The Luftwaffe's Last Hope: The Attack on Allied Airfields New Year's Day 1945*, Hikoki Publications, Crowborough, 2004, pg.12-42

9 Manrho and Pütz, pg. 28

10 Bernd Barbas notes.

11 Eric Mombeek, *Defenders*

12 NAARS/Microfilm T-321/Roll 10: Das Oberkommando der Luftwaffe Kriegstagebuch 1.Februar-7.April 1945. See also UKNA/AIR20/7708 OKL Daily Situation Reports, 1-14 February 1945

13 '*Wieder ein 'Modell mit Geschichte' – 'Volksjäger' He 162 A2 'weiße 1'*, Hans Lächler, Modell Magazin, 5/80

14 Prien, Jochen & Rodeike, Peter, *Jagdgeschwader 1 und 11 – Teil 3 1944-1945*, pg. 1572

15 Prien & Rodeike, pg. 1572

16 Kommando der Erprobungsstellen Rechlin, 430/45, *8-161 – Besprechung am 11.2.1945 in Wien-Schwechat*, (13.2.1945)

17 Smith & Creek, *Close-Up*, pg. 12 and *'Wieder ein 'Modell mit Geschichte' – 'Volksjäger' He 162 A2 'weiße 1'*, Hans Lächler, Modell Magazin, 5/80

18 UKNA/AIR40/2422 ADI(K) Report No. 287/1945

19 Stephen Ransom and Hans-Hermann Cammann, *Me 163 Rocket Interceptor Volume Two*, Classic Publications, Hersham, 2003, pg. 379 & 382

20 UKNA/AIR20/7709 OKL Daily Situation Reports, 15-28 February 1945

21 Oberkommando der Luftwaffe Kriegstagebuch 1.Februar-7.April 1945 (NAARS/Microfilm T-321/Roll 10) and OKL, Lw. Organisationsstab, Genst.Gen.Qu.2.Abt. (IIB), Betr. Besprechung bei 6. Abt am 29.1.1945, (30.1.1945)

22 Wollenweber, *Thunder*, pg. 101-104

23 Prien & Rodeike, pg. 1573

24 Smith & Creek, *Jet Planes* pg. 312

25 Eric Mombeek, *Defenders* pg. 292

26 Smith & Creek, *Jet Planes* pg. 314

27 Prien & Rodeike pg. 1573

28 Wollenweber, *Thunder*, pg. 110

29 Wollenweber, *Thunder*, pg. 113

30 UKNA/DEFE/CX/MSS/T505/1 (via Nick Beale)

31 Smith & Creek Close-Up pg. 12 and 'Wieder ein 'Modell mit Geschichte' – 'Volksjäger' He 162 A2 'weiße 1', Hans Lächler, Modell Magazin, 5/80

32 Wollenweber, *Thunder*, pg. 114

33 Künnecke *Flugbuch*

34 Hanf *Flugbuch* and '*Ich flog die He 162*' Gerhard Hanf, Flugzeug 6/92

35 Eric Mombeek, *Defenders*, pg. 292

36 Hanf *Flugbuch*

37 Schmitt *Flugbuch* and *'Wieder ein 'Modell mit Geschichte' – 'Volksjäger' He 162 A2 'weiße 1'*, Hans Lächler, Modell Magazin, 5/80

38 Künnecke and Berger *Flugbuch*

39 *Flugbuch* Riehl and Prien & Rodeike, various refs.

40 Schmitt *Flugbuch*; for reference to 'Lulu' see '*Die letzten Wochen des 'Volksjägers'*', Hans Lächler, Modell Magazin 7/84, pg. 36

41 Prien & Rodeike, *Teil 2 1944*, pg 678 & Teil 3 1944-1945, pg 1587

42 Künnecke and Kirchner *Flugbuch*

43 *Flugbuch* states 'Schlarb' with no reference to rank, first name or *Staffel*. However in Prien, Jochen & Rodeike, Peter, *Jagdgeschwader 1 und 11 – Teil 3 1944-1945*, pg 1649 there is a pilot listed as 'Lt Adalbert Schlarp'.

44 Berger and Wollenweber *Flugbuch*

45 Quoted in Eric Mombeek, *Defenders* pg. 292-93

46 '*Die Abschüsse der He 162*', Die Redaktion, Modell Magazin, 8/80 and Prien, Jochen & Rodeike, Peter, *Jagdgeschwader 1 und 11 – Teil 3 1944-1945*, pg 1590

47 Eric Mombeek, *Defenders*, pg. 292

48 Künnecke *Flugbuch*

49 Mombeek and Prien quote the raid as being by the RAF on the 8th, but this was unlikely as RAF Bomber Command was not active during the day on the 8th and attacked only Molbis on 7/8 April and Hamburg, Lützkendorf and Travemünde on 8/9 April (see *The Bomber Command War Diaries – An Operational Reference Book 1939-1945*: Martin Middlebrook and Chris Everitt, Penguin, 1985, pg 692). The USAAF 8th AF however, did bomb Parchim as part of its operations on 7 April.

50 Schmitt Flugbuch

51 SSD LBKW 1358 6/4 (2315)

52 Quoted in Eric Mombeek, *Reichsverteidigung – Die Geschichte des Jagdgeschwaders 1 'Oesau'*, Eric Mombeek, 1993, pg 300

53 Wilhelm Harder, *Beitrag zur Geschichte der II./JG 1*, 27.05.85

54 Quoted in Eric Mombeek, *Defenders of the Reich – Jagdgeschwader 1: Volume Three 1944-1945*, Classic Publications, Hersham, 2003, pg. 293-94

55 Wilhelm Harder, *Beitrag zur Geschichte der II./JG 1*, 27.05.85

56 Quoted in Eric Mombeek, *Defenders of the Reich – Jagdgeschwader 1:* Volume Three 1944-1945, Classic Publications, Hersham, 2003, pg. 293-94

57 Wollenweber and Kirchner *Flugbuch*

58 Müller, pg 269

59 UKNA/CX/MSS/T521/20, 16/4/45 (Via Nick Beale)

60 Wollenweber *Flugbuch*; Eric Mombeek pg. 300 and Prien & Rodeike, pg. 1577

61 Wollenweber *Flugbuch*
62 Künnecke and Riehl Flugbuch
63 Eric Mombeek pg. 300
64 H. Essame, *The Battle for Germany*, Batsford, London, 1969 pg. 205
65 Max Hastings, *Armageddon – The Battle for Germany 1944-45*, Macmillan, London, 2004 pg. 491
66 *Geschwaderstab und I. Gruppe des JG 1*, Jägerblatt, Date ?
67 Prien, Jochen & Rodeike, Peter, *Jagdgeschwader 1 und 11 – Teil 3 1944-1945*, pg 1579 and '*Wieder ein 'Modell mit Geschichte' – 'Volksjäger' He 162 A2 'weiße 1'*, Hans Lächler, Modell Magazin, 5/80
68 Quoted in Eric Mombeek, *Defenders* pg. 296
69 Müller, pg. 270
70 All information from respective *Flugbuch*
71 Quoted in Eric Mombeek, *Defenders*, pg. 293
72 Schmitt *Flugbuch*
73 Eric Mombeek, *Reichsverteidigung*, pg. 300
74 Prien & Rodeike pg. 1649
75 Riehl *Flugbuch*
76 Kirchner *Flugbuch*; Prien & Rodeike pg. 1587 and Eric Mombeek, *Defenders*, pg. 293
77 Christopher Shores & Chris Thomas, *2nd Tactical Air Force Volume Three: From the Rhine to Victory January to May 1945*, Classic Publications, Hersham, 2006, pg 497
78 135 Wing Personal Combat Report No. 68, F/O G. Walkington, 222 (Natal) Sqn (via Steve Coates)
79 Shores & Thomas, pg 498
80 See Roger A. Freeman, *Mighty Eighth War Diary*, pg. 494 and Kenn C. Rust, *The 9th Air Force in World War II*, pg. 171
81 Wollenweber and Dosch *Flugbuch*; Steeb *Flugbuch* and '*Die letzten Wochen des 'Volksjägers'*, Hans Lächler, Modell Magazin 7/84
82 OKL, 1889 g.Kdos, 19.4.45 (teleprint signal)
83 Wollenweber *Flugbuch*, and correspondence quoted in Prien, Jochen & Rodeike, Peter, *Jagdgeschwader 1 und 11 – Teil 3 1944-1945*, pg 1588-89
84 Berger *Flugbuch*
85 Hanf *Flugbuch* and Gerhard Hanf '*Ich flog die He 162 'Nervenklau*'', Jägerblatt Nr. 4/XL, September/Oktober 1992
86 chmitt *Flugbuch* and Prien & Rodeike, pgs. 1589 & 1649
87 Steeb *Flugbuch*
88 Dosch *Flugbuch*
89 Künnecke, Hanf, Berger, Riehl and Wollenweber *Flugbuch*
90 Hanf Flugbuch
91 Dosch *Flugbuch*; Prien & Rodeike, pg 1649 and Eric Mombeek, *Defenders* pg. 292
92 Künnecke *Flugbuch*
93 Wilhelm Harder, *Beitrag zur Geschichte der II./JG 1*, 27.05.85
94 Prien & Rodeike, pg. 1584 and Beauvais et al, *German Secret Flight Test Centres to 1945*, pg. 228
95 Wiesinger, Günter & Schroeder, Walter, *Die Österreichischen Ritterkreuzträger in der Luftwaffe 1939-45*, H. Weishaupt Verlag, Graz, 1986, pg 57
96 Wilhelm Harder, *Beitrag zur Geschichte der II./JG 1*, 27.05.85
97 Schmitt *Flugbuch* and information from Eric Mombeek, 13.7.1999
98 Eric Mombeek, *Defenders*, pg. 293
99 Berger *Flugbuch* and Eric Mombeek, *Reichsverteidigung*, pg. 303
100 Hanf *Flugbuch*
101 Prien & Rodeike, pg. 1649
102 '*Wieder ein 'Modell mit Geschichte' – 'Volksjäger' He 162 A2 'weiße 1'*, Hans Lächler, Modell Magazin, 5/80
103 Hanf *Flugbuch*
104 Dürr *Flugbuch*
105 Wilhelm Harder, *Beitrag zur Geschichte der II./JG 1*, 27.05.85
106 Hanf *Flugbuch*
107 Prien & Rodeike, pg. 1649
108 Schlarb *Flugbuch*
109 Dürr *Flugbuch*
110 Eric Mombeek, *Defenders*, pg. 296
111 Prien & Rodeike, pg. 1649
112 Eric Mombeek, *Defenders*, pg. 296
113 *Geschwaderstab und I. Gruppe des JG 1*, Jägerblatt, Date ?
114 '*Wieder ein 'Modell mit Geschichte' – 'Volksjäger' He 162 A2 'weiße 1'*, Hans Lächler, Modell Magazin, 5/80
115 Dosch *Flugbuch*
116 via Eric Mombeek
117 Schmitt *Flugbuch*
118 '*Abschuß mit He 162 – JA oder NEIN?*', A.R.Chapman, Flugzeug, 1/89
119 Eric Mombeek, *Defenders*, pg. 293
120 *Geschwaderstab und I. Gruppe des JG 1*, Jägerblatt, Date ?
121 '*Wieder ein 'Modell mit Geschichte' – 'Volksjäger' He 162 A2 'weiße 1'*, Hans Lächler, Modell Magazin, 5/80 and Eric Mombeek Defenders, pg. 296
122 via Eric Mombeek
123 *Dissolution of the Luftwaffe: The Work of the British Air Forces of Occupation Germany*, HMSO London, 1995, pg. 52
124 '*Die letzten Wochen des 'Volksjägers'*, Hans Lächler, Modell Magazin 7/84, pg. 36
125 via Eric Mombeek
126 Information from A.R. Chapman to author, October 2008 based on interviews conducted by Gerhard Roletschek
127 Based partly on *Heinkel He 162s at Leck, Germany May 6, 1945*, compiled by David E. Brown, November 2005 & Leck, 08 May 1945. He 162s of I./JG 1 by R.L.Reid

Chapter Four

1 *He 162 with Argus tube* – Heinkel report 30.3.45, TPA3/TIB Translation No. GDC 18/59T
2 IWM: Rheinmetall Borsig Aktengesellschaft Werk Unterlüss *Bewaffnung Schneller Jagdflugzeuge*, Josef Schoetz, 27.7.1945 (as Halstead Exploiting Centre: Developments of German Fighter Armament for the attack of Bombers, BIOS/Gr.2/HEC/10787, UNT 5T)

3 EHW TD 134 Dir. Fr./Nie., dated 14.10.44, Topic 3 (via E. Oliver)
4 IWM: Rheinmetall Borsig Aktengesellschaft Werk Unterlüss *Bewaffnung Schneller Jagdflugzeuge*, Josef Schoetz, 27.7.1945 (as Halstead Exploiting Centre: Developments of German Fighter Armament for the attack of Bombers, BIOS/Gr.2/HEC/10787, UNT 5T)
5 Air Min AI2(g) Report 2383 of January 1946, pg.51 (via E. Oliver)
6 *Mistelanordnung: 8-162 mit Verbrauchsflugzeug E377a auf Startwagen*, Entwurfsabteilung 30.11.44 and research carried out for Robert Forsyth *Mistel – German Composite Aircraft and Operations*, Classic Publications, Crowborough, 2001
7 Fritz Hahn: *Deutsche Geheimwaffen 1939-1945 – Flugzeugbewaffnungen*, Erich Hoffman Verlag, Heidenheim (1963), pg.307 (ref via E. Oliver)

Chapter Five

1 *Visit to select German aeroplanes of Category 1 May 29th-June 3rd, 1945*, G.M.Buxton, Central Fighter Establishment, CFE/S.960/Eng., 8th June 1945
2 *Mastering Heinkel's Minimus*, Captain Eric Brown, CBE, DSC, AFC, RN, Air Enthusiast, June 1972
3 *Enemy Aircraft Flight, Central Fighter Establishment: Report of work on German orthodox and jet aircraft in Germany from 18.5.45 to 13.6.45*, F/Lt. R.T.H.Collis, DFC, OC, EA Flight, EAF/S.50/AIR, 13th June 1945
4 Eric Mombeek *Defenders*, pg. 297
5 From *Visit to select German aeroplanes of Category 1 May 29th-June 3rd, 1945*, G.M.Buxton, Central Fighter Establishment, CFE/S.960/Eng., 8th June 1945
6 *Enemy Aircraft Flight, Central Fighter Establishment: Report of work on German orthodox and jet aircraft in Germany from 18.5.45 to 13.6.45*, F/Lt. R.T.H.Collis, DFC, OC, EA Flight, EAF/S.50/AIR, 13th June 1945
7 Phil Butler *War Prizes – An Illustrated survey of German, Italian and Japanese aircraft brought to Allied countries during and after the Second World War*, Midland Counties Publications, Leicester, pg. 75
8 From *Visit to select German aeroplanes of Category 1 May 29th-June 3rd, 1945*, G.M.Buxton, Central Fighter Establishment, CFE/S.960/Eng., 8th June 1945
9 Combined Intelligence Objectives Sub-Committee – Evaluation Report 166a Jet Fighter Heinkel 162 (Volksjäger) [Target No. 5/55] By: Dr Ernst Heinkel and Karl Frydag, 7 July 1945
10 A reference to *Fl.Stabs.Ing. Dipl.-Ing.* Helmut Schelp, leader of the *Technisches Amt* GL/C-E3/VII responsible for policy covering jet engine development.
11 Probably a reference to the 'Wimbledon Cage', a main interrogation centre for senior German officers and personalities.
12 Heinkel, *He 1000*, pgs. 274-75
13 Butler *War Prizes*, pgs. 89-90
14 Butler *War Prizes*, pg. 188
15 www.wospweb.com/site/RAF-Brize-Norton/History-1942-1950.htm
16 *Mastering Heinkel's Minimus*, Captain Eric Brown, CBE, DSC, AFC, RN, Air Enthusiast, June 1972
17 Smith, J. Richard & Creek, Eddie J., *Me 262 Volume Four* pgs. 805-06
18 Butler *War Prizes*, pg. 213
19 Captain Eric 'Winkle' Brown *Wings on my Sleeve*, Weidenfeld & Nicolson, London, 2006, pgs. 72 & 131 and Richard Dennis, *Royal Aircraft Establishment at War*, Tutor Publications, Dorchester, 2008, pg. 194
20 *He-162: The Plywood Coffin* Robert Trimble *Air Combat*, date unknown
21 Butler *War Prizes*, pgs. 89-90
22 Dennis, *RAE at War*, pgs. 100 01
23 Dennis, *RAE at War*, pg. 114
24 Brown *Wings on my Sleeve*, Weidenfeld & Nicolson, London, 2006, pg. 131
25 Butler *War Prizes*, pg. 90
26 *Dissolution of the Luftwaffe*, pg. 86
27 *The Salamander in France* (Part 1), Philippe Couderchon, *Aeroplane*, April 2006
28 *Dissolution of the Luftwaffe*, pg. 86 and *The Salamander in France* (Part 1), Philippe Couderchon, *Aeroplane*, April 2006
29 Butler *War Prizes*, pg. 89
30 www.wospweb.com/site/RAF-Brize-Norton/History-1942-1950.htm
31 www.airpages.ru
32 Balous, Miroslav & Bily, Miroslav *Heinkel He 162 Spatz*, MBI, Praha, 2004, pg. 43
33 Carl-Fredrik Geust *Under the Red Star – Luftwaffe Aircraft in the Soviet Air Force*, Airlife, Shrewsbury, 1993, pgs. 70-71. NOTE: Phil Butler in *War Prizes* states that one He 162 was captured in Austria (pg. 308)
34 C-F Geust and G Petrov *Red Stars Vol. 2 – German Aircraft in the Soviet Union*, Apali Oy, Tampere, 1998
35 www.airpages.ru
36 Balous, Miroslav & Bily, Miroslav, pg. 45
37 C-F Geust and G Petrov *Red Stars Vol. 2*
38 UKNA/AIR40/164 *Interim Report No. 1 on the German Jet Fighter Heinkel 162*, Interim Report No. F-IM -1113A-ND, HQ, Air Materiel Command, 14 May 1946
39 Butler *War Prizes*, pgs. 89-90
40 *The Salamander in France* (Part 1), Philippe Couderchon, *Aeroplane*, April 2006
41 *The Salamander in France* (Part 2), Philippe Couderchon, *Aeroplane*, May 2006
42 Butler *War Prizes*, pgs. 89-90
43 *The Salamander in France* (Part 2), Philippe Couderchon, *Aeroplane*, May 2006
44 Butler *War Prizes*, pg. 90
45 Brown *Wings on my Sleeve*, pg. 131

APPENDIX 1: Specification and Performance

Heinkel He 162 A-1 (Standard configuration)

Crew	1
Engine: BMW 003 jet engine, model 003 E	
Ground level thrust, 30 sec military rating	920 kg
Ground level thrust, normal performance	800 kg
Thrust performance at 800 km/h at 11000 m (30 sec boost)	332 kg
Thrust performance at 800 km/h at 11000 m (normal)	265 kg
Actual fuel consumption at normal rating	1.61 kg/kg h
Actual fuel consumption at 30 sec rating	1.96 kg/kg h
Span	7.2 m
Length	9.05 m
Height	2.6 m
Wing area	11.16 m^2
Wing loading	265 kg/m^2
Power loading	3.18 kg/kg
Aspect ratio	4.65
Empty weight	1663 kg
Auxiliary equipment	95 kg
Structural weight (inc Auxiliary equipment)	1758 kg
Weapons (2 x MK 108)	157 kg
Ammunition (2 x 50 rpg)	58 kg
Armour	57 kg
Crew	100 kg
Undercarriage, flaps and trims (with 61 kg trimming ballast)	983 kg
Engine with tank and cowling/fairing	680 kg
Fuel (excluding starter fuel)	675 kg
Take-off weight	2805 kg
Taxying and Warming up fuel	80 kg
Starting fuel	22 kg
Taxying weight	2907 kg

Maximum speed at	0 m	790 km/h normal	890 km/h (30 sec boost)
	6000 m	838 km/h	905 km/h
	11000 m	765 km/h	845 km/h
Full throttle endurance at	0 m	30 mins	28 mins
	6000 m	48 mins	46 mins
	11000 m	83 mins	81 mins
Full throttle range at	0 m	390 km	370 km
	6000 m	620 km	596 km
	11000 m	975 km	945 km
Climb Performance at	0 m	19.2 m/sec	26.5 m/sec
	6000 m	9.9 m/sec	16.0 m/sec
	11000 m	1.6 m/sec	5.8 m/sec
Take-off distance		850 m	740 m
Take-off distance to	15 m	980 m	810 m
Landing distance from	15 m	950 m	950 m
Landing speed		190 km/h	190 km/h

P.1073 ('*Jagdeinsitzer*') with BMW 003 A-1 engine (8.9.1944)

Measurements:	
Wing area	11 m^2
Span	7 m
Length	9.05 m

Engine: BMW 003	
Ground-level thrust	800 kg
Thrust at 800 km/h at 11 km	265 kg
Actual fuel consumption at this rating	1.61 kg/kp h

Weights	
Weapons (2 x MG 151/20)	148 kg
Ammunition (2 x 150 rpg)	67 kg
Armour	50 kg
Equipment (without weapons and armour)	145 kg
Crew	90 kg
(Military weight	500 kg)
Undercarriage, flaps and trims	725 kg
Engine	725 kg
Tank	75 kg
Fuel	475 kg
Take-off weight	2500 kg
Landing weight with 20% fuel	2120 kg

Flight Performance		
Maximum performance	at 0 km	810 km/h
	at 6 km	860 km/h
	at 11 km	800 km/h
Cal. endurance (full power)	at 0 km	20 mins
	at 6 km	33 mins
Calculated range (full power)	at 0 km	270 km
	at 6 km	440 km
Maximum range	at 12 km	730 km
Maximum climb at mean weight	at 0 km	22.0 m/sec
	at 6 km	13.5 m/sec
	at 11 km	4.5 m/sec
Climbing time from take-off		
	to 6 km	6.4 mins
	to 11 km	19.5 mins
Take-off distance		650 m
Landing speed with 20% fuel		166 km/h
Take-off distance with 1000 kg total thrust		320 m

Detailed military load options:

Weapons	2 x MG 151/20 (20 mm)	2 x MK 108 (30 mm)
RPG	2 x 150	2 x 50
Weapons weight	148 kg	200 kg
Ammunition weight	67 kg	60 kg
(Total weight	215 kg	260 kg)
Armour	50 kg	50 kg
Radio equipment	85 kg	85 kg
Engine & Nav. Equip.	23 kg	23 kg
Oxygen & Safety Equip.	12 kg	12 kg
Catapult seat	25 kg	25 kg
Crew	90 kg	90 kg
Total weight	500 kg	545 kg

He 162 with Heinkel-Hirth HeS 011 engine (3.11.1944)

Measurements:	
Wing area	11.16 m^2
Span	7.2 m
Length	9.05 m
Engine: HeS 011	
Ground-level thrust	1100 kg
Thrust at 800 km/h at 11 km	372 kg
Actual fuel consumption at this rating	1.425 kg/kp h

Weights

Weapons (2 x MK 108)	152 kg
Ammunition (2 x 50 rpg)	58 kg
Armour	67 kg
Equipment (without weapons and armour)	93 kg
Crew	100 kg
(Military weight	470 kg)
Undercarriage, flaps and trims	900 kg
Engine with tank	865 kg
Fuel (including 120 kg for taxying and take-off)	675 kg
Take-off weight	2910 kg
Landing weight with 20% fuel	2370 kg

Flight Performance

Maximum performance	at 0 km	850 km/h
	at 6 km	890 km/h
	at 11 km	850 km/h
	at 13 km	830 km/h
Cal. endurance (full power)	at 0 km	25 mins
	at 6 km	40 mins
	at 11 km	66 mins
	at 13 km	90 mins
Cal. range (full power)	at 0 km	350 km
	at 6 km	570 km
	at 11 km	900 km
	at 13 km	1150 km
Maximum range	at 14 km	1350 km

Maximum climb at mean weight	at 0 km	30.0 m/sec
	at 6 km	20.0 m/sec
	at 11 km	9.5 m/sec
Climbing time from take-off		
	to 6 km	4.7 mins
	to 11 km	11.7 mins
Take-off distance		650 m
Landing speed		169 km/h
Flight performance with supplementary fuel		
Cal. endurance (full power)	at 0 km	41 mins
	at 13 km	145 mins
Cal. range (full power)	at 0 km	530 km
	at 13 km	1900 km
Take-off distance		870 m

With 2 x 30 mm MK 108 cannon and unprotected tank with 960 litres of fuel

Undercarriage, flaps and trims	900 kg
Engine with tank	865 kg
Standard equipment	12 kg
(Empty weight	1777 kg)
Safety equipment	8 kg
Signal/flare equipment	1 kg
Radio equipment	72 kg
Weapons	152 kg
Armour	67 kg
(Equipped weight	2077 kg)
Crew	100 kg
Fuel (excluding 120 kg for taxying and take-off)	675 kg
Ammunition	58 kg
(Load weight	833 kg)
(Total take-off weight	2910 kg)

With 2 x 30 mm MK 108 cannon and unprotected tank with 1450 litres of fuel

Undercarriage, flaps and trims	900 kg
Engine with tank	895 kg
Standard equipment	12 kg
(Empty weight	1807 kg)
Auxiliary equipment weight (as above)	300 kg
(Equipped weight	2107 kg)
Crew	100 kg
Fuel (excluding 120 kg for taxying and take-off)	1085 kg
Ammunition	58 kg
(Load weight	1243 kg)
(Total take-off weight	3350 kg)

Heinkel He 162 A-1 (Standard configuration A-1/A-2 – revised 4.10.1944)

Measurements

Wing area	11.16 m²
Span	7.2 m
Length	9.05 m

Engine: BMW 003 A-1

Ground-level thrust	800 kg
Thrust at 800 km/h to 11 km	265 kg
Actual fuel consumption at this rating	1.61 kg/kgh

Weights

Weapons (2 x MK 108)	180 kg
Ammunition (2 x 50 rpg)	58 kg
Armour	70 kg
Equipment (without weapons and armour)	100 kg
Crew	100 kg
(Military weight	508 kg)
Undercarriage, flaps and trims	839 kg
Engine with tank	673 kg
Fuel	475 kg
Take-off weight	2495 kg
Landing weight with 20% fuel	2190 kg

Flight Performance

Maximum performance	at 0 km	790 km/h
	at 6 km	840 km/h
	at 11 km	780 km/h
Cal. endurance at (full power)	at 0 km	20 mins
	at 6 km	33 mins
	at 11 km	57 mins
Cal. range (full power)	at 0 km	285 km
	at 6 km	430 km
	at 11 km	660 km
Maximum range at	11.7 km	700 km
Maximum climb with mean weight	at 0 km	21.5 m/sec
	at 6 km	12.5 m/sec
	at 11 km	3.5 m/sec
Climbing time from take-off	to 6 km	6.6 mins
	to 11 km	20.0 mins
Take-off distance without Rato	850 m	
Take-off distance with 1000 kg Rato	320 m	
Landing speed	165 km/h	
Flight performance with 200 kg supplementary fuel		
Cal. endurance (full power)	at 0 km	30 mins
	at 11 km	85 mins
Cal. range (full power)	at 0 km	390 km
	at 13 km	1000 km
Take-off distance without Rato	800 m	
Take-off distance with 1000 kg Rato	380 m	

Heinkel He 162 A-1 (with Jumo 004 D/E – 16.3.1945)

Measurements				
Wing area		11.16 m^2		
Span		7.2 m		
Length		9.05 m		

Engine: Jumo 004 D/E (Performance based as at January 1945)				
Ground-level thrust		1000 kg		
Thrust at 800 km/h at 11 km		315 kg		
Actual fuel consumption at this rating		1.89 kg/kg h		

Weights				
Weapons (2 x MK 108)		157 kg		
Ammunition (2 x 50 rpg)		58 kg		
Armour		57 kg		
Equipment (without weapons and armour)		95 kg		
Crew		100 kg		
(Military weight		467 kg)		
Undercarriage, flaps and trims		983 kg		
Engine with tank and cowling/fairing		800 kg		
Fuel (not including take-off allowance		475 kg	675 kg	865 kg
Take-off weight		2725 kg	2925 kg	3115 kg
Taxying and Warming up fuel		80 kg	80 kg	80 kg
Starting fuel		22 kg	22 kg	22 kg
Take-off weight		2827 kg	3027 kg	3317 kg
Landing weight with 20% fuel		2335 kg	2385 kg	2423 kg

Flight Performance at mean weight				
Maximum performance at 0 km		885 km/h	885 km/h	885 km/h
	at 6 km	888 km/h	887 km/h	886 km/h
	at 11 km	826 km/h	824 km/h	821 km/h
Calculated endurance	at 0 km	15 mins	22 mins	28 mins
(Full power)	at 6 km	26 mins	38 mins	49 mins
	at 11 km	40 mins	59 mins	77 mins
Calculated range	at 0 km	225 km	320 km	410 km
(Full power)	at 6 km	360 km	530 km	685 km
	at 11 km	495 km	750 km	985 km
Maximum calculated endurance (throttled back)				
	at 0 km	34 mins	47 mins	59 mins
	at 6 km	51 mins	73 mins	92 mins
	at 11 km	48 mins	68 mins	89 mins
- associated performance				
	at 0 km	490 km	500 km	510 km
	at 6 km	510 km	520 km	530 km
	at 11 km	715 km	728 km	740 km
Maximum range	540 km	830 km	1080 km	
at average height	12.5 km	12.3 km	12.1 km	
Maximum climb with average flight weight				
	at 0 km	30.8 m/s	30.3 m/s	29.8 m/s
	at 6 km	16.1 m/s	15.7 m/s	15.3 m/s
	at 11 km	5.2 m/s	4.9 m/s	4.7 m/s
Climbing time from take-off				
	to 6 km	5.3 mins	5.8 mins	6.3 mins
	to 11 km	15.5 mins	17.6 mins	19.9 min
Take-off distance without Rato		660 m	760 m	860 m
Take-off distance with 1000 kg Rato		310 m	330 m	350 m
Landing speed		165 km/h	166 km/h	168 km/h

Glossary

Armée de l'Air	French Air Force
Bauaufsicht Luft (BAL)	*Luftwaffe* aircraft inspection/acceptance department
Baukreise	Building (construction) groups
CFE	Central Fighter Establishment
Centre d'Expériences Aériennes Militaires (CEAM)	Military Aeronautical Testing Centre
Direction des Études et Fabrications d'Armement	Armament Study and Development Directorate
EHAG	Ernst Heinkel Aktiengesellschaft
Entwicklungs Hauptkommission Flugzeuge	Chief Development Commission for Aircraft
Entwurfbüro	Development Office
Erprobungskommando (E.Kdo)	Test Command/Unit
Erprobungsstelle (E-Stelle)	Experimental station
General der Jagdflieger	General of Fighter Arm
Generalkommissar	General Commissioner
Gruppe	Group
Hauptauschuss Flugzeugbau	Main Committee for Aircraft Construction
Jagdgeschwader	Fighter Wing
Jägerstab	Fighter Staff
Kommandeur der Erprobungsstellen (K.d.E.)	Commander of Experimental Stations *(Luftwaffe)*
Letno-Islyedovatel'skiy Institut Narodny Kommisariat Aviatsionoy Promishlinosti (LII NKAP)	Flight Research Institute of the People's Commissariat for the Aircraft Industry
Luftflotte	Air Fleet
Luftflottenkommando	Air Fleet Command (usually a smaller command than a Luftflotte)
Materialprüfungskommission	Equipment assessment commission
Nationalsozialistisches Fliegerkorps (NSFK)	National Socialist Flying Corps
RAE	Royal Aeronautical Establishment (Farnborough)
Reichsluftfahrtministerium (RLM)	German Air Ministry
SS-Reichssicherheitshauptamt	SS Main Administration Office
Societé Nationale de Construction Aéronautique du Centre (SNCAC)	National Centre for Aeronautical Construction
Stabsstaffel	Staff Squadron
Tsentral'niy Aero-Gidrodinamicheskiy Institut (TsAGI)	Central Aero-Hydrodynamics Institute

Ranks

The following table lists the appoximately similar rankings of wartime *Luftwaffe*, Royal Air Force and US Army Air Force personnel.

Luftwaffe		**RAF**		**USAAF**	
Generalfeldmarschall	*Gen.Feldm.*	Marshal of the RAF	—	General (five star)	Gen
Generaloberst	*Gen.Oberst.*	Air Chief Marshal	ACM	General (four star)	Gen
General	*Gen.*	Air Marshal	AM	Lieutenant General	Lt Gen
Generalleutnant	*Gen.Lt.*	Air Vice-Marshal	AVM	Major General	Maj Gen
Generalmajor	*Gen.Maj.*	Air Commodore	Air Cmdre	Brigadier General	Brig Gen
Oberst	—	Group Captain	Grp Capt	Colonel	Col
Oberstleutnant	*Oberstlt.*	Wing Commander	Wing Cdr	Lieutenant Colonel	Lt Col
Major	*Maj.*	Squadron Leader	Sqn Ldr	Major	Maj
Hauptmann	*Hptm.*	Flight Lieutenant	Flt Lt	Captain	Capt
Oberleutnant	*Oblt.*	Flying Officer	F/O	First Lieutenant	1st Lt
Leutnant	*Lt.*	Pilot Officer	P/O	Second Lieutenant	2nd Lt
Hauptfeldwebel	*Hptfw.*	Warrant Officer	W/O	Flight Officer	Flt Off
Oberfeldwebel	*Obfw.*	Flight Sergeant	F/S	Master Sergeant	M/Sgt
Feldwebel	*Fw.*	Sergeant	Sgt	Technical Sergeant	T/Sgt
Unteroffizier	*Uffz.*	Corporal	Cpl	Staff Sergeant	S/Sgt
Hauptgefreiter	*Hptgefr.*	—	—	Sergeant	Sgt
Obergefreiter	*Ogefr.*	Leading Aircraftman	LAC	Corporal	Cpl
Gefreiter	*Gefr.*	Aircraftman First Class	AC1	Private First Class	Pfc
Flieger	*Flg.*	Aircraftman Second Class	AC2	Private	Pvt

The *Luftwaffe* also recognised three officer candidate grades, commencing with *Fahnenjunker*, prefixed to the normal NCO rank, e.g. *Fhj.Ofw.*, and rising to *Fähnrich* (*Fhr.*) and *Oberfähnrich* (*Ofhr.*), both of which were used as ranks in their own right. These candidate grades were equivalent to the ranks of *Unterfeldwebel*, *Feldwebel* and *Oberfeldwebel* respectively.

Organisational Ranks

The titles given to *Luftwaffe* personnel in operational units should not be confused with the ranks they held within the unit, e.g. a *Gruppenkommandeur* could hold the rank of *Major* or *Hauptmann* and a *Staffelkapitän* or *Staffelführer* could hold the rank of *Hauptmann*, *Oberleutnant* or even *Leutnant*.

Geschwaderkommdore		Wing Commander
Gruppenkommandeur	*Gr.Kdr.*	Group Captain
Staffelkapitän	*St.Kpt.*	Squadron Leader
Staffelführer	*St.Fhr.*	Squadron Leader (acting)
Stabsoffizier		Administrative Officer
Adjutant	*Adj.*	Adjutant
Stabsarzt		Doctor attached to squadron staff
Einsatzoffizier (Ia)		Operations officer
Nachrichtenoffizier (Ic)	NO	Signals officer
Technische Offizier	TO	Technical officer

APPENDIX 2: Identified He 162 *Werknummern*

Place of Build: W = Wien L = Languste H = Heidfeld R = Rostock B = Bernburg

Werknummer	Place of Build	Variant	Code/Tactical Code	Unit	Notes
200 001	W-L/H	V1/M1	VI+IA	-	First prototype. MK 108. First flight 6.12.44. Flown by Peter. Crashed 10.12.44, Peter killed.
200 002	W-L/H	V2/M2	VI+IB	-	First flight 22.12.44. Francke and Bader. Strengthened nose. MK 108.
200 003	W-L/H	V3/M3	VI+IC	-	First flight 16.1.45. Increased tail span. Modified rudder, hydraulics and controls. Later fitted with an enlarged tail unit. Flown by Full. Flown by Gollob 11.2.45. MK 108.
200 004	W-L/H	V4/M4	VI+ID	-	First flight 16.1.45. Then fitted with wing 'ears' and refitted with new wings. Stability, dive and taxying trials and plans for night vision camera. MG 151.
200 005	W-L/H	V5/M5	Code not assigned officially	-	Aircraft never flown. Engaged in static tests.
200 006	W-L/H	M6	VI+IF	-	Flight-ready 17.1.45. First flight 23.1.45. Extra weight added for rudder control. Crashed 4.2.45. Test pilot Weydemeyer killed. MK 108.
200 007	W-L/H	M7	VI+IG	-	MG 151. Stability tests. Brake parachute. Wing 'ears'.
200 008	W-L/H	M8/A-1	VI+IH	-	MG 151, refitted with MK 108. Completed 29.1.45. Crashed and destroyed 12.3.45. Flown by Wanke.
200 009	W-L/H	M9	VI+II(?)	-	Completed 15.2.45. Blown up to avoid capture, April 1945.
200 010	W-L/H	M10	VI+IJ	-	Blown up to avoid capture, April 1945.
220 001	W-L/H	A-01?/A-2/M18	VI+IK	-	MG 151. Flight-ready 10.1.45. First flight 24.1.45.
220 002	W-L/H	A-02?/M19	VI+IL	-	First flight 28.1.45. Ballast in nose. Plans for V-tail. Flown by Tautz. Aircraft destroyed 14.3.45.
220 003	W-L/H	A-03?/M20	VI+IM	-	Fitted with wing 'ears'. First flight 10.2.45. Tested centre of gravity issues, flaps and rudders. Flown by Francke. MG 151. Found by Allies at Munich-Riem.
220 004	W-L/H	A-2/M21	VI+IN	-	First flight 22.2.45. Flown by Gleuwitz to 955 km/h. MG 151.
220 005	W-L/H	A-2/M22	VI+IO	-	Tested redesigned wing root fillets. First flight 22.2.45. 15% damaged 4.3.45. Flown by Denzin.
220 006	W-L/H	M23 (A-06)	VI+IP	-	Flight ready 24.1.45. Trialled new wing/fuselage joints with the wings of the M19. Flown by Gleuwitz. Found by Allies at Munich-Riem.
220 007	W-L/H	A-07?/M24	VI+IQ	-	First flight 10.2.45. Taxying trials and general flight-testing. MG 151.
220 008	W-L/H	A-08?/M25	VI+IR	-	Flight ready 29.1.45. First flight 17.2.45. Flown by Gleuwitz.
220 009	W-L/H	A-2/M26	VI+IS	-	Extended fuselage. Flight-ready 30.1.45. First flight 17.2.45. Flown by Gleuwitz 12.3.45., 60% damaged.
220 010	W-L/H	A-010/M27	VI+IT/E2+52	K.d.E.	First flight 1.2.45. Strengthened airframe and tail. 60% damaged 2.3.45. Flown by Pawolka.
220 011	W-L/H	A-011?/M28	VI+IU	Listed as '*Stabsstaffel Hachtel*'	Strengthened airframe. MK 108. Extended and strengthened airframe. Additional fuel tank. First flight 18.2.45.
220 012	W-L/H	A-012?/M29	VI+IV	Listed as '*Stabsstaffel Hachtel*'	Completed 8.2.45. MK 108. Reserve aircraft for weapons-testing. Extended and strengthened airframe. First flight 18.2.45.
220 013	W-L/H	A-013?/M30	VI+IW/WA+51	-	Completed 8.2.45. MG 151. Weapons testing and EZ 42 gunsight. First flight 24.2.45.
220 014	W-L/H	A-2/M31	VI+IX/recoded VH+HC	-	Completed 8.2.45. MG 151. Reserve aircraft. First flight 24.2.45. Trials with a gyroscopic gunsight. Damaged in air raid 13.2.45.
220 015	W-L/H	A-015?/M14	Not assigned		Assigned for installation of Heinkel-Hirth HeS 011 engine.
220 016	W-L/H	A-015?/M15	Not assigned		
220 017	W-L/H	A-017?/M11	E2+51	K.d.E.	MK 108. Proposed Jumo 004. Used for engine and undercarriage tests. Destroyed by bombing, March 1945. Never flown.
220 018	W-L/H	M12		-	Destroyed by bombing, March 1945. Never flown.
220 019	W-L/H	A-2/M16			Planned as two-seat, powered trainer, early Feb. 1945. Never built.
220 020	W-L/H	A-2/M17/			Also briefly known as M32?
220 021	W-L/H	M33		-	First flight 14.3.45. Flown by Gleuwitz. Reserve aircraft.
220 022	W-L/H	A-2/M34	E3+51		Flown by Borsdorff.
220 023	W-L/H	A-2/M35			
220 024	W-L/H	A-2/M36			
220 025	W-L/H	A-2/M37			
220 026	W-L/H	A-2/M38			
220 027	W-L/H	A-2/M39			
220 028	W-L/H	A-2/M40			
220 029	W-L/H	A-2/M41			
220 030	W-L/H	A-2/M42		-	Ready for engine-testing purposes 29.3.45.

Werknummer	Place of Build	Variant	Code/Tactical Code	Unit	Notes
220 102			E2+53	K.d.E.	
220 103			E5+E4	K.d.E.	
120 001	R				First flight 14.1.45.
120 002	R		White 1	To 1./JG 1	At Leck, May 1945
120 003	R				
120 013	R		White 1?	To 2./JG 1	Flown by Schmitt of 2./JG 1, 4.4.45.
120 015	R	A-2	White 21	To 1./JG 1	At Leck, May 1945. Transferred to French. Assigned code 'No. 2' by French. To Musée de l'Air de France, Le Bourget.
120 017	R		Yellow 6	To 3./JG 1	At Leck, May 1945. Shipped to USA in 1946. Became T-2-494.
120 020	R				Possibly commandeered by the Russians.
120 028	R	A-2	White 3	To I./JG 1	Flown by Kirchner of JG 1, 5.4.45. At Leck, May 1945.
120 031	R		White 1	To JG 1	At Leck, May 1945. Assigned to Schmitt of JG 1?
120 067	R	A-2	White 4	To 1./JG 1	At Leck, May 1945. Shipped to USA in 1946.
120 068	R			To 2./JG 1	Flight-tested 29.3.45. Also flown by Schmitt of JG 1, 7.4.45.
120 069	R				Flight-tested 13.4.45.
120 070	R				Flight-tested 31.3.45.
120 072	R	A-2	Yellow 3	To I./JG 1	Flown by Kirchner of JG 1, 10.4.45. Also flown by Stiemer. At Leck, May 1945. Commandeered by British. Became AM 61. To RAE Farnborough. Crashed, killing British pilot, Marks, 9.11.45.
120 074	R	A-2	Yellow 11	To I./JG 1	Flown by Demuth and Wollenweber of JG 1, 15.4.45. At Leck, May 1945. Assigned to Demuth. Commandeered by British. Became AM 60. To RAE Farnborough. Struck off RAF charge by 14.8.47.
120 076	R		Yellow 4	To 3./JG 1	Flight-tested 31.3.45. & 9.4.45. At Leck, May 1945. Commandeered by British. Became AM 59. To RAE Farnborough. Flown by Falk, 29.6.45 and Martindale, 6.7.45. Shipped to Canada, August 1946.
120 077	R	A-2	Red 1	To 2./JG 1	Flown by Hanf of JG 1. At Leck, May 1945. Commandeered by Americans. Shipped to USA IN 1946. Test-flown by Hoover in California. Later transferred to Kansas. Then to Planes of Fame Museum, Chino, California.
120 082	R				Flight-tested 28.3.45.
120 083	R				Flight-tested 12.4.45.
120 085	R				Flight-tested 13.4.45.
120 086	R			To II./JG 1	Flown by Dürr of JG 1, 30.4.45. Commandeered by British. Became AM 62. To RAE Farnborough. Shipped to Canada, August 1946. Then to Canadian Aviation Museum, Ottawa.
120 091	R	A-2	Red 5?	To 2./JG 1	At Leck, May 1945. Commandeered by British. Became AM 66. To RAE Farnborough, then to Science Museum, London.
120 092	R				Flight-tested 17.4.45.
120 093	R	A-2	White 2	To JG 1	At Leck, May 1945. Transferred to French. Assigned code 'No. 3' by French.
120 095	R	A-2	White 20	To JG 1	At Leck, May 1945. Commandeered by British. Became AM 63. To RAE Farnborough. Struck off RAF charge by 14.8.47.
120 097	R	A-2	White 3?	To JG 1	At Leck, May 1945. Commandeered by British. Became AM 64. To RAE Farnborough. In scrap area at Farnborough by 15.12.46.
120 098	R	A-2	White 2?	To JG 1	At Leck, May 1945. Commandeered by British. Became AM 67. To RAE Farnborough. Flown by Brown, 7.9.45. Flown again at RAE 18.9.45, 29.& 30.11.45. In scrap area at Farnborough by 15.12.46.
120 099	R			To JG 1	Flown by Schlarb of JG 1, 30.4.45.
120 108	R			To II./JG 1	Flown by Dürr of JG 1, 28.4.45.
120 221	R		White 21?		At Leck, May 1945. Commandeered by British. Became AM 58. To RAE Farnborough. In scrap area at Farnborough by 15.12.46.
120 222	R		White or Yellow 7?	To JG 1	At Leck, May 1945. Later provided tail section to W.Nr. 120 230 in USA.
120 223	R	A-2	Yellow 1		Flown by Wollenweber of JG 1, 22.4.45. Transferred to French. Assigned code 'No. 1' by French. Flown by Nicolle, Longuet and Schlienger in France.
120 227	R		Red 2	To 2./JG 1	At Leck, May 1945. Commandeered by British. Became AM 65. To RAE Farnborough. At Central Gunnery School in 1949, then at St. Athan and RAF Museum, Hendon, London.
120 230	R	A-2	White 23	To 1./JG 1	At Leck, May 1945. Shipped to USA in 1946 with tail section of W.Nr. 120 222. Became T-2-504.
120 231	R	A-2	White 6	To 1./JG 1	At Leck, May 1945.
120 233	R				At Leck, May 1945.
120 235	R		Yellow 6?	To 3./JG 1?	At Leck, May 1945.
310 001	B				First flight 15.2.45. Flown again by Steckhan on 27.3.45., 85% damaged.
310 002	B			To JG 1	Flown by Steckhan 21.2.45. and Strauss of JG 1, 1.4.45.
310 003	B	A-1	Yellow 5	To 2./JG 1	At Leck, May 1945. Transferred to French.
310 004	B				Flown by Steckhan 22.2.45.
310 005	B	A-1	Red 7		At Leck? Transferred to French.
310 006	B			To JG 1	Flown by Büttner, JG 1, 1.4.45.
310 007	B				Flown by Steckhan 24.2.45.
310 008	B				Flown by Steckhan 22.2.45.

Werknummer	Place of Build	Variant	Code/Tactical Code	Unit	Notes
310 010	B				Flown by Osterwald 9.4.45.
310 012	B		Yellow 5?	To 3./JG 1?	Flown by Steckhan 6.3.45. At Leck, May 1945.
310 013	B				Flown by Steckhan 8.3.45.
310 014	B				Flown by Steckhan 6.3.45.
310 018	B		White 5	To JG 1	Flown by Osterwald 27.3.45. and Dobrath of JG 1, 1.4.45. At Leck, May 1945.
310 020	B				Found at Bernburg by Allies.
310 021	B				Flown by Osterwald 9.4.45., 12.4.4.5
310 023	B			To JG 1	Flown by Wollenweber of JG 1, 11.4.45.
310 027	B	A-1			Found at Bernburg by Allies.
310 078	B	A-1	White 5	To JG 1	Flown by Wollenweber of JG 1, 6.4.45. Also flown by Künnecke.
310 079	B				Flown by Osterwald 4.4.45.
310 081	B				Flown by Osterwald 4.4.45.

Sources and Bibliography

By far the bulk of original source material used in this book was taken from the large collection of papers from Ernst Heinkel Aktiengesellschaft (EHAG). These comprise several hundred pages of reports, letters, file notes, cables and teleprint messages mainly despatched from EHAG from late 1944 to May 1945. Those documents used are cited in the endnotes to each chapter.

In addition, the following selected documents proved most useful:

UK National Archives:

AIR20/7708 *OKL Daily Situation Reports, 1-14 February 1945*
AIR20/7709 *OKL Daily Situation Reports, 15-28 February 1945*
AIR34/274 Air Ministry: Central Interpretation Unit, Interpretation reports: L204 - L299, 1944 June - 1945 Apr.
AIR40/164 Günter, S and Hohbach *History and Experiences of He 162 and He 162 Report No. 2 Performances with Jumo-004 (Heinkel Report)*, Translation No. F-TS-672-RE, Headquarters Air Materiel Command, Wright Field, Dayton, Oh., October 1946
AIR40/164 *Interim Report No. 1 on the German Jet Fighter Heinkel 162*, Interim Report No. F-IM -1113A-ND, HQ, Air Materiel Command, 14 May 1946
AIR40/2421: ADI(K) Report No. 185/1945 *Heinkel – Wien/Schwechat and Ludwigslust*, July 1945
AIR40/2422 ADI(K) Interrogation of German and Italian Prisoners of War : Reports 138-262 Vol 26, 1945 Feb.-Mar. Report No. 287/1945
AIR40/2423: ADI(K) Report No. 379/1945 – *Some Notes on the German Aircraft Industry and German Aircraft Production during the War*
HW13/47 War Department, *Military Intelligence Service, German Technical Aid to Japan*, 31 August 1945
WO208/4170 CSDIC Reports 1201 – 1350, 1945 May-Sept

Imperial War Museum

GDC/18/205 EHAG Aktenvermerk Nr. 5/44, *162 Konstruktionbespechung*, 7.10.44
CIOS Evaluation Report 40, 29.5.1945
GDC/18 64, EHAG Wien, *Prüfmappe Flugzeug 162*, 1.2.45
GDC 18/106: OKL-Chef-TLR-Fl-E-10/IV, *Vorläufige Dichtungsvorschrift für Flächentankraum Baumuster 8-162*, 12.3.1945
Rheinmetall Borsig Aktengesellschaft Werk Unterlüss *Bewaffnung Schneller Jagdflugzeuge*, Josef Schoetz, 27.7.1945 (as Halstead Exploiting Centre *Developments of German Fighter Armament for the Attack of Bombers*, BIOS/Gr.2/HEC/10787, UNT 5T)
He 162 with Argus tube – Heinkel report 30.3.45, TPA3/TIB Translation No. GDC 18/59T
CIOS: '*Jet-Fighter Heinkel 162 (Volksjäger)*'. Evaluation Report 166a, 7 July 1945

Miscellaneous Allied documents

Air P/W Interrogation Unit, Main Headquarters Second TAF *Trends of Development in the GAF – Part IV – The Story of the 8-162*, AP/WIU (2nd TAF) 87/1945, 12.7.1945
ADI(K) Report No. 309B/1945, 16 May 1945
ADI(K) Report No. 340/1945, *Arguments for and against the Volksjäger*, 26 June 1945
APWIU (2nd Air Disarmament Wing) 63/1945, *A View on the Volksjäger He 162*, 14 June 1945
Farren Mission to Germany: *He. 162 – An Achievement in Rapid Aircraft Development and Manufacture* (undated report)
Visit to select German aeroplanes of Category 1 May 29th-June 3rd, 1945, G.M.Buxton, Central Fighter Establishment, CFE/S.960/Eng., 8th June 1945
Enemy Aircraft Flight, Central Fighter Establishment: *Report of work on German orthodox and jet aircraft in Germany from 18.5.45 to 13.6.45*, F/Lt. R.T.H.Collis, DFC, OC, EA Flight, EAF/S.50/AIR, 13th June 1945
USSAFE Tech. Intelligence Report No.I-66, 10 June 1945: '*Interrogation of Dipl.-Ing. Fritz Stenzel, Gothe (sic), Germany M51-J06, on a new method of aircraft construction as developed by the subject engineer.*'

Miscellaneous German documents (not part of EHAG collection)

NAARS/Microfilm T-321/Roll 10: Das Oberkommando der Luftwaffe *Kriegstagebuch* 1.Februar-7.April 1945
Projekt Volksjäger – Stellungnahme zum Projekt Volksjäger von Dr. Vogt (Blohm & Voss) unter Berücksichtigung des Entwurfs Heinkel He 162 (undated)
Der Reichsminister für Rüstung und Kriegsproduktion: Entwicklungshauptkommission Flugzeuge, B.Nr. 181/44, *Bericht über die Besprechung am 24.10.44 betr. Schulflugzeuge*, 27.10.1944
Chef TLR Fl.Nr.8582/44 (E-2), *Flugzeug-Baureihen-Blatt 8-162*, 1.11.44
Erprobungsstelle der Luftwaffe, Tarnewitz, various *Schwerpunkterprobungsberichte* 1944-45
Kommando der Erprobungsstellen Rechlin, 430/45 8-161 – *Besprechung am 11.2.1945 in Wien-Schwechat*, (13.2.1945)
OKL, Gen.d.Fl.Ausb/V.u.L.Abt. IC Br.B.Nr. 3608/44 *Besprechungsbericht Nr 379*, 19.11.44

OKL, Lw.Organisationsstab, Genst.Gen.Qu. 2.Abt. (IIB), 30.1.1945
Mistelanordnung: 8-162 mit Verbrauchsflugzeug E377a auf Startwagen, Entwurfsabteilung 30.11.44
Der Chef des SS-Hauptamtes, 9. November 1944 and Bra/H. 2091/44 betr: Baumuster Me 162, 25. November 1944

Flugbuch:

Hans Berger
Heinz Borsdorff
Herbert Dosch
Alfred Dürr
Gerhard Hanf
Günther Kirchner
Heinz Künneke
Heinrich Osterwald
Helmut Riehl
Adalbert Schlarb
Rudolf Schmitt
Hermann Steckhan
Erwin Steeb
Wolfgang Wollenweber

Published articles

Heinkels Verschleißjäger – Die Entwicklung der He 162 (Teil 1), Manfred Griehl *Flugzeug* 5/95
Heinkel – Die Zeitschrift der Heinkel-Werke, Heft 1, 1 Dezember 1962
Heinkel He 162, P. Lloyd, Aero Modeller, October 1968
Henschel Hs 132, Hans Redemann, *Flug Revue*, 3/1970
'*Wieder ein 'Modell mit Geschichte' – 'Volksjäger' He 162 A2 'weiße 1'*, Hans Lächler, *Modell Magazin*, 5/80
'*Die letzten Wochen des 'Volksjägers'*', Hans Lächler, *Modell Magazin* 7/84
'*Ich flog die He 162 'Nervenklau'*", Gerhard Hanf, *Jägerblatt* Nr. 4/XL, September/Oktober 1992
'*Abschuß mit He 162 – JA oder NEIN?*', A.R.Chapman, *Flugzeug*, 1/89
Mastering Heinkel's Minimus, Captain Eric Brown, CBE, DSC, AFC, RN, *Air Enthusiast*, June 1972
He-162: The Plywood Coffin Robert Trimble *Air Combat*, date unknown
The Salamander in France (Part 1), Philippe Couderchon, *Aeroplane*, April 2006
The Salamander in France (Part 2), Philippe Couderchon, *Aeroplane*, May 2006
Ta 152H & He 162, John Melson, *Luftwaffe Verband*, Issue Number 5, January 1996
Ta 152H & He 162, John Melson, *Luftwaffe Verband*, Issue Number 8, October 1996
Heinkel 162, *Luftwaffe Verband*, Issue Number 10, April 1997
Heinkel 162, *Luftwaffe Verband*, Issue Number 11, July 1997
Heinkel 162 – JG 1, *Luftwaffe Verband*, Issue Number 12, October 1997

Unpublished drafts and studies

Smith, J. Richard & Norton, Mike *Heinkel He 162 – A Bird of a Different Feather*, unpub. Draft
Heinkel He 162s at Leck, Germany May 6, 1945, compiled by David E. Brown, November 2005
Diagram: Leck, 08 May 1945. He 162s of I./JG 1 by R.L.Reid, undated

Published books

Balous, Miroslav & Bily, Miroslav *Heinkel He 162 Spatz*, MBI, Praha, 2004
Baumbach, Werner, *Broken Swastika – The defeat of the Luftwaffe*, Hale, London, 1986
Beauvais, Heinrich; Kössler, Karl; Mayer, Max & Regel, Christoph, *German Secret Flight Test Centres to 1945*, Midland Publishing, Hinckley, 2002
Captain Eric 'Winkle' Brown *Wings on my Sleeve*, Weidenfeld & Nicolson, London, 2006
Brütting, Georg, *Das Buch der deutschen Fluggeschichte: Band 3*, Drei Brunnen Verlag, Stuttgart, 1979
Phil Butler *War Prizes – An Illustrated survey of German, Italian and Japanese aircraft brought to Allied countries during and after the Second World War*, Midland Counties Publications, Leicester, 1994
Caldwell, Donald & Muller, Richard *The Luftwaffe over Germany – Defense of the Reich*, Greenhill Books, London, 2007
Dahl, Walter *Rammjäger*, Orion Verlag, Heusenstamm, 1961
Richard Dennis, *Royal Aircraft Establishment at War*, Tutor Publications, Dorchester, 2008
H. Essame *The Battle for Germany*, Batsford, London, 1969
Galland, Adolf *The First and The Last*, Methuen, London, 1955
Carl-Fredrik Geust *Under the Red Star – Luftwaffe Aircraft in the Soviet Air Force*, Airlife, Shrewsbury, 1993
C-F Geust and G Petrov *Red Stars Vol. 2 – German Aircraft in the Soviet Union*, Apali Oy, Tampere, 1998
Forsyth, Robert *Jagdwaffe – Defending the Reich 1944-1945*, Classic Publications, Hersham, 2005
Freeman, Roger A. *Mighty Eighth War Diary* Janes, London, 1981
Gilbert, Martin *Second World War* Weidenfeld and Nicolson, London, 1989
Griehl, *Heinkel He 162* Schiffer Military History, Atglen, 2001
Hammel, Eric *Air War Europa – America's Air War against Germany in Europe and North Africa: Chronology 1942-1945*, Pacifica Press, 1994
Max Hastings *Armageddon – The Battle for Germany 1944-45*, Macmillan, London, 2004
Heinkel, *He 1000*, Hutchinson & Co., London, 1956
Hiller, *Heinkel He 162 'Volksjäger' – Entwicklung – Produktion – Einsatz*, Verlag Dr. Alfred Hiller, Wien, 1984

Heinz Höhne *The Order of the Death's Head*, Secker & Warburg, London, 1980
Dissolution of the Luftwaffe: The Work of the British Air Forces of Occupation Germany, HMSO London, 1995
Kay, Antony L. *German Jet Engine and Gas Turbine Development 1930-1945*, Airlife Publishing, Shrewsbury, 2002
Koos, Volker *Heinkel Raketen- und Strahlflugzeuge*, Aviatic Verlag, Oberhaching, 2008
Manrho, John and Pütz, Ron *Bodenplatte – The Luftwaffe's Last Hope: The Attack on Allied Airfields New Year's Day 1945*, Hikoki Publications, Crowborough, 2004
Mombeek, Eric *Defending the Reich, The History of Jagdgeschwader 1 'Oesau'*, JAC Publications, Norwich, 1992
Eric Mombeek *Reichsverteidigung – Die Geschichte des Jagdgeschwaders 1 'Oesau'*, Eric Mombeek, 1993
Eric Mombeek *Defenders of the Reich – Jagdgeschwader 1: Volume Three 1944-1945*, Classic Publications, Hersham, 2003
Müller, Peter *Heinkel He 162 'Volksjäger' – Last-Ditch Effort by the Luftwaffe*, History Facts, Andelfingen, 2006
Obermaier, Ernst *Die Ritterkreuzträger der Luftwaffe 1939-1945 – Band I Jagdflieger*, Verlag Dieter Hoffmann, Mainz, 1966
Prien, Jochen & Rodeike, Peter *Jagdgeschwader 1 und 11 – Teil 3 1944-1945* Eutin, undated
Ransom, Stephen and Cammann, Hans-Hermann *Me 163 Rocket Interceptor, Volume One*, Classic Publications, Crowborough, 2002
Stephen Ransom and Hans-Hermann Cammann *Me 163 Rocket Interceptor Volume Two*, Classic Publications, Hersham, 2003
Ries, Karl *Luftwaffen Story 1935-1939*, Verlag Dieter Hoffmann, Mainz, 1974
Kenn C. Rust *The 9th Air Force in World War II*, Aero Publishers Inc., Fallbrook, Ca, 1970
Schick & Meyer, *Luftwaffe Secret Projects – Fighters 1939-1945*, Midland Publishing, Leicester, 1997
Christopher Shores & Chris Thomas *2nd Tactical Air Force Volume Three: From the Rhine to Victory January to May 1945*, Classic Publications, Hersham, 2006
Smith & Creek, *Jet Planes of the Third Reich*, Monogram Aviation Publications, Boylston, 1982
Smith, J. Richard & Creek, Eddie J., *Volksjäger*, Monogram Close-Up 11, Monogram Aviation Publications, Boylston, 1986
Smith, J. Richard and Creek, Eddie J. Me 262 *Volume One*, Classic Publications, Burgess Hill, 1997
Smith, J. Richard and Creek, Eddie J. Me 262 *Volume Two*, Classic Publications, Burgess Hill, 1998
Smith, J. Richard and Creek, Eddie J. Me 262 *Volume Four*, Classic Publications, Crowborough, 2000
Smith, J. Richard & Creek, Eddie J. with Rolotschek, Gerhard, *Dornier Do 335 Pfeil*, Classic Publications, Hersham, 2007
Albert Speer, *Inside the Third Reich*, Weidenfeld & Nicolson, London 1970
Speer, *The Slave State - Heinrich Himmler's Masterplan for SS Supremacy*, Weidenfeld & Nicolson, London, 1981
Dan van der Vat, *The Good Nazi – The Life and Lies of Albert Speer*, Weidenfeld & Nicolson, London, 1997
Wiesinger, Günter & Schroeder, Walter *Die Österreichischen Ritterkreuzträger in der Luftwaffe 1939-45*, H. Weishaupt Verlag, Graz, 1986
Wollenweber, Wolfgang, *Thunder over the Reich: Flying the Luftwaffe's He 162 Jet Fighter*, Hikoki Publications/Crecy Publishing, Manchester, 2014

INDEX

German Personnel

Allied Personnel